McGraw-Hill's
GED
Mathematics

The Most Comprehensive and Reliable
Study Program for the GED Math Test

Jerry Howett

McGraw·Hill

New York   Chicago   San Francisco   Lisbon   London   Madrid   Mexico City
Milan   New Delhi   San Juan   Seoul   Singapore   Sydney   Toronto

CD-ROM for Windows
To install:
Insert the CD-ROM into your CD-ROM drive. The CD will start automatically. If it does not, double-click on MY COMPUTER; find and open your CD-ROM disk drive, then double-click on the **install.exe** icon. The CD-ROM includes audio instruction as well as a comprehensive User's Guide to guide you in using this program effectively.

Minimum System Requirements
Computer: Windows 95, 98, NT, 2000, XP
Pentium II, AMD K6-2, or better
64 MB RAM
14" color monitor
8× or better CD-ROM
Sound card
Installation: necessary free hard-drive space: 150 MB
Settings: 800 × 600 screen resolution
256 (8-bit) colors (minimum)
Thousands (24- or 32-bit) of colors (preferred)

Call 800-722-4726 if the CD-ROM is missing from this book.
For technical support go to http://books.mcgraw-hill.com/techsupport.

1 2 3 4 5 6 7 8 9 0 QPD/QPD 0 9 8 7 6 5

ISBN 0-07-146935-4 (book with CD)
ISBN 0-07-146936-2 (book alone)
Library of Congress Control Number 2005936542

McGraw-Hill books are available at special quantity discounts to use as premiums and sales promotions or for use in corporate training programs. For more information, please write to the Director of Special Sales, Professional Publishing, McGraw-Hill, Two Penn Plaza, New York, NY 10121-2298. Or contact your local bookstore.

Reviewers
Karen L. Kuenn, Coordinator, GED/Adult Basic Education, Moraine Valley Community College, Palos Hills, Illinois.
Blair Liddicoat, ABE Program Director, Rio Salado College, Tempe, Arizona
Debbie Milledge, Lead Teacher/Supervisor, Adult Literacy Program, DeKalb Technical College, Clarkston, Georgia
Gregory K. Spooner, Lead Teacher, Independent Learning Center, Long Beach School for Adults, Long Beach, California
Julie Zimmerman-Kelly, Curriculum Coordinator, Adult Education Department, St. Johns River Community College, Palatka, Florida

Table of Contents

To the Student

If you're studying to pass the GED Tests, you're in good company. In 1999, the most recent year for which figures are available, the American Council on Education GED Testing Service reported that more than 750,700 adults took the GED Test battery worldwide. Of this number, more than 526,400 (70 percent) actually received their certificates. About 14 percent of those with high school credentials, or about one in seven, have a GED diploma. One in 20 (5 percent) of those students in their first year of college study is a GED graduate.

The average age of GED test-takers in the United States was over 24 in 1999, but nearly three quarters (70 percent) of GED test-takers were 19 years of age or older. Two out of three GED test-takers report having completed the tenth grade or higher, and more than a third report having completed the eleventh grade before leaving high school.

Why do so many people choose to take the GED tests? Some do so to get a job, to advance to a better job, to attend college, or to qualify for military service. More than two out of every three GED graduates work toward college degrees or attend trade, technical, or business schools. Still others pursue their GED diplomas to feel better about themselves or to set good examples for their children.

More than 14 million adults earned the GED diploma between 1942 and 1999. Some well-known graduates include country music singers Waylon Jennings and John Michael Montgomery, comedian Bill Cosby, Olympic gold medalist Mary Lou Retton, Delaware Lieutenant Governor Ruth Ann Minner, Colorado's U.S. Senator Ben Nighthorse Campbell, Wendy's founder Dave Thomas, Famous Amos Cookies creator Wally Amos, and Triple Crown winner jockey Ron Turcotte.

This book has been designed to help you, too, succeed on the test. It will provide you with instruction in the skills you need to pass and plenty of practice with the kinds of test items you will find on the real test.

What Does GED Stand For?

GED stands for the Tests of **General Educational Development**. The GED Test Battery is a national examination developed by the GED Testing Service of the American Council on Education. The certificate earned for passing the test is widely recognized by colleges, training schools, and employers as equivalent to a high school diploma. The American Council reports that almost all (more than 95 percent) of employers in the nation employ GED graduates and offer them the same salaries and opportunities for advancement as high school graduates.

The GED Test reflects the major and lasting outcomes normally acquired in a high school program. Since the passing rate for the GED is based on the performance of graduating high school seniors, you can be sure your skills are comparable. In fact, those who pass the GED Test actually do better than one-third of those graduating seniors. Your skills in communication, information processing, critical thinking, and problem solving are keys to success. The test also places special emphasis on questions that prepare you for entering the workplace or higher education. Much that you have learned informally or through other types of training can help you pass the test.

Special editions of the GED Test will include the Canadian-French language, Spanish-language, Braille, large print, and audiocassette formats. If you need special accomodations because of a learning or physical disability, your adult education program and testing center can assist you.

What Should You Know to Pass the Test?

The GED Test consists of five examinations called Language Arts, Writing; Social Studies; Science; Language Arts, Reading; and Mathematics. On all five tests, you are expected to demonstrate the ability to think about many issues. You are tested on knowledge and skills you have acquired from life experiences, television, radio, books and newspapers, consumer products, and advertising. Your work or business experiences may be helpful during the test. You can expect the subjects to be interrelated. This is called *interdisciplinary* material. For example, a mathematics problem may include a scientific diagram. Or a social studies question may require some mathematical skills.

Keep these facts in mind about specific tests:

1. The **Language Arts, Writing Test** requires you in Part I to recognize or correct errors, revise sentences or passages, and shift constructions in the four areas of organization, sentence structure, usage, and mechanics (capitalization and punctuation). Letters, memos, and business-related documents are likely to be included.

    In Part II you will write an essay presenting an opinion or an explanation on a topic familiar to most adults. You should plan and organize your ideas before you write, and revise and edit your essay before you are finished.

2. Three of the five tests—**Social Studies, Science**, and **Mathematics**— require you to answer questions based on reading passages or interpreting graphs, charts, maps, cartoons, diagrams, or photographs. Developing strong reading and critical thinking skills is the key to succeeding on these tests. Being able to interpret information from graphic sources, such as a map or cartoon, is essential.

3. The **Language Arts, Reading Test** asks you to read literary text and show that you can comprehend, apply, analyze, synthesize, and evaluate concepts. You will also read nonfiction and show that you can understand the main points of what you are reading.

4. The **Mathematics Test** consists mainly of word problems to be solved. Therefore, you must be able to combine your ability to perform computations with problem-solving skills.

   Part I of the Mathematics Test will permit the use of the Casio *fx*-260 calculator, which will be provided at the test site. The calculator will eliminate the tediousness of making complex calculations. Part II will not permit the use of the calculator. Both parts of the test will include problems without multiple-choice answers. These problems will require you to mark your answers on bubble-in number grids or on coordinate plane graphs.

Who May Take the Tests?

About 3,500 GED Testing Centers are available in the fifty United States, the District of Columbia, eleven Canadian provinces and territories, U.S. and overseas military bases, correctional institutions, Veterans Administration hospitals, and certain learning centers. People who have not graduated from high school and who meet specific eligibility requirements (age, residency, and so on) may take the tests. Since eligibility requirements vary, you should contact your local GED testing center or the director of adult education in your state, province, or territory for specific information.

What Is a Passing Score on the GED Test?

A passing score varies from area to area. The scoring range varies from 200 to 800 per test. To find out what you need to pass each test, contact your local GED testing center. However, you should keep two scores in mind. One score represents the minimum score you must get on each test. The other is the minimum average score on all five tests. Both of these scores will be set by your state and must be met in order to pass the GED Test.

Can You Retake the Test?

You are allowed to retake some or all of the tests. The regulations governing the number of times that you may retake the tests and the time you must wait before retaking them are set by your state, province, or territory. Some states require you to take a review class or to study on your own for a certain amount of time before retaking the test.

THE GED TESTS

Tests	Minutes	Questions	Content/Percentages
Test 1: Language Arts, Writing			
Part I: Editing (multiple choice)	75	50	Organization 15% Sentence Structure 30% Usage 30% Mechanics 25%
Part II: the Essay	45	1 topic: appx. 250 words	
Test 2: Social Studies	70	50	World History 15% U.S. History 25% Civics and Government 25% Economics 20% Geography 15%
Test 3: Science	80	50	Earth and Space Science 20% Life Science 45% Physical Science 35% (Physics and Chemistry)

Test 4: Language Arts, Reading	65	40	Literary Text 75%
			    Poetry 15%
			    Drama 15%
			    Fiction 45%
			Nonfiction 25%
			    Informational Text
			    Literary Nonfiction
			    Reviews of Fine and Performing Arts
			    Business Documents

Test 5: Mathematics			Number Operations and Numbers Sense 20–30% Measurement and Geometry 20–30% Data Analysis, Statistics, and Probability 20–30% Algebra, Functions, and Patterns 20–30%
Part I Calculator	45	25	
Part II No Calculator	45	25	
	Total: $7\frac{1}{4}$ hours	Total: 240 questions and essay	

How Can You Best Prepare for the Test?

Many community colleges, public schools, adult education centers, libraries, churches, community-based organizations, and other institutions offer GED preparation classes. While your state may not require you to take part in a preparation program, it's a good idea if you've been out of school for some time, if you had academic difficulty when you were in school, or if you left before completing the eleventh grade. Some television stations broadcast classes to prepare people for the test. If you cannot find a GED preparation class locally, contact the director of adult education in your state, province, or territory.

What Are Some Test-Taking Tips?

1. **Prepare physically.** Get plenty of rest and eat a well-balanced meal before the test so that you will have energy and will be able to think clearly. Intense studying at the last minute probably will not help as much as having a relaxed and rested mind.

2. **Arrive early.** Be at the testing center at least 15 to 20 minutes before the starting time. Make sure you have time to find the room and to get situated. Keep in mind that many testing centers refuse to admit latecomers. Some testing centers operate on a first come, first served basis; so you want to be sure that there is an available seat for you on the day that you're ready to test.

3. **Think positively.** Tell yourself you will do well. If you have studied and prepared for the test, you should succeed.

4. **Relax during the test.** Take half a minute several times during the test to stretch and breathe deeply, especially if you are feeling anxious or confused.

5. **Read the test directions carefully**. Be sure you understand how to answer the questions. If you have any questions about the test or about filling in the answer form, ask before the test begins.

6. **Know the time limit for each test.** The Mathematics Test has a time limit of 45 minutes for Part I with the calculator. If you have extra time, go back and check your answers before you must hand in Part I. Part II without the use of a calculator also has a time limit of 45 minutes. Again, if you have extra time, go back and check your answers before you hand in your test.

7. **Have a strategy for answering questions.** You should read through the reading passages or look over the materials once and then answer the questions that follow. Read each question two or three times to make sure you understand it. It is best to refer back to the passage or graphic in order to confirm your answer choice. Don't try to depend on your memory of what you have just read or seen. Some people like to guide their reading by skimming the questions before reading a passage. Use the method that works best for you.

8. **Don't spend a lot of time on difficult questions.** If you're not sure of an answer, go on to the next question. Answer easier questions first and then go back to the harder questions. However, when you skip a question, be sure that you have skipped the same number on your answer sheet. Although skipping difficult questions is a good strategy for making the most of your time, it is very easy to get confused and throw off your whole answer key.

   Lightly mark the margin of your answer sheet next to the numbers of the questions you did not answer so that you know what to go back to. To prevent confusion when your test is graded, be sure to erase these marks completely after you answer the questions.

9. **Answer every question on the test.** If you're not sure of an answer, take an educated guess. When you leave a question unanswered, you will always lose points, but you can possibly gain points if you make a correct guess.

   If you must guess, try to eliminate one or more answers that you are sure are not correct. Then choose from the remaining answers. Remember that you greatly increase your chances if you can eliminate one or two answers before guessing. Of course, guessing should be used only when all else has failed.

10. **Clearly fill in the circle for each answer choice.** If you erase something, erase it completely. Be sure that you give only one answer per question; otherwise, no answer will count.

11. **Practice test-taking.** Use the exercises, reviews, and especially the Posttest and Practice Test in this book to better understand your test-taking habits and weaknesses. Use them to practice different strategies such as skimming questions first or skipping hard questions until the end. Knowing your own personal test-taking style is important to your success on the GED Test.

How to Use This Book

This book has been designed to give you the necessary skills to succeed on the GED Mathematics Test. Study the examples provided with each lesson and practice the mathematical skills in the exercises. Your everyday experiences with math may help you understand the practical applications of these skills.

Before beginning this book, you should take the Pretest. This will give you a preview of what the Mathematics Test includes, but, more importantly, it will help you identify which areas you need to concentrate on most. Use the chart at the end of the Pretest to pinpoint the types of questions you have answered incorrectly and to determine which skills you need the most work in. You may decide to concentrate on specific areas or to work through the entire book. We strongly suggest you *do* work through the whole book to best prepare yourself for the GED Test.

This book has a number of features designed to help make the task of test preparation easier and more effective.

- **Alternate format questions** using the number grid and the coordinate plane grid are practiced throughout the book.

- Throughout the lessons, step-by-step explanations for **calculator use** make it easy to understand how to work the examples with the Casio *fx*-260 calculator.

- Math **Tips** throughout the book offer useful hints in areas that can sometimes be troublesome.

- **Rules** are explained in simple language and are contained in highlighted boxes to make them easy to find.

- Each chapter concludes with a **Review and GED Practice** exercise. Like the GED Mathematics Test, the exercise is divided into Part I, which uses the calculator, and Part II, which uses paper and pencil only.

- At the back of the book, the **Formulas** page similar to the one used with the GED Mathematics Test contains all the formulas used in lessons and exercises. The **Using a Calculator** page gives a quick review of calculations with the Casio *fx*-260 used on the GED Mathematics Test. The **Glossary** offers a ready reminder of mathematical definitions used throughout the book.

- The **Answer Key** shows the solutions for the exercises and will help you figure out where you went wrong. If you make a mistake, you can learn from it by studying the solution provided and then reviewing the problem to analyze your error.

- Throughout the chapters you'll see references to **www.GEDMath.com**. This website has been designed to accompany this book. Check it out for additional instruction and practice!

After you have worked through the eleven chapters in this book, you should take the Posttest. The Posttest is a simulated GED Test that presents problems in the format, at the level of difficulty, and in the percentages found on the actual GED Test. The Posttest will help you determine whether you are ready for the GED Mathematics Test. The evaluation chart at the end of the test will help you locate the areas of the book you need to review.

After you have reviewed, the Practice Test can be used as a final indicator of your readiness for the GED Test. This test has the same format, level of difficulty, and percentages as the Posttest and the GED Mathematics Test.

Mathematics

Directions: This test will help you evaluate your strengths and weaknesses in mathematics. The test is in three parts. Part 1 includes number operations (arithmetic) as well as data analysis, probability, and statistics. Part 2 tests measurement and geometry, and Part 3 tests algebra. Included below is a table of formulas that you may use during the test.

Solve every problem that you can. Skip problems that you cannot solve. You will not be given a grade on this Pretest.

When you finish, check the answers and solutions that follow the test. Then look at the evaluation chart that follows the answers. Use the chart as a guide to tell you the areas where you need the most work.

Even if you do well on the Pretest, work through the entire book. Each section includes problems and tips that will help you on the GED Mathematics Test.

Pretest Formulas

Refer to this list of formulas as you work through the parts of the Pretest.

Area of a square	area = side^2
Area of a rectangle	area = length $\times$ width
Circumference of a circle	circumference = $\pi \times$ diameter; π is approximately 3.14.
Volume of a rectangular solid	volume = length $\times$ width $\times$ height
Pythagorean relationship	$a^2 + b^2 = c^2$; a and b are legs and c is the hypotenuse of a right triangle.
Simple interest	interest = principal $\times$ rate $\times$ time
Distance	distance = rate $\times$ time
Total cost	total cost = (number of units) $\times$ (price per unit)
Slope of a line	slope = $\dfrac{y_2 - y_1}{x_2 - x_1}$; (x_1, y_1) and (x_2, y_2) are two points on a line.
Distance between two points	distance = $\sqrt{(x_2 - x_1)^2 + (y_2 - y_1)^2}$; (x_1, y_1) and (x_2, y_2) are two points in a plane.
Trigonometric ratios	$\sin = \dfrac{\text{opposite}}{\text{hypotenuse}}$
	$\cos = \dfrac{\text{adjacent}}{\text{hypotenuse}}$
	$\tan = \dfrac{\text{opposite}}{\text{adjacent}}$
Mean	mean = $\dfrac{x_1 + x_2 + \ldots + x_n}{n}$, where the x's are the values for which a mean is desired, and n is the total number of values for x.

PRETEST

Pretest Answer Grid, Part 1

1 _____

2 _____

3 _____

4 _____

5 _____

6 _____

7 _____

8 _____

9 _____

10 _____

11 _____

12 _____

13 ① ② ③ ④ ⑤

14 ① ② ③ ④ ⑤

15 ① ② ③ ④ ⑤

16 ① ② ③ ④ ⑤

17 ① ② ③ ④ ⑤

18 ① ② ③ ④ ⑤

19 ① ② ③ ④ ⑤

20 ① ② ③ ④ ⑤

21 ① ② ③ ④ ⑤

22 ① ② ③ ④ ⑤

23 ① ② ③ ④ ⑤

24 ① ② ③ ④ ⑤

25 ① ② ③ ④ ⑤

26 ① ② ③ ④ ⑤

27 ① ② ③ ④ ⑤

28 ① ② ③ ④ ⑤

29 ① ② ③ ④ ⑤

30 ① ② ③ ④ ⑤

31 ① ② ③ ④ ⑤

32 ① ② ③ ④ ⑤

33 ① ② ③ ④ ⑤

PRETEST

Part 1

Number Operations, Data Analysis, Statistics, and Probability

Directions: Solve each problem.

1. For the numbers 385, 4012, and 856 first round each number to the nearest hundred. Then add the rounded numbers.

2. Round 214.0853 to the nearest thousandth.

3. Find the sum of $9\frac{1}{2}$, $3\frac{2}{3}$, and $6\frac{5}{6}$.

4. What percent of 40 is 24?

5. What is 35% of 91?

6. Find the interest on $1000 at 18% annual interest for 8 months.

7. On Thursday Maria had $483.27 in her checking account. On Friday she deposited her paycheck of $743.80. The following Wednesday she wrote a check for $635 to pay the rent and a check for $52.81 to pay her phone bill. What was the balance left in her account?

8. A plane flew for 6 hours. For 2 hours the average speed was 260 mph, and for 4 hours the average speed was 430 mph. How many miles did the plane travel in 6 hours?

9. What is the value of 80^2?

10. In 1980 the population of Central County was 2.3 million; in 1990 it was 2.6 million; and in 2000 it was 3 million. By how many did the population of the county increase from 1980 to 2000?

11. Express the ratio 36:48 in simplest form.

12. In a GED class of 18 students, there are 10 women. What is the ratio of the number of men to the number of women?

Directions: Choose the correct answer to each problem.

13. In the number 3,427,500 what is the value of the digit 2?

    (1)   20
    (2)   200
    (3)   2,000
    (4)   20,000
    (5) 200,000

14. Which of the following is the approximate product of 726 and 68?

    (1) 70,000
    (2) 49,000
    (3) 35,000
    (4) 4,900
    (5) 3,500

15. Which of the following is the same as $3(7 - 5)$?

    (1) $3(7) - 5$
    (2) $3 - 3(7)$
    (3) $3(7) - 3(5)$
    (4) $7(3) - 7(5)$
    (5) $5(3) - 5(7)$

16. Allen makes $36,425 a year. Which expression represents Allen's monthly salary?

    (1) 12 × $36,425

    (2) 4 × $36,425

    (3) $\frac{\$36,425}{52}$

    (4) $\frac{\$36,425}{12}$

    (5) $\frac{\$36,425}{4}$

17. Jake planned to install 20 sections of fencing to enclose his vegetable garden. By sunset, Jake had installed 16 sections. Which of the following does *not* represent the part of the total job that Jake completed by sunset?

    (1) $\frac{4}{5}$

    (2) 0.8

    (3) 80%

    (4) $\frac{16}{20}$

    (5) $\frac{8}{100}$

18. Sally has to drive her pickup truck 306 miles to bring her daughter home from college. Sally gets 24.7 miles per gallon with her truck. Which expression best estimates the number of gallons of gasoline Sally will need to make the trip?

    (1) $\frac{300}{25}$

    (2) $\frac{25}{300}$

    (3) 25 × 300

    (4) $\frac{25 \times 300}{2}$

    (5) 25 + 300

19. The answer to $\sqrt{1804}$ is between which of the following pairs of numbers?

    (1) 20 and 30

    (2) 30 and 40

    (3) 40 and 50

    (4) 50 and 60

    (5) 60 and 70

20. Bill worked 3 hours of overtime on Thursday and 4 hours of overtime on Friday. He makes $16 an hour for overtime work. Which of the following expresses the amount Bill made for overtime work on those 2 days?

    (1) 16 × 3 + 4

    (2) 16(3 + 4)

    (3) 3(16 + 4)

    (4) 4 × 3 × 16

    (5) 16(3 × 4)

21. Grace spent $32 for 18 gallons of gasoline. To the nearest cent, what was the price of one gallon of gasoline?

    (1) $1.68

    (2) $1.69

    (3) $1.70

    (4) $1.77

    (5) $1.78

22. Which expression is equal to the quotient of 8 divided by $2\frac{2}{3}$?

    (1) $\frac{1}{8} \times \frac{8}{3}$

    (2) $\frac{8}{1} \times \frac{8}{3}$

    (3) $\frac{1}{8} \times \frac{3}{8}$

    (4) $\frac{8}{1} \times \frac{3}{8}$

    (5) $\frac{8}{1} \times \frac{2}{3}$

PRETEST

23. The mean distance from the planet Mercury to the sun is 36,000,000 miles. Which of the following expresses this distance in scientific notation?

    (1) 36×10^2
    (2) 36×10^4
    (3) 3.6×10^5
    (4) 3.6×10^6
    (5) 3.6×10^7

24. Which of the following fractions is less than $\frac{1}{2}$?

    (1) $\frac{5}{9}$

    (2) $\frac{4}{7}$

    (3) $\frac{3}{8}$

    (4) $\frac{7}{12}$

    (5) $\frac{2}{3}$

25. From a pipe 4 meters long, Nick cut a piece that was $1\frac{3}{4}$ meters long. Assuming no waste, which of the following expresses the length of the remaining piece?

    (1) $4 - 1.75$

    (2) $4 - \frac{3}{4}$

    (3) $\frac{3}{4} - 4$

    (4) $4 - 1.34$

    (5) $4 - 1.25$

26. The Chungs spend $\frac{1}{4}$ of their income on rent and $\frac{1}{3}$ on food. They take home $2400 a month. How much do the Chungs have left each month after paying for rent and food?

    (1) $ 600
    (2) $ 800
    (3) $1000
    (4) $1200
    (5) $1400

27. Sam bought a raffle ticket at the Uptown Community Center. His wife bought three tickets, and his son bought two. Altogether, 300 tickets were sold. What is the probability that someone in Sam's family will win the grand prize?

    (1) $\frac{1}{300}$

    (2) $\frac{1}{150}$

    (3) $\frac{1}{75}$

    (4) $\frac{1}{50}$

    (5) $\frac{1}{25}$

28. Find the mean of the following test scores: 75, 82, 93, and 86.

    (1) 75
    (2) 82
    (3) 84
    (4) 86
    (5) 93

Directions: For problems 29 and 30, use the graph below.

CAR SALES BY SIZE AND TYPE

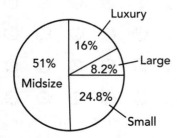

29. The number of small cars sold was about how many times the number of large cars sold?

    (1) $1\frac{1}{2}$

    (2) 2

    (3) 3

    (4) $21\frac{1}{2}$

    (5) $31\frac{1}{2}$

30. At Stan's Autos 789 cars were sold one year. The sales followed the pattern shown in the graph. About how many of the cars sold at Stan's were midsize?

    (1) 200
    (2) 300
    (3) 400
    (4) 500
    (5) 600

Directions: For problems 31–33, use the passage below.

Carla started a new job with a gross salary of $2650 a month. Her employer will deduct 20% of her salary for taxes and social security. After a year Carla will be eligible for a raise of 8% of her gross salary.

31. Which of the following tells the amount Carla's employer withholds each month from her gross salary?

    (1) $530
    (2) $480
    (3) $420
    (4) $390
    (5) Not enough information is given.

32. What is the ratio of Carla's net pay to her gross pay?

    (1) 2:3
    (2) 3:4
    (3) 4:5
    (4) 5:6
    (5) 6:7

33. What will Carla's gross monthly salary be during her second year of employment?

    (1) $2915
    (2) $2862
    (3) $2782
    (4) $2650
    (5) Not enough information is given.

Answers are on page 13.

PRETEST

Pretest Answer Grid, Part 2

1 _____

2 _____

3 _____

4 _____

5 ① ② ③ ④ ⑤   11 ① ② ③ ④ ⑤

6 ① ② ③ ④ ⑤   12 ① ② ③ ④ ⑤

7 ① ② ③ ④ ⑤   13 ① ② ③ ④ ⑤

8 ① ② ③ ④ ⑤   14 ① ② ③ ④ ⑤

9 ① ② ③ ④ ⑤   15 ① ② ③ ④ ⑤

10 ① ② ③ ④ ⑤   16 ① ② ③ ④ ⑤

Part 2

Measurement and Geometry

Directions: For problems 1–4, solve each problem.

1. What fraction of a yard is 27 inches?

2. Three kilometers are equal to how many meters?

3. What is the distance in centimeters between point *A* and point *B* on the 5-centimeter ruler?

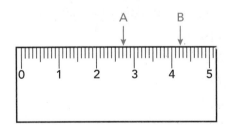

4. At a price of $5.40 per pound, what is the cost of 1 lb 12 oz of smoked turkey?

Directions: Choose the correct answer to each problem.

5. Which expression represents the weight, in pounds, of four tubes of toothpaste that each weigh 6 ounces?

   (1) $4 \times 6 \times 16$

   (2) $\frac{4 \times 16}{6}$

   (3) $\frac{6 \times 16}{4}$

   (4) $\frac{4 \times 6}{16}$

   (5) $\frac{4 + 6}{16}$

6. To the nearest square meter, what is the area of the rectangle?

   (1) 8
   (2) 10
   (3) 12
   (4) 14
   (5) 16

   2.2 m

   4.5 m

7. What is the volume, in cubic feet, of a rectangular container that is 10 feet long, 4 feet wide, and 1 yard high?

   (1) 40
   (2) 80
   (3) 120
   (4) 160
   (5) 200

8. The shaded part of the diagram represents the walkway around a square pool that measures 30 feet on each side. Which expression tells the area in square feet of the walkway?

   (1) $(40)(50) - 30^2$

   (2) $(40)(50)(30)$

   (3) $2(40 + 50) - 4(30)$

   (4) $(30)(40) - 50^2$

   (5) $\frac{40 + 50 + 30}{2}$

40 ft
50 ft

9. To the nearest meter, what is the circumference of this circle?

   (1) 16
   (2) 20
   (3) 24
   (4) 28
   (5) 32

d = 6.5 m

10. What is the measurement of $\angle AOB$ in the diagram?

    (1) 32.5°
    (2) 57.5°
    (3) 67.5°
    (4) 147.5°
    (5) 157.5°

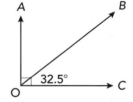
A   B
32.5°
O   C

11. In the diagram $\angle a = 72°$. Find the measurement of $\angle d$.

    (1) 18°
    (2) 28°
    (3) 72°
    (4) 108°
    (5) 118°

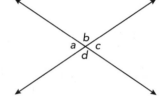
b
a   c
d

12. What is the length, in inches, of side XY in this triangle?

    (1) 6
    (2) 8
    (3) 10
    (4) 12
    (5) 14

Y
12 in.
Perimeter = 34 in.
X   Z
10 in.

13. In the diagram, $\angle A = \angle D$ and $\angle C = \angle F$. Side $AC = 24$, side $DF = 15$, and side $EF = 10$. Find the length of side BC.

    (1) 12
    (2) 16
    (3) 20
    (4) 24
    (5) 28

B
E
A   C   D   F

PRETEST

14. In △MNO, MN = 9 and MO = 12. Find the length of NO.

    (1) 9
    (2) 12
    (3) 15
    (4) 18
    (5) 21

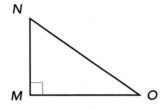

15. What is the slope of a line that passes through points A and B in the diagram?

    (1) $\frac{2}{3}$

    (2) $\frac{3}{2}$

    (3) $\frac{3}{4}$

    (4) $\frac{4}{3}$

    (5) 1

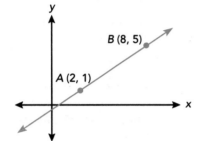

16. Which ratio represents sin x for this triangle?

    (1) $\frac{17}{15}$

    (2) $\frac{17}{8}$

    (3) $\frac{15}{17}$

    (4) $\frac{8}{15}$

    (5) $\frac{8}{17}$

Answers are on page 14.

PRETEST

Pretest Answer Grid, Part 3

1 _____

2 _____

3 _____

4 _____

5 _____

6 ① ② ③ ④ ⑤

7 ① ② ③ ④ ⑤

8 ① ② ③ ④ ⑤

9 ① ② ③ ④ ⑤

10 ① ② ③ ④ ⑤

11 ① ② ③ ④ ⑤

12 ① ② ③ ④ ⑤

13 ① ② ③ ④ ⑤

14 ① ② ③ ④ ⑤

15 ① ② ③ ④ ⑤

16 ① ② ③ ④ ⑤

Part 3

Algebra

Directions: Solve each problem.

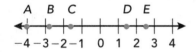

$$A \quad B \quad C \qquad D \quad E$$
$$-4 \ -3 \ -2 \ -1 \quad 0 \quad 1 \quad 2 \quad 3 \quad 4$$

1. Which point on the number line corresponds to $\frac{5}{2}$?

2. Simplify $+9 - (-4) + (-6) - 8$.

3. Simplify $-\frac{30}{6} + 4(-10)$.

4. Is the point $(2, 5)$ on the graph of the equation $y = 4x - 3$?

5. Solve for x in $12x - 4 = 3x + 11$.

Directions: Choose the correct answer to each problem.

6. Yolanda weighs w pounds. Which of the following expresses her weight after she loses 12 pounds?

    (1) $12w$

    (2) $12 - w$

    (3) $w - 12$

    (4) $\frac{w}{12}$

    (5) $w + 12$

7. Which expression represents the distance from point A to point B?

    (1) $5x + 4$

    (2) $6x + 4$

    (3) $6x - 4$

    (4) $6x + 2$

    (5) $5x - 1$

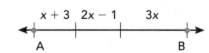

$$x + 3 \quad 2x - 1 \qquad 3x$$
$$A \qquad\qquad\qquad B$$

8. James makes $6 an hour more than his wife. Which expression tells their combined income for a 40-hour work week?

(1) $40x + 6$

(2) $40(2x + 6)$

(3) $x(6 + 40)$

(4) $x + x + 6$

(5) $40 + 6x$

9. Which of the following expresses the sum of a number and three times the same number all multiplied by five?

(1) $5n$

(2) $n(5 + 3)$

(3) $5(n + 3)$

(4) $5(3n + 3)$

(5) $5(n + 3n)$

10. The ratio of Antonio's age to his son's age is 9:2. Together their ages add up to 55. How old is Antonio?

(1) 30

(2) 35

(3) 40

(4) 45

(5) 50

11. The area of a rectangle is 147 square inches. The length is three times the width. Find the length, in inches, of the rectangle.

(1) 17

(2) 21

(3) 27

(4) 31

(5) 37

12. Which of the following is equal to $\sqrt{75}$?

(1) 15

(2) 10

(3) 5

(4) $3\sqrt{5}$

(5) $5\sqrt{3}$

13. Which of the following is *not* a solution to $6(m - 2) > 5(m + 5)$?

(1) $m = 36$

(2) $m = 38$

(3) $m = 40$

(4) $m = 42$

(5) $m = 44$

14. Which of the following is equal to the expression $a^2 - 6a$?

(1) $a(-6a)$

(2) $a(a + 6)$

(3) $-6(a + 1)$

(4) $a(a - 6)$

(5) $-a(a + 6)$

15. What are the coordinates of the y-intercept of the equation $y = 4x - 7$?

(1) $(7, 0)$

(2) $(-7, 0)$

(3) $(0, 4)$

(4) $(0, 7)$

(5) $(0, -7)$

16. Which of the following values is a solution to the equation $x^2 - 5x + 6 = 0$?

(1) $+1$

(2) -1

(3) $+3$

(4) -3

(5) $+6$

Answers are on page 14.

Answer Key

Part 1

Number Operations, Data Analysis, Statistics, and Probability

1. 5300 $\quad$ $385\rightarrow\ 400$
   $4012\rightarrow\ 4000$
   $856\rightarrow\ \underline{\ 900}$
   $\qquad\quad 5300$

2. 214.085 $\quad$ $214.08\underline{5}3\rightarrow214.085$

3. 20 $\quad$ $9\frac{1}{2}=9\frac{3}{6}$
   $\qquad 3\frac{2}{3}=3\frac{4}{6}$
   $\quad +6\frac{5}{6}=6\frac{5}{6}$
   $\qquad\quad 18\frac{12}{6}=20$

4. 60% $\quad$ $\frac{24}{40}=\frac{3}{5}=60\%$

5. 31.85 $\quad\qquad 91$
   $\qquad\quad\underline{\times.35}$
   $\qquad\quad\ 455$
   $\qquad\quad\underline{273\ \ }$
   $\qquad\ 31.85$

6. $120 $\quad$ 8 months $=\frac{8}{12}=\frac{2}{3}$ year
   $i=\frac{\overset{10}{\cancel{1000}}}{1}\times\frac{\overset{6}{\cancel{18}}}{\cancel{100}}\times\frac{2}{\underset{1}{\cancel{3}}}=\frac{120}{1}=120$

7. $539.26 $\quad$ $ 483.27
   $\qquad\qquad\quad \underline{+\ 743.80}$
   $\qquad\qquad\quad\ 1227.07$
   $\qquad\qquad\quad \underline{-\ 635.00}$
   $\qquad\qquad\qquad\ 592.07$
   $\qquad\qquad\qquad \underline{-\ 52.81}$
   $\qquad\qquad\qquad 539.26

8. 2240 miles $\quad$ $d=260\times2+430\times4$
   $\qquad\qquad\qquad d=520+1720$
   $\qquad\qquad\qquad d=2240$

9. 6400 $\quad$ $80^2=80\times80=6400$

10. 0.7 million $\quad$ $3.0-2.3=0.7$ million

11. 3:4 $\quad$ $36:48=3:4$

12. 4:5 $\quad$ $18-10=8$ men
    men:women $=8:10=4:5$

13. (4) $\quad$ 20,000 $\quad$ 2 is in the ten thousands place.

14. (2) $\quad$ 49,000 $\quad$ $726\rightarrow700$ and $68\rightarrow70$
    $\qquad\qquad\qquad\quad 700\times70=49,000$

15. (3) $\quad$ $3(7)-3(5)$
    This is the distributive property of multiplication over subtraction.

16. (4) $\quad$ $\frac{$36,425}{12}$ $\quad$ Salary divided by 12 months.

17. (5) $\quad$ $\frac{8}{100}$ $\quad$ Each of the other answers is equal to $\frac{4}{5}$.

18. (1) $\quad$ $\frac{300}{25}$ $\quad$ $306\rightarrow300$ and $24.7\rightarrow25$

19. (3) $\quad$ 40 and 50 $\quad$ $40^2=1600$ and $50^2=2500$

20. (2) $\quad$ $16(3+4)$

21. (5) $\quad$ $1.78 $\quad$ $\frac{32}{18}=$1.777\rightarrow$1.78$

22. (4) $\quad$ $\frac{8}{1}\times\frac{3}{8}$ $\quad$ $8\div2\frac{2}{3}=\frac{8}{1}\div\frac{8}{3}=\frac{8}{1}\times\frac{3}{8}$

23. (5) $\quad$ 3.6×10^7

24. (3) $\quad$ $\frac{3}{8}$ $\quad$ In each of the other fractions, the numerator is more than half of the denominator.

25. (1) $\quad$ $4-1.75$ $\quad$ $1\frac{3}{4}=1.75$

26. (3) $\quad$ $1000 $\quad$ $\frac{1}{4}\times$2400=600 and
    $\qquad\qquad\qquad \frac{1}{3}\times$2400=\ 800
    $\qquad\qquad\qquad $600+$800=1400
    $\qquad\qquad\qquad $2400-$1400=1000

27. (4) $\quad$ $\frac{1}{50}$ $\quad$ tickets bought by Sam and his family
    $\qquad\qquad\qquad =1+3+2=6$
    $\qquad\qquad\qquad \frac{6}{300}=\frac{1}{50}$

28. (3) $\quad$ 84 $\quad$ $75+82+93+86=336$
    $\qquad\qquad\qquad \frac{336}{4}=84$

29. (3) $\quad$ 3 $\quad$ $\frac{24.8\%}{8.2\%}$ is approximately 3

30. (3) $\quad$ 400 $\quad$ $789\rightarrow800$
    $\qquad\qquad\qquad$ midsize $=51\%\rightarrow50\%=\frac{1}{2}$
    $\qquad\qquad\qquad \frac{1}{2}\times800=400$

31. (1) $530   20% = 0.2   0.2 × $2650 = $530.00

32. (3) 4:5 $2650 − 530 = $2120 net pay

$$\frac{2120}{2650} = \frac{4}{5} \text{ or } 4:5$$

33. (2) $2862   8% = 0.08
0.08 × $2650 = $212
$2650 + $212 = $2862

Part 2

Measurement and Geometry

1. $\frac{3}{4}$ $\frac{27}{36} = \frac{3}{4}$

2. 3000   1 km = 1000 m   3 × 1000 = 3000

3. 1.5 cm   4.2 − 2.7 = 1.5 cm

4. $9.45 $\frac{12 \text{ oz}}{16 \text{ oz}} = \frac{3}{4}$ lb $1\frac{3}{4} = 1.75$ lb
1.75 × $5.40 = $9.45

5. (4) $\frac{4 \times 6}{16}$ 16 oz = 1 lb

6. (2) 10   A = lw = 4.5 × 2.2 = 9.9→10

7. (3) 120   1 yard = 3 feet
V = lwh = (10)(4)(3) = 120 cu ft

8. (1) $(40)(50) − 30^2$ area of rectangle = (40)(50);
area of square = 30^2

9. (2) 20   C = πd = 3.14 × 6.5 =
20.41→20

10. (2) 57.5°   90° − 32.5° = 57.5°

11. (4) 108°   180° − 72° = 108°

12. (4) 12   34 − 12 − 10 = 12

13. (2) 16 $\frac{24}{x} = \frac{15}{10}$
15x = 240
x = 16

14. (3) 15 $a^2 + b^2 = c^2$
$9^2 + 12^2 = c^2$
$81 + 144 = c^2$
$225 = c^2$
$\sqrt{225} = c$
$15 = c$

15. (1) $\frac{2}{3}$ slope $= \frac{y_2 - y_1}{x_2 - x_1} = \frac{5 - 1}{8 - 2} = \frac{4}{6} = \frac{2}{3}$

16. (5) $\frac{8}{17}$ $\sin = \frac{\text{opposite}}{\text{hypotenuse}} = \frac{8}{17}$

Part 3

Algebra

1. E $\frac{5}{2} = 2\frac{1}{2}$

2. −1   +9 − (−4) + (−6) − 8 =
+9 + 4 − 6 − 8 =
13 − 14 = −1

3. −45 $-\frac{30}{6} + 4(-10) =$
−5 − 40 = −45

4. yes   Substitute 2 for x in the equation y = 4x − 3.
y = 4(2) − 3 = 8 − 3 = 5
The point (2, 5) is on the graph.

5. $1\frac{2}{3}$ 12x − 4 = 3x + 11
9x   = 15
x $= 1\frac{6}{9} = 1\frac{2}{3}$

6. (3)   w − 12

7. (4) 6x + 2   x + 3 + 2x − 1 + 3x = 6x + 2

8. (2) 40(2x + 6)
wife's wage = x and James's wage = x + 6
40(x + x + 6) = 40(2x + 6)

9. (5) 5(n + 3n)   n = number
3 × n = 3n
sum multiplied by 5 = 5(n + 3n)

10. (4) 45
Antonio's age = 9x and son's age = 2x
9x + 2x = 55
11x = 55
x = 5
Antonio's age = 9(5) = 45

11. (2) 21   width $= x$ and length $= 3x$

$$\text{Area } = lw$$
$$147 = 3x \cdot x$$
$$147 = 3x^2$$
$$49 = x^2$$
$$\sqrt{49} = x$$
$$7 = x$$
$$\text{length } = 3(7) = 21$$

12. (5) $5\sqrt{3}$ $\sqrt{75} = \sqrt{25 \cdot 3} = 5\sqrt{3}$

13. (1) $m = 36$ $6(m - 2) > 5(m + 5)$
$$6m - 12 > 5m + 25$$
$$m \qquad > \qquad 37$$

The other answers are each greater than 37.

14. (4) $a(a - 6)$

15. (5) $(0, -7)$ Substitute 0 for x. $y = 4(0) - 7$
$$y = -7$$

16. (3) $+3$ Substitute each value of x.
If $x = 1$, $x^2 - 5x + 6 =$
$$1^2 - 5(1) + 6 =$$
$$1 - 5 + 6 = 2, \text{ not } 0.$$
If $x = -1$, $x^2 - 5x + 6 =$
$$(-1)^2 - 5(-1) + 6 =$$
$$1 + 5 + 6 = 12, \text{ not } 0.$$
If $x = 3$, $x^2 - 5x + 6 =$
$$3^2 - 5(3) + 6 =$$
$$9 - 15 + 6 = 0.$$
$$x = 3 \text{ is a solution.}$$

Evaluation Chart

On the chart below, circle the number of the problems you got wrong. To the right of the problem numbers, you will find the sections and starting pages that cover the skills you need to solve the problems.

Pretest 1 Number Operations, Data Analysis, Statistics, and Probability

Problem	Section	Starting Page
1, 9, 13, 14, 15, 19, 20	Whole Numbers	17
7, 8, 16, 17, 18	Word Problems	51
2, 10, 21, 23, 25	Decimals	75
3, 17, 22, 24, 26	Fractions	103
11, 12, 32	Ratio and Proportion	137
4, 5, 6, 31, 33	Percent	149
27, 28, 29, 30	Data Analysis, Statistics, and Probability	197

Pretest 2 Measurement and Geometry

Problem	Section	Starting Page
1, 4, 5	Customary Measures	183
2	Metric Measures	186
3	Scales	190
6, 7, 8, 9	Perimeter, Circumference, Area, and Volume	234
10, 11	Angles	223
12, 13, 14	Triangles	259
15	Slope	331
16	Trigonometric Ratios	343

Pretest 3 Algebra

Problem	Section	Starting Page
1, 2, 3	Signed Numbers	281
6, 7, 8, 9	Expressions	292
4, 5, 12	Equations	294
10, 11	Word Problems	315
13	Inequalities	304
14	Factoring	339
15	Coordinate Plane	323
16	Quadratic Equations	346

Chapter 1

Whole Numbers

Whole numbers are written with the **digits** 0, 1, 2, 3, 4, 5, 6, 7, 8, and 9. You can think of a whole number as a number that 1 divides into with no remainder. The number 27 is a whole number. The number $3\frac{1}{2}$ is not. In this chapter you will review operations with whole numbers.

Number Values and Facts

Place Value

The number 307 is a three-digit number. The number 3700 is a four-digit number. **Place value** means that the position of each digit determines its value. The diagram below shows the names of the first 10 whole number places.

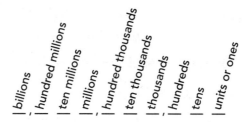

Compare the value of the digit 3 in two different numbers. The 3 in 307 is in the hundreds place. It has a value of 3 × 100 or 300. The 3 in 3700 is in the thousands place. It has a value of 3 × 1000 or 3000.

EXERCISE 1

Directions: Answer each problem below.

1. Circle the three-digit numbers in this list.

   27   389   2,056   417   16,210

2. Circle the four-digit numbers in this list.

   2,100   19,307   1,456   158,300   88,400

3. Circle the five-digit numbers in this list.

   75,000   8,640   127,200   998   32,312

4. Underline the digit in the tens place in each number.

   45   217   80,320   6,654   209

5. Underline the digit in the thousands place in each number.

   52,600   168,420   9,712   1,253,840   27,610

6. In what place is the digit 3 in 435,780?

7. In what place is the digit 5 in 85,460,000?

8. What is the value of the digit 8 in the number 26,803?

9. What is the value of the digit 6 in the number 469,551?

10. What is the value of the digit 2 in 86,420?

11. What is the value of the digit 9 in 2,925,000?

12. What is the value of the digit 4 in 34,783,000?

Answers are on page 383.

Arithmetic Facts

The building blocks of mathematics are the arithmetic facts.

You need to know that $9 + 7 = 16$ and that $7 + 9 = 16$ to do addition problems. You also need to know the *opposite* facts, $16 - 9 = 7$ and $16 - 7 = 9$, to do subtraction problems.

You need to know that $6 \times 9 = 54$ and that $9 \times 6 = 54$ to do multiplication problems. You also need to know the *opposite* facts, $54 \div 9 = 6$ and $54 \div 6 = 9$, to do division problems.

The Addition Facts

The answer to an addition problem is called the **sum**. Exercise 2 is a review of facts you use to add and subtract.

EXERCISE 2

Directions: In each box in the grid labeled "Addition Facts," write the *sum* of the number on the top and the number on the side. A few answers have been filled in as examples.

Addition Facts

	1	3	8	4	6	9	7	10	2	5
8	9									
1		4								
3										
6										
4					10					
9										
5										
7								17		
2										
10										

Answers are on page 383.

The Multiplication Facts

The answer to a multiplication problem is call the **product**. Knowing the multiplication (and division) facts is also essential for your work in mathematics.

Directions: In each box in the grid labeled "Multiplication Facts," write the *product* of the number on the top and the number on the side. Again, a few answers have been filled in as examples.

Multiplication Facts

	12	3	1	4	10	9	7	5	6	8	11	0	2
9													
7													
4		12											
5													
2							14						
1													
8													
10													
12			12										
0													
11													
3													
6													

Answers are on page 383.

Now is the time to review any addition or multiplication facts that you got wrong. Memorize any fact that you missed before you continue to work with whole numbers.

Types of Whole Numbers

Mathematics is a kind of specialized language. Terms are used in mathematics in ways that are different from their use in ordinary speech. This lesson introduces some of the specialized words used to describe **whole numbers**. Whole numbers include 0 and all **positive** numbers.

An **odd** number is not evenly divisible by 2. The units digit of an odd number is 1, 3, 5, 7, or 9. The numbers 23 and 49 are odd numbers. The numbers 8 and 56 are not.

An **even** number is evenly divisible by 2. The units digit of an even number is 0, 2, 4, 6, or 8. The numbers 12 and 198 are even numbers. The numbers 11 and 243 are not.

Consecutive numbers follow one after the other. The three consecutive numbers that follow 12 are 13, 14, and 15. The two consecutive even numbers that follow 20 are 22 and 24.

A **prime** number is evenly divisible by only itself and 1. For example, the number 7 is a prime number because only 7 and 1 divide into 7 evenly. The number 15 is not a prime number. Besides 15 and 1, the numbers 3 and 5 also divide evenly into 15.

A **factor** is another word for a divisor. A factor is a number that divides evenly into another number. The factors of 15 are 1, 3, 5, and 15. The factors of 12 are 1, 2, 3, 4, and 6.

EXERCISE 4

Directions: Answer each problem below.

1. Circle the even numbers in this list: 12   56   87   100   241   1026

2. Circle the odd numbers in this list: 9   41   58   63   241   302

3. What are the first two consecutive numbers after 15?

4. List the first three consecutive even numbers that follow 40.

5. List all the prime numbers between 10 and 30.

6. What is the first prime number after 30?

7. Which of the following is *not* a factor of 24?   2   4   6   8   12   16

8. Which of the following is a prime factor of 56?   4   7   8   18

9. List the four factors of the number 8.

10. List the three prime factors of the number 30.

Answers are on page 383.

The Basic Operations

The four basic operations in arithmetic are **addition, subtraction, multiplication,** and **division**. This book assumes that you have a basic understanding of these four operations. If you have trouble following the examples or if you miss more than a couple of problems in the next exercise, take the time to practice these four basic skills in another book such as Contemporary's *Number Power* series.

Addition

Recall that the answer to an addition problem is called the **sum**, or **total**. The symbol for addition is the $+$ sign.

Example 1 $2723 + 8 + 925 =$

Step 1 Line up the numbers with units under units, tens under tens, and so on.	$\begin{array}{r} {\overset{\scriptstyle 1\ \ 1}{2723}} \\ 8 \\ +\ 925 \\ \hline 3656 \end{array}$
Step 2 Add each column, and carry the digit on the left of each sum to the next column. (You may know this as **regrouping**.)	

To check the answer to an addition problem, add the numbers from the bottom to the top. The sum should equal your original sum. For the last example, $925 + 8 + 2723 = 3656$.

Subtraction

The answer to a subtraction problem is called the **difference.** The symbol for subtraction is the $-$ sign. To find the difference between two numbers, put the larger number on top.

Example 2 Find the difference between 982 and 6039.

Step 1 Put the larger number, 6039, on top. Line up the digits with units under units, tens under tens, and so on. Start subtracting with the units: $9 - 2 = 7$.	$\begin{array}{r} {\overset{\scriptstyle 5\,9}{}}{\overset{\scriptstyle 1\ 1}{6039}} \\ -\ 982 \\ \hline 5057 \end{array}$
Step 2 Borrow (or regroup) to subtract the other columns.	

To check the answer to a subtraction problem, add the difference (the answer) $+$ the bottom number in the original problem. The sum should equal the top number of the original problem. For the last example, $5057 + 982 = 6039$.

Multiplication

The answer to a multiplication problem is called the **product**. The $\times$ sign and the raised dot $\cdot$ mean to multiply. Numbers in parentheses with no signs between the number and the parentheses also mean to multiply.

Look at these four ways of writing the problem "4 times 5 equals 20."

$$4 \times 5 = 20 \qquad 4 \cdot 5 = 20 \qquad 4(5) = 20 \qquad (4)(5) = 20$$

Example 3 Find the product of 127 and 32.

Step 1 Put the number with more digits, 127, on top, and multiply each digit in 127 by the 2 in 32 to find the first partial product.

$$
\begin{array}{r}
127 \\
\times\ 32 \\
\hline
254 \leftarrow \text{partial product} \\
381 \leftarrow \text{partial product} \\
\hline
4064
\end{array}
$$

Step 2 Multiply each digit in 127 by the 3 in 32, and start the second partial product under the 3.

Step 3 Add the partial products.

One way **to check the answer to a multiplication problem** is to divide the product by one of the numbers you multiplied by. The result should equal the other number in the original problem. For the last example, $4064 \div 32 = 127$.

Division

The answer to a division problem is called the **quotient.** The $\div$ sign, the $\overline{)}$ sign, the fraction bar, and the slash / all mean to divide.

In the problem "21 divided by 7 equals 3," 21 is called the **dividend**, 7 is the **divisor,** and 3 is the **quotient.**

Look at these four ways of writing the problem "21 divided by 7 equals 3."

$$21 \div 7 = 3 \qquad 7\overline{)21}^{\ 3} \qquad \frac{21}{7} = 3 \qquad 21/7 = 3$$

The four steps to solving a division problem are to divide, multiply, subtract, and bring down the next number. Repeat these steps until you have completed the division.

Example 4 Find the quotient of 156 divided by 9.

Step 1 In this problem, 156 is the dividend and 9 is the divisor. Start by dividing 9 into 15, the first two digits of 156.

$$
\begin{array}{r}
17\ \text{r}\ 3 \\
9\overline{)156} \\
9 \\
\hline
66 \\
63 \\
\hline
3
\end{array}
$$

Step 2 Continue to multiply, subtract, and bring down the next number. Then divide 9 into 66.

Step 3 Multiply and subtract. The remainder is 3.

To check the answer to a division problem, multiply the divisor and the quotient. Then add the remainder if there is one. The result should equal the original dividend. For the last example, $17 \times 9 = 153$. Then $153 + 3 = 156$.

EXERCISE 5

Directions: Solve and check each problem.

1. $25,624 + 92,183 =$

2. $60,845 - 2,926 =$

3. Find the difference between 49,005 and 6,774.

4. $83 + 2096 + 194 =$

5. $6 \times 5708 =$

6. What is the product of 349 and 74?

7. $872(409) =$

8. Find the product of 65 and 50,000.

9. $446 \div 17 =$

10. $2464/8 =$

11. Find the quotient of 54,036 divided by 6.

12. $30,045 - 15,586 =$

13. Find the sum of 194, 8, 2366, and 850.

14. $(96)(500) =$

15. What is the difference between 3,000,000 and 816,000?

16. $7 \cdot 29,058 =$

17. $\dfrac{37,600}{800} =$

18. What is the product of 8000 and 74?

19. What is the difference between 5,040,000 and 264,500?

20. What is the quotient of 10,710 divided by 35?

21. Find the product of 8 and 5090.

22. How much is 5076 divided by 12?

23. What is the difference between 88 and 7000?

24. $400,300 - 9,216 =$

25. 2820/4 =

26. 346(450) =

27. 2,900 + 857 + 11,630 + 405 =

28. 56,423 ÷ 7 =

29. 1,300,500 − 807,631 =

30. $\frac{14,060}{19}$ =

Answers are on page 383.

GED Test-Taking Shortcuts

Rounding

Think about the number 472. Is 472 closer to 400 or to 500? The numbers 400 and 500 are called **round numbers** because they end with zeros. 472 is closer to 500 than to 400. 472 rounded to the nearest hundred is 500.

—————————————————— R U L E ——————————————————

To round a whole number, follow these steps:
1. Underline the digit in the place you are rounding to.
2. a. If the digit to the right of the underlined digit is *greater than or equal to 5*, add 1 to the underlined digit.
   b. If the digit to the right of the underlined digit is *less than 5*, leave the underlined digit as is.
3. Change all the digits to the right of the underlined digit to zeros.

Example 1   Round 274 to the nearest hundred.

Step 1   Underline the digit in the hundreds place, 2. $\underline{2}74 \rightarrow 300$

Step 2   The digit to the right of 2 is 7. Since 7 is greater than 5, add 1 to 2: $2 + 1 = 3$.

Step 3   Change the digits to the right of 3 to zeros.

Example 2   Round 86,492 to the nearest thousand.

Step 1   Underline the digit in the thousands place, 6. $8\underline{6},492 \rightarrow 86,000$

Step 2   The digit to the right of 6 is 4. Since 4 is less than 5, leave 6 as is.

Step 3   Change the digits to the right of 6 to zeros.

<u>Example 3</u>   Round 298,406 to the nearest ten thousand.

Step 1   Underline the digit in the ten thousands   298,406 → 300,000
place, 9.

Step 2   The digit to the right of 9 is 8. Since 8 is greater
than 5, add 1 to 9: $9 + 1 = 10$.

Step 3   Write 0 in the ten thousands place, and add 1
to the hundred thousands: $1 + 2 = 3$. Then
change the digits to the right of 3 to zeros.

EXERCISE 6

Directions: Solve each problem below.

1. Round each number to the nearest ten.
    76   243   6128   297

2. Round each number to the nearest hundred.
    13,719   4,266   548   5,952

3. Round each number to the nearest thousand.
    5,375   49,721   92,483

4. Round each number to the nearest ten thousand.
    73,996   408,000   2,695,000

5. Last year Angela made $26,812. What was her income to the
    nearest thousand?

6. Mark's monthly car payment is $119. What is the payment to the
    nearest ten?

Answers are on page 384.

Estimating

Estimating means finding an approximate answer. Estimating is a convenient
way to decide whether an answer is reasonable. Most estimation methods
involve rounding numbers.

One way to get an estimate is to round each number in a problem to the
same place. The symbol ≈ in the next examples means "approximately equals."

Example 1   Estimate the answer to the problem 13,581 + 2,617 + 466 by first rounding each number to the nearest hundred.

Step 1   Round each number to the nearest hundred.

$$13{,}581 + 2{,}617 + 466 \approx$$

Step 2   Add the rounded numbers. The exact answer is 16,664.

$$13{,}600 + 2{,}600 + 500 = 16{,}700$$

Another way to estimate is called **front-end estimation.** Round each number in a problem to the *left-most place.* Then do the arithmetic operation with the rounded numbers.

Example 2   Use front-end estimation to estimate the answer to 59,416 − 6,834.

Step 1   Round 59,416 to the nearest ten thousand, and round 6,834 to the nearest thousand.

$$59{,}416 - 6{,}834 \approx$$

Step 2   Subtract the rounded numbers. The exact answer is 52,582.

$$60{,}000 - 7{,}000 = 53{,}000$$

Rounding each number to the same place in a problem or using front-end estimation works well with addition, subtraction, and multiplication. Division, however, is more difficult.

Think about the number of digits in the answer to any division problem.

Example 3   How many digits are in the answer to the problem 4756 ÷ 82?

Step 1   Set the problem up for division.

Step 2   The digits of the quotient will be above the 5 and the 6 in the dividend 4756. The answer will have two digits.

$$82\overline{)4756}^{\,\text{xx}}$$

If you use front-end estimation to estimate the answer to the last problem, you get the new problem 5000 ÷ 80, but this division does not come out evenly. Look for **compatible pairs** of numbers. Compatible pairs divide evenly. Although 80 does not divide evenly into 5000, 80 does divide evenly into 4800. The numbers 80 and 4800 are a compatible pair.

Compare the pairs of number in the following list:

incompatible pairs	related compatible pairs
8 and 43	8 and 40 or 8 and 48
6 and 40	6 and 36 or 6 and 42
78 and 610	80 and 640
53 and 277	50 and 300

Example 4   Use compatible pairs to estimate the answer to the
problem $4756 \div 82$.

(1) 28   (2) 42   (3) 58   (4) 92

Step 1   Round 82 to 80 and 4756 to 4800 and divide. $4800 \div 80 = 60$

Step 2   Among the choices, the answer that is closest
to 60 is choice (3) 58.

EXERCISE 7

Directions: For problems 1–4, use front-end estimation to estimate each
answer.

1. $216 + 98 + 4730 =$ $7{,}309 + 826 + 39{,}276 =$ $88 + 19 + 278 =$

2. $38{,}506 - 8{,}917 =$ $196{,}209 - 42{,}520 =$ $2945 - 881 =$

3. $41 \times 783 =$ $68 \times 912 =$ $508 \times 73 =$

4. $7238 + 496 + 121 =$ $93{,}276 - 14{,}318 =$ $92 \times 1243 =$

For problems 5–7, state the number of digits in each answer.

5. The answer to the problem $2340 \div 9$ has how many digits?

6. The answer to the problem $8\overline{)9704}$ as how many digits?

7. The answer to the problem $63\overline{)882}$ has how many digits?

8. The answer to the problem $1926 \div 3$ is between

(1) 60 and 70   (2) 80 and 90   (3) 600 and 700   (4) 1000 and 2000

9. The answer to $72\overline{)864}$ is between

(1) 100 and 200   (2) 50 and 60   (3) 10 and 20   (4) 5 and 10

10. The answer to $38\overline{)52{,}136}$ is between

(1) 1000 and 2000   (2) 500 and 1000
(3) 300 and 400   (4) 200 and 300

Use compatible pairs to choose the correct answer.

11. 9)5238

(1) 692 (2) 582 (3) 402 (4) 372

12. 23,072 ÷ 32 =

(1) 721 (2) 632 (3) 76 (4) 61

13. 487)30,681

(1) 41 (2) 63 (3) 327 (4) 637

14. 12,296 ÷ 58 =

(1) 142 (2) 182 (3) 212 (4) 292

Answers are on page 384.

Using a Calculator

The GED Mathematics Test permits the use of a calculator on half of the mathematics test. The Casio *fx*-260 solar is the only calculator permitted with the test.

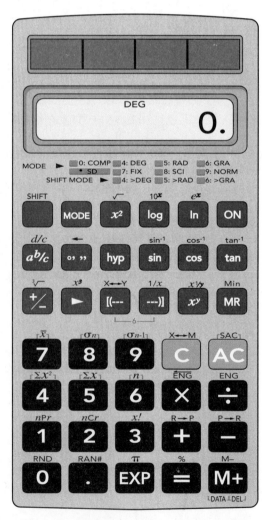

The calculator directions throughout this book refer specifically to the Casio *fx*-260. Other calculators may not work the same way.

To turn the calculator on, press the **ON** key at the upper right or the red **AC** key. A small "DEG" will appear at the top center of the display, and "0." will appear at the right of the display.

To perform any arithmetic operation, first press **AC** (all clear) to clear the display. Then enter the numbers and operating signs. Then press **=** (the equals sign) key when you are finished.

Example 1   Use a calculator to find the sum of $9 + 7$.

Press **AC**.

Press **9** **+** **7** **=**.

The display should read   16.

Example 2   Use the calculator to find the difference of $28 - 9$.

Press **AC**.

Press **2** **8** **−** **9** **=**.

The display should read   19.

Example 3   Use a calculator to find the product of 8×56.

Press **AC**.

Press **8** **×** **5** **6** **=**.

The display should read   448.

Example 4   Use a calculator to find the quotient of $9\overline{)243}$.

Press **AC**.

Press **2** **4** **3** **÷** **9** **=**.

The display should read   27.

EXERCISE 8

Directions: Solve all the problems in Exercise 7, page 27, with a calculator. Use the original numbers, not rounded numbers.

Answers are on page 385.

Special Topics with Whole Numbers

Mean and Median

A **mean** is a number that represents a set of numbers. *Mean* is another name for "average."

───────────────────────── RULE ─────────────────────────

To find the mean of a set of numbers, add the numbers in the set and divide by the number of numbers in the set.

───

Example 1 Find the mean of 10, 15, 23, and 28.

Step 1 Find the sum by adding the four numbers.

$$10 + 15 + 23 + 28 = 76$$

Step 2 Divide the sum by 4, the number of numbers in the set. The mean, or average, of the four numbers is 19.

$$76 \div 4 = 19$$

Finding a mean is a common application of arithmetic skills. Look at the next example.

Example 2 Houses on the block where the Garcias live recently sold for $140,000, $143,000, and $152,000. What was the mean selling price of the houses?

Step 1 Find the sum by adding the cost of each house.

$$\begin{array}{r} \$140,000 \\ 143,000 \\ + 152,000 \\ \hline \$435,000 \end{array}$$

$$\begin{array}{r} \$145,000 \\ 3\overline{)\$435,000} \end{array}$$

Step 2 Divide by the number of houses, 3. The mean selling price was $145,000.

Example 3 Use the calculator to find the mean of 17, 29, and 23.

Press [AC].

Press [1] [7] [+] [2] [9] [+] [2] [3] [=].

The display should read [69.].

Press [÷] [3] [=]

The display should read [23.].

A **median** is a number in the middle of a group of numbers. Half of the numbers in a group are greater than the median, and half are less. For the house prices in Example 2 the median is $143,000.

RULE

To find the median for a group of numbers, arrange the numbers in order from smallest to largest. The number in the middle is the median.

Example 4   Lorenzo had scores of 90, 72, 88, 85, and 93 on five math tests. What was his median score?

Step 1   Arrange the scores in order   72 85 **88** 90 93
from smallest to largest.

Step 2   Find the number in the middle.
The median score is 88.

Sometimes there are two numbers in the middle of a group of numbers. The median is the mean, or average, of these two numbers.

Example 5   Ruby had scores of 78, 97, 72, and 84 on four Spanish quizzes. What was her median score?

Step 1   Arrange the scores in order   72 **78 84** 97
from smallest to largest.

Step 2   Find the sum of the two   78 + 84 = 162
middle scores, 78 and 84.

Step 3   Divide the sum by 2.   162 ÷ 2 = 81
Ruby's median score was 81.

EXERCISE 9

Directions: Use the calculator to solve each problem.

1. Find both the mean and the median for 353, 19, and 207.

2. Find both the mean and the median for 2046, 971, 3113, and 1850.

3. Find both the mean and the median for 240, 313, 189, and 270.

4. Ramon weighs 187 pounds. His brother Manny weighs 159 pounds. What is their average weight in pounds?

5. The noon temperature Monday was 69°F. Tuesday the noon temperature was 71°F. Wednesday it was 56°F, Thursday it was 63°F, and Friday it was 66° F. What was the mean noon temperature for these days?

6. Last year Fran's salary was $33,900. This year her salary is $34,700. Next year her salary will be $35,800. Find her average salary for these years.

7. After expenses were paid, the Mini-Mart had a profit of $2566 in January, $3327 in February, and $1928 in March. Find the average profit for these months.

Answers are on page 385.

Powers

The mathematical expression 5^2 is read as "five to the second power." The 5 is called the **base**. The 2 is called the **exponent.** The exponent tells how many times to write the base in a multiplication problem.

─────────── R U L E ───────────

To find a power, follow these steps:
1. Write the base as many times as the exponent indicates.
2. Multiply.

___

Example 1   What is the value of 5^2 ?

Write 5 two times and multiply. $5^2 = 5 \times 5 = 25$

A number raised to the second power is sometimes called the **square** of a number. For the last example, you can say, "5 squared equals 25."

Example 2   Evaluate 4^3.

Write 4 three times and multiply. $4^3 = 4 \times 4 \times 4 = 64$
The first product is $4 \times 4 = 16$.
The second product is $16 \times 4 = 64$.

A number raised to the third power is sometimes called the cube of a number. For the last example, you can say, "4 cubed equals 64."

Study the next three examples carefully.

─────────── R U L E ───────────

Any number to the first power equals that number.

___

Example 3   What is 7^1?

There is no multiplication in this problem. $7^1 = 7$
Raising 7 to the first power means to write
7 one time.

——————————————————————— R U L E ———————————————————————

1 raised to any power equals 1.

———

Example 4   What is 1^3?

Write 1 three times and multiply. $1^3 = 1 \times 1 \times 1 = 1$

——————————————————————— R U L E ———————————————————————

Any number to the zero power equals 1.

———

Example 5   What is 7^0?

Raising a number to the zero power is like $7^0 = 1$
dividing a number by itself. $\dfrac{7}{7} = 1$

To square a number with a Casio *fx*-260 calculator, enter the number
followed by the $\boxed{x^2}$ key.

Example 6   Use the calculator to find 38^2.

Press $\boxed{AC}$.

Press $\boxed{3}$ $\boxed{8}$ $\boxed{x^2}$.

The display should read $\boxed{\qquad 1444.}$.

You can use the calculator $\boxed{x^y}$ key to raise a number to the third power
or higher.

Example 7   Use the calculator to find 6^5.

Press $\boxed{AC}$.

Press $\boxed{6}$ $\boxed{x^y}$ $\boxed{5}$ $\boxed{=}$.

The display should read $\boxed{\qquad 7776.}$.

EXERCISE 10

Directions: Find the value of each expression. Use the calculator to check your answers.

1. $6^2 =$ $1^3 =$ $2^4 =$

2. $5^3 =$ $3^5 =$ $10^2 =$

3. $9^4 =$ $15^2 =$ $8^0 =$

4. $20^2 =$ $30^5 =$ $16^1 =$

5. $25^2 =$ $8^4 =$ $50^2 =$

6. The first six places in our number system are units, tens, hundreds, thousands, ten thousands, and hundred thousands. Units can be written as 10^0. Tens can be written as 10^1. Write the name of the next four places in our number system as powers of 10.

Answers are on page 385.

Square Roots

Just as subtraction is the opposite of addition and division is the opposite of multiplication, finding powers has an opposite operation. The opposite of raising a number to the second power is finding the **square root** of a number. The square root is indicated with the symbol $\sqrt{\ }$.

To find the square root of a number, ask yourself, "What number multiplied by itself equals this number?"

Example 1   Find $\sqrt{25}$.

5 multiplied by itself equals 25. $\sqrt{25} = 5$

Example 2   Find $\sqrt{144}$.

12 multiplied by itself equals 144. $\sqrt{144} = 12$

Following is a list of common perfect square roots. Take the time now to memorize this list.

$\sqrt{1} = 1$	$\sqrt{36} = 6$	$\sqrt{121} = 11$	$\sqrt{400} = 20$
$\sqrt{4} = 2$	$\sqrt{49} = 7$	$\sqrt{144} = 12$	$\sqrt{900} = 30$
$\sqrt{9} = 3$	$\sqrt{64} = 8$	$\sqrt{169} = 13$	$\sqrt{1600} = 40$
$\sqrt{16} = 4$	$\sqrt{81} = 9$	$\sqrt{196} = 14$	$\sqrt{2500} = 50$
$\sqrt{25} = 5$	$\sqrt{100} = 10$	$\sqrt{225} = 15$	$\sqrt{3600} = 60$

There are several methods for finding the square roots of larger numbers. One method is to guess. Then divide your guess into the number for which you are trying to find the square root. The average of your guess and the answer to the division problem is often the square root you are looking for. Study the example carefully.

Example 3 Find $\sqrt{484}$.

Step 1 Guess a round number you think may be close to the correct answer. For example, 50 is a bad guess because $50 \times 50 = 2500$, which is much too large. But 20 is a good guess because $20 \times 20 = 400$, which is closer to 484.

Step 2 Divide 20 into 484 and ignore the remainder. $484 \div 20 = 24r\_$

Step 3 Find the average of the division answer, 24, with the guess, 20.

$24 + 20 = 44$
$$\frac{44}{2} = 22$$

Step 4 Check by multiplying 22 by itself. $22 \times 22 = 484$
The square root of 484 is 22.

Another method of finding a square root is to use the answers provided in a multiple-choice question. Substitute each answer until you find the correct square root.

Example 4 Which of the following is the solution to $\sqrt{841}$?

(1) 21   (2) 29   (3) 31   (4) 39   (5) 41

Multiply each answer choice by itself.
For choice (1), $21 \times 21 = 441$.
For choice (2), $29 \times 29 = 841$.
Choice (2) is correct. $\sqrt{841} = 29$

To find a square root on a Casio *fx*-260 calculator, you need to use two keys, the [SHIFT] key at the upper left followed by the [x^2] key. The [SHIFT] key changes the operation from finding a second power to finding a square root.

Example 5 Use a calculator to find $\sqrt{841}$.

Press [AC].

Press [8] [4] [1] [SHIFT] [x^2].

The display should read [29.].

EXERCISE 11

Directions: For problems 1–4, use the answer choices to find each square root.

1. $\sqrt{196} =$ (1) 12   (2) 14   (3) 24   (4) 26

2. $\sqrt{441} =$ (1) 11   (2) 19   (3) 21   (4) 29

3. $\sqrt{1024} =$ (1) 18   (2) 22   (3) 28   (4) 32

4. $\sqrt{1521} =$ (1) 21   (2) 29   (3) 31   (4) 39

For problems 5–8, try the method of guessing, dividing, and averaging to find each square root.

5. $\sqrt{361} =$

6. $\sqrt{676} =$

7. $\sqrt{1849} =$

8. $\sqrt{3364} =$

9. Suppose the letter s represents the square root of 6889. Which of the following statements is true about the letter s?

(1) $s + s = 6889$

(2) $s \times s = 6889$

(3) $s - s = 6889$

(4) $s \div s = 6889$

For problems 10–12, use a calculator to find each square root.

10. $\sqrt{5184} =$

11. $\sqrt{2704} =$

12. $\sqrt{1089} =$

Answers are on page 386.

Number Sequences and Patterns

A **number sequence**, or **number series**, is a list of numbers in a special order or pattern. The numbers 1, 2, 3, 4, 5, 6, . . . form the most familiar sequence. The number 7 is the next **term** in the sequence.

––––––––––– R U L E –––––––––––

To find a missing number in a number sequence, first find the pattern that changes the numbers from left to right.

Example 1   Find the next term in the sequence 5, 8, 11, 14, . . .

    Step 1   Find how the sequence changes.
                This sequence changes by adding 3.

$$\underset{+3 \quad +3 \quad +3}{5 \quad 8 \quad 11 \quad 14}$$

    Step 2   Add 3 to the last term. $14 + 3 = 17$

Example 2   Find the next term in the sequence
                2, 7, 4, 9, 6, 11, . . .

    Step 1   Find how the pattern changes.
                The sequence increases by 5
                and then decreases by 3.

$$\underset{+5 \quad -3 \quad +5 \quad -3 \quad +5}{2 \quad 7 \quad 4 \quad 9 \quad 6 \quad 11}$$

    Step 2   Subtract 3 from the last term. $11 - 3 = 8$

TIP
Pay attention to the term you are asked to find. You may not be asked to find the next term.

Example 3   What is the seventh term in the sequence 1, 3, 9, 27, 81, . . . ?

    Step 1   Find how the pattern changes.
                The sequence changes by
                multiplying by 3.

$$\underset{\times 3 \quad \times 3 \quad \times 3 \quad \times 3}{1 \quad 3 \quad 9 \quad 27 \quad 81}$$

    Step 2   Find the sixth term. Multiply 81 by 3. $81 \times 3 = 243$

    Step 3   Find the seventh term. Multiply 243 by 3. $243 \times 3 = 729$

          Number sequence problems may be in the form of word problems where you need to find a pattern.

Example 4   One day in June the temperature at 9:00 A.M. was 62°F. The temperature at 10:00 A.M. was 67°F, and the temperature at 11:00 A.M. was 72°F. If the temperature change continued in the same pattern, what was the temperature at noon?

    Step 1   Find how the temperature changes each hour.
                The temperature goes up 5° each hour.

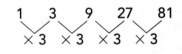

    Step 2   Add 5 to the last term. $72° + 5° = 77°$

EXERCISE 12

Directions: Solve each problem.

1. Find the next term in the sequence 6, 12, 24, 48, . . .

2. What is the sixth term in the sequence 81, 84, 87, 90, . . . ?

3. What is the next term in the sequence 32, 29, 26, 23, . . . ?

4. Find the seventh term in the sequence 13, 17, 21, 25, . . .

5. What is the next term in the sequence 10, 5, 15, 10, 20, 15, . . . ?

6. Find the eighth term in the sequence 100, 81, 64, 49, 36, 25, . . .

7. Find the next term in the sequence 5, 9, 17, 33, . . .

8. What is the eighth term in the sequence 2, 3, 5, 8, 12, 17, . . . ?

9. Find the next term in the sequence 320, 160, 80, 40, 20, . . .

10. Find the ninth term in the sequence 4, 8, 7, 14, 13, 26, 25, . . .

11. Every month a committee is withdrawing money from the building fund at the rate shown in the table below. How much will be in the account in August?

Month	March	April	May	June
Balance	$30,000	$24,000	$18,000	$12,000

12. The table below shows the population of Bridge Creek. If the population continues in the same pattern, what will be the population of Bridge Creek in the year 2010?

Year	1910	1930	1950	1970	1990
Population	1,500	3,000	6,000	12,000	24,000

Answers are on page 386.

Properties of Numbers

There are three **properties**, or characteristics, of numbers that you should know. These properties describe the way arithmetic operations such as addition and multiplication are performed. You do not have to memorize the names of these properties, but you should be able to understand them and apply them to problems.

The Commutative Property

The commutative property applies to both addition and multiplication. For addition, the commutative property means that you can add two numbers in any order. The sums will be the same. For example, $6 + 3$ and $3 + 6$ both add up to 9.

Mathematicians often write properties with letters instead of numbers. You will get more practice using letters when you work with algebra. The letters a and b stand for any two numbers.

COMMUTATIVE PROPERTY FOR ADDITION

In addition the numbers can be added in any order.
$a + b = b + a$

The commutative property for multiplication means that you can multiply two numbers in any order. The products will be the same. For example, both 5×7 and 7×5 equal 35.

COMMUTATIVE PROPERTY FOR MULTIPLICATION

The commutative property for multiplication can be written in two ways.
$a \times b = b \times a$ or $ab = ba$

Notice the expression $ab = ba$. When two letters stand next to each other with no signs between them, this indicates multiplication. Again, remember that a and b stand for any two numbers.

Example 1   Which of the following is the same as $9 + 8$?

   (1) 9×8

   (2) 8×9

   (3) $8 + 9$

   (4) $9 - 8$

Answer (3) $8 + 9$ is the correct choice. $9 + 8$ and $8 + 9$ both add up to 17. This is an example of the commutative property for addition.

Notice that the commutative property does *not* apply to subtraction or division. The problem $6 - 4$ is not the same as $4 - 6$. Also, the problem $\frac{20}{5}$ is not the same as $\frac{5}{20}$.

The Associative Property

The associative property also works for addition and multiplication. For addition, the associative property means that when you add three numbers, you can first add any two of the numbers and then add the third.

ASSOCIATIVE PROPERTY FOR ADDITION

First add any two of the numbers and then add the third.
$(a + b) + c = a + (b + c)$

The parentheses group numbers together. Suppose you want to add $2 + 5 + 6$. You could first add 2 and 5 to get 7, and then add 7 and 6 to get 13. Or you could first add 5 and 6 to get 11, and then add 2 and 11 to get 13. The results are the same.

If you replace a with 2, b with 5, and c with 6, the associative property of addition looks like this:

$$(a + b) + c = a + (b + c)$$
$$(2 + 5) + 6 = 2 + (5 + 6)$$
$$7 + 6 = 2 + 11$$
$$13 = 13$$

ASSOCIATIVE PROPERTY FOR MULTIPLICATION

First multiply two numbers and then multiply that product by the third number.
$(a \times b) \times c = a \times (b \times c)$ or $(ab)c = a(bc)$

Again, the parentheses group numbers together. Suppose you want to solve the multiplication problem $2 \times 3 \times 4$. You could first multiply 2×3 to get 6, and then multiply 6×4 to get 24. Or you could first multiply 3×4 to get 12, and then multiply 2×12 to get 24. The results are the same.

If you replace a with 2, b with 3, and c with 4, the associative property of multiplication looks like this:

$$(ab)c = a(bc)$$
$$(2 \times 3) \times 4 = 2 \times (3 \times 4)$$
$$6 \times 4 = 2 \times 12$$
$$24 = 24$$

<u>**Example 2**</u>   Which of the following is the same as (10 + 12) + 15?

> (1) 10(12 + 15)
> (2) (10 + 12)15
> (3) 10 + 15 + 12 + 15
> (4) 10 + (12 + 15)

Answer (4) is the correct choice. You could first add 10 and 12 to get 22, and then add 22 and 15 to get 37. Or, you could first add 12 and 15 to get 27, and then add 10 and 27 to get 37. This is an example of the associative property for addition.

The Distributive Property

The distributive property is about multiplying a sum or a difference. It means that multiplication is distributive *over* addition and subtraction. For example, if you want to solve (4 + 5) × 3, you can first add 4 and 5 to get 9 and then multiply 3 by 9 to get 27. Or, you can multiply 3 by 4 to get 12, multiply 3 by 5 to get 15, and then add 12 and 15 to get 27. The results are the same.

DISTRIBUTIVE PROPERTY

The distributive property applies to both addition and subtraction.
$a(b + c) = ab + ac$
$a(b - c) = ab - ac$

If you replace a with 3, b with 5, and c with 4, the distributive property looks like this with addition:

$$a(b + c) = ab + ac$$
$$3(5 + 4) = (3 \times 5) + (3 \times 4)$$
$$3(9) = 15 + 12$$
$$27 = 27$$

The distributive property looks like this with subtraction:

$$a(b - c) = ab - ac$$
$$3(5 - 4) = (3 \times 5) - (3 \times 4)$$
$$3(1) = 15 - 12$$
$$3 = 3$$

EXERCISE 13

Directions: Apply what you have learned about properties to choose the correct answer. (Hint: To check your answers, work through each alternative.)

1. Which of the following is equal to 20 + 30?

    (1) 30 × 20
    (2) 30 − 20
    (3) 30 + 30
    (4) 30 + 20

2. Which of the following is the same as 9 × 3?

    (1) 9 − 3
    (2) 9 + 3
    (3) 3 × 9
    (4) 9 ÷ 3

3. Which of the following is the same as (9 + 7) + 4?

    (1) 4(9 + 7)
    (2) 9 + (7 + 4)
    (3) 9(7 + 4)
    (4) 7(9 + 4)

4. Which of the following is *not* equal to (5 + 2) + 6?

    (1) 7 + 6
    (2) 5 + 8
    (3) 2 + 11
    (4) 7 + 8

5. Which of the following is equal to (5 × 2) × 4?

    (1) (5 + 2) × 4
    (2) 5 × (2 × 4)
    (3) 5 × (2 + 4)
    (4) 5 + 2 × 4

6. Which of the following is *not* equal to (3 × 4) × 5?

    (1) 12 × 5
    (2) 3 × 20
    (3) 12 × 20
    (4) 15 × 4

7. Which of the following is equal to 16(14 + 27)?

    (1) 16 + 14 + 27
    (2) 14(16 + 27)
    (3) 16 × 14 + 27
    (4) (16 × 14) + (16 × 27)

8. Which of the following is *not* equal to 4(3 + 7)?

    (1) 4 × 21
    (2) 4(10)
    (3) 12 + 28
    (4) 4 × 3 + 4 × 7

9. Which of the following is *not* equal to 3(8 − 2)?

    (1) 24 − 6
    (2) 3 × 8 − 2
    (3) 3 × 8 − 3 × 2
    (4) 3 × 6

10. Which of the following is the same as (3 × 15) − (3 × 6)?

    (1) 3 − (15 × 6)
    (2) 3 × 15 × 6
    (3) 3 × 15 − 6
    (4) 3(15 − 6)

Answers are on page 386.

Order of Operations

Solving a math problem often requires more than one operation. Mathematicians have agreed on the correct order to perform these operations. It is important that you know these rules. To see what can happen if you perform operations in the wrong order, look at the example below.

Find the value of 10 + 4 × 2.

METHOD 1

If you work left to right, 10 + 4 = 14. Then 14 × 2 = 28.

METHOD 2

If you multiply first, 4 × 2 = 8. Then 10 + 8 = 18.

The second method is correct.

Memorize the following steps. Whenever you come across a problem with more than one operation, you will need to know the correct order in which to perform them.

ORDER OF OPERATIONS

When solving a problem, follow these steps in order:

1. Do operations in grouping symbols.

2. Do powers from left to right.

3. Do multiplication or division from left to right.

4. Do addition or subtraction from left to right.

The **grouping symbols** in the first line of the order of operations are *parentheses*, which you saw in the last lesson, and the *fraction bar*.

Example 1   What is the value of the expression $5(2 + 8)$?

Step 1   Perform the operations inside the parentheses first. Add $2 + 8$.

$5(2 + 8)$
$5(10)$

Step 2   Multiply 5 by 10. The answer is 50.

50

Remember that the fraction bar works as a grouping symbol. Combine numbers above or below the fraction bar first.

Example 2   Evaluate the expression $\frac{21 - 9}{4}$.

Step 1   Perform the operation above the fraction bar first. Subtract 9 from 21.

$\frac{21 - 9}{4} = \frac{12}{4}$

Step 2   Divide 12 by 4. The answer is 3.

$\frac{12}{4} = 3$

Example 3   Evaluate the expression $7^2 + (19 - 7)$.

Step 1   First perform the operation inside the parentheses.

$19 - 7 = 12$

Step 2   Next perform the powers operation.

$7^2 = 7 \times 7 = 49$

Step 3   Add 12 and 49. The answer is 61.

$12 + 49 = 61$

TIP

To remember the order of operations, remember "<u>P</u>lease <u>E</u>xcuse <u>M</u>y <u>D</u>ear <u>A</u>unt <u>S</u>ally," which stands for <u>P</u>arentheses, <u>E</u>xponents (power signs), <u>M</u>ultiply, <u>D</u>ivide, <u>A</u>dd, <u>S</u>ubtract.

If you are using the Casio *fx*-260 calculator, the order of operations is programmed into it. (Many calculators do NOT have this capability.) Be sure to key in the numbers, symbols, and operations as they occur in the problem. If a number precedes an open parenthesis, (use a ⨯ key before the parenthesis ⦗--- key.

<u>Example 4</u>   Use a calculator to find the value of 5(2 + 8).

Press `AC`.

Press `5` `×` `[(--` `2` `+` `8` `--)]` `=`.

The display should read ⌷   50. ⌷.

The Casio *fx*-260 calculator has no symbol for the extended division bar. You will need to add the open parenthesis key `[(--` and the close parenthesis key `--)]` to indicate an operation that is to be calculated first. In the next example, notice how the numbers that are grouped above the fraction bar, 21 − 9, are grouped with the `[(--` and `--)]` keys on the calculator.

<u>Example 5</u>   Use a calculator to find the value of $\frac{21 - 9}{4}$.

Press `AC`.

Press `[(--` `2` `1` `−` `9` `--)]` `÷` `4` `=`.

The display should read ⌷   3. ⌷.

EXERCISE 14

Directions: Use the order of operations to find the value of each expression. If your calculator does order of operations, check your answers with the calculator.

1. $\frac{5 + 9}{2} =$ $2 \times 6 + 4 \times 3 =$ $3(9 + 5) =$

2. $\frac{11 - 5}{3 - 1} =$ $11 \times 2 - 5 \times 3 =$ $7(12 - 3) =$

3. $\frac{8 + 4 + 9}{3} =$ $3 \cdot 5^2 =$ $4 + 6 \times 5 =$

4. $12(3 + 4) =$ $2(9 - 4) =$ $\frac{20 + 10}{20 - 10} =$

5. $(4 + 7)(5 - 2) =$ $\frac{20 - 9 + 4}{5} =$ $4 \cdot 3^2 =$

6. $10^2 - 3 \cdot 7 =$ $2(8 - 2)^2 =$ $(6 + 1) - (5 - 4) =$

Answers are on page 387.

Using a Number Grid

At the end of each chapter in this book, you will find a section called "Review and GED Practice." Each of these sections has two parts like the GED math test itself. Part I permits the use of a calculator. Part II does not.

A few problems in each part of the review ask you to mark your answers on an alternate format called a **number grid.** Each grid has five blanks above a column of numbers and symbols.

Example   Find the quotient of 5513 divided by 37. Then round your answer to the nearest ten and mark the rounded quotient on the number grid.

Step 1   Use a calculator to divide 5513 by 37. $5513/37 = 149$

Step 2   Round 149 to the nearest ten. $149 \rightarrow 150$
The answer is 150.

   To answer the question on a number grid, write the correct answer in the blank boxes at the top of each column. Use a separate column for each digit. Then fill in one circle below each column that corresponds to the digit that you wrote on top.

   Below are three correctly filled in grids with the answer 150. The first answer starts at the left side of the grid. The second answer is centered. And the third answer uses the right side of the grid.

Correct Answers

   Be careful when you fill in a number grid. Below are two incorrectly filled in grids for the last example. On the first grid, the circles were not filled in. On the second grid, all the circles were filled in the first column.

Incorrect Answers

Whole Numbers Review

PART I

Directions: Use a calculator to solve problems 1–12.

1. What is 7488 divided by 18?

2. Find the difference between 905,246 and 387,529.

3. 34,510 + 97,286 =

4. Find the difference between 32,070 and 9,958.

5. What is the quotient of 666 divided by 18?

6. Find the product of 6000 and 58.

7. 81,206 − 7,395 =

8. 356 × 48 =

9. What is the difference between 2,309,000 and 586,900?

For problems 10–12, mark each answer on the corresponding number grid.

10. 79 + 3148 + 307 =

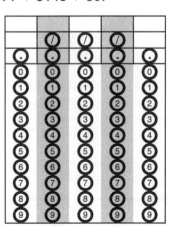

11. What is the product of 58 and 37 rounded to the nearest hundred?

12. 30,550/650 =

PART II

Directions: Solve each of the following problems without a calculator. Choose the correct answer to each problem.

13. What is the solution to $\sqrt{5184}$?

   (1) 58
   (2) 62
   (3) 68
   (4) 72
   (5) 78

14. Round 36,498 to the nearest thousand.

   (1) 36,000
   (2) 36,500
   (3) 37,000
   (3) 37,500
   (5) 38,000

15. Which of the following is *not* a factor of 24?

   (1) 2
   (2) 4
   (3) 6
   (4) 8
   (5) 10

16. Find the next term in the sequence 2, 4, 3, 6, 5, 10, . . .

   (1) 9
   (2) 11
   (3) 15
   (4) 19
   (5) 20

17. The quotient to 33,108/62 is between which of the following?

   (1) 50 and 60
   (2) 90 and 100
   (3) 200 and 300
   (4) 300 and 400
   (5) 500 and 600

18. Which of the following is equal to 35^2?

   (1)   70
   (2) 140
   (3) 625
   (4) 925
   (5) 1225

19. The table below shows the number of homes in Central County with Internet access. If the pattern continues, how many thousands of homes will have Internet access in 2004?

Year	1994	1996	1998	2000	2002	2004
Homes with Internet access (in thousands)	1	3	7	15	31	

   (1) 63
   (2) 62
   (3) 47
   (4) 32
   (5) 31

20. Which of the following is the same as
$(4 \times 9) + (4 \times 15)$?

(1) $4 \times 9 \times 15$

(2) $4(9 + 15)$

(3) $4 + 9 + 15$

(4) $9(4 + 15)$

(5) $16(4 + 9)$

21. Each day for 5 days Sam timed his trip home from work. His trips took 27, 36, 28, 39, and 40 minutes. What is the average number of minutes for these trips?

(1) 28

(2) 30

(3) 32

(4) 34

(5) 36

22. What is the smallest prime number greater than 20?

(1) 21

(2) 23

(3) 25

(4) 27

(5) 29

For problems 23–25, mark each answer on the corresponding number grid.

23. Following are the attendance figures for each of four nights at a high school basketball tournament: 1024, 1263, 1137, 1440. Find the median attendance for the four nights.

24. Evaluate the expression $\dfrac{70 \times 2}{50 - 30}$.

25. Find the value of the expression
$30 \div 6 + (8 - 4)$.

Answers are on page 387.

You should have gotten at least 20 problems right on the last exercise. If you did not get 20 problems right, review your whole-number skills before you go on. If you got 20 or more right, correct any problem you got wrong. Then go on to the next chapter.

Chapter 2
Word Problems

Word problems often scare people, but they should not. There is no secret to solving word problems. Experience and practice are the best help.

RULE

Use these five steps to organize your thinking about word problems:

1. Understand the question—what is being asked for?

2. Decide what information you need to answer the question.

3. Choose the arithmetic operation (or operations)—addition, subtraction, multiplication, or division.

4. Solve the problem and check your work.

5. Make sure that you answered the question and that your answer makes sense.

Example Laura works at a part-time job 20 hours a week. She makes $9 an hour. How much money does she make a week?

Step 1 *Question:* How much money does she make a week?

Step 2 *Information:* 20 hours at $9 an hour

Step 3 *Arithmetic:* Since she makes $9 in one hour, and she works 20 hours, multiply.

Step 4 *Solve:* 20 hours × $9 = $180.

Step 5 *Make sense:* $180 is a sensible amount of money to make in one week for a part-time job. You have answered the question asked.

The exercises in this chapter will give you a chance to improve your skills in solving word problems.

Five Steps to Solving Word Problems

Step 1: Understanding the Question

After you have read the problem, the first step in solving a word problem is to get a clear understanding of what the question is asking you to find. You will use this knowledge to select necessary information and later to see if your answer makes sense.

TIP
One good strategy is to try to put the question in your own words. Sometimes this can help you visualize the problem clearly.

Which of the answer choices below accurately restates what you are being asked to find?

Sarah bought 3 pounds of meat, 5 pounds of fruit, and 7 pounds of vegetables. What was the total weight of her purchases?

(1) Find the difference in weight between the fruit and the vegetables.

(2) Find how much Sarah's purchases weighed altogether.

(3) Find the combined weight of the meat and the vegetables Sarah bought.

Answer choice (2) means the same thing as "What was the total weight of her purchases?"

EXERCISE 1

Directions: Which choice best expresses the question asked in each problem? *Do not solve these problems now.* You will have a chance to solve them in Exercise 4, page 60.

1. In a recent election Mr. Sanders got 67,576 votes, and his opponent got 62,881 votes. How many more votes did Mr. Sanders get than his opponent?

   (1) Find how many people voted.
   (2) Find how many registered voters turned up at the polls.
   (3) Find the difference between the number of votes Mr. Sanders received and the number of votes his opponent received.

2. A television was on sale for $198. This was $60 less than the original price. Find the original price.

   (1) What was the sale price of the TV?
   (2) How much more did the TV cost before it was on sale?
   (3) How much did the TV cost before it was on sale?

3. Manny makes monthly payments of $290 for a new car. How much does Manny pay in 1 year for the car?

   (1) Find how how much more Manny owes on his car.
   (2) Find Manny's total car payments for 12 months.
   (3) Find the down payment Manny made for his car.

4. Pancho drove 460 miles and used 20 gallons of gasoline. On the average, how far did he drive on 1 gallon of gasoline?

   (1) Find how much 20 gallons of gasoline cost.
   (2) Find how far Pancho can drive on 20 gallons of gasoline.
   (3) Find how far Pancho drove on 1 gallon of gasoline.

5. In September after a long diet, Gordon weighed 178 pounds. He went off his diet, and by the end of December he had gained 33 pounds. Find Gordon's weight at the end of December.

   (1) How much did Gordon weigh before his diet?
   (2) How much did Gordon weigh at the end of December?
   (3) How much did Gordon weigh in early September?

6. Together Marilyn and Calvin Howard take home $22,200 a year. Find their monthly take-home pay.

   (1) How much does Marilyn Howard take home in a month?
   (2) How much do both Marilyn and Calvin take home in a month?
   (3) How much do both Marilyn and Calvin make in a year?

7. On the open road Carmen's car gets 24 miles to the gallon. How far can she drive on the highway with 13 gallons of gas?

   (1) Find how many miles Carmen gets on one gallon of gas.
   (2) Find the number of gallons Carmen's gas tank holds.
   (3) Find the distance Carmen can drive with 13 gallons of gas.

8. Gloria is saving for a color TV listed at $385. So far she has saved $290. Find the additional amount Gloria has to save.

   (1) How much more does Gloria need to save for the TV?
   (2) How much has Gloria saved already?
   (3) What is the list price of the color TV?

Answers are on page 388.

Step 2: Using the Right Information

Step 2 of the five steps to solving word problems is: *Decide what information you need.* Some word problems contain more information than you need.

Example 1   The Chung family made $27,400 last year. They paid $4,380 for rent and $5,265 in taxes. After paying taxes, how much money did the Chungs have left for all their other expenses?

Question: How much was left after taxes?

Information needed: income of $27,400 and taxes of $5,265. Notice that you do not need the rent of $4,380.

Operation: Subtract the amount the Chungs paid in taxes from the amount they made in a year.

Solution: $27,400 − $5,265 = $22,135

Example 2   The fish that Anna bought cost $12.50. What was the price of 1 pound of the fish?

Question: Find the price of a pound of fish.

Information needed: the price of the fish and the weight of the fish.

Solution: Not enough information is given.

In this example you do not know the weight of the fish. On the GED Test you will sometimes see the answer choice *Not enough information is given.*

Warning: Be sure that you cannot solve the problem with the information that is given before you choose the answer *Not enough information is given.*

The next exercise is not typical of problems that you will see on the GED Test, but it gives you practice thinking about the information you need to solve a word problem.

EXERCISE 2

Directions: For each problem state the information that you need to solve the problem. If you cannot solve the problem with the information that is given, write *Not enough information is given.* Use a calculator to solve each problem that you can.

1. In March last year 8,248 people in Center City were officially unemployed. In June of that year 9,307 people were unemployed, and in September 10,549 were unemployed. By how many people did the official unemployment count rise from March to September?

   a. *Information needed:*
   b. *Solution:*

2. Paul paid $134.40 for 64 feet of floor joists that weigh 4 pounds per foot. What was the price per foot of the joists?

   a. *Information needed:*

   b. *Solution:*

3. A child's ticket to the circus costs $6, and an adult's ticket costs $10. Altogether, 1230 children attended the circus one weekend. Find the total value of the tickets to the circus that were sold that weekend.

   a. *Information needed:*

   b. *Solution:*

4. Of the 543 cars sold in Midvale last month, 387 were made in the United States. Of the foreign cars sold that month, 98 were made in Japan. How many of the cars sold in Midvale last month were made outside the U.S.?

   a. *Information needed:*

   b. *Solution:*

5. Huey drove 132 miles in 3 hours. Before leaving he paid $18 to fill his gas tank. Find his average driving speed in miles per hour.

   a. *Information needed:*

   b. *Solution:*

6. In the last problem, what was Huey's average gasoline consumption in miles per gallon?

   a. *Information needed:*

   b. *Solution:*

7. Of the 2500 adults in Cripple Creek, 1950 finished high school and 750 of those finishing high school also finished college. How many adults in Cripple Creek did not finish high school?

   a. *Information needed:*

   b. *Solution:*

8. The three most populous states in the U.S. are California, Texas, and New York. In a recent year the population of California was 32,667,000, the population of Texas was 19,760,000, and the population of New York was 18,175,000. How many more people lived in the most populous state than in the second most populous state?

   a. *Information needed:*

   b. *Solution:*

9. Adrienne earns $2600 a month. She pays $625 a month for rent and $380 a month for food. How much more does she pay for rent than for food each month?

   a. *Information needed:*

   b. *Solution:*

10. At her children's clothing shop Cary charges $12 each for shirts and $16 each for jeans. The difference between the price Cary charges her customers and the amount she pays her supplier is called the *markup*. Find the markup that Cary puts on shirts and jeans.

    a. *Information needed:*

    b. *Solution:*

Answers are on page 388.

Step 3: Choosing the Operation

The third step in solving word problems is: *Choose the arithmetic operation (or operations).* This step requires that you read problems carefully and find important clues.

This lesson reviews some of the key words, phrases, and situations that suggest the arithmetic operations of addition, subtraction, multiplication, and division.

Addition

Words such as *sum, total, combined,* and *altogether* suggest addition.

Example 1   Ruby makes $720 a week, and her daughter Marie makes $360. What is their combined weekly income?

Question: Find *combined* income.

Operation: Add Ruby's income and Marie's income.

Solution: $720 + $360 = $1080

Subtraction

Phrases such as *How much more? How much less? How much greater? How much smaller? Find the difference,* and *Find the balance* all suggest subtraction.

Example 2   A freight elevator can hold 2500 pounds. A table saw weighing 375 pounds is loaded onto the elevator. How much more weight can the elevator hold?

Question: How much more weight can the elevator hold?

Operation: Subtract the weight of the saw from the total weight the elevator can hold.

Solution: 2500 − 375 = 2125 pounds

The words *gross* and *net* suggest subtraction. *Gross* refers to an amount before subtracting something from it. *Net* refers to the amount that is left after something is subtracted from the gross amount.

Example 3   Mark's gross monthly salary is $3000. His employer withholds $600 for taxes and social security. What is Mark's net salary each month?

Question: Find Mark's *net* monthly salary.

Operation: Subtract the amount withheld from the gross salary.

Solution: $3000 − $600 = $2400

Multiplication

A problem may give you *information for one thing* and ask you to calculate an amount *for several things*. This suggests multiplication. These problems often give you a rate such as *dollars per pound* or *miles per gallon* or *rent per month*.

Example 4   On a highway Jack can drive 24 miles on 1 gallon of gasoline. How far can he drive with 10 gallons of gasoline?

Question: Find the distance Jack can drive with 10 gallons of gasoline.

Operation: Multiply the rate of 24 *miles* on 1 *gallon* by 10 gallons.

Solution: 24 mpg (miles per gallon) × 10 gallons = 240 miles

Division

A problem may give you *information about several things* and ask you to calculate an amount *for one thing*. This suggests division. In these problems you are looking for a rate such as a *price per pound, miles per gallon,* or *income per month*.

Notice that these problems are the *opposite* of multiplication problems. In multiplication problems you are often *given* a rate. In division problems you are often *looking for* a rate.

Example 5   Last year the Soto family paid $4800 in rent. What was their monthly rent?

Question: Find the monthly rent. *Monthly* rent means "rent per month."

Operation: Divide the yearly rent by the number of months in a year, 12, to find the *rent per month*. The situation in this problem suggests division.

Solution: $4800 ÷ 12 = $400

The words *sharing equally* and *dividing equally* suggest division. You may be asked to find how many of a small number of items fit into a larger number of items. This situation also means to divide.

Example 6   One carton contains 24 cans of tomatoes. How many cartons are used to hold 400 cans of tomatoes?

Question: Find the number of cartons needed. How many times does 24 go into 400?

Operation: Divide 400 by 24, the number of cans in one carton.

Solution: $400 \div 24 = 16$ with 16 cans remaining. 17 cartons will be needed to hold all 400 cans.

EXERCISE 3

Directions: For each problem, rewrite or rephrase the question. Tell what operation you need to use to solve the problem. Then use a calculator to find the solution.

1. Pete is 37 years old. His son Chris is 8. How much older is Pete than his son?

   a. *Question:*

   b. *Operation:*

   c. *Solution:*

2. Connie earns $440 for a 40-hour week. How much does she earn in 1 hour?

   a. *Question:*

   b. *Operation:*

   c. *Solution:*

3. An auditorium has 33 rows of seats. Each row contains 28 seats. What are the total number of seats in the auditorium?

   a. *Question:*

   b. *Operation:*

   c. *Solution:*

4. In a recent election for county clerk Mr. Ellis got 92,965 votes, and his opponent got 72,557 votes. How many votes were cast for county clerk?

   a. *Question:*

   b. *Operation:*

   c. *Solution:*

5. Nolan makes monthly mortgage payments of $859 for his house. How much in mortgage payments does Nolan make in one year?

   a. *Question:*

   b. *Operation:*

   c. *Solution:*

6. In November the Johnsons' utility bills were $42 for electricity, $55 for telephone, and $73 for heating oil. What is the total cost for their November utilities?

   a. *Question:*

   b. *Operation:*

   c. *Solution:*

7. Kim inputs 85 words per minute on her computer. How long does it take her to type a letter that contains 1700 words?

   a. *Question:*

   b. *Operation:*

   c. *Solution:*

8. Cheryl's gross salary for the year is $28,296. Her deductions come to a total of $6,780. What is her net income for the year?

   a. *Question:*

   b. *Operation:*

   c. *Solution:*

9. A group of citizens in Cicero hope to raise $10,000 for improvements to their youth center. If everyone gives an average of $25, how many contributors will they need?

   a. *Question:*

   b. *Operation:*

   c. *Solution:*

10. The beef Mrs. Robinson is buying for a barbecue costs $6 per pound. How much will she pay for 15 pounds of beef?

    a. *Question:*

    b. *Operation:*

    c. *Solution:*

11. Fatima and three colleagues from her job bought lottery tickets. They won $200. If Fatima shares the winnings equally with her colleagues, how much will each person receive?

    a. *Question:*

    b. *Operation:*

    c. *Solution:*

12. Andy bought a telephone answering machine on sale for $69. The sale price was $20 less than the original price. What was the original price of the answering machine?

   a. *Question:*

   b. *Operation:*

   c. *Solution:*

Answers are on page 389.

Step 4: Solving Word Problems

Step 4 of the five steps to solving word problems is: *Solve the problem and check your work.* This is where your skills in the basic arithmetic operations play an important part. Be sure to do your math neatly and accurately. All the good planning in the world will not give you a correct answer if you make mistakes in your computation.

EXERCISE 4

Directions: Go back to Exercise 1 on page 52 and solve problems 1–8.

Answers are on page 389.

Step 5: Thinking About the Answer

Step 5 of the five steps to solving word problems is: *Make sure that you answered the question and that your answer makes sense.*

The example below is problem 12 in Exercise 3. Think about the answer.

<u>Example 1</u>   Andy bought a telephone answering machine on sale for $69. The sale price was $20 less than the original price. What was the original price of the answering machine?

The phrase *less than* often means to subtract. But in this problem it does not. Think about the size of the answer. The sale price of the machine is $69, and this is $20 *less than* the original price. The original price must be $20 *more than* the sale price. The situation suggests addition: $69 + $20 = $89.

For the last problem, an answer less than $69 would not make sense.

You can use front-end estimation (or compatible pairs in division problems) to help you choose the most reasonable answer among a set of answer choices.

Example 2   The Wilson family wants to divide a 57-acre parcel of land into building lots each with 3 acres. Which of the following tells the number of lots that can be made from the original parcel?

    (1) 49

    (2) 39

    (3) 29

    (4) 19

    (5) 9

Step 1   Round 57 to the nearest 10. $57 \rightarrow 60$

Step 2   Find how many times 3 divides into 60. $\frac{60}{3} = 20$

Step 3   Choose the answer that is closest to 20.
Choice (4) 19 is correct.

To check the last problem, divide 57 by 3. $\frac{57}{3} = 19$

If you need to review front-end estimation and compatible pairs, return to page 26.

EXERCISE 5

Directions: Estimate to choose the best answer to each problem. Use front-end estimation or compatible pairs to make each estimate. Then use a calculator to figure exact answers.

1. Bert drove for 5 hours at an average speed of 62 miles per hour. How many miles did he drive?

    (1) 248

    (2) 310

    (3) 430

    (4) 640

    (5) 860

2. On Friday 437 people attended a play at the local high school. On Saturday 739 people attended, and on Sunday 496 people attended. Find the total attendance for those days.

    (1) 1482

    (2) 1512

    (3) 1672

    (4) 1852

    (5) 2092

3. The Central County Historical Society building was constructed in 1847. How many years old was the building in 2002?

   (1) 295
   (2) 255
   (3) 205
   (4) 155
   (5) 105

4. The CD player Marvin bought was on sale for $198. He saved $58 by buying the player on sale. What was the original price?

   (1) $270
   (2) $256
   (3) $240
   (4) $156
   (5) $140

5. Maria paid $1156 for 4 armchairs for the waiting room of her accounting office. What was the price for each chair?

   (1) $149
   (2) $199
   (3) $229
   (4) $289
   (5) $369

6. Sam makes $34,080 in a year. How much does he make each month?

   (1) $2840
   (2) $2130
   (3) $1960
   (4) $1530
   (5) $1240

7. To hear a jazz band, 112 people paid $18 each. What was the total amount of the ticket sales?

   (1) $ 916
   (2) $1016
   (3) $1526
   (4) $2016
   (5) $2826

8. From a board 96 inches long, Paul cut a piece 27 inches long. Assuming no waste, how many inches long was the leftover piece?

    (1) 99

    (2) 79

    (3) 69

    (4) 59

    (5) Not enough information is given.

9. The profit at the end of the year for a trucking company was $187,560. The 6 partners plan to share the profit equally. How much will each receive?

    (1) $46,890

    (2) $39,512

    (3) $31,260

    (4) $23,445

    (5) Not enough information is given.

10. In addition to his regular 40 hours, Fred worked 12 hours at the overtime rate of $22 an hour. How much did Fred make altogether that week?

    (1) $244

    (2) $264

    (3) $374

    (4) $484

    (5) Not enough information is given.

Answers are on page 389.

GED Problem Solving

Multistep Problems

Problems often require that you perform more than one operation to find a solution. Think about each step and work carefully. Each part of the solution must be accurate.

Example   Mike drove for 3 hours on the highway at an average speed of 65 mph. Then he drove for 2 hours in the city at an average speed of 15 mph. Altogether, how far did he drive?

Step 1   Find the highway distance. Multiply the average speed, 65 mph, by the time, 3 hours. $65 \times 3 = 195$ miles

Step 2   Find the city distance. Multiply the average speed, 15 mph, by the time, 2 hours. $15 \times 2 = 30$ miles

Step 3   Add the two distances. $195 + 30 = 225$ miles

EXERCISE 6

Directions: Use a calculator to solve each problem.

1. Each year the Upperville school district spends $7,800 to educate each child. The Central City school district spends $2,100 per child. Find the difference between the costs of educating 30 children in Upperville and 30 children in Central City.

2. For her store Mrs. Rivera ordered 4 cases of green beans, 6 cases of canned corn, and 10 cases of beets. If there are 20 cans in each case, what is the total number of cans in Mrs. Rivera's order?

3. Jamal works 35 hours a week for $10.50 an hour and 6 hours a week for $15.75 an hour. How much does he make in one week?

4. Mrs. Enright paid $150 down and $45 a month for 18 months for new living room furniture. What total amount did she pay for the furniture?

5. Grace can type 75 words per minute. How long will it take her to input both a 1000-word letter and a 500-word memo?

6. Mr. and Mrs. Diaz have signed a 2-year lease on an apartment. Rent for the first year will be $450 a month. Rent for the second year will be an additional $24 a month. Find the total amount of rent they will pay for 2 years.

7. One machine at Paul's Plastics can produce 100 handles in an hour. An older machine produces 65 handles in 1 hour. How many handles do the machines produce in a day when they both run for 12 hours?

8. Carlos drove a truckload of vegetables from his farm to a market in Los Angeles. The distance from his farm to the edge of town is 178 miles. The distance to the market is another 32 miles. The entire trip took 5 hours. Find his average driving speed in miles per hour.

Answers are on page 390.

Item Sets

An **item set** is a passage—maybe a few sentences or a few short paragraphs—that gives enough information to produce several questions. To answer each question based on an item set, be sure you are using only the information that you need.

Below is an item set about a couple comparing two apartments. The two questions that follow are answered as examples.

Laura and Tim have seen two apartments that they like. Apartment A has monthly rent of $480 for the first year. The rent for the second year will be an additional $48 a month. The rent for apartment A includes heat. The rent for apartment B is $412 a month for 2 years. The rent for apartment B does not include heat. The landlord for apartment B says that the heating bill for the apartment averages $84 a month.

Example 1 Find the yearly rent for apartment A for the second year.

Step 1 Add the monthly increase for the second year. $480 + $48 = $528

Step 2 Multiply the monthly rent by 12. $528 × 12 = $6336

Example 2 Assuming the landlord's estimate for heating bills is correct, find the total rent and heating costs for one year in apartment B.

Step 1 Add the monthly rent and heating bill. $412 + $84 = $496

Step 2 Multiply the monthly total by 12. $496 × 12 = $5952

In the last example, you could multiply the monthly rent by 12, multiply the monthly heating bill by 12, and add the two results. The total will be the same.

EXERCISE 7

Directions: Use a calculator to solve these problems. For problems 1 and 2, use the information from the item set above.

1. For the first year, the monthly rent for apartment A is how much less than the combined monthly rent and heating bill for apartment B?

2. Laura and Tim take home $2230 each month. How much will they have left each month of the second year of their lease if they choose apartment A?

Use the passage below to answer questions 3–7.

Family Furniture sells a set of living room furniture for $1199. The store offers a $100 rebate for paying cash. It will also sell the furniture for $150 down and monthly installments of $45 for 3 years. Today's Furniture sells the same furniture for $1279. The store offers no rebate for paying cash. It will sell the furniture for $200 down and monthly installments of $54 for 2 years.

3. Mrs. Allen is considering paying cash for the furniture. How much can she save by buying the furniture at Family Furniture rather than at Today's Furniture?

4. What is the total price of the furniture from Family Furniture if it is purchased in installments?

5. What is the total price of the furniture purchased in installments from Today's Furniture?

6. Mrs. Allen decided to buy the furniture from the store with the lower total cost under the installment plan. How much money did she save?

7. How much more does Family Furniture get for the furniture from a buyer who pays in installments than from a buyer who pays cash?

Use the passage below to answer questions 8–10.

Steve is a builder. He tells the Smiths that he can build a garage for them for $18,000. He estimates that, working with an assistant, he can complete the job in 80 hours. Steve pays his assistant $18 an hour. Steve estimates that materials and expenses, not including his assistant's wages, will cost him $13,500.

8. If the work is done in 80 hours as planned, how much will the assistant get paid?

9. Steve's estimates were correct. How much was left for him after paying for materials, expenses, and his assistant?

10. Although his assistant worked only 80 hours on the garage, Steve actually worked for 90 hours. Calculate his hourly wage.

Answers are on page 390.

Formulas

A **formula** is a mathematical rule. A formula usually has an = sign and words or letters for which you substitute number values. A complete list of the formulas that you will see on the GED Mathematics Test is on page 439.

To use any formula, you substitute values you *do* know for certain letters in the formula. When you **substitute**, you replace a letter with a number.

A common formula that you use often without thinking about it is the total cost formula:

$$\text{total cost} = (\text{number of units}) \times (\text{price per unit})$$

The formula means, "Total cost equals the number of units multiplied by the cost per unit." You have already used this formula in earlier exercises.

The total cost formula can also be written with letters: $c = nr$, where c is the total cost, n is the number of units or items, and r is the rate or cost per unit. Remember, when there is no arithmetic operation sign between two letters, you need to multiply.

Example 1 Use the cost formula to find the cost of 3 pounds of coffee at $5.99 per pound.

Step 1 Choose the correct formula. $c = nr$

Step 2 Substitute 3 for *n* and $5.99 for *r* $c = 3 \times \$5.99$
in the formula $c = nr$.

Step 3 Multiply 3 by $5.99. $c = \$17.97$

Another common formula is the distance formula:

$$\text{distance} = \text{rate} \times \text{time}$$

With letters, the distance formula is $d = rt$, where d is the distance, r is the rate (usually in miles per hour), and t is the time (usually in hours).

Example 2 Use the distance formula to find the distance a trucker traveled if he drove at an average speed of 65 mph for 5 hours.

Step 1 Choose the correct formula. $d = rt$

Step 2 Substitute 65 for *r* and 5 for *t* in $d = 65 \times 5$
the formula.

Step 3 Multiply 5 by 65. $d = 325$ miles

Notice the formula for **mean**, or average, on the formula page. The sum of the numbers that make up the mean is written as $x_1 + x_2 + \ldots + x_n$. The small numbers and letter *n* are called **subscripts.** This is a mathematical way of referring to the different values in an average.

EXERCISE 8

Directions: Solve the problems below with a calculator. Use the total cost formula to solve problems 1–3.

1. What is the cost of 3 shirts that cost $25 each?

2. What is the total cost of 6 replacement windows that cost $198 each?

3. Find the total cost of 4 gallons of paint that are priced at $19 each.

Use the distance formula to solve problems 4–6.

4. Carlos drove for 4 hours at an average speed of 55 mph. How far did he drive?

5. A train traveled for 3 hours at an average speed of 64 mph. How far did the train travel?

6. How far can a plane travel in 2 hours at an average cruising speed of 415 mph?

Use the formulas given below to solve problems 7–10.

7. The formula for finding the mean of three items is $m = \frac{a+b+c}{3}$, where a, b, and c are three items. Find Harriet's mean score for three tests on which she got 82, 76, and 94.

8. The formula for finding the approximate Fahrenheit temperature from a Centigrade temperature is *Fahrenheit* $\approx$ *2 × Centigrade + 30*. What Fahrenheit temperature is approximately equivalent to a Centigrade temperature of 11°?

9. The formula for finding unit cost is *rate = total cost/number of items*. What is the cost of one hammer if 36 hammers cost $396?

10. The formula $n = c/r$ tells the number of items, n, that you can buy with c dollars if the items cost r each. A pair of children's shorts cost $12. How many pairs of children's shorts can Maria buy with $50?

Answers are on page 390.

Set-up Answers

On multiple-choice math tests like the GED, you must sometimes choose an answer that shows a method of solution rather than an actual answer. For example, if you are asked how far Marvin can drive in 2 hours at an average speed of 48 mph, the answer choices could include 2 × 48.

Example   Shirley worked for 8 hours at her regular rate of $12 an hour and then for 2 hours at her overtime rate of $18 an hour. Which of the following expresses her earnings in dollars for that day?

(1) 12(8 + 2)

(2) 8 × 12 + 2 × 18

(3) 10(8 + 2)

(4) 8 × 12 − 2 × 18

(5) $\frac{8 + 2}{12}$

Choice (2) is the correct choice. The expression shows 8 hours at her regular rate and 2 hours at her overtime rate.

EXERCISE 9

Directions: Choose the correct solution to each problem.

1. On Saturday afternoon 265 people were at the Uptown Movie Theatre. On Saturday night 304 people were there. Everyone paid $6 for a ticket. Which of the following represents the ticket sales that day and night?

    (1) 6 × 265 × 304

    (2) 6(265 + 304)

    (3) 265(6 + 304)

    (4) 6 + 265 + 304

    (5) 265 + 6(304)

2. In June, Herb's Furniture sold 5 patio table sets. In July the store sold 10 table sets. The table sets cost $200 each. Which expression represents the total value of table sets sold those 2 months?

    (1) 200(5 + 10)

    (2) 5(200 + 10)

    (3) 10(200 + 5)

    (4) 200(5 × 10)

    (5) 200(10 − 5)

3. In a typical week Martha works 40 hours for $13 an hour. Her employer deducts $125 for taxes and social security. Which expression tells Martha's weekly take-home pay?

   (1) 40 + 13 + 125
   (2) 40(13 + 125)
   (3) 13(40 + 125)
   (4) 40 × 13 − 125
   (5) 40 × 13 + 125

4. A machine at Gaston & Sons can mold 45 cylinders in 1 minute. A slower machine molds 30 cylinders in a minute. With both machines running at the same time, which of the following expressions gives the number of cylinders Gaston produces in 5 minutes?

   (1) $\frac{45 - 30}{5}$

   (2) $\frac{45 + 30}{5}$

   (3) 5(45 + 30)

   (4) (5 × 45) − (5 × 30)

   (5) (45 ÷ 5) + (30 ÷ 5)

5. Sharon drove for 4 hours at an average speed of 55 mph and then for 3 hours at an average speed of 40 mph. Which of the following expressions represents the total distance she drove?

   (1) 7(55 + 40)
   (2) 55(3 + 4)
   (3) (3 × 55) + (4 × 40)
   (4) (4 × 55) + (3 × 40)
   (5) 40(3 + 4)

6. Monday morning there were 50 dozen eggs at Mariano's grocery store. By Monday night all but 10 dozen were sold. Which expression represents the number of individual eggs that were sold that day?

   (1) 12(50 − 10)
   (2) 50(12 − 10)
   (3) 10(50 − 12)
   (4) (12 × 50) − (10 × 50)
   (5) 12(50 + 10)

7. Sam bought 3 shirts for $16 each and 2 pairs of pants for $24 each. Which expression represents the total price he paid for these items?

   (1) $(2 + 16) \times (3 + 24)$
   (2) $(3 \times 16) + (2 \times 24)$
   (3) $(2 \times 16) + (3 \times 24)$
   (4) $(16 + 24) + (2 + 3)$
   (5) $(2 \times 3) + (16 \times 24)$

8. Marge works part-time as a waitress in a coffee shop. On Wednesday she made $34 in tips. On Thursday she made $80, and on Friday she made $65. Which expression represents her average daily tips for those days?

   (1) $\dfrac{34 + 80 + 65}{3}$

   (2) $\dfrac{34 + 80}{3}$

   (3) $\dfrac{34 + 80 + 65}{2}$

   (4) $34 + 80 + 65$

   (5) $2 \times (34 + 80 + 65)$

Answers are on page 390.

Word Problems Review

PART I

Directions: Use a calculator to solve problems 1–6. Mark each answer to problems 1 and 2 on the corresponding number grid.

1. A publisher has to ship a large order of workbooks to a program that teaches English as a second language. Each box holds 48 workbooks. How many boxes are needed to ship an order of 7488 workbooks?

2. Of the 420 employees at Tess's Textiles, 63 regularly walk to work and 187 take public transportation. How many employees at Tess's do not regularly walk to work?

3. In one month the leading U.S. car manufacturer sold 259,056 cars. The second largest manufacturer sold 120,947 cars. How many more cars did the leading manufacturer sell than the second largest manufacturer?

   (1) 128,109
   (2) 138,009
   (3) 138,109
   (4) 139,009
   (5) 139,109

4. Sandy is the bookkeeper for a senior citizen's center. At the beginning of the week the center's checking account had a balance of $2453.18. That week Sandy wrote a rent check for $658.00 and paid the electric bill of $49.57. She also deposited a grant check from the county for $860.00. What was the balance in the account at the end of the week?

   (1) $1745.67
   (2) $1795.18
   (3) $2605.61
   (4) $2655.18
   (5) $2704.75

Questions 5 and 6 refer to the following information.

Sandy is shopping for a new conference table and 12 chairs for the senior citizens' center. Below is a comparison of the prices for the table and chairs from two stores.

store	table	chairs
Bob's	$495	$59 each
Max's	$525	$115 for 2

5. Find the total cost of the table and 12 chairs at Max's.

   (1) $1185
   (2) $1203
   (3) $1215
   (4) $1253
   (5) $1905

6. Bob's store offers a discount for paying cash. If Sandy pays cash, how much will the table and 12 chairs cost at Bob's?

   (1) $1033
   (2) $1133
   (3) $1203
   (4) $1253
   (5) Not enough information is given.

PART II

Directions: Solve each of the following problems without a calculator. Use any formulas on page 439 that you need. Mark each answer for problems 7 and 8 on the corresponding number grid.

7. Craig got an oil change for $19 and bought 10 gallons of gasoline for $1.69 a gallon. To the nearest dollar, how much did Craig spend for oil and gasoline?

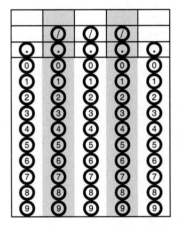

8. Sylvia paid $200 down and $56 a month for 15 months for a new washer and dryer. What total amount did she pay for the appliances?

9. A grant of $12,500,000 is to be shared equally by 5 Central City programs. How much will each of the programs receive?

   (1) $2,500,000
   (2) $1,250,000
   (3) $ 750,000
   (4) $ 250,000
   (5) $ 125,000

10. Fred works part-time for $12 an hour. He worked for 9 hours on Monday and 6 hours on Wednesday. Which expression tells how many dollars Fred made on those two days?

   (1) 12(9 + 6)
   (2) 9(12 + 6)
   (3) 6(12 + 9)
   (4) (12 × 9) + (6 + 9)
   (5) (12 × 9) + 9

11. A year's profit of $81,480 was divided evenly among the 84 employees of the Central Electric Cooperative. In addition each employee received a bonus of $200. Which operations should you use to find how much money each employee received?

   (1) Add 81,480 and 200; then divide by 84.
   (2) Multiply 81,480 by 84; then add 200.
   (3) Divide 81,480 by 84; then add 200.
   (4) Divide 81,480 by 84; then divide 200 by 84.
   (5) Add 84 and 200; then subtract the total from 81,480.

12. Rafael drove for 6 hours at an average speed of 55 mph. After he got to a big city, he drove for 2 hours at an average speed of 20 mph. How many miles did he drive altogether?

   (1) 330
   (2) 370
   (3) 390
   (4) 410
   (5) 440

Answers are on page 391.

You should have gotten at least 9 problems right on the last exercise. If you did not get 9 problems right, review your word problems skills before you go on. If you got 9 or more right, correct any problem you got wrong. Then go on to the next chapter.

Chapter 3

Decimals

A **decimal** is a kind of fraction. A decimal expresses a part of a whole. With decimals, the whole is divided into ten parts, or one hundred parts, or one thousand parts, or any power of ten.

A decimal point separates whole numbers from fractional parts of whole numbers. In our money system, dollars are represented by whole numbers, and they are written to the left of the decimal point. The first place to the right of the decimal point represents *tenths* of a dollar, or dimes. The second place to the right of the decimal point represents *hundredths* of a dollar, or pennies.

The digit 6 in $6.29 represents 6 whole dollars. The digit 2 is in the dimes place and has a value of 20 cents. The digit 9 is in the pennies place and has a value of 9 cents.

Understanding Decimals

Place Value

As you saw with dollars and cents, the first place to the right of the decimal point is the tenths place. (A dime is one of the ten equal parts of a dollar.) The second place to the right of the decimal point is the hundredths place. (A penny is one of the hundred equal parts of a dollar.)

Below is a diagram of the first six whole number places and the first six decimal places. The decimal point separates whole numbers from decimal places.

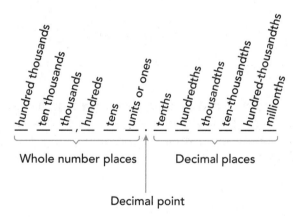

Notice that all the decimal place names end in *-ths*. They represent fractions or parts of one unit.

TIP
To learn the decimal place names, remember that 10 has one zero and tenths has one place, 100 has two zeros and hundredths has two places, 1000 has three zeros and thousandths has three places.

Example 1   Which digit is in the thousandths place in the number 18.406?

Thousandths is the third place to the right of the decimal point. The digit 6 is in the thousandths place.

Example 2   What is the value of the 3 in $5.43?

The digit 3 is in the pennies place. The 3 has a value of 3 cents.

EXERCISE 1

Directions: Answer each problem below.

1. Circle the digit in the tenths place in each number.
   0.3   2.986   12.7   4.1509   428.63

2. Circle the digit in the hundredths place in each number.
   0.27   0.018   4.26   0.8597   23.584

3. Circle the digit in the thousandths place in each number.
   0.138   0.0256   4.1498   0.0076   0.0412

4. Circle the digit in the units place in each number.
   8.1   13.46   124.95   2.008   1045.6

For problems 5–8, fill in the blank to correctly complete each sentence.

5. The digit 7 in the number 0.174 has a value of seven _____ .

6. The digit 3 in the number 26.3 has a value of three _____ .

7. The digit 5 in the number 0.258 has a value of five _____ .

8. The digit 9 in the number 1.4893 has a value of nine _____ .

Answers are on page 391.

Reading Decimals

Remember that decimals get their names from the number of decimal places (digits to the right of the decimal point) in each number.

First read a decimal as though it were a whole number. Then give the decimal a name according to the number of places. In mixed decimals the word *and* separates whole numbers from decimal fractions.

Examples

decimal	number of decimal places	words
0.04	two	*four hundredths*
0.027	three	*twenty-seven thousandths*
6.3	one	*six and three tenths*
14.0012	four	*fourteen and twelve ten-thousandths*

EXERCISE 2

Directions: For problems 1–3, fill in the blank to complete the name of the decimal or mixed decimal.

1. 0.9 = nine _____   0.18 = eighteen _____

2. 0.016 = sixteen _____   4.7 = four and seven _____

3. 0.0002 = two _____   10.03 = ten and three _____

For problems 4–9, write each decimal or mixed decimal in words.

4. 0.031 = _____

5. 0.00018 = _____

6. 1.203 = _____

7. 0.0208 = _____

8. 42.5 = _____

9. 30.80 = _____

Answers are on page 392.

Zeros

Think about the zeros in the decimal 08.0070 and decide which zeros are necessary.

The zero to the *left* of 8 is unnecessary.

The two zeros to the *right* of the decimal point are necessary. They keep 7 in the thousandths place.

The zero to the *right* of 7 is unnecessary.

The number 08.0070 can be rewritten as 8.007 and read as *eight and seven thousandths*.

One exception to the rule of dropping unnecessary zeros is in our monetary system. We write $4.50 (*four dollars and fifty cents*) because our monetary system is based on hundredths of a dollar. Another exception is a decimal such as 0.4 (*four tenths*). The zero in the units place is often written to show that there is no whole number.

Warning: Do not confuse the period at the end of a sentence with a decimal point.

EXERCISE 3

Directions: Rewrite each number, keeping only the necessary zeros.

1. 0.06700   03.405   08.09060   06.3

2. 80.0250   0124.0090   007.50   0.002300

3. 5.0   0.37080   029.300   060.0502

Answers are on page 392.

Writing Decimals

When you write a decimal, think about the number of decimal places that you need. Use zeros to hold places where necessary. Remember that the word *and* separates whole numbers from decimal fractions in mixed decimals.

Examples

words	number of decimal places	decimal
three hundredths	two	0.03
fifty-two thousandths	three	0.052
twenty-three and nine tenths	one	23.9

EXERCISE 4

Directions: Write each group of words as a decimal or as a mixed decimal.

1. four tenths   six and three tenths

2. eighteen hundredths   ninety-five and four tenths

3. nine thousandths   five and fifteen thousandths

4. one hundred six thousandths   eight and twenty-nine
                                   ten-thousandths

5. thirty-four ten-thousandths   five hundred twelve and seven
                                   hundredths

6. forty-five millionths   seventy and three hundred six
                                   thousandths

Answers are on page 392.

Comparing Decimals

It is easy to compare $0.20 and $0.04. You know that 20 cents is more than 4 cents. Both decimals have two decimal places.

To compare decimals, give each decimal the same number of places by adding zeros. Remember that zeros to the right of other digits in a decimal do not change the value of the decimal.

Example   Which decimal is larger, 0.08 or 0.3?

Step 1   Put a zero to the right of 0.3 to give it $0.3 = 0.30$
             two decimal places.

Step 2   Since 30 is larger than 8,   0.3 is larger
             0.3 is larger than 0.08.

EXERCISE 5

Directions: For problems 1–3, circle the larger number in each pair.

1. 0.08 or 0.7   0.62 or 0.062   0.33 or 0.403

2. 0.0029 or 0.001 0.01 or 0.101   0.895 or 0.9

3. 0.8 or 0.098   5.2 or 5.23   0.4 or 0.268

For problems 4 and 5, order each set of decimals from *smallest* to *largest*.

4. 0.62, 0.062, 0.602, 0.26

5. 0.43, 0.0034, 0.34, 0.403

For problems 6 and 7, order each set of decimals from *largest* to *smallest*.

6. 0.7, 0.77, 0.67, 0.701

7. 0.5, 0.505, 0.55, 0.511

For problems 8 and 9, use the information given to answer the questions.

8. Ben has to stack cans on the shelves of the Corner Store. He wants to put the heaviest cans on the lowest shelves and increasingly lighter cans on the upper shelves. Following are the weights of the different cans Ben has to shelve.

   can A weighs 0.475 kilogram
   can B weighs 0.5 kilogram
   can C weighs 2 kilograms
   can D weighs 1.75 kilograms
   can E weighs 0.34 kilogram

   Which list orders the cans from lower to upper shelves?

   (1) D, A, E, B, C
   (2) C, D, B, A, E
   (3) D, B, E, C, A
   (4) D, B, A, E, C
   (5) C, E, B, D, A

9. Below are the lengths of five pieces of galvanized pipe that Thelma wants to organize.

   piece A: 0.8 meter
   piece B: 0.95 meter
   piece C: 0.85 meter
   piece D: 0.09 meter
   piece E: 0.085 meter

   Which list orders the lengths of pipe from smallest to largest?

   (1) A, E, D, C, B
   (2) D, A, C, B, E
   (3) B, C, A, D, E
   (4) E, D, A, C, B
   (5) A, D, C, E, B

Answers are on page 392.

Rounding Decimals

Rounding is a useful tool for estimating answers to decimal problems.

—————————— R U L E ——————————

To round a decimal, follow these steps:
1. Underline the digit in the place you are rounding to.
2. a. If the digit to the right of the underlined digit is *greater than or equal to 5*, add 1 to the underlined digit.
   b. If the digit to the right of the underlined digit is *less than 5*, leave the underlined digit as is.
3. Drop the digits to the right of the underlined digit.

Example 1   Round 4.27 to the nearest tenth.

Step 1   Underline 2, the digit in the tenths place.   4.2̲7 → 4.3

Step 2   The digit to the right of 2 is 7. Since 7 is greater than 5, add 1 to 2. 2 + 1 = 3

Step 3   Drop the digit to the right of 3.

Example 2   Round 0.863 to the nearest hundredth.

Step 1   Underline 6, the digit in the hundredths place.   0.86̲3 → 0.86

Step 2   The digit to the right of 6 is 3. Since 3 is less than 5, leave 6 as is.

Step 3   Drop the digit to the right of 6.

EXERCISE 6

Directions: Answer each problem below.

1. Round each number to the nearest tenth.   0.48   5.726   29.55

2. Round each number to the nearest hundredth.   0.125   0.072   2.596

3. Round each number to the nearest thousandth.   0.0594   0.1268   0.0382

4. Round each number to the nearest unit.   12.94   3.278   98.6

5. Round each amount to the nearest cent.

$1.588 $0.029 $28.695

6. Round each amount to the nearest dollar.

$12.72 $3.49 $146.855

7. A gallon of unleaded gasoline costs $1.599. What is the price to the nearest cent?

Answers are on page 392.

Adding and Subtracting Decimals

Adding Decimals

The operations of adding and subtracting with decimals are much like adding and subtracting whole numbers.

R U L E

To add decimals, line up the decimals with *decimal point under decimal point*. Remember that a whole number is understood to have a decimal point at the right. To be sure decimals are lined up correctly, you can give each number the same number of decimal places.

Example 1 $3.8 + 47 + 1.83 =$

Step 1 Line up the decimals with point under point. Notice the decimal point at the right of 47.

Step 2 Add each column and bring the decimal straight down into each answer. Notice how the tenths carry over to the units column.

$$
\begin{array}{r}
3.8 \\
47. \\
+\ 1.83 \\
\hline
52.63
\end{array}
\quad \text{or} \quad
\begin{array}{r}
3.80 \\
47.00 \\
+\ 1.83 \\
\hline
52.63
\end{array}
$$

To solve a decimal problem on a calculator, press the [·] key for the decimal point. Do not confuse the decimal point key with the raised dot that means multiplication. The multiplication key looks like [×].

Example 2   Solve $5.6 + 0.94$ with a calculator.

Press [AC].

Press [5] [·] [6] [+] [·] [9] [4] [=].

The display should read ⌐ 6.54 ⌐.

EXERCISE 7

Directions: Solve each problem. For problems 1–4, check your answers with the calculator.

1. $0.6 + 0.9 =$ $\qquad$ $0.57 + 0.8 =$

2. $16 + 9.24 + 170.3 =$ $\qquad$ $25.34 + 4 + 1.816 =$

3. $12.3 + 4.8 + 0.625 =$ $\qquad$ $4.036 + 2.19 + 18.7 =$

4. $8.9 + 12.66 + 0.742 =$ $\qquad$ $0.73 + 0.0094 + 0.085 =$

5. To estimate the answer to $4.32 + 12.78 + 1.936$, first round each number to the nearest *tenth*. Then add the rounded numbers.

6. To estimate the answer to $0.197 + 4.3826 + 0.0179$, first round each number to the nearest *hundredth*. Then add the rounded numbers.

7. To estimate the answer to $0.0165 + 0.1426 + 0.0872$, first round each number to the nearest *thousandth*. Then add the rounded numbers.

8. To estimate the answer to $3.9 + 20.85 + 6.17$, first round each number to the nearest *unit*. Then add the rounded numbers.

9. Use a calculator to find the exact sum for problems 5–8.

10. Find the combined weight of a book that weighs 1.6 pounds, another book that weighs 2.15 pounds, and a carton that weighs 0.45 pound.

11. What is the total thickness of a tabletop that consists of a piece of wood that is 2.8 centimeters thick and a veneer that is 0.12 centimeter thick?

12. Fran is 65.5 inches tall. Her daughter Beth is 2.5 inches taller. How tall is Beth?

Answers are on page 392.

Subtracting Decimals

---------- R U L E ----------

To subtract decimals, put the larger number on top and line up the decimals with *point under point*. Use zeros to give each number the same number of decimal places. Then subtract and bring down the decimal point.

Example 1 What is the difference between 0.254 and 0.7?

Step 1 Line up the decimals point under point. Write two zeros to the right of 0.7 and put that decimal on the top since 0.7 is larger than 0.254.

$$\begin{array}{r} 0.700 \\ -\ 0.254 \\ \hline 0.446 \end{array}$$

Step 2 Subtract and bring down the decimal point.

To subtract decimals on the calculator, enter the larger number first.

Example 2 What is the difference between 0.0652 and 0.6528?

Press [AC].

Press [.] [6] [5] [2] [8] [−] [.] [0] [6] [5] [2] [=].

The display should read [0.5876].

EXERCISE 8

Directions: Solve each problem. For problems 1–4, check your answers with the calculator.

1. $0.8 - 0.26 =$ $0.5 - 0.345 =$

2. $18 - 0.32 =$ $4.09 - 2.076 =$

3. $0.3 - 0.094 =$ $1.004 - 0.0025 =$

4. $12.3 - 8.094 =$ $7 - 6.93 =$

5. To estimate the answer to $4.28 - 1.375$, first round each number to the nearest *tenth*. Then subtract the rounded numbers.

6. To estimate the answer to $1.367 - 0.4592$, first round each number to the nearest *hundredth*. Then subtract the rounded numbers.

7. To estimate the answer to $0.3857 - 0.0938$, first round each number to the nearest *thousandth*. Then subtract the rounded numbers.

8. To estimate the answer to 14.8 − 9.57, first round each number to the nearest *unit*. Then subtract the rounded numbers.

9. Use a calculator to find the exact answers for problems 5–8.

10. A sheet of metal was 0.36 centimeter thick when it was manufactured. After the sheet was polished, it was 0.012 centimeter thinner. What was the thickness of the polished sheet?

11. From a bottle that contained 23.15 grams of salt, a pharmacist used 1.6 grams of salt. Find the weight of the salt left in the bottle.

12. The yearly budget for Green County is $14.8 million. By the end of June the county had spent $9.57 million. How much was left in the budget for the year?

Answers are on page 392.

Multiplying and Dividing Decimals

Multiplying Decimals

--- RULE ---

To multiply decimals, you do not have to line up the numbers with point under point. Put the number with more digits on the top, and multiply as you would multiply whole numbers. Count the number of decimal places (places to the right of the decimal point) in the numbers you are multiplying. Counting from the right, insert the decimal point so that you have this total number of decimal places in your answer.

Example 1 What is the product of 3.26 and 0.4?

Step 1 Put the number with more digits (3.26) on top.

$$3.26 \leftarrow \text{two places}$$
$$\times\, 0.4 \leftarrow \text{one place}$$
$$\overline{1.304} \leftarrow \text{three places}$$

Step 2 Multiply.

Step 3 Put the total number of decimal places (three) in the answer.

You may have to put additional zeros in your answer to get enough decimal places.

Example 2   What is the product of 2.04 and 0.006?

Step 1   Put 2.04 on top.

Step 2   Multiply.

$$\begin{array}{r} 2.04 \leftarrow \text{two places} \\ \times\ 0.006 \leftarrow \text{three places} \\ \hline 0.01224 \leftarrow \text{five places} \end{array}$$

Step 3   Put the total number of decimal places (five) in the answer. The zero to the right of the decimal point gives the answer five decimal places.

To multiply decimals on the calculator, enter the numbers in either order.

Example 3   What is the product of 4.72 and 0.65?

Press [AC].

Press [4] [.] [7] [2] [×] [.] [6] [5] [=].

The display should read [3.068].

OR
Press [AC].

Press [.] [6] [5] [×] [4] [.] [7] [2] [=].

The display should read [3.068].

TIP

Follow these shortcuts for multiplying a decimal or mixed decimal by 10, 100, or 1000:

- To multiply by 10, move the decimal point one place to the right.

  Example: $0.34 \times 10 = 0.3\,4 = 3.4$

- To multiply by 100, move the decimal point two places to the right.

  Example: $5.6 \times 100 = 5.60 = 560$

- To multiply by 1000, move the decimal point three places to the right.

  Example: $7.8 \times 1000 = 7.800 = 7800$

EXERCISE 9

Directions: Solve problems 1–4. Then check your answers with the calculator.

1. $0.8 \times 0.7 =$ $9.3 \times 0.4 =$

2. $1.6 \times 0.03 =$ $15 \times 0.4 =$

3. $2.56 \times 0.08 =$ $0.107 \times 0.9 =$

4. $7.4 \times 0.25 =$ $6.9 \times 0.12 =$

Use the shortcut of moving the decimal point to solve problems 5–7.

5. $4.2 \times 10 =$ $10 \times 0.95 =$ $2.08 \times 10 =$

6. $100 \times 3.5 =$ $0.72 \times 100 =$ $100 \times 0.128 =$

7. $1.97 \times 1000 =$ $0.685 \times 1000 =$ $1000 \times 0.4 =$

8. To estimate the answer to 12.8×4.2, first round each number to the nearest *unit*. Then multiply the rounded numbers.

9. To estimate the answer to 0.39×1.82, first round each number to the nearest *tenth*. Then multiply the rounded numbers.

10. To estimate the answer to 289×0.62, use *front-end estimation*. Then multiply the rounded numbers. (Hint: Round 289 to the nearest *hundred* and 0.62 to the nearest *tenth*.)

11. Use a calculator to find the exact answers for problems 8–10.

12. Evaluate each power. $(0.6)^2 =$ $(1.5)^2 =$ $(0.13)^2 =$

13. Bill bought 11 gallons of gasoline at $1.699 per gallon. To the nearest cent how much did he pay for the gasoline?

14. In an election for shop steward 384 people voted. Marla got 0.75 of the votes. How many votes did she get?

Answers are on page 393.

Dividing Decimals by Whole Numbers

Remember the parts of a division problem. The **dividend** is the number being divided. The **divisor** is the number that divides into the dividend. The **quotient** is the answer.

───────────────── R U L E ─────────────────

To divide a decimal by a whole number, bring the decimal point up in the quotient directly above its position in the dividend. Divide as you would with whole numbers.

───

Example 1   Find 4.5 ÷ 3.

Step 1   Set the problem up with 4.5 as the dividend and 3 as the divisor.

Step 2   Bring the decimal point up in the quotient and divide.

$$\begin{array}{r} 1.5 \\ 3\overline{)4.5} \\ 3 \\ \overline{} \\ 15 \\ 15 \\ \overline{} \end{array}$$

You may need to use zeros to hold decimal places.

Example 2   What is the quotient of 0.168 divided by 2?

Step 1   Set the problem up with 0.168 as the dividend and 2 as the divisor.

Step 2   Bring the decimal point up in the quotient, put a zero in the tenths place, and divide.

$$\begin{array}{r} 0.084 \\ 2\overline{)0.168} \\ 16 \\ \overline{} \\ 08 \\ 8 \\ \overline{} \end{array}$$

Sometimes adding a zero makes a division problem come out evenly.

Example 3   Solve 2.7 ÷ 5.

Step 1   Set the problem up with 2.7 as the dividend and 5 as the divisor.

Step 2   Bring the decimal point up in the quotient, add a zero, and divide. Notice that the zero to the right of 7 makes the division come out even.

$$\begin{array}{r} 0.54 \\ 5\overline{)2.70} \\ 25 \\ \overline{} \\ 20 \\ 20 \\ \overline{} \end{array}$$

Some division problems never come out even. You can round these answers.

Example 4   What is 0.2 ÷ 3 to the nearest hundredth?

Step 1   Set the problem up with 0.2 as the dividend and 3 as the divisor.

Step 2   Bring the decimal point up in the quotient, add zeros, and divide. Notice that the division does not come out evenly when you add more zeros.

$$
\begin{array}{r}
0.066 \rightarrow 0.07 \\
3\overline{)0.200} \\
\underline{18} \\
20 \\
\underline{18} \\
2
\end{array}
$$

Step 3   Divide to the thousandths place and round to the nearest hundredth.

To divide with a calculator, first enter the dividend and then the divisor.

Example 5   Solve 4.44 ÷ 8.

Press ⟨AC⟩.

Press ⟨4⟩ ⟨.⟩ ⟨4⟩ ⟨4⟩ ⟨÷⟩ ⟨8⟩ ⟨=⟩.

The display should read ⟨ 0.555 ⟩.

TIP

Follow these shortcuts for dividing a decimal or mixed decimal by 10, 100, or 1000:

- To divide by 10, move the decimal point one place to the left.

  Example: $14.3 \div 10 = 1\,4.3 = 1.43$

- To divide by 100, move the decimal point two places to the left.

  Example: $2.75 \div 100 = 02.75 = 0.0275$

- To divide by 1000, move the decimal point three places to the left.

  Example: $9.4 \div 1000 = 009.4 = 0.0094$

EXERCISE 10

Directions: Solve problems 1–3. Then check your answers with the calculator.

1. $0.039 \div 3 =$ $0.0168 \div 7 =$

2. $\dfrac{5.36}{8} =$ $\dfrac{75.6}{9} =$

3. $10.5/14 =$ $518.4/12 =$

For problems 4 and 5, round your answers to the nearest *hundredth*.

4. $4.2 \div 9 =$ $2.59 \div 8 =$

5. $3.4 \div 3 =$ $3.1 \div 7 =$

Use the shortcut of moving the decimal point to solve problems 6–8.

6. $0.04 \div 10 =$ $20.6 \div 10 =$ $1.9 \div 10 =$

7. $5.6 \div 100 =$ $12.7 \div 100 =$ $4.23 \div 100 =$

8. $195 \div 1000 =$ $4.8 \div 1000 =$ $520.6 \div 1000 =$

Use a calculator to solve problems 9–12.

9. Find $20 \div 7$ to the nearest thousandth.

10. $\sqrt{0.64} =$ $\sqrt{0.0144} =$

11. In Green County four summer programs shared $1.5 million equally. How much did each program receive?

12. At his food coop Steve divided 82.5 pounds of new potatoes equally into 10 bags. What was the weight of the potatoes in each bag?

Answers are on page 393.

Dividing Decimals by Decimals

RULE

To divide a decimal by a decimal, make the divisor a whole number. Move the decimal point in the divisor to the right as far as it will go. Also move the point in the dividend the same number of places that you moved the point in the divisor. Then divide.

For example, $20 \div 0.5$ is the same as $200 \div 5$. The numbers in the second problem are each ten times greater than the numbers in the first problem, but the answers are the same.

Study the following examples carefully.

Example 1   What is 2.4 divided by 0.3?

Step 1   Set the problem up with 2.4 as the dividend and 0.3 as the divisor. Then move the decimal point in the divisor to make 0.3 a whole number.

$$0.3\overline{)2.4}$$

Step 2   Move the decimal point in the dividend the same number of places that you moved the point in the divisor (one).

$$0.3\overline{)2.4}$$

Step 3   Bring the decimal point up above its new position and divide.

$$0.3\overline{)2.4} = 8.$$

You may have to add zeros to the dividend.

Example 2   What is 5.6 divided by 0.07?

Step 1   Set the problem up with 5.6 as the dividend and 0.07 as the divisor. Then move the decimal point in the divisor to make 0.07 a whole number.

$$0.07\overline{)5.6}$$

Step 2   Move the decimal point in the dividend the same number of places that you moved the point in the divisor (two). Notice the extra zero.

$$0.07\overline{)5.60}$$

Step 3   Bring the decimal point up to its new position and divide.

$$0.07\overline{)5.60} = 80.$$

To divide decimals by decimals on a calculator, enter the dividend first and then the divisor. You do not have to move the decimal point. The calculator does that for you.

Example 3   What is the quotient of 9.9 ÷ 0.44?

Press ⟨AC⟩.

Press ⟨9⟩ ⟨.⟩ ⟨9⟩ ⟨÷⟩ ⟨.⟩ ⟨4⟩ ⟨4⟩ ⟨=⟩.

The display should read [22.5].

EXERCISE 11

Directions: Solve each problem. For problems 1–4, check your answers with the calculator.

1. 8.4 ÷ 0.2 =   5.25 ÷ 0.5 =

2. $\frac{3.24}{0.04}$ = $\frac{90.6}{0.03}$ =

3. 8.74/2.3 =   2.888/3.8 =

4. 0.42 ÷ 0.028 =   6.7 ÷ 0.134 =

For problem 5, round each answer to the nearest tenth.

5. 4 ÷ 0.7 =   0.8 ÷ 0.9 =

For problem 6, round each answer to the nearest hundredth.

6. 0.0195 ÷ 0.3 =   0.836 ÷ 0.6 =

7. Use a calculator to find 1.5 ÷ 0.7 to the nearest thousandth.

8. Tom cut a wire 18 inches long into pieces that were each 1.5 inches long. Assuming no waste, how many pieces did Tom cut?

9. Marcia paid $12.25 for 2.5 pounds of cheese. Find the price per pound.

Answers are on page 393.

Scientific Notation with Large Numbers

To avoid writing many zeros in very large numbers, scientists and mathematicians often use a shortened method of writing these numbers called **scientific notation**. The method uses powers of ten. (Using scientific notation to write small numbers will be covered in Chapter 4.)

Study the following chart carefully. Notice that the names refer to the names of the first seven places in our whole number system.

Name	Number Value	Power
unit or one	1	10^0
ten	10	10^1
hundred	100	10^2
thousand	1,000	10^3
ten thousand	10,000	10^4
hundred thousand	100,000	10^5
million	1,000,000	10^6

Scientific notation is a number between 1 and 10 multiplied by a power of ten.

RULE

To write a large number in scientific notation, follow these steps:
1. Move the decimal point in the number to get a number between 1 and 10.
2. Write a multiplication problem with the new decimal multiplied by a power of ten. The power corresponds to the number of places that the decimal had to move.

Example 1 Write 7,300,000 in scientific notation.

Step 1 Move the decimal point between 7 and 3 because 7.3 is between 1 and 10. $7,300,000 = 7.3 \times 10^6$

Step 2 Since the decimal moved six places to the left, multiply the new decimal by 10^6.

RULE

To change a number in scientific notation to a whole number, move the decimal point to the right as many places as the power indicates.

Example 2   Write 2.15×10^4 as a whole number.

Step 1   Remember that multiplying by 10^4 means $2.15 \times 10^4 = 21,500$
moving the decimal point four places
to the right.

Step 2   Move the decimal point in 2.15 four places to
the right. Add two zeros in order to move four places.

When you are working on a calculator, you may have a number with too many digits for the calculator to display. The number will automatically be changed to scientific notation. It will look unusual because the " $\times 10$" will not be displayed. Only the number between 1 and 10 and the exponent will be shown.

Example 3 $717,000 \times 1,000,000 =$
The display should read $\boxed{\qquad 7.17^{\,11}}$.

EXERCISE 12

Directions: For problems 1 and 2, express each number in
scientific notation.

1. $740 =$ $18,000 =$ $6,930,000 =$

2. $95,000,000 =$ $450,000 =$ $206,000,000 =$

For problems 3 and 4, write each number in scientific notation as a whole number.

3. $2.74 \times 10^5 =$ $9.3 \times 10^3 =$ $4.6 \times 10^6 =$

4. $8.1 \times 10^4 =$ $6.35 \times 10^7 =$ $1.2 \times 10^5 =$

Solve problems 5–8.

5. Some experts believe that the population of the world in the year 2010 will be 7,240,000,000. Write the estimated population in scientific notation.

6. The temperature of the core of the sun is 27,000,000°F. Write this temperature using scientific notation.

7. The distance across the sun is 8.65×10^5 miles. Write this distance as a whole number.

8. The planet Pluto is 3,675,000,000 miles from the sun. Write this distance in scientific notation.

Answers are on page 393.

Decimal Word Problems

The next exercise gives you a chance to apply your decimals skills to word problems. Be sure that you understand each question before you start. Then decide what information you need to solve the problem and what operations you need to use. Again, be sure that your answer makes sense.

On the GED Test, you will be asked to answer word problems like these and write the answers on number grids.

Example   From a pipe 3 meters long, Thomas cut a piece 1.8 meters long. What was the length, in meters, of the remaining piece? Put your answer on the number grid.

Subtract: 3.0 − 1.8 = 1.2 meters

To write the answer on a grid, write the numbers in the blank boxes at the top of each column. Use a separate column for each digit and the decimal point. Then fill in one circle below each column that corresponds to the digit or the symbol that you wrote at the top.

EXERCISE 13

Directions: Solve each problem. For the first three problems, fill in each corresponding number grid.

1. Tito rode his bicycle for 1.5 hours at an average speed of 15 mph. How many miles did he travel in that time?

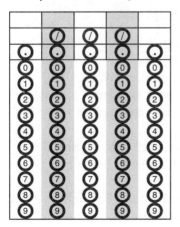

2. A sign at a highway tunnel says, "Height Limit = 11.5 feet." When the air is low in the tires of Mark's truck, the truck is 10.65 feet tall. When the tires are full, the truck is an additional 0.2 feet high. By how much does Mark's truck clear the ceiling of the tunnel when the truck tires are full?

3. The population of Capital City is 1.3 million. The population of the surrounding suburbs is another 1.12 million. What is the population in millions of the entire metropolitan area of Capital City and its suburbs?

Use a calculator to solve problems 4–10.

4. A post office can process 1300 pieces of mail in 8 hours. To the nearest whole number, how many pieces of mail can the post office process in 1 hour?

5. Find the cost of 1.15 pounds of cheese that costs $6.49 per pound. Round the answer to the nearest cent.

6. One pound equals 0.45 kilogram. Sam weighs 175 pounds. What is Sam's weight in kilograms? Round your answer to the nearest unit.

7. To pay for a new sports center, the town of Troy raised $1.35 million from the state, $0.85 million from the county, and $1.05 million from local businesses and individuals. The total estimated cost of the project is $4 million. How much more money does the town need?

8. In basketball a scoring average is the number of points a player gets divided by the number of games he plays. Basketball scoring averages are measured in *tenths*. Find the scoring average for a player who scored 1786 points in 82 games.

9. A plane flew at an average speed of 394 mph for 1.75 hours. To the nearest mile, how far did the plane fly?

10. Charlene makes $18.60 an hour when she works overtime. One week her paycheck stub listed $269.70 for overtime work. How many hours did she work overtime that week?

For problems 11 and 12, choose the correct answer.

11. Senta drove for 2.5 hours at an average speed of 60 mph and for 1.5 hours at an average speed of 48 mph. Which expression shows the total distance that she drove?

    (1) 2.5(60) + 1.5(48)
    (2) (2.5 + 1.5) + (60 + 48)
    (3) 60 × 48 × 4
    (4) 2.5(60 + 48)
    (5) 60 + 48

12. Nick cut two lengths of copper tubing each 1.45 meters long from the piece shown below. Which of the following expressions shows the length of the remaining piece?

    (1) 4 − 2 − 1.45
    (2) 2(4 − 1.45)
    (3) 4 − 2(1.45)
    (4) 4(2 − 1.45)
    (5) 4 − 1.45

←——————— 4 meters ———————→

Answers are on page 394.

Decimals Review

PART I

Directions: Use a calculator to solve problems 1–15.

1. $36 + 2.93 + 0.065 =$

2. $0.08 - 0.0063 =$

3. $3.2 \times 0.005 =$

4. $0.405/15 =$

5. $9/0.045 =$

6. $3 - 0.586 =$

For problems 7–9, mark each answer on the corresponding number grid.

7. Find $3.96/0.7$ to the nearest tenth.

8. $(2.8)^2 =$

9. David drove 223 miles on 12 gallons of gasoline. To the nearest tenth, what is the average number of miles he drove on one gallon of gasoline?

10. A baseball batting average is the number of hits a player gets divided by the number of times he goes to bat. Last season Bill was at bat 75 times, and he made 22 hits. Find Bill's batting average to the nearest *thousandth*.

    (1) .356

    (2) .333

    (3) .320

    (4) .299

    (5) .293

11. Maria bought 5 yards of 36-inch wide material for $7.80 a yard and 2.5 yards of 42-inch wide material for $8.40 a yard. How much did she pay altogether for the material?

    (1) $81.00

    (2) $63.36

    (3) $60.00

    (4) $55.80

    (5) $50.00

For problems 12–14, refer to the following information and diagram.

Alfonso drove from El Paso to Dallas in 13 hours. Then he drove from Dallas to Houston in 4 hours. Finally he drove from Houston back to El Paso in 15.5 hours. For the entire trip he bought 70 gallons of gasoline at a cost of $1.64 per gallon.

12. Find the total number of hours Alfonso spent driving on his trip.

    (1) 17

    (2) 19.5

    (3) 28.5

    (4) 30

    (5) 32.5

13. How much did Alfonso spend for gasoline on his trip?

    (1) $ 70.00

    (2) $ 84.80

    (3) $ 94.80

    (4) $114.80

    (5) $168.00

14. To the nearest whole number, what was Alfonso's average speed, in miles per hour, from El Paso to Dallas?

    (1) 42

    (2) 48

    (3) 50

    (4) 55

    (5) 58

15. The chart below shows the hourly electricity costs for various household appliances. The Walek family has the television turned on for an average of 52 hours a week. To the nearest cent, how much do they spend each week to operate their television?

    (1) $1.77
    (2) $1.98
    (3) $2.60
    (4) $5.40
    (5) $8.60

Electricity (cost per hour)	
iron	$0.050
television	$0.034
clock	$0.010
radio	$0.022

PART II

Directions: Solve the following problems without a calculator.

16. In what place is the digit 8 in the number 426.385?

17. Rewrite 060.04300 and omit unnecessary zeros.

18. Write four hundred eight and fifteen ten-thousandths as a decimal.

19. Arrange the decimals 0.6, 0.06, 0.606, and 0.066 in order from smallest to largest.

20. Write 2.3×10^5 as a whole number.

For problems 21 to 23, mark each answer on the corresponding number grid.

21. Write seven and sixteen thousandths as a decimal.

22. In 2000 the population of Florida was 15.23 million. In 2010 the population is expected to be 2.07 million more. What is the population of Florida, in millions, expected to be in 2010?

23. From board A below, Allen cut off a piece the length of board B. What was the length, in yards, of the remaining piece?

A

3 yards

B

1.75 yards

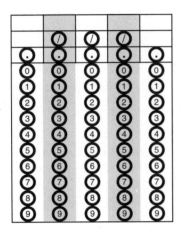

24. Pete is a builder. He charges $125 for a small bookcase and $190 for a large one. One month he sold 5 small bookcases and 3 large ones. Which expression represents the gross amount Pete received for the bookcases?

(1) (125 + 5)(190 + 3)

(2) 125(3 + 5) + 190

(3) 3(125) + 5(190)

(4) 5(125) + 3(190)

(5) 125(190) + 3(5)

25. Arrange the following boxes in order from lightest to heaviest.

   Box A: 1.8 kilograms
   Box B: 0.75 kilogram
   Box C: 1.75 kilograms
   Box D: 0.125 kilogram
   Box E: 1.125 kilograms

   (1) A, B, D, C, E

   (2) A, B, C, E, D

   (3) D, B, C, E, A

   (4) D, B, E, C, A

   (5) B, D, E, C, A

Answers are on page 394.

You should have gotten at least 20 problems right on the last exercise. If you did not get 20 right, review your decimal skills before you go on. If you got 20 or more right, correct any problem you got wrong. Then go on to the next chapter.

Chapter 4

Fractions

A **fraction**, like a decimal, describes a part of a whole. A fraction is written as a quotient of two whole numbers.

A day is one of the seven equal parts of a week. One day is $\frac{1}{7}$ (one-seventh) of a week. A penny is one of the one hundred equal parts of a dollar. One penny is $\frac{1}{100}$ (one-hundredth) of a dollar. Two feet are two of the three equal parts of a yard. Two feet are $\frac{2}{3}$ (two-thirds) of a yard.

A fraction is written with a **numerator** on top and a **denominator** on the bottom.

$\frac{\text{numerator}}{\text{denominator}}$ tells how many parts you have
            tells the number of equal parts in the whole

The fraction $\frac{3}{4}$ describes the part of the figure at the right that is shaded. There are 3 shaded parts. The whole figure has 4 equal parts.

You can think of a fraction in three ways:

1. as part of a whole

    $\frac{3}{4}$ of the circle is shaded.

2. as part of a group

    The Dawson family has four members, and three of them work in the construction business. $\frac{3}{4}$ of the Dawson family works in the construction business.

3. as a division problem

    The fraction $\frac{3}{4}$ means 3 *divided by* 4.

Understanding Fractions

Forms of Fractions

In a **proper fraction** the numerator is *less than* the denominator. The value of a proper fraction is always less than 1.

Examples of proper fractions: $\frac{2}{5}, \frac{3}{10}, \frac{99}{100}$

In an **improper fraction** the numerator is *equal to* or *larger than* the denominator. The value of an improper fraction is equal to 1 when the numerator and the denominator are the same. The value of an improper fraction is greater than 1 when the numerator is greater than the denominator.

Examples of improper fractions: $\frac{6}{5}, \frac{9}{9}, \frac{3}{2}$

A **mixed number** is a whole number and a proper fraction.

Examples of mixed numbers: $1\frac{1}{2}, 5\frac{2}{3}, 20\frac{9}{10}$

Remember that fractions can be written vertically, with the numerator over the denominator, as in $\frac{2}{3}$, or horizontally with a slash, as in 2/3.

EXERCISE 1

Directions: Solve each problem.

1. Circle the proper fractions. $\frac{5}{8}$ $\frac{7}{7}$ $\frac{1}{6}$ $\frac{9}{2}$ $\frac{19}{20}$

2. Circle the improper fractions. $\frac{2}{2}$ $\frac{7}{4}$ $\frac{4}{7}$ $\frac{8}{3}$ $\frac{5}{16}$

3. Which of the following have a value greater than 1?

   $\frac{3}{3}$ $3\frac{1}{2}$ $\frac{9}{8}$ $\frac{7}{8}$ $\frac{1}{6}$

4. A foot has 12 inches. What fraction of a foot is 5 inches?

5. Pete got 7 items wrong out of 50 on a test. What fraction of the total number of problems did Pete get wrong?

Answers are on page 395.

Reducing Fractions

Reducing means writing a fraction with smaller numbers. Reducing a fraction does not change the value of the fraction. A quarter is $\frac{25}{100}$ of a dollar. A quarter is also $\frac{1}{4}$ of a dollar. The fraction $\frac{25}{100}$ reduces to $\frac{1}{4}$.

To reduce a fraction, divide both the numerator and the denominator of the fraction by the same number. Check the reduced fraction to see whether another number divides evenly into the new numerator and the new denominator.

When a fraction cannot be reduced further, it is reduced to **lowest terms**.

TIP
If both the numerator and denominator are even numbers, you can reduce by 2.

Example 1   Reduce $\frac{6}{10}$ to lowest terms.

Step 1   Find a number that divides evenly into both 6 and 10. 6 and 10 are even numbers. Divide both by 2.

$$\frac{6 \div 2}{10 \div 2} = \frac{3}{5}$$

Step 2   Check to see if another number divides evenly into both 3 and 5. Since no other number divides evenly into both 3 and 5, the fraction $\frac{3}{5}$ is reduced to lowest terms.

Example 2   Reduce $\frac{25}{30}$ to lowest terms.

Step 1   Find a number that divides evenly into both 25 and 30. 5 divides evenly into both 25 and 30.

$$\frac{25 \div 5}{30 \div 5} = \frac{5}{6}$$

Step 2   Check to see if another number divides evenly into both 5 and 6. Since no other number divides evenly into both 5 and 6, the fraction $\frac{5}{6}$ is reduced to lowest terms.

Example 3   Reduce $\frac{16}{32}$ to lowest terms.

Step 1   Find a number that divides evenly into both 16 and 32. 4 divides evenly into both 16 and 32.

$$\frac{16 \div 4}{32 \div 4} = \frac{4}{8}$$

Step 2   Check to see if another number divides evenly into both 4 and 8. 4 divides evenly into both 4 and 8.

$$\frac{4 \div 4}{8 \div 4} = \frac{1}{2}$$

Step 3   Check to see if another number divides evenly into both 1 and 2. Since no other number divides evenly into 1 and 2, the fraction $\frac{1}{2}$ is reduced to lowest terms.

Example 4   Reduce $\frac{70}{80}$ to lowest terms.

Step 1   Cancel the zeros one-for-one. This is the same as reducing by 10.

$$\frac{7\cancel{0}}{8\cancel{0}} = \frac{7}{8}$$

Step 2   Check to see if another number divides evenly into both 7 and 8. Since no other number divides evenly into both 7 and 8, the fraction $\frac{7}{8}$ is reduced to lowest terms.

> ### TIP
>
> Tips for reducing fractions:
>
> - If both the numerator and the denominator are even numbers, reduce by 2.
>
> - If both numbers end in zero, cancel the zeros one-for-one.
>
> - If one number ends in 5 and the other in 0, reduce by 5.
>
> - See whether the numerator divides evenly into the denominator.

To check a reduced fraction, find the **cross products**. The cross products are the numerator of the first fraction multiplied by the denominator of the second and the denominator of the first fraction multiplied by the numerator of the second.

Look at the fractions from Example 1.

$$\frac{6}{10} \times \frac{3}{5}$$

The first cross product is $6 \times 5 = 30$.

The second cross product is $10 \times 3 = 30$.

Since the cross products are the same, $\frac{3}{5}$ is equal to $\frac{6}{10}$. Checking cross products does not guarantee that a fraction is reduced to lowest terms. If the cross products are equal, the fractions are equal.

You can use the Casio *fx*-260 to reduce fractions. The key for entering a fraction is $\boxed{\text{a b/c}}$.

Example 5   Use a calculator to reduce $\frac{16}{32}$.

Press $\boxed{\text{AC}}$.

Press $\boxed{1}$ $\boxed{6}$ $\boxed{\text{a b/c}}$ $\boxed{3}$ $\boxed{2}$ $\boxed{=}$.

The display should read $\boxed{\qquad 1 \lrcorner 2.}$.

The symbol $\lrcorner$ represents the fraction bar. The answer is $\frac{1}{2}$.

EXERCISE 2

Directions: Reduce each fraction to lowest terms. Then check your answers with the Casio *fx*-260 calculator.

1. $\dfrac{6}{10} =$ $\dfrac{4}{6} =$ $\dfrac{14}{20} =$ $\dfrac{4}{32} =$

2. $\dfrac{18}{36} =$ $\dfrac{18}{24} =$ $\dfrac{25}{35} =$ $\dfrac{45}{50} =$

3. $\dfrac{15}{40} =$ $\dfrac{45}{60} =$ $\dfrac{30}{45} =$ $\dfrac{10}{25} =$

4. $\dfrac{70}{100} =$ $\dfrac{50}{60} =$ $\dfrac{80}{160} =$ $\dfrac{40}{200} =$

5. $\dfrac{30}{200} =$ $\dfrac{50}{250} =$ $\dfrac{7}{28} =$ $\dfrac{9}{30} =$

6. $\dfrac{27}{45} =$ $\dfrac{22}{33} =$ $\dfrac{17}{34} =$ $\dfrac{13}{39} =$

Answers are on page 396.

Writing Fractions

Remember that a fraction represents a **part** over a **whole**. When you write a fraction, be sure that the numerator represents the part and the denominator represents the whole.

Example   Rose got 2 problems wrong and 8 problems right on a quiz. What fraction of the problems did she get right?

Step 1   The whole is the number of problems on the quiz.
2 wrong + 8 right = 10 total

Step 2   Make a fraction with the problems right as the numerator and the total number of problems as the denominator.

$\dfrac{\text{right}}{\text{total}}$ $\dfrac{8}{10} = \dfrac{4}{5}$

Step 3   Reduce to lowest terms. Rose got $\dfrac{4}{5}$ of the problems right.

EXERCISE 3

Directions: Solve each problem. Be sure each fraction is reduced to lowest terms.

1. There are 6 women and 9 men in Martin's night school math class.

   a. What fraction of the class is women?

   b. What fraction of the class is men?

   c. One night 3 students were absent. What fraction of the class was absent?

2. Last season the Consolidated Electric softball team played 24 games and won 18.

   a. What fraction of the games did the team win?

   b. What fraction of the games did they lose?

3. Ellen bought a dress for $60. This was $30 off the original price.

   a. What was the original price?

   b. What fraction of the original price did Ellen save?

   c. What fraction of the original price did Ellen pay?

4. The Jacksons are driving from Carver City to Westerville. They stop to eat after driving 175 miles. They still have another 125 miles to go.

   a. What is the total distance from Carver City to Westerville?

   b. What fraction of the drive had they completed when they stopped to eat?

   c. What fraction of the drive do they have left?

5. Uta takes home $2400 a month. Each month she spends $600 for rent, $450 for food, and $150 on a car payment.

   a. What fraction of her monthly income does Uta spend for rent?

   b. What fraction of her monthly income does she spend for food?

   c. What fraction of her monthly income does she spend on a car payment?

   d. Uta saves $200 every month. What fraction of her monthly income does she save?

Answers are on page 396.

Working with Fractions

Raising Fractions to Higher Terms

The *opposite* of reducing fractions is raising fractions to higher terms. This is a skill you need when you add or subtract fractions. To reduce the fraction $\frac{6}{8}$, you *divide* both the numerator and the denominator by 2 to get $\frac{3}{4}$. To raise $\frac{3}{4}$ to eighths, you *multiply* both the numerator and the denominator by 2.

This operation is an example of using opposite operations. You will hear more about opposite operations when you review the algebra chapter.

RULE

To raise a fraction to higher terms, follow these steps:
1. Divide the original denominator into the new denominator to find the multiplier.
2. Multiply the original numerator by the multiplier.

Example Change $\frac{2}{3}$ to a fraction with a denominator of 15. $\frac{2}{3} = \frac{}{15}$

Step 1 Divide the original denominator, 3, into the new denominator, 15. The new denominator is 5 times the original denominator. $15 \div 3 = 5$

Step 2 Multiply the original numerator, 2, by the multiplier, 5. $\frac{2 \times 5}{3 \times 5} = \frac{10}{15}$

To check the answer, reduce $\frac{10}{15}$ to get $\frac{2}{3}$, or find the cross products.

EXERCISE 4

Directions: Raise each fraction to higher terms by finding the missing numerator. Check by finding the cross products.

1. $\frac{3}{5} = \frac{}{20}$ $\frac{5}{12} = \frac{}{24}$ $\frac{7}{8} = \frac{}{40}$ $\frac{3}{4} = \frac{}{16}$

2. $\frac{5}{11} = \frac{}{44}$ $\frac{13}{20} = \frac{}{40}$ $\frac{7}{10} = \frac{}{60}$ $\frac{19}{20} = \frac{}{100}$

3. $\frac{3}{4} = \frac{}{100}$ $\frac{5}{9} = \frac{}{36}$ $\frac{1}{8} = \frac{}{24}$ $\frac{1}{3} = \frac{}{36}$

Answers are on page 396.

Changing Improper Fractions to Whole or Mixed Numbers

The figure at the right shows two rectangles, each of which is divided into thirds. You can say that $\frac{5}{3}$ of the rectangles are shaded or that $1\frac{2}{3}$ rectangles are shaded. The improper fraction $\frac{5}{3}$ is equivalent to the mixed number $1\frac{2}{3}$.

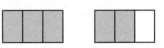

Remember that the fraction bar (—) or slash (/) means to divide. The improper fraction $\frac{5}{3}$ means "5 divided by 3."

──────────────── RULE ────────────────

To change an improper fraction to a whole or mixed number, follow these steps:
1. Divide the denominator into the numerator.
2. Write the remainder as a fraction. Put the remainder over the original denominator.
3. Reduce the remaining fraction if necessary.

───────────────────────────────────────

Example 1   Change $\frac{20}{6}$ to a mixed number.

Step 1   Divide 20 by 6.

Step 2   Write the remainder, 2, over the denominator, 6.

$$3\frac{2}{6} = 3\frac{1}{3}$$
$$6\overline{)20}$$
$$\underline{18}$$
$$2$$

Step 3   Reduce $\frac{2}{6}$ to $\frac{1}{3}$.

You can use the ⬚ a b/c ⬚ key on the Casio *fx*-260 calculator to change an improper fraction to a whole or mixed number.

Example 2   Change $\frac{19}{4}$ to a mixed number.

Press ⬚ AC ⬚.

Press ⬚ 1 ⬚ ⬚ 9 ⬚ ⬚ a b/c ⬚ ⬚ 4 ⬚ ⬚ = ⬚

The display should read ⬚ 4 ⌐3⌐4. ⬚.

The answer is $4\frac{3}{4}$.

EXERCISE 5

Directions: Change each improper fraction to a whole or mixed number, and reduce any remaining fractions. Check your answers with a calculator.

1. $\dfrac{15}{9} =$ $\dfrac{36}{8} =$ $\dfrac{13}{5} =$ $\dfrac{31}{6} =$

2. $\dfrac{6}{2} =$ $\dfrac{28}{16} =$ $\dfrac{15}{15} =$ $\dfrac{24}{18} =$

3. $\dfrac{7}{4} =$ $\dfrac{21}{3} =$ $\dfrac{50}{12} =$ $\dfrac{21}{6} =$

4. $\dfrac{12}{5} =$ $\dfrac{28}{9} =$ $\dfrac{19}{2} =$ $\dfrac{73}{10} =$

Answers are on page 396.

Changing Whole Numbers and Mixed Numbers to Improper Fractions

When you multiply and divide mixed numbers, you will need to change the mixed numbers to improper fractions.

Remember that a fraction is a kind of division problem. Any whole number can be written as an improper fraction with a denominator of 1. When you divide the denominator into the numerator, the result is the original whole number.

<u>Example 1</u>   Write 3 as an improper fraction with a denominator of 1.

Step 1   Write a fraction with 3 as the numerator $3 = \dfrac{3}{1}$
and 1 as the denominator.

Step 2   Check by dividing 1 into 3.

The figure at the right shows $2\frac{1}{3}$ shaded circles. Each completely shaded circle represents $\frac{3}{3}$. You can also say that $\frac{7}{3}$ of the circles are shaded.

━━━━━━━ R U L E ━━━━━━━

To change a mixed number to an improper fraction, follow these steps:
1. Multiply the denominator by the whole number.
2. Add the numerator.
3. Write the total over the denominator.

When you use these steps, you first change the whole number to an improper fraction. Then you add the fraction part of the mixed number.

Think about the shaded circles above. The two completely shaded circles can be written as $\frac{6}{3}$. $\dfrac{6}{3} + \dfrac{1}{3} = \dfrac{7}{3}$

Example 2   Change $3\frac{1}{4}$ to an improper fraction. $3\frac{1}{4} = \frac{}{4}$

Step 1   Multiply the denominator, 4, by the whole number, 3. $4 \times 3 = 12$

Step 2   Add the numerator, 1, to 12. $12 + 1 = 13$

Step 3   Write the total, 13, over the denominator, 4. $3\frac{1}{4} = \frac{13}{4}$

To check your answer, change the improper fraction back to a mixed number.

You can use the **SHIFT** and **d/c** keys on the Casio *fx*-260 calculator to change a whole or mixed number to an improper fraction.

Example 3   Change $4\frac{3}{4}$ to an improper fraction.

Press **AC**.

Press **4** **a b/c** **3** **a b/c** **4** to enter the mixed number.

Press **SHIFT** **d/c**.

The display should read ⌐ 19 ⌐ 4. ⌐.

The answer is $\frac{19}{4}$.

EXERCISE 6

Directions: For problems 1–3, rewrite the numbers as fractions.

1. Change each whole number to an improper fraction with a denominator of 1.
   4 =   10 =   9 =   16 =   50 =

2. Write 6 as an improper fraction with a denominator of 2.

3. Write 5 as an improper fraction with a denominator of 4.

For problems 4–6, change each mixed number to an improper fraction. Check your answers with the Casio *fx*-260 calculator.

4. $2\frac{2}{3} =$ $1\frac{5}{8} =$ $8\frac{2}{5} =$ $3\frac{3}{4} =$ $3\frac{5}{6} =$

5. $5\frac{4}{7} =$ $3\frac{1}{2} =$ $7\frac{1}{3} =$ $6\frac{2}{9} =$ $10\frac{1}{3} =$

6. $12\frac{3}{4} =$ $9\frac{1}{4} =$ $13\frac{2}{3} =$ $15\frac{1}{3} =$ $4\frac{3}{8} =$

Answers are on page 396.

Comparing and Rounding Fractions

In a proper fraction the numerator is less than the denominator. The size of the numerator *compared to* the size of the denominator tells something about the size of the fraction.

A fraction is *equal to* $\frac{1}{2}$ when the numerator is half of the denominator.

Examples $\frac{3}{6} = \frac{1}{2}$ because 3 is half of 6.

$\frac{17}{34} = \frac{1}{2}$ because 17 is half of 34.

A fraction is *less than* $\frac{1}{2}$ when the numerator is *less than* $\frac{1}{2}$ of the denominator. The symbol $<$ means "is less than."

Examples $\frac{2}{9} < \frac{1}{2}$ because 2 is less than half of 9.

$\frac{13}{30} < \frac{1}{2}$ because 13 is less than half of 30.

A fraction is *greater than* $\frac{1}{2}$ when the numerator is *greater than* $\frac{1}{2}$ of the denominator. The symbol $>$ means "is greater than."

Examples $\frac{5}{8} > \frac{1}{2}$ because 5 is more than half of 8.

$\frac{12}{19} > \frac{1}{2}$ because 12 is more than half of 19.

When you add, subtract, multiply, or divide fractions, you can estimate answers by rounding to the nearest whole number. For a mixed number with a fraction of $\frac{1}{2}$ or more, round to the next whole number.

Examples $8\frac{5}{5} \rightarrow 9$ $1\frac{7}{8} \rightarrow 2$ $4\frac{1}{2} \rightarrow 5$

For a mixed number with a fraction of less than $\frac{1}{2}$, drop the fraction and use the whole number.

Examples $6\frac{2}{5} \rightarrow 6$ $10\frac{2}{9} \rightarrow 10$ $4\frac{5}{16} \rightarrow 4$

EXERCISE 7

Directions: Answer each problem below.

1. Which fractions are *equal to* $\frac{1}{2}$? $\frac{2}{7}$ $\frac{6}{12}$ $\frac{9}{18}$ $\frac{5}{9}$

2. Which fractions are *less than* $\frac{1}{2}$? $\frac{6}{11}$ $\frac{4}{9}$ $\frac{21}{50}$ $\frac{17}{30}$

3. Which fractions are *more than* $\frac{1}{2}$? $\frac{2}{3}$ $\frac{6}{13}$ $\frac{12}{24}$ $\frac{23}{40}$

4. Round each of the following mixed numbers to the nearest whole number.

$7\frac{5}{6}$ $4\frac{1}{3}$ $9\frac{2}{7}$ $11\frac{1}{2}$

$6\frac{1}{4}$ $20\frac{8}{9}$ $14\frac{3}{20}$ $2\frac{7}{8}$

Answers are on page 396.

Finding a Common Denominator

A **common denominator** is a number that can be divided evenly by all the denominators in a problem. The *smallest* number that can be divided evenly by all the denominators in a problem is the **lowest common denominator**, or **LCD**. In order to add and subtract fractions, you need to know how to find the LCD.

--- RULE ---

To find the lowest common denominator for two or more fractions, follow these steps:
1. Try the largest denominator to see whether the other denominators divide into it evenly.
2. If that doesn't work, go through the multiplication table of the largest denominator until you find a number that the other denominators divide into evenly.

Example 1   Find the lowest common denominator for $\frac{3}{4}$ and $\frac{5}{8}$.

Since 4 divides evenly into 8, the lowest common denominator is 8.

$$\frac{3}{4} = \frac{6}{8} \qquad \frac{5}{8} = \frac{5}{8}$$

Example 2   Find the lowest common denominator for $\frac{7}{9}$, $\frac{1}{12}$, and $\frac{5}{6}$.

Step 1   The largest denominator in the group is 12. 6 divides evenly into 12, but 9 does not.

Step 2   Go through the multiplication table of 12 until you find a number that both 9 and 6 will divide into evenly.

$1 \times 12 = 12$, which is not evenly divisible by 9.

$2 \times 12 = 24$, which is not evenly divisible by 9.

$3 \times 12 = 36$, which is evenly divisible by both 9 and 6.

The lowest common denominator for the three fractions is 36.

$$\frac{7}{9} = \frac{28}{36} \qquad \frac{1}{2} = \frac{18}{36} \qquad \frac{5}{6} = \frac{30}{36}$$

EXERCISE 8

Directions: For problems 1 and 2, find the lowest common denominator for each pair of fractions.

1. $\frac{2}{5}$ and $\frac{7}{10}$ $\frac{5}{6}$ and $\frac{3}{4}$ $\frac{3}{4}$ and $\frac{4}{9}$ $\frac{1}{2}$ and $\frac{1}{3}$

2. $\frac{1}{2}$ and $\frac{5}{9}$ $\frac{5}{8}$ and $\frac{3}{20}$ $\frac{2}{9}$ and $\frac{5}{6}$ $\frac{5}{6}$ and $\frac{5}{8}$

3. What is the lowest common denominator for the fractions $\frac{7}{12}$ and $\frac{5}{8}$?

4. Raise both $\frac{7}{12}$ and $\frac{5}{8}$ to higher terms using the lowest common denominator.

5. Which fraction is larger, $\frac{7}{12}$ or $\frac{5}{8}$?

For problems 6 and 7, find the lowest common denominator for each group of fractions.

6. $\frac{1}{2}, \frac{3}{5},$ and $\frac{3}{4}$ $\frac{5}{6}, \frac{3}{4},$ and $\frac{2}{3}$ $\frac{3}{8}, \frac{5}{6},$ and $\frac{7}{12}$

7. $\frac{4}{9}, \frac{5}{6},$ and $\frac{1}{2}$ $\frac{5}{8}, \frac{11}{20},$ and $\frac{1}{2}$ $\frac{8}{9}, \frac{7}{12},$ and $\frac{2}{3}$

8. Raise $\frac{5}{8}, \frac{11}{20},$ and $\frac{1}{2}$ to higher terms using the lowest common denominator.

9. Which fraction is largest, $\frac{5}{8}, \frac{11}{20},$ or $\frac{1}{2}$?

10. Raise $\frac{8}{9}, \frac{7}{12},$ and $\frac{2}{3}$ to higher terms using the lowest common denominator.

11. Which fraction is smallest, $\frac{8}{9}, \frac{7}{12},$ or $\frac{2}{3}$?

Answers are on page 396.

Adding Fractions

When you add decimals, you must add tenths to tenths, hundredths to hundredths, and so on. Fractions are similar. You must add like fractions. **Like fractions** are fractions with the same denominators. To add like fractions, add the numerators of each fraction and put the sum over the denominator. If the answer is an improper fraction, change it to a mixed number. Reduce if you can.

Example 1 $\frac{7}{8} + \frac{3}{8} =$

Step 1 Add the numerators and put the total, 10, over the denominator, 8.

$\frac{7}{8} + \frac{3}{8} = \frac{10}{8}$

Step 2 Change the sum, $\frac{10}{8}$, to a mixed number.

$\frac{10}{8} = 1\frac{2}{8}$

Step 3 Reduce $1\frac{2}{8}$ to $1\frac{1}{4}$.

$1\frac{2}{8} = 1\frac{1}{4}$

In the last example you can first reduce $\frac{10}{8}$ to $\frac{5}{4}$ and then change the improper fraction to the mixed number $1\frac{1}{4}$. The result is the same.

To add mixed numbers, first add the whole numbers and fractions separately. Then combine them to simplify the answer.

Example 2   Add $7\frac{5}{12}$ and $8\frac{11}{12}$.

Step 1 Add the numerators and put the total over the denominator.

$$7\frac{5}{12}$$
$$+ \, 8\frac{11}{12}$$
$$\overline{15\frac{16}{12}}$$

Step 2 Add the whole numbers.

Step 3 Change the improper fraction to a mixed number.

$\frac{16}{12} = 1\frac{4}{12}$

Step 4 Add the whole number part of the answer to the mixed number and reduce.

$15 + 1\frac{4}{12} = 16\frac{4}{12} = 16\frac{1}{3}$

— R U L E —

To estimate the answer to an addition problem, round each mixed number to the nearest whole number. Then add the rounded numbers.

Example 3   Estimate an answer to the problem $7\frac{5}{12} + 8\frac{11}{12}$.

Step 1 Round each mixed number to the nearest whole.

$7\frac{5}{12} \rightarrow 7$

$8\frac{11}{12} \rightarrow 9$

Step 2 Add the rounded numbers. Notice that the estimate is close to the answer $16\frac{1}{3}$.

$7 + 9 = 16$

Unlike fractions have different denominators. When the fractions in an addition problem do not have the same denominators, first raise each fraction to an equivalent fraction with the lowest common denominator. Then add.

Example 4 $5\frac{2}{3} + 3\frac{7}{9} =$

Step 1 The LCD for 3 and 9 is 9.
Raise $\frac{2}{3}$ to ninths.

$$5\frac{2}{3} = 5\frac{6}{9}$$
$$+ 3\frac{7}{9} = 3\frac{7}{9}$$
$$8\frac{13}{9}$$

Step 2 Add the numerators.

Step 3 Add the whole numbers.

Step 4 Change the improper fraction to a mixed number.

$$\frac{13}{9} = 1\frac{4}{9}$$

Step 5 Add the whole number part of the answer to the mixed number.

$$8 + 1\frac{4}{9} = 9\frac{4}{9}$$

EXERCISE 9

Directions: Add. Be sure each answer is reduced to lowest terms.

1. $\frac{2}{9} + \frac{4}{9} =$ $\frac{8}{15} + \frac{11}{15} =$ $\frac{5}{8} + \frac{5}{8} =$

2. $6\frac{5}{9} + 7\frac{8}{9} =$ $1\frac{7}{8} + 20\frac{3}{8} =$ $\frac{5}{16} + \frac{7}{16} =$

3. $\frac{3}{4} + \frac{1}{4} + \frac{3}{4} =$ $2\frac{7}{12} + 4\frac{11}{12} + 9\frac{5}{12} =$ $5\frac{4}{9} + 4\frac{5}{9} + 3\frac{8}{9} =$

4. $\frac{5}{6} + \frac{7}{12} =$ $\frac{2}{3} + \frac{3}{4} =$ $\frac{2}{5} + \frac{5}{6} =$

For problems 5 and 6, first estimate the answer by rounding each mixed number to the nearest whole number and adding the rounded numbers. Then find the exact answer.

5. $9\frac{2}{3} + 4\frac{1}{2} =$ $10\frac{1}{8} + 3\frac{1}{3} =$ $9\frac{1}{2} + 8\frac{3}{4} =$

6. $2\frac{5}{6} + 4\frac{1}{2} + 1\frac{2}{3} =$ $\frac{1}{2} + \frac{1}{4} + \frac{3}{5} =$ $4\frac{1}{3} + 1\frac{5}{6} + 6\frac{5}{8} =$

Answers are on page 397.

Subtracting Fractions

When you subtract fractions, the denominators must be the same.

Example 1 Subtract $3\frac{9}{16}$ from $10\frac{15}{16}$.

$$10\frac{15}{16}$$
$$- 3\frac{9}{16}$$
$$7\frac{6}{16} = 7\frac{3}{8}$$

Step 1 Subtract the numerators and put the difference over the denominator.

Step 2 Subtract the whole numbers and reduce.

When the fractions in a subtraction problem do not have the same denominators, first raise each fraction to an equivalent fraction with the lowest common denominator. Then subtract.

Example 2 $7\frac{2}{3} - 3\frac{4}{9} =$

Step 1 The LCD for 3 and 9 is 9.
Raise $\frac{2}{3}$ to ninths.

$$7\frac{2}{3} = 7\frac{6}{9}$$
$$- 3\frac{4}{9} = 3\frac{4}{9}$$
$$\overline{\qquad 4\frac{2}{9}}$$

Step 2 Subtract the numerators.

Step 3 Subtract the whole numbers.

Example 3 Estimate the answer to the previous example.

Step 1 Round each mixed number to the nearest whole number.

$$7\frac{2}{3} \rightarrow 8$$
$$3\frac{4}{9} \rightarrow 3$$

Step 2 Subtract the rounded numbers.

$$8 - 3 = 5$$

EXERCISE 10

Directions: Subtract. Be sure each answer is reduced to lowest terms.

1. $\frac{5}{8} - \frac{1}{8} =$ $\qquad$ $8\frac{5}{6} - 2\frac{1}{6} =$ $\qquad$ $4\frac{7}{8} - 2\frac{3}{8} =$

2. $10\frac{4}{5} - 8\frac{1}{5} =$ $\qquad$ $\frac{19}{20} - \frac{13}{20} =$ $\qquad$ $6\frac{13}{15} - 2\frac{4}{15} =$

3. $\frac{25}{36} - \frac{4}{9} =$ $\qquad$ $8\frac{5}{6} - 1\frac{1}{3} =$ $\qquad$ $4\frac{17}{18} - 4\frac{1}{6} =$

For problem 4, first estimate the answer by rounding each mixed number to the nearest whole number and subtracting the rounded numbers. Then find the exact answer.

4. $7\frac{5}{8} - 2 =$ $\qquad$ $9\frac{3}{4} - 1\frac{5}{12} =$ $\qquad$ $10\frac{1}{2} - 6\frac{3}{16} =$

Answers are on page 397.

Borrowing

In some subtraction problems there is no fraction in the top number or the fraction in the top number is too small to subtract from. You have to **borrow** or **regroup** or **rename** the top number. Study these examples carefully.

Example 1 $9 - 2\frac{1}{4} =$

Step 1   Since there is nothing to subtract $\frac{1}{4}$ from, you must borrow. Borrow 1 from 9 and change the 1 to $\frac{4}{4}$ because 4 is the LCD.

$$\begin{array}{r} 9 = 8\frac{4}{4} \\ -\ 2\frac{1}{4} = 2\frac{1}{4} \\ \hline 6\frac{3}{4} \end{array}$$

Step 2   Subtract the fractions and the whole numbers.

Example 2 $4\frac{5}{8} - 1\frac{7}{8} =$

Step 1   Since you cannot take $\frac{7}{8}$ from $\frac{5}{8}$, you must borrow. Borrow 1 from 4 and change the 1 to $\frac{8}{8}$ because 8 is the LCD.

$$\begin{array}{r} 4\frac{5}{8} = 3\frac{5}{8} + \frac{8}{8} \\ -\ 1\frac{7}{8} = \\ \hline \end{array}$$

Step 2   Add $\frac{5}{8}$ to $\frac{8}{8}$.

$$3\frac{5}{8} + \frac{8}{8} = 3\frac{13}{8}$$

Step 3   Subtract the fractions and the whole numbers.

$$\begin{array}{r} 3\frac{13}{8} \\ -\ 1\frac{7}{8} \\ \hline \end{array}$$

Step 4   Reduce.

$$2\frac{6}{8} = 2\frac{3}{4}$$

Example 3   Subtract $5\frac{3}{4}$ from $8\frac{1}{3}$.

Step 1   Raise each fraction to 12 because 12 is the LCD.

$$\begin{array}{r} 8\frac{1}{3} = 8\frac{4}{12} \\ -\ 5\frac{3}{4} = 5\frac{9}{12} \\ \hline \end{array}$$

Step 2   Borrow 1 from 8 and change the 1 to $\frac{12}{12}$ because 12 is the LCD.

$$8\frac{4}{12} = 7\frac{4}{12} + \frac{12}{12}$$

Step 3   Add $\frac{4}{12}$ to $\frac{12}{12}$.

$$\begin{array}{r} 7\frac{4}{12} + \frac{12}{12} = 7\frac{16}{12} \\ -\ 5\frac{9}{12} \\ \hline 2\frac{7}{12} \end{array}$$

Step 4   Subtract the fractions and the whole numbers.

EXERCISE 11

Directions: Subtract. Be sure each answer is reduced to lowest terms. Watch for problems in which you do not have to borrow.

1. $9 - 1\frac{2}{3} =$ $11 - 3\frac{5}{8} =$ $8 - 5\frac{7}{12} =$

2. $8\frac{3}{8} - 4\frac{7}{8} =$ $9\frac{1}{3} - 7\frac{2}{3} =$ $7\frac{3}{10} - 4\frac{9}{10} =$

3. $5\frac{7}{12} - 2\frac{11}{12} =$ $15\frac{1}{6} - 13\frac{5}{6} =$ $20\frac{5}{9} - 7\frac{7}{9} =$

4. $\frac{7}{10} - \frac{1}{2} =$ $3\frac{2}{3} - 1\frac{3}{4} =$ $\frac{5}{8} - \frac{3}{5} =$

5. $8\frac{1}{5} - 3\frac{3}{4} =$ $11\frac{3}{5} - 9\frac{1}{2} =$ $9\frac{1}{2} - 5\frac{2}{3} =$

For problem 6, first estimate the answer by rounding each mixed number to the nearest whole number and subtracting the rounded numbers. Then find the exact answer.

6. $16\frac{1}{4} - 7\frac{5}{8} =$ $7\frac{11}{12} - 3\frac{5}{8} =$ $8\frac{9}{10} - 2\frac{3}{4} =$

Answers are on page 397.

Multiplying Fractions

When you multiply fractions, you find a *fraction of a fraction*. The product (answer) is smaller than the fractions you multiply. The phrase *a fraction of* means to multiply.

In the illustration, $\frac{3}{4}$ of a rectangle is shaded. One-half of the shaded part is $\frac{3}{8}$. In other words, $\frac{1}{2}$ of $\frac{3}{4}$ is $\frac{3}{8}$.

Multiplying fractions means finding *a part of a part*.

| $\frac{1}{8}$ | $\frac{1}{8}$ | $\frac{1}{8}$ | $\frac{1}{8}$ |
| $\frac{1}{8}$ | $\frac{1}{8}$ | $\frac{1}{8}$ | $\frac{1}{8}$ |

$\frac{1}{4}$ $\frac{1}{4}$ $\frac{1}{4}$

---- **RULE** ----

To multiply fractions, follow these steps:
1. Multiply the numerators together.
2. Multiply the denominators together.
3. Reduce the answer if possible.

Example Find the product of $\frac{3}{8}$ and $\frac{7}{10}$.

Step 1 Multiply the numerators. $\frac{3}{8} \times \frac{7}{10} = \frac{21}{80}$

Step 2 Multiply the denominators.

Step 3 Try to reduce. $\frac{21}{80}$ is already reduced to lowest terms.

EXERCISE 12

Directions: Multiply. Be sure each answer is reduced to lowest terms.

1. $\frac{3}{4} \times \frac{5}{7} =$ $\frac{2}{3} \times \frac{1}{3} =$ $\frac{1}{10} \cdot \frac{3}{8} =$

2. $\frac{7}{8} \times \frac{1}{5} =$ $\frac{1}{4} \times \frac{5}{16} =$ $\frac{3}{10} \cdot \frac{3}{5} =$

3. $\frac{2}{9} \times \frac{4}{5} =$ $\frac{1}{5} \times \frac{1}{6} =$ $\frac{3}{5} \times \frac{1}{2} =$

Answers are on page 398.

Canceling

A shortcut for multiplying fractions is called **canceling**. To cancel, find a number that divides evenly into the numerator of one fraction and the denominator of the other.

Canceling is much like reducing. In both operations, you divide a numerator and a denominator by the same number.

Example 1 Find the product of $\frac{3}{4}$ and $\frac{8}{15}$.

Step 1 Divide 3 and 15 by 3.

$$\frac{\overset{1}{\cancel{3}}}{\underset{1}{4}} \times \frac{\overset{2}{\cancel{8}}}{\underset{5}{\cancel{15}}} = \frac{2}{5}$$

Step 2 Divide 4 and 8 by 4.

Step 3 Multiply the new numerators and denominators. Be sure the answer is reduced to lowest terms. $\frac{2}{5}$ is reduced.

Example 2 $\frac{5}{8} \times \frac{8}{9} \times \frac{7}{10} =$

Step 1 Divide 5 and 10 by 5.

$$\frac{\overset{1}{\cancel{5}}}{\underset{1}{\cancel{8}}} \times \frac{\overset{1}{\cancel{8}}}{9} \times \frac{7}{\underset{2}{\cancel{10}}} = \frac{7}{18}$$

Step 2 Divide 8 and 8 by 8.

Step 3 Multiply the new numerators. $1 \times 1 = 1$ and $1 \times 7 = 7$

Step 4 Multiply the new denominators. $1 \times 9 = 9$ and $9 \times 2 = 18$. $\frac{7}{18}$ is reduced to lowest terms.

EXERCISE 13

Directions: Multiply. Be sure each answer is reduced to lowest terms.

1. $\frac{3}{4} \times \frac{6}{7} =$ $\frac{14}{15} \times \frac{3}{7} =$ $\frac{4}{5} \cdot \frac{5}{6} =$

2. $\frac{4}{9} \times \frac{3}{8} =$ $\frac{5}{8} \times \frac{2}{15} =$ $\frac{9}{10} \cdot \frac{2}{3} =$

3. $\frac{3}{20} \times \frac{1}{3} =$ $\frac{4}{5} \times \frac{5}{24} =$ $\frac{2}{3} \times \frac{9}{20} =$

4. $\frac{6}{7} \times \frac{7}{8} \times \frac{4}{5} =$ $\frac{9}{10} \times \frac{1}{4} \times \frac{8}{9} =$ $\frac{3}{4} \times \frac{2}{9} \times \frac{15}{16} =$

Answers are on page 398.

Multiplying Fractions, Whole Numbers, and Mixed Numbers

All the numbers in a multiplication of fractions problem should be written in fraction form.

A whole number can be written as a fraction with a denominator of 1. Remember that any number divided by 1 is that number.

Remember that the phrase *a fraction of* means to multiply.

Example 1   Find $\frac{3}{4}$ of 24.

Step 1   Write 24 as a fraction. $24 = \frac{24}{1}$

Step 2   Divide 4 and 24 by 4. $\frac{3}{4} \times \frac{\overset{6}{24}}{1} = \frac{18}{1} = 18$

Step 3   Multiply across.

Step 4   Change the improper fraction to a whole number.

Notice in the last example that the result of finding *a fraction of* a whole number is a *smaller* whole number. For example, $\frac{3}{4}$ of 24 is 18.

To review how to change mixed numbers to improper fractions, see page 111.

Example 2 $1\frac{1}{3} \times \frac{5}{6} =$

Step 1   Change $1\frac{1}{3}$ to an improper fraction. $1\frac{1}{3} = \frac{4}{3}$

Step 2   Divide 4 and 6 by 2. $\frac{\overset{2}{4}}{3} \times \frac{5}{\underset{3}{6}} =$

Step 3   Multiply across. $\frac{\overset{2}{4}}{3} \times \frac{5}{\underset{3}{6}} = \frac{10}{9} = 1\frac{1}{9}$

Step 4   Change the improper fraction to a mixed number.

EXERCISE 14

Directions: Multiply. Be sure each answer is reduced to lowest terms.

1. $\frac{1}{2} \times 16 =$ $10 \times \frac{2}{3} =$ $\frac{3}{8} \times 12 =$

2. $8 \times \frac{7}{10} =$ $\frac{2}{5} \times 10 =$ $9 \times \frac{11}{20} =$

3. $\frac{5}{6} \times 9 =$ $15 \times \frac{7}{100} =$ $\frac{2}{3} \times 4 =$

4. $4\frac{2}{3} \times \frac{15}{16} =$ $2\frac{1}{4} \times \frac{8}{9} =$ $\frac{1}{4} \times 1\frac{1}{2} =$

For problem 5, first estimate the answer by rounding each mixed number to the nearest whole number and multiplying the rounded numbers. Then find the exact answer.

5. $3\frac{3}{4} \times 6\frac{2}{3} =$ $\qquad$ $1\frac{1}{5} \times 2\frac{1}{3} =$ $\qquad$ $4\frac{3}{8} \times 3\frac{3}{7} =$

Answers are on page 398.

Dividing Fractions

Dividing Fractions, Whole Numbers, and Mixed Numbers

Remember the parts of a division problem. The number that is being divided is the **dividend**. The number that divides into the dividend is the **divisor**. The answer is called the **quotient**.

The whole number division problem, $8 \div 2 = 4$, has the same answer as the fraction multiplication problem, $8 \times \frac{1}{2} = 4$.

$$8 \div 2 = 4$$

In division problems with fractions or mixed numbers, you must **invert** the divisor. The fraction $\frac{1}{2}$ is the **reciprocal**, or the **inverse**, of the improper fraction $\frac{2}{1}$.

$$\frac{\overset{4}{\cancel{8}}}{1} \times \frac{1}{\cancel{2}} = \frac{4}{1} = 4$$

--- **R U L E** ---

To divide with fractions, whole numbers, or mixed numbers, follow these steps:
1. Write each number in fraction form.
2. Invert the divisor and change the $\div$ sign to a $\times$ sign.
3. Follow the rules for multiplying fractions.

Example 1 $4 \div \frac{2}{3} =$

Step 1   Write 4 as an improper fraction with a denominator of 1. $\frac{4}{1} \div \frac{2}{3}$

Step 2   Invert $\frac{2}{3}$ to $\frac{3}{2}$ and change the $\div$ sign to a $\times$ sign. $\frac{4}{1} \times \frac{3}{2}$

Step 3   Follow the rules for multiplication. $\frac{\overset{2}{\cancel{4}}}{1} \times \frac{3}{\cancel{2}} = \frac{6}{1} = 6$

Example 2 $4\frac{1}{2} \div 1\frac{1}{2} =$

Step 1   Change both $4\frac{1}{2}$ and $1\frac{1}{2}$ to improper fractions.

$$\frac{9}{2} \div \frac{3}{2}$$

Step 2   Invert the divisor $\frac{3}{2}$ to $\frac{2}{3}$ and change the $\div$ sign to a $\times$ sign.

$$\overset{3}{\underset{1}{\cancel{\frac{9}{2}}}} \times \overset{1}{\underset{1}{\cancel{\frac{2}{3}}}} = \frac{3}{1} = 3$$

Step 3   Follow the rules for multiplication.

EXERCISE 15

Directions: Divide. Be sure each answer is reduced to lowest terms.

1. $\frac{1}{3} \div \frac{1}{6} =$ $5 \div \frac{5}{6} =$ $4\frac{1}{2} \div \frac{3}{4} =$

2. $\frac{1}{3} \div \frac{2}{3} =$ $4 \div \frac{3}{8} =$ $\frac{5}{9} \div \frac{3}{4} =$

3. $5\frac{5}{6} \div \frac{7}{8} =$ $\frac{9}{10} \div \frac{3}{5} =$ $3\frac{1}{3} \div \frac{1}{3} =$

4. $10 \div 1\frac{1}{2} =$ $1\frac{1}{3} \div 3\frac{1}{5} =$ $6 \div 1\frac{1}{3} =$

5. $21 \div 4\frac{1}{5} =$ $2\frac{2}{9} \div 2 =$ $\frac{9}{10} \div 3 =$

6. $5\frac{5}{6} \div 7 =$ $2\frac{1}{4} \div 1\frac{1}{8} =$ $2\frac{1}{2} \div 4\frac{3}{4} =$

Answers are on page 399.

Fractions and Decimals

Changing Decimals to Fractions

Decimals and fractions are both ways of describing parts of a whole. Decimals and fractions can be easily interchanged. Remember that a decimal gets its name from the number of decimal places (the digits to the right of the decimal point).

--- R U L E ---

To change a decimal to a fraction or a mixed decimal to a whole number, follow these steps:
1. Write the digits in the decimal as the numerator.
2. Write the denominator that corresponds to the number of places.
3. Reduce the fraction to lowest terms.

Example 1   Change 0.25 to a fraction.

Step 1   Write the digits in the decimal, 25, as the numerator.

$0.25 = \frac{25}{100}$

Step 2   Since two decimal places mean *hundredths*, write 100 as the denominator.

Step 3   Reduce $\frac{25}{100}$ to lowest terms.

$\frac{25}{100} = \frac{1}{4}$

Example 2   Change 3.8 to a mixed number.

Step 1   Write the digit in the decimal, 8, as the numerator.

$3.8 = 3\frac{8}{10}$

Step 2   Since one decimal place means *tenths*, write 10 as the denominator.

Step 3   Reduce $\frac{8}{10}$ to lowest terms.

$3\frac{8}{10} = 3\frac{4}{5}$

You can use the a b/c key on the Casio *fx*-260 calculator to change a decimal to a fraction.

Example 3   Change 4.75 to a mixed number.

Press AC.

Press 4 a b/c 7 5 a b/c 1 0 0 =.

The display should read 4⌐3⌐4.

The answer is $4\frac{3}{4}$.

EXERCISE 16

Directions: Change each decimal to a fraction or a mixed number and reduce to lowest terms.

1. 0.6 =   0.5 =   0.45 =   0.80 =

2. 0.125 =   0.065 =   0.15 =   0.96 =

3. 0.024 =   0.0002 =   0.010 =   0.34 =

4. 2.5 =   3.75 =   4.001 =   6.05 =

Answers are on page 399.

Changing Fractions to Decimals

Remember that the fraction bar means to divide. The fraction $\frac{1}{4}$ means one out of four parts. It also means *one divided by four*.

──────── RULE ────────

To change a fraction to a decimal, follow these steps:
1. Divide the denominator into the numerator.
2. Write a decimal point and zeros to the right of the decimal point in the dividend. Often two zeros are enough.

Example 1　Change $\frac{1}{4}$ to a decimal.

Step 1　Divide 4 into 1. Write a decimal point and two zeros to the right of the decimal point.

$$\frac{1}{4} = 4\overline{)1.00}^{\,0.25}$$

$$\begin{array}{r} 0.25 \\ 4\,\overline{)1.00} \\ \underline{8} \\ 20 \\ \underline{20} \end{array}$$

Step 2　Divide and bring up the decimal point.

Sometimes the division doesn't come out evenly no matter how many zeros you write.

Example 2　Change $\frac{1}{3}$ to a decimal.

Step 1　Divide 3 into 1. Write a decimal point and two zeros to the right of the decimal point.

$$\frac{1}{3} = 3\,\overline{)100}$$

$$\begin{array}{r} 0.33\frac{1}{3} \\ 3\,\overline{)100} \\ \underline{9} \\ 10 \\ \underline{9} \\ 1 \end{array}$$

Step 2　Divide and bring up the decimal point.

If you continue to write zeros in the last example, you continue to get another 3 in the quotient. You can stop after two places as in the example. Or you can round the answer. $\frac{1}{3}$ to the nearest tenth is 0.3. $\frac{1}{3}$ to the nearest hundredth is 0.33. $\frac{1}{3}$ to the nearest thousandth is 0.333.

A calculator is a useful tool for changing fractions to decimals.

Example 3　Use a calculator to change $\frac{3}{16}$ to a decimal.

Press [AC].

Press [3] [÷] [1] [6] [=].

The display should read [＿＿0.1875＿＿].

EXERCISE 17

Directions: Change each of these fractions to decimals.

1. $\dfrac{3}{4} =$ $\qquad$ $\dfrac{9}{20} =$ $\qquad$ $\dfrac{7}{10} =$ $\qquad$ $\dfrac{5}{8} =$

2. $\dfrac{1}{2} =$ $\qquad$ $\dfrac{1}{20} =$ $\qquad$ $\dfrac{4}{25} =$ $\qquad$ $\dfrac{3}{8} =$

Use a calculator to change these fractions to decimals. Then round each answer to the nearest hundredth.

3. $\dfrac{5}{6} =$ $\qquad$ $\dfrac{4}{9} =$ $\qquad$ $\dfrac{1}{12} =$ $\qquad$ $\dfrac{2}{3} =$

4. $\dfrac{2}{7} =$ $\qquad$ $\dfrac{1}{6} =$ $\qquad$ $\dfrac{5}{12} =$ $\qquad$ $\dfrac{5}{16} =$

For these pairs of fractions, use a calculator to change each fraction to a decimal. Then circle the larger fraction in each pair.

5. $\dfrac{3}{8}$ or $\dfrac{2}{5}$ $\qquad$ $\dfrac{2}{3}$ or $\dfrac{3}{5}$ $\qquad$ $\dfrac{13}{20}$ or $\dfrac{7}{10}$ $\qquad$ $\dfrac{1}{6}$ or $\dfrac{2}{9}$

Answers are on page 399.

Scientific Notation with Small Numbers

On page 93 you learned to write large numbers in **scientific notation**. Mathematicians and scientists use scientific notation to write small numbers as well.

You learned earlier that whole number places can be written as powers of ten. The decimal places can also be written as powers of ten. Decimal places are indicated with a negative exponent. A negative exponent represents a **reciprocal**, or inverse. For example, the reciprocal of 10 is 0.1. In scientific notation
$0.1 = 10^{-1}$.

Study the following chart carefully. Notice that the names refer to the names of the first six decimal places in our number system.

name	decimal	fraction	power
one tenth	0.1	$\dfrac{1}{10}$	10^{-1}
one hundredth	0.01	$\dfrac{1}{100}$	10^{-2}
one thousandth	0.001	$\dfrac{1}{1000}$	10^{-3}
one ten-thousandth	0.0001	$\dfrac{1}{10,000}$	10^{-4}
one hundred-thousandth	0.00001	$\dfrac{1}{100,000}$	10^{-5}
one millionth	0.000001	$\dfrac{1}{1,000,000}$	10^{-6}

Scientific notation is a number that is between 1 and 10 multiplied by a power of ten.

--- RULE ---

To write a small number in scientific notation, follow these steps:
1. Move the decimal point in the number to get a number between 1 and 10.
2. Write a multiplication problem with the new decimal multiplied by a negative power of 10. The power corresponds to the number of places that the decimal had to move.

Example 1   Write 0.0057 in scientific notation.

Step 1   Move the decimal point between 5 and 7 $0.0057 = 5.7 \times 10^{-3}$
because 5.7 is between 1 and 10.

Step 2   Since the decimal moved three places
to the right, multiply the new decimal by 10^{-3}.

Example 2   Change 2.38×10^{-6} to a decimal.

Step 1   Remember that multiplying by $2.38 \times 10^{-6} = 0.00000238$
10^{-6} means moving the decimal
point six places to the left.

Step 2   Move the decimal point in 2.38
six places to the left.

EXERCISE 18

Directions: For problems 1 and 2, express each decimal in scientific notation.

1. 0.008 =   0.0446 =   0.000091 =

2. 0.0000015 =   0.027 =   0.00034 =

For problems 3 and 4, write each number in scientific notation as a decimal.

3. 1.98×10^{-5} = 1.1×10^{-6} = 9.2×10^{-2} =

4. 5.1×10^{-3} = 7.33×10^{-4} = 4.09×10^{-5} =

Solve each problem.

5. A sheet of plastic has a thickness of 0.0019 centimeter. Write this number in scientific notation.

6. A virus is 1.8×10^{-7} meter long. Write the length of the virus as a decimal.

Answers are on page 400.

Fraction Word Problems

The next exercise gives you a chance to apply your fraction skills to word problems. On the GED Test you will be asked to write your answers to some fraction questions on a grid.

Example 1 Matt gets 15 days of paid vacation each year. So far this year he has used 9 of his vacation days. What fraction of his yearly vacation has Matt used?

Step 1 Make a fraction with vacation days used in the numerator and total vacation days in the denominator.

$$\frac{9}{15} = \frac{3}{5}$$

Step 2 Divide 9 and 15 by 3. Matt has used $\frac{3}{5}$ of his vacation days.

To answer the last example on a grid, write the correct answer in the blank boxes at the top of each column. Use a separate column for each digit and the fraction bar. Notice that the grid uses a slash / for the fraction bar.

The grid at the right is filled in correctly. As you learned with whole numbers (page 46), an answer on a grid may be centered (like this one), shifted to the left, or shifted to the right.

Do not forget to fill in the circles below each column. And do not leave blank columns between digits and symbols.

Example 2   In the last example, what fraction of his yearly vacation days does Matt have left for the rest of the year?

Step 1   Find the number of vacation days that Matt still has. Subtract the days he has used, 9, from the total, 15.

$15 - 9 = 6$

Step 2   Make a fraction with the vacation days remaining in the numerator and the total in the denominator.

$\frac{6}{15} = \frac{2}{5}$

Step 3   Divide 6 and 15 by 3. Matt has $\frac{2}{5}$ of his vacation days left.

There is another way to think about the last example. Think of the 15 vacation days as *one whole*. Matt has used $\frac{3}{5}$ of his vacation days. Subtract the fraction that he has used from 1. Write 1 as the improper fraction $\frac{5}{5}$ since 5 is the denominator. Then subtract $\frac{3}{5}$ from $\frac{5}{5}$. Again, Matt has $\frac{2}{5}$ of his vacation days left.

$1 - \frac{3}{5}$

$\frac{5}{5} - \frac{3}{5} = \frac{2}{5}$

Division problems sometimes cause trouble. Remember that the amount being divided is the dividend. The dividend comes first when you divide fractions.

Example 3   How many boards each $1\frac{1}{2}$ feet long can Phil cut from a board that is 8 feet long?

Step 1   The 8-foot board is being divided. Divide 8 by $1\frac{1}{2}$.

$8 \div 1\frac{1}{2}$

Step 2   Change both 8 and $1\frac{1}{2}$ to improper fractions.

$\frac{8}{1} \div \frac{3}{2}$

Step 3   Invert $\frac{3}{2}$ to $\frac{2}{3}$ and change the $\div$ sign to a $\times$ sign.

$\frac{8}{1} \times \frac{2}{3}$

Step 4   Follow the rules for multiplication.

$\frac{8}{1} \times \frac{2}{3} = \frac{16}{3} = 5\frac{1}{3}$

The quotient is a mixed number $5\frac{1}{3}$. This means that Phil can cut 5 small boards from the 8-foot board. Ignore the leftover fraction.

EXERCISE 19

Directions: Solve each problem. For the first three problems fill in each corresponding number grid.

1. Melanie wants to make a recipe that calls for $\frac{1}{4}$ cup of sugar. She wants to make only one-half of the amount in the recipe. How much sugar should she use?

2. José has to drive 60 miles to deliver a refrigerator. He stops for gasoline after driving 45 miles. What fraction of the total distance has he driven?

3. What fraction of the total distance does José, in the last problem, have left to drive after he buys gasoline?

4. Jeff paid $38 for $9\frac{1}{2}$ yards of lumber. What was the price for one yard?

5. Mrs. Vega bought $2\frac{1}{2}$ pounds of chicken, $2\frac{5}{8}$ pounds of ground beef, $1\frac{3}{4}$ pounds of sausage, and $3\frac{1}{4}$ pounds of oranges. Find the total weight of these purchases.

6. At the last minute Mrs. Vega decided that she also needed 10 pounds of potatoes. However, she cannot carry more than 20 pounds of groceries. Will she ask to have the groceries delivered? Why or why not?

7. One cubic foot of water weighs $62\frac{1}{2}$ pounds. Find the weight of three cubic feet of water.

8. The MacDonalds are dividing a 90-acre field into $4\frac{1}{2}$-acre building lots. How many lots can they make from the 90-acre field?

9. Sandra had a $\frac{3}{4}$-pound bar of cooking chocolate. She used $\frac{1}{2}$ pound of the bar to bake a cake. How much chocolate was left?

For problems 10–13, choose the correct answer.

10. Five hundred questionnaires were sent out asking people their reaction to a plan to build a new cement plant in their community. In one month about $\frac{1}{6}$ of the questionnaires were returned. Approximately how many of the questionnaires were returned in one month?

    (1) 40   (2) 80   (3) 120   (4) 150   (5) 200

11. Two months after mailing the questionnaires in the last problem, 294 were filled out and returned. About what fraction of the total were returned in two months?

    (1) $\frac{1}{4}$ (2) $\frac{2}{5}$ (3) $\frac{1}{2}$ (4) $\frac{3}{5}$ (5) $\frac{3}{4}$

12. Marlene needs $2\frac{1}{4}$ yards of material to make a dress for her youngest daughter. How many dresses can she make from 10 yards of material?

    (1) 2   (2) 3   (3) 4   (4) 5   (5) 6

13. On a snowy evening about 12 of the students in Mrs. Thompson's English class were absent. There are 35 students registered for her class. About what fraction of the class was absent that evening?

    (1) $\frac{1}{12}$ (2) $\frac{1}{6}$ (3) $\frac{1}{4}$ (4) $\frac{1}{3}$ (5) $\frac{1}{2}$

Answers are on page 400.

GED PRACTICE
Fractions Review

PART I

Directions: Solve each problem. Use a calculator whenever possible for problems 1–7. Mark each answer for problems 1 and 2 on the corresponding number grid.

1. Reduce $\frac{48}{60}$ to lowest terms.

2. Change $\frac{6}{25}$ to a decimal.

For problems 3–5, refer to the information below.

Alfredo's employer withholds $\frac{1}{5}$ of his gross wages for federal tax, $\frac{1}{8}$ for state tax, and $\frac{1}{10}$ for social security. Alfredo's weekly gross pay is $720.

3. What fraction of his gross wages does Alfredo take home?

   (1) $\frac{23}{40}$

   (2) $\frac{17}{40}$

   (3) $\frac{9}{10}$

   (4) $\frac{7}{8}$

   (5) $\frac{4}{5}$

4. How much of Alfredo's salary is withheld each week for federal tax?

   (1) $ 46
   (2) $ 72
   (3) $ 80
   (4) $100
   (5) $144

5. Alfredo spends $\frac{1}{6}$ of his take-home pay for food. How much does he spend on food each week?

   (1) $ 27
   (2) $ 69
   (3) $ 80
   (4) $ 90
   (5) $120

6. Anna spent $41.40 for $4\frac{1}{2}$ yards of material. What was the cost of one yard of the material?

   (1) $ 2.30

   (2) $ 4.60

   (3) $ 8.60

   (4) $ 9.20

   (5) $10.20

7. Find the cost of $1\frac{1}{2}$ pounds of coffee that sells for $5.90 a pound.

   (1) $ 6.65

   (2) $ 7.75

   (3) $ 8.85

   (4) $ 9.95

   (5) $10.15

PART II

Directions: Solve the following problems without a calculator. For problems 8–10, mark each answer on the corresponding number grid.

8. Change 0.35 to a fraction and reduce.

9. Change $7\frac{2}{3}$ to an improper fraction.

10. Change $5\frac{2}{3}$ to a mixed decimal and round to the nearest hundredth.

11. Change $\frac{52}{8}$ to a mixed number and reduce to lowest terms.

12. Which fractions are *less than* $\frac{1}{2}$?

    $\frac{5}{8}$ $\frac{7}{15}$ $\frac{9}{20}$ $\frac{19}{36}$

13. Round each mixed number to the nearest whole number.

    $3\frac{7}{8}$ $6\frac{1}{4}$ $9\frac{2}{3}$ $12\frac{3}{10}$

14. Which fraction is smaller: $\frac{5}{9}$ or $\frac{2}{3}$?

15. $7\frac{3}{8} + 3\frac{5}{8} + 4\frac{7}{8} =$

16. $12\frac{1}{5} - 8\frac{4}{5} =$

17. $5\frac{3}{4} + 6\frac{1}{2} + 8\frac{7}{10} =$

18. $8\frac{5}{12} - 3\frac{2}{3} =$

19. $\frac{3}{8} \times \frac{1}{6} \times \frac{4}{5} =$

20. $5 \times \frac{3}{10} =$

21. $3\frac{3}{4} \times 3\frac{1}{3} =$

22. $\frac{3}{4} \div \frac{1}{8} =$

23. $24\frac{1}{2} \div 3\frac{1}{2} =$

Choose the correct answer to each of the following problems.

24. From a log that was $8\frac{1}{2}$ feet long, Jed sawed a piece that was $3\frac{3}{4}$ feet long. What was the length in feet of the remaining piece of the log?

    (1) $8\frac{1}{2}$

    (2) $5\frac{3}{4}$

    (3) $4\frac{3}{4}$

    (4) $4\frac{1}{4}$

    (5) $3\frac{3}{4}$

25. This year there are 1189 cellular phones in the rural county where Mark lives. Five years ago there were only 423 cellular phones in the county. The number of cell phones 5 years ago was approximately what fraction of the number in the county this year?

    (1) $\frac{1}{8}$

    (2) $\frac{1}{6}$

    (3) $\frac{1}{4}$

    (4) $\frac{1}{3}$

    (5) $\frac{1}{2}$

26. From a 10-pound bag of flour Janina first took $3\frac{1}{2}$ pounds and then another $\frac{3}{4}$ pound. Which expression represents the weight, in pounds, of the flour that is left in the bag?

(1) $(0.75 + 10) - 3.5$

(2) $3.5 - 10 - 0.75$

(3) $10 + 3.5 + 0.75$

(4) $10 - 3.5 - 0.75$

(5) $10 \times 3.5 \times 0.75$

27. Which of the following is equal to 3.4×10^{-4}?

(1) 0.34

(2) 0.034

(3) 0.0034

(4) 0.00034

(5) 3.4

Answers are on page 401.

You should have gotten at least 22 problems right on the last exercise. If you did not get 22 right, review your fractions skills before you go on. If you got 22 or more right, correct any problem you got wrong.
Then go on to the next chapter.

Chapter 5

Ratio and Proportion

In mathematics we often compare numbers. Imagine a factory where there are 150 men and 100 women working. One way to compare these facts is to subtract. There are 50 more men than women working in the factory. (150 − 100 = 50)

Another way to compare these facts is to write a **ratio.** The ratio of men to women working in the factory is 150 to 100 or, in reduced form, 3 to 2. In other words, for every three men working in the factory, there are two women.

Ratio and proportion are useful tools for solving many word problems.

Ratio

A ratio is a comparison of numbers by division. A ratio can be written with the word *to*, with a colon (:), or as a fraction. Like a fraction, a ratio always should be reduced. Reducing a ratio is sometimes called **simplifying**.

Following are the three ways to write the ratio of the number of men to the number of women working in the factory.

150 to 100 = 3 to 2 or 150:100 = 3:2 or $\frac{150}{100} = \frac{3}{2}$

The numbers in a ratio *must* be written in the order the problem asks for. For the example of the factory workers, the ratio of men to women is 3 to 2, *not* 2 to 3.

Example   Evelyn earns $2400 a month. She pays $600 a month in rent. What is the ratio of her income to her rent?

Make a ratio with her income first (in the numerator) and her rent second. Then reduce.

$\frac{\text{income}}{\text{rent}}$ $\frac{2400}{600} = \frac{4}{1}$

The ratio of Evelyn's income to her rent is 4 to 1 or 4:1 or $\frac{4}{1}$.

TIP
Always reduce a ratio to lowest terms. However, when a ratio is an improper fraction, do not change it to a mixed number.

EXERCISE 1

Directions: For problems 1 and 2, simplify each ratio.

1. 24:30 =   200:125 = $\frac{28}{21}$ =

2. $\frac{3.4}{1.7}$ =   4 to 1000 = $560 to $320 =

Solve each problem below.

3. Alvaro makes $600 a week and saves $60 each week. What is the ratio of the amount he makes to the amount he saves?

4. For Alvaro, in problem 3, what is the ratio of the amount he saves to the amount he makes?

5. There are 24 students in Sam's English class. Four of the students speak Armenian as a first language. What is the ratio of Armenian speakers to the total number of students in the class?

6. Anna drove 110 miles on 22 gallons of gas. What is the ratio of the distance she drove to the number of gallons of gas she used?

Answers are on page 402.

Two-Step Ratio Problems

A problem may not directly state both numbers that you need to set up a ratio. You may have to determine one of the numbers. Read the next example carefully.

Example   On a test with 20 problems, Maceo got 2 problems wrong. What was the ratio of the number of problems he got right to the total number of problems?

Step 1   Find the number of problems he got right. $20 - 2 = 18$
Subtract the number he got wrong, 2, from the total number of problems on the test, 20.

Step 2   Make a ratio of the number of problems he got right, 18, to the total number of problems, 20. Then reduce. $\frac{\text{right}}{\text{total}} \quad \frac{18}{20} = \frac{9}{10}$

EXERCISE 2

Directions: Solve each problem.

1. A GED class of 20 students has 12 women.

   a. What is the ratio of the number of women to the total number of students?
   b. What is the ratio of the number of men to the total number of students?
   c. What is the ratio of the number of men to the number of women?
   d. What is the ratio of the number of women to the number of men?

2. At Baxter Electronics there are 105 union workers and 45 nonunion workers.

   a. What is the ratio of the number of union workers to the total number of workers?
   b. What is the ratio of the number of nonunion workers to the total number of workers?
   c. What is the ratio of the number of union workers to the number of nonunion workers?
   d. What is the ratio of the total number of workers to the number of union workers?

3. From a total yearly budget of $18,000,000, the city of McHenry spends $3,000,000 on education. What is the ratio of the amount spent on education to the amount not spent on education?

4. A math test of 50 questions included 15 fraction problems and 5 decimal problems. What is the ratio of the total number of fraction and decimal problems to the number of questions on the test?

5. There are 1213 registered voters in Paul's village. During the last election 887 people actually voted. Which of the following is approximately the ratio of the number of people who voted to the total number of registered voters in the village?

   (1) 1 to 2
   (2) 2 to 3
   (3) 3 to 4
   (4) 5 to 6

Answers are on page 402.

Proportion

A **proportion** is a statement that says two ratios (or two fractions) are equal. The statement 2:4 = 1:2 is a proportion. The statement $\frac{2}{4} = \frac{1}{2}$ is also a proportion.

You learned that the **cross products** of equal fractions are equal.

For example, the cross products are $2 \times 2 = 4$ and $4 \times 1 = 4$. $\frac{2}{4} \diagdown\diagup \frac{1}{2}$

Each of the four numbers in a proportion is called an **element** or a **term.** In many proportion problems one term is missing. A letter usually represents the missing term.

──────── R U L E ────────

To solve a proportion, follow these steps:
1. Write a statement with two equal cross products.
2. Divide both sides of the statement by the number in front of the missing term.

Note: This is an example of writing in the language of algebra. If a missing term in a proportion is represented by the letter n and the other term that makes the cross product with n is 12, then the cross product of $12 \times n$ is $12n$.

Example 1   Find the missing term in $\frac{n}{8} = \frac{9}{12}$.

Step 1   The cross product of n and 12 is $12n$. $12n = 72$
The cross product of 8 and 9 is 72.
Write a statement that the cross products are equal.

Step 2   Divide both sides of the statement by 12. $\frac{12n}{12} = \frac{72}{12}$

The missing term is 6. $n = 6$

Example 2   Solve for c in $\frac{3}{7} = \frac{8}{c}$.

Step 1   The cross product of 3 and c is $3c$. $3c = 56$
The cross product of 7 and 8 is 56.
Write a statement that the cross products are equal.

Step 2   Divide both sides of the statement by 3. $\frac{3c}{3} = \frac{56}{3}$

The missing term is $18\frac{2}{3}$. $c = 18\frac{2}{3}$

Example 3   Solve for y in the proportion $5:y = 2:8$.

Step 1   Rewrite the proportion with fractions. The first term in each ratio becomes a numerator.

$$\frac{5}{y} = \frac{2}{8}$$

Step 2   The cross product of y and 2 is $2y$.
The cross product of 5 and 8 is 40.
Write a statement that the cross products are equal.

$$2y = 40$$

Step 3   Divide both sides of the statement by 2.

$$\frac{2y}{2} = \frac{40}{2}$$

The missing term is 20.

$$y = 20$$

EXERCISE 3

Directions: For problems 1–3, find the missing term in each proportion.

1. $\frac{m}{6} = \frac{10}{15}$ $\frac{3}{a} = \frac{5}{6}$ $\frac{4}{9} = \frac{y}{3}$ $\frac{8}{7} = \frac{4}{x}$

2. $\frac{1}{3} = \frac{s}{5}$ $\frac{3}{6} = \frac{w}{5}$ $\frac{2}{11} = \frac{4}{p}$ $\frac{2}{8} = \frac{9}{x}$

3. $4:e = 6:8$ $3:7 = 4:y$ $15:40 = x:60$ $30:a = 12:16$

For problems 4 and 5, choose the answer that is set up correctly.

4. If $\frac{x}{7} = \frac{4}{9}$, then $x =$

    (1) $\frac{4 \times 7}{9}$

    (2) $\frac{4 + 7}{9}$

    (3) $4(9 \times 7)$

    (4) $4(9 + 7)$

5. If $\frac{5}{12} = \frac{c}{3}$, then $c =$

    (1) $12 \times 5 \times 3$

    (2) $\frac{12}{5 \times 3}$

    (3) $\frac{5 \times 3}{12}$

    (4) $\frac{3 \times 12}{5}$

Answers are on page 403.

Proportion Word Problems

Proportion is a useful tool for solving many word problems. The key to setting up a proportion is making sure that the amounts being compared are in the same position on either side of the = sign. Study the examples carefully.

Example 1   If 12 yards of lumber cost $40, how much do 30 yards of lumber cost?

Step 1   This problem compares *yards* to *cost.* $\frac{\text{yards}}{\text{cost}} \quad \frac{12}{40} = \frac{30}{c}$
Set up two ratios of yards to cost.
Here *c* represents the cost you are looking for.

Step 2   Find both cross products. $\frac{12c}{12} = \frac{1200}{12}$

Step 3   Divide both sides of 12*c* = 1200 by 12. $c = \$100$
The cost of 30 yards of lumber is $100.

TIP

Any letter can represent the unknown you are looking for in a proportion. In these examples, the first letter of the quantity you are looking for represents the unknown. The letter *c* represents cost in the last example. The letter *m* represents men in the next example.

Example 2   The ratio of the number of men to the number of women working in the county hospital is 2:3. If 480 women work in the hospital, how many men work there?

Step 1   This problem compares *men* to *women.* $\frac{\text{men}}{\text{women}} \quad \frac{2}{3} = \frac{m}{480}$
Set up two ratios of men to women.
Here *m* represents the number of men.

Step 2   Find both cross products. $\frac{3m}{3} = \frac{960}{3}$

Step 3   Divide both sides of 3*m* = 960 by 3. $m = 320$
There are 320 men working in the hospital.

Be sure that the parts in a proportion correspond to the question that is asked. Read the next example carefully.

Example 3   Carlos got 2 problems wrong for every 5 problems right on a test. How many problems did Carlos get wrong if there were 35 problems on the test?

Step 1	The ratio in the question is *problems wrong* to *total problems*. Carlos got 2 *wrong* for every 5 *right*. The ratio of wrong to total is 2:7. (2 wrong + 5 right = 7 total)	$\dfrac{\text{wrong}}{\text{total}} \ \dfrac{2}{7}$
Step 2	Set up two ratios of wrong to total. Here *w* represents problems wrong.	$\dfrac{2}{7} = \dfrac{w}{35}$
Step 3	Find both cross products.	$7w = 70$
Step 4	Divide both sides of $7w = 70$ by 7. Carlos got 10 problems wrong.	$\dfrac{7w}{7} = \dfrac{70}{7}$ $w = 10$

Some problems may ask you to choose the correct set-up for a proportion problem.

Example 4   Manny drove 110 miles in 2 hours. Which expression shows the distance he can travel in 5 hours if he drives at the same speed?

(1) $\dfrac{5 \times 2}{110}$ (2) $\dfrac{110 \times 2}{5}$ (3) $\dfrac{110 \times 5}{2}$ (4) $\dfrac{110 + 5}{2}$

Step 1	Set up two ratios of *miles* to *hours*. Here *m* represents miles.	$\dfrac{\text{miles}}{\text{hours}} \ \dfrac{110}{2} = \dfrac{m}{5}$
Step 2	Write both cross products, but write the cross product of 110 and 5 as a set-up.	$2m = 110 \times 5$
Step 3	Divide both sides by 2. Choice (3) is correct.	$m = \dfrac{110 \times 5}{2}$

In the last example, notice that choice (4) is wrong because it shows the sum of 110 and 5 rather than the product.

EXERCISE 4

Directions: Solve each problem.

1. For every $13 that Helen earns, she takes home $10. Helen's gross pay each month is $1950. How much does she take home each month?

2. Pat's softball team won 5 games for every 3 games they lost. Altogether, the team played 32 games. How many games did they win?

3. The ratio of the number of men to the number of women working at Apex, Inc., is 7:2. Altogether, there are 360 workers at the company. How many of the workers are women?

4. The ratio of good parts to defective parts coming off the assembly line at Apex, Inc., is 20:1. Every day the factory produces 10,500 parts. How many of these parts are defective?

5. The ratio of the number of workers who voted to strike to the number of workers who voted not to strike at Apex was 3:2. If 360 workers voted, how many voted to strike?

6. Recently 300 people in Central County took a civil service examination. For every 6 people who took the exam, 5 people passed. How many people passed the exam?

7. The picture shown at the right is to be enlarged. The short side will measure 20 inches. Find the measurement of the long side.

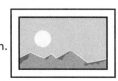

4 in.

6 in.

8. The illustration below shows the ratio of blue paint to gray paint in a special color mix. How many gallons of gray paint are needed to make a total of 30 gallons of mix?

9. A recipe calls for 2 cups of sugar for every 3 cups of flour. Which expression below shows the number of cups of sugar a cook needs with 12 cups of flour?

(1) $\dfrac{2 \times 3}{12}$

(2) $\dfrac{3 + 12}{2}$

(3) $\dfrac{3 \times 12}{2}$

(4) $\dfrac{2 \times 12}{3}$

(5) $\dfrac{2 + 12}{3}$

10. Apples cost 90 cents a dozen. Which expression below represents the cost, in cents, of 8 apples?

(1) $(12 \times 8) \times 90$

(2) $\dfrac{90 \times 8}{12}$

(3) $\dfrac{90}{12 \times 8}$

(4) $\dfrac{90 \times 12}{8}$

(5) $\dfrac{90 + 12}{8}$

Answers are on page 403.

Ratio and Proportion Review

PART I

Directions: Use a calculator to solve problems 1–10.

1. Simplify the ratio 48:60.

2. Write the ratio 1.6 to 6.4 in simplest terms.

3. Express the ratio 75:35 in reduced form.

4. Solve for *x* in the proportion *x*:9 = 12:36.

5. Solve for *s* in the proportion $\frac{2}{7} = \frac{20}{s}$.

6. Find the value of *n* in 8:*n* = 5:18.

Choose the correct answer for problems 7 and 8.

7. Among the seniors at Cripple Creek High School, 2 students said that they planned to leave Cripple Creek within 2 years for every 3 students who said that they planned to stay. There are 110 seniors at the school. How many of them said that they plan to leave within 2 years?

   (1) 22
   (2) 33
   (3) 44
   (4) 55
   (5) 66

8. One seat was empty for every 4 that were occupied at an open meeting in the town hall about a proposal to build a new firehouse. The meeting room in the town hall can seat 140 people. How many seats were empty at the meeting?

   (1) 21
   (2) 28
   (3) 35
   (4) 42
   (5) 49

For problems 9 and 10, mark each answer on the corresponding number grid.

9. The Towsons planted a 35-acre field that yielded 3150 bushels of wheat. At the same rate, how many acres would they need to produce 1890 bushels?

10. At the Central County Municipal Airport the ratio of delayed flights to flights that leave on time is 2:7. During a normal week there are 108 scheduled flights leaving the Central County Airport. How many of those flights are likely to be delayed?

PART II

Directions: Solve problems 11–20 without a calculator.

For problems 11–13, refer to the following information. Write each answer in fraction form and mark your answer on the corresponding number grid.

A survey shows that 42 families on Maple Avenue own their homes and 28 families rent their homes.

11. What is the ratio of the number of families who own their homes to the number who rent?

12. What is the ratio of the number of families who rent their homes to the total number of families on Maple Avenue?

13. Find the ratio of the number of families who own their homes to the total number who live on Maple Avenue.

Choose the correct answer for each of the following problems.

14. Which of the following ratios is *not* equal to the ratio 12:36?

    (1) 3:9
    (2) 5:15
    (3) 9:36
    (4) 10:30
    (5) 16:48

15. If 6 feet of wire cost $3.40, how much do 9 feet of wire cost?

    (1) $1.70
    (2) $2.55
    (3) $3.40
    (4) $4.60
    (5) $5.10

16. The scale on a map says that 2 inches = 150 miles. If two cities are actually 325 miles apart, how many inches apart will they be on the map?

    (1) $3\frac{1}{4}$
    (2) $4\frac{1}{3}$
    (3) $5\frac{7}{8}$
    (4) 7
    (5) 15

17. How many hours will a plane take to go 1200 miles if it travels 450 miles in 2 hours?

    (1) $2\frac{3}{4}$
    (2) $4\frac{1}{2}$
    (3) $5\frac{1}{3}$
    (4) 9
    (5) 12

18. To make a certain color of paint, the ratio of green paint to white paint is 5:2. How many gallons of green paint are required to mix with 14 gallons of white paint?

    (1) 14
    (2) 21
    (3) 28
    (4) 35
    (5) 42

19. A snapshot that was 3 inches wide and 5 inches long was enlarged to be 12 inches long. Which expression represents the width of the enlargement?

   (1) $\dfrac{3 + 12}{5}$

   (2) $\dfrac{5 \times 12}{3}$

   (3) $\dfrac{3 \times 12}{5}$

   (4) $\dfrac{3 \times 5}{12}$

   (5) $\dfrac{5 + 12}{3}$

20. A worker can make 15 motor parts in 2 hours. Which expression represents the time the worker needs to make 100 parts?

   (1) $\dfrac{2 \times 100}{15}$

   (2) $\dfrac{15 \times 100}{2}$

   (3) $\dfrac{15 \times 2}{100}$

   (4) $\dfrac{15 + 2}{100}$

   (5) $\dfrac{2}{15 \times 100}$

Answers are on page 403.

You should have gotten at least 16 problems right on this exercise. If you did not get 16 right, review your ratio and proportion skills before you go on. If you got 16 or more right, correct any problem you got wrong. Then go on to the next chapter.

Chapter 6

Percent

A **percent**, like a decimal or a fraction, describes a part of a whole.

A decimal divides one whole into tenths, hundredths, thousandths, ten-thousandths, and so on. The number of parts in the whole depends on the number of decimal places — digits to the right of the decimal point.

A fraction divides one whole into halves, thirds, fourths, fifths, and so on. With fractions any integer except zero can be the denominator.

With percent, one whole is always divided into 100 parts. A percent is indicated by the % sign. *Percent* means "out of 100" or "per 100." Percent can be expressed as a two-place decimal or a fraction with a denominator of 100.

Understanding Percent

One whole is 100%. For example, if every registered student comes to class, the attendance is 100%. If only half of the registered students come to class, the attendance is $\frac{1}{2}$ of 100%, or 50%.

A percent *greater than* 50% is *greater than* $\frac{1}{2}$. For example, three quarters are 75 of the 100 equal parts of a dollar, or 3 of the 4 equal parts of a dollar, or 75% of a dollar.

A percent *less than* 50% is *less than* $\frac{1}{2}$. For example, one nickel is one of the 20 equal parts of a dollar, or $\frac{1}{20}$ of a dollar, or 5% of a dollar.

A percent *greater than* 100% is *greater than* one whole. For example, suppose that Tom started his career as a carpenter making $15,000. Now he makes twice as much, or 2 × $15,000 = $30,000. His salary today is 2 × 100%, or 200% of his starting salary.

EXERCISE 1

Directions: For problems 1–3, circle the correct answers.

1. Which of the following percents have a value *greater than* $\frac{1}{2}$?
   20%   40%   60%   75%   99%

2. Which of the following percents have a value *greater than* 1?
   35%   50%   75%   110%   200%

3. Which of the following percents have a value *less than* $\frac{1}{2}$?
   4%   15%   20%   51%   85%

For problems 4–8, fill in each blank.

4. *Percent* means that a whole has been divided into _____ equal parts.

5. Thirty-five percent of something means 35 of the _____ equal parts of something.

6. If Frank gets every question right on a Spanish test, then his score is _____ %.

7. If Maria gets only half the questions right on a Spanish test, then her score is _____ %.

8. If town A has a population that is three times the population of town B, then the population of town A is _____ % of the population of town B.

Answers are on page 405.

Percents, Decimals, and Fractions

Changing a Percent to a Decimal

In some problems you may need to change a percent to a decimal to make the amounts easier to work with. When you work with percent, first change each percent to an equivalent decimal or fraction. A percent is like *hundredths*, a two-place decimal.

--- RULE ---

To change a percent to a decimal, follow these steps:
1. Drop the percent sign (%).
2. Move the decimal point two places to the *left*.

TIP
Remember that a whole number written without a decimal point is understood to have a decimal point to the right of the units digit. Notice in the examples that you sometimes add zeros to get two places.

Example

Percent	Decimal
45% = 45	0.45
8% = 08	0.08
$37\frac{1}{2}$% = $37\frac{1}{2}$	$0.37\frac{1}{2}$
250% = 250	2.5

Notice that the decimal point in $37\frac{1}{2}$% is understood to be at the right of the digit 7.

EXERCISE 2

Directions: Change each percent to a decimal or a whole number.

1. 9% =   24% =   100% =   0.3% =

2. $87\frac{1}{2}$% = $8\frac{1}{3}$% =   0.15% =   275% =

3. 2.7% =   3.95 % =   57% =   1000% =

4. 150% =   12% =   99% =   4% =

Answers are on page 405.

Changing a Decimal to a Percent

In some problems you may need to change a decimal to a percent to make amounts easier to work with.

RULE

To change a decimal to a percent, follow these steps:
1. Move the decimal point two places to the *right*.
2. Write the percent sign after the last digit.

You may have to write extra zeros to the right of the digits to move the decimal point two places.

Example

Decimal	Percent
0.25 = 0 25	25%
0.6 = 0 60	60%
$0.04\frac{1}{4}$ = $0\ 04\frac{1}{4}$	$4\frac{1}{4}$%
3.5 = 3 50	350%
36 = 36 00	3600%

EXERCISE 3

Directions: Change each decimal to a percent.

1. 0.81 = $0.37\frac{1}{2}$ =   0.5 =   0.004 =

2. 0.09 =   0.217 =   0.03 = $0.33\frac{1}{3}$ =

3. 2.1 =   4.85 =   3.25 =   0.015 =

4. 0.16 =   0.4 =   1.75 =   4.5 =

Answers are on page 405.

Changing a Percent to a Fraction

Percent means "out of 100." A percent is like a fraction with a denominator of 100.

─────────────── R U L E ───────────────

To change a percent to a fraction, follow these steps:
1. Drop the % sign.
2. Write 100 as the denominator.
3. Then reduce.

───

Example 1 Change 35% to a fraction.

Step 1 Write 35 as the numerator and 100 as the denominator. $35\% = \frac{35}{100}$

Step 2 Reduce the fraction by dividing by 5. $\frac{35 \div 5}{100 \div 5} = \frac{7}{20}$

The answer is $\frac{7}{20}$.

You can use the Casio *fx*-260 calculator to change 35% to a fraction.

Example 2 Use the calculator to change 35% to a fraction.

Press AC .

Press 3 5 a b/c 1 0 0 =

The display should read ⌐ 7 ⌐ 20. ⌐.

To change a percent such as $16\frac{2}{3}\%$ to a fraction, divide the percent by 100. Remember: The fraction bar means to divide.

Example 3   Change $16\frac{2}{3}\%$ to a fraction.

Step 1   Write $16\frac{2}{3}$ as the numerator and 100 as the denominator.

$16\frac{2}{3}\% = \dfrac{16\frac{2}{3}}{100}$

Step 2   Divide $16\frac{2}{3}$ by 100.

$16\frac{2}{3} \div 100$

Step 3   Change $16\frac{2}{3}$ to the fraction $\frac{50}{3}$ and invert $\frac{100}{1}$ to $\frac{1}{100}$.

$\dfrac{50}{3} \times \dfrac{1}{100}$

Step 4   Multiply.
The answer is $\frac{1}{6}$.

$\overset{1}{\underset{}{\dfrac{50}{3}}} \times \dfrac{1}{\underset{2}{100}} = \dfrac{1}{6}$

You can use the Casio *fx*-260 calculator to change $16\frac{2}{3}\%$ to a fraction.

Example 4   Use the calculator to change $16\frac{2}{3}\%$ to a fraction.

Press `AC`.

Press `1` `6` `a b/c` `2` `a b/c` `3` `÷` `1` `0` `0` `=`

The display should read ⌷⌷⌷⌷$1 \lrcorner 6.$⌷ .

EXERCISE 4

Directions: Change each percent to a fraction or a mixed number and reduce.

1. $45\% =$ $37\frac{1}{2}\% =$ $8\% =$ $2\% =$

2. $83\frac{1}{3}\% =$ $24\% =$ $33\frac{1}{3}\% =$ $80\% =$

3. $150\% =$ $12\frac{1}{2}\% =$ $96\% =$ $5\% =$

4. $90\% =$ $325\% =$ $1\frac{1}{2}\% =$ $85\% =$

Answers are on page 405.

Changing a Fraction to a Percent

METHOD 1

To change a fraction to a percent, multiply the fraction by 100%.

Example 1   Change $\frac{3}{4}$ to a percent.

Multiply $\frac{3}{4}$ by 100%.
The answer is 75%.

$\dfrac{3}{\underset{1}{4}} \times \dfrac{\overset{25}{100}}{1} = \dfrac{75}{1} = 75\%$

Example 2   On the Casio *fx-260*, change $\frac{1}{3}$ to a percent.

Press ⬛ AC ⬛.

Press ⬛ 1 ⬛ ⬛ a b/c ⬛ ⬛ 3 ⬛ ⬛ × ⬛ ⬛ 1 ⬛ ⬛ 0 ⬛ ⬛ 0 ⬛ ⬛ = ⬛.

The display should read ⬛ 33⏌1⏌3. ⬛.

The answer is $33\frac{1}{3}$%.

METHOD 2

To change a fraction to a percent, divide the denominator into the numerator. Then move the decimal point two places to the right.

Example 3   Change $\frac{1}{9}$ to a percent.

Divide 9 into 1 and move the decimal point two places to the right.

$$\frac{0.11\frac{1}{9}}{9)1.00^9} = 0\underset{\smile}{\,}11\frac{1}{9} = 11\frac{1}{9}\%$$

The answer is $11\frac{1}{9}$%.

Example 4   On the Casio *fx-260*, change $\frac{2}{5}$ to a percent.

Press ⬛ AC ⬛.

Press ⬛ 2 ⬛ ⬛ ÷ ⬛ ⬛ 5 ⬛ ⬛ = ⬛.

The display should read ⬛ 0.4 ⬛.

Move the decimal point two places to the right.
The answer is 40%.

EXERCISE 5

Directions: Change each fraction or mixed number to a percent. Use either method from above.

1. $\frac{1}{5} =$ $\frac{5}{6} =$ $\frac{3}{8} =$ $\frac{2}{3} =$

2. $\frac{7}{4} =$ $\frac{9}{10} =$ $\frac{5}{12} =$ $\frac{6}{7} =$

3. $\frac{1}{6} =$ $2\frac{1}{2} =$ $\frac{1}{12} =$ $3\frac{1}{4} =$

4. $1\frac{1}{2} =$ $\frac{9}{8} =$ $\frac{4}{3} =$ $5\frac{1}{10} =$

Answers are on page 406.

Common Fractions, Decimals, and Percents

The values in the following chart are the most commonly used fractions, decimals, and percents. After you fill in the chart, check your answers. Then take the time to memorize the values in the chart.

EXERCISE 6

Directions: Fill in the missing values in this chart. The first line has been completed as an example.

Percent	Decimal	Fraction
25%	0.25	$\frac{1}{4}$
50%		
75%		
$12\frac{1}{2}\%$		
$37\frac{1}{2}\%$		
$62\frac{1}{2}\%$		
$87\frac{1}{2}\%$		
20%		
40%		
60%		
80%		
10%		
90%		
$33\frac{1}{3}\%$		
$66\frac{2}{3}\%$		

Answers are on page 406.

Solving Percent Problems

Finding a Percent of a Number

When you worked with fractions, you learned that finding a **fraction of** a number means to multiply. Finding a **percent of** a number also means to multiply.

RULE

To find a percent of a number, follow these steps:
1. Change the percent to a decimal or a fraction.
2. Then multiply.

Example 1 Find 20% of 60.

Step 1 Change 20% to a decimal. $20\% = 0.2$

Step 2 Multiply 60 by 0.2. $60 \times 0.2 = 12$
20% of 60 is 12.

To find a percent of a number on the Casio *fx*-260 calculator, press
[SHIFT] [%]. The % symbol is just above the [=] key.

Example 2 Use the calculator to find 20% of 60.

First press [AC].

Then press [6] [0] [×] [2] [0] [SHIFT] [%].

The display should read [12.].

Note: For the last example, you can first change 20% to a decimal in your head. Then use the calculator to do a decimal multiplication.

First press [AC].

Then press [6] [0] [×] [.] [2] [=].

The display should read [12.].

Example 3 What is $62\frac{1}{2}\%$ of 56?

Step 1 Change $62\frac{1}{2}\%$ to a fraction. $62\frac{1}{2}\% = \frac{5}{8}$
(See the chart on page 155.)

Step 2 Multiply 56 by $\frac{5}{8}$. $\frac{5}{\underset{1}{8}} \times \frac{\overset{7}{56}}{1} = \frac{35}{1} = 35$
$62\frac{1}{2}\%$ of 56 is 35.

If you do not know the fractional equivalent of a percent, multiply the improper fraction form of the percent, and put the other number over 100.

<u>Example 4</u>   Find $6\frac{2}{3}\%$ of 210.

Step 1   Change the percent to an improper fraction. $6\frac{2}{3} = \frac{20}{3}$

Step 2   Write 210 over 100 and multiply. $\frac{\overset{1}{\cancel{20}}}{\underset{1}{\cancel{3}}} \times \frac{\overset{70}{\cancel{210}}}{\underset{5}{\cancel{100}}} = \frac{70}{5} = 14$
$6\frac{2}{3}\%$ of 210 is 14.

EXERCISE 7

Directions: For problems 1–4, change each percent to a decimal. Then solve each problem. Use a calculator to check your answers.

1.   25% of 80 =   60% of 75 =

2.   50% of 260 =   10% of 420 =

3.   90% of 600 =   200% of 35 =

4.   4.5% of 400 =   12.5% of 96 =

For problems 5–9, change each percent to a fraction. Then solve each problem.

5. $37\frac{1}{2}\%$ of 240 = $16\frac{2}{3}\%$ of 120 =

6. $33\frac{1}{3}\%$ of 150 = $87\frac{1}{2}\%$ of 64 =

7.   150% of 80 = $66\frac{2}{3}\%$ of 87 =

8.   Which of the following does *not* give the correct solution to 50% of 24?

(1) $\frac{1}{2} \times 24$

(2) 0.5×24

(3) $\frac{24}{2}$

(4) $\frac{2}{24}$

9.   Sally wants a new computer that costs $900. She has saved 75% of the price. How much has she saved?

10.   Residents of Green Acres were asked whether they would like to have a recycling center built in their neighborhood. Of the 120 people who were interviewed, 80% said, "No, not in my backyard." How many people said no?

Answers are on page 406.

Using Shortcuts

Look at the percents and fractions in the chart below. Each percent in the list is equal to a fraction with a numerator of 1.

50%	$33\frac{1}{3}\%$	25%	20%	$16\frac{2}{3}\%$	$12\frac{1}{2}\%$	10%
$\frac{1}{2}$	$\frac{1}{3}$	$\frac{1}{4}$	$\frac{1}{5}$	$\frac{1}{6}$	$\frac{1}{8}$	$\frac{1}{10}$

To find a percent of a number using any percent in this list, divide the number by the denominator of the equivalent fraction. Look at Method 3 in the example, where 36 is divided by 4, the denominator of $\frac{1}{4}$.

Example 1   Find 25% of 36.

METHOD 1

Change 25% to a decimal and multiply. $0.25 \times 36 = 9$

METHOD 2

Change 25% to a fraction and multiply. $\frac{1}{4} \times \frac{\overset{9}{\cancel{36}}}{1} = \frac{9}{1} = 9$

METHOD 3

Divide 36 by 4. $36 \div 4 = 9$

Notice that the shortcut in Method 3 is the same as the canceling in Method 2.

When you studied decimals, you learned that a quick way to divide by 10 is to move the decimal point one place to the left. (See page 89.) Finding 10% of a number is the same as dividing a number by 10.

To find a multiple of 10% of a number such as 20% or 30% or 40%, first find 10% of the number by moving the decimal point. Then multiply by 2 or 3 or 4.

Example 2   What is 30% of 420?

Step 1   Find 10% of 420 by moving the   10% of 420 = 42.0 = 42
decimal point one place to the left.

Step 2   Multiply 42 by 3. $42 \times 3 = 126$
30% of 420 is 126.

EXERCISE 8

Directions: Use a shortcut method to solve each problem.

1. 25% of 48 =   50% of 280 =

2. 20% of 65 = $33\frac{1}{3}$% of 360 =

3. 10% of 80 = $16\frac{2}{3}$% of 180 =

4. 50% of 150 =   10% of 390 =

5. 20% of 50 = $33\frac{1}{3}$% of 210 =

6. $16\frac{2}{3}$% of 720 = $12\frac{1}{2}$% of 24 =

7. 40% of 460 =   30% of 1200 =

8. 80% of $110 =   60% of $2000 =

Answers are on page 407.

Finding What Percent One Number Is of Another

With fractions you learned that to find what fraction one number is of another, you must first make a fraction with the **part** over the **whole.** (See page 107.) Percent problems are similar.

---------------------------- R U L E ----------------------------

To find what percent one number is of another, follow these steps:
1. First make a fraction. Put the part (usually the smaller number) over the whole and reduce.
2. Then change the fraction to a percent.

Example 1   27 is what percent of 45?

Step 1   Write a fraction with the part over the $\frac{27}{45} = \frac{3}{5}$
whole and reduce.

Step 2   Change $\frac{3}{5}$ to a percent. $\frac{3}{5} \times 100\% = 60\%$

The answer is 60%.

You can use the Casio *fx*-260 calculator to find percents.

Example 2   Use the calculator to find what percent 27 is of 45.

First press ⬚AC⬚.

Press ⬚2⬚ ⬚7⬚ ⬚÷⬚ ⬚4⬚ ⬚5⬚ ⬚SHIFT⬚ ⬚%⬚

The display should read ⬚⬚⬚⬚⬚60.⬚.

The answer is 60%.

Notice that the calculator instruction uses the ⬚÷⬚ key. This is another reminder that a fraction is a kind of division problem.

EXERCISE 9

Directions: Solve each problem. Use a calculator to check your answers.

1. 9 is what percent of 36?   7 is what percent of 35?

2. 50 is what percent of 75?   16 is what percent of 40?

3. 120 is what percent of 160?   17 is what percent of 34?

4. 23 is what percent of 230?   240 is what percent of 300?

5. 15 is what percent of 45?   70 is what percent of 420?

6. 57 is what percent of 57?   110 is what percent of 55?

7. The Melino family was on vacation for 12 days. It rained 3 of those days. On what percent of their vacation days did it rain?

8. Bill paid $2 sales tax on a $40 shirt. The tax was what percent of the list price?

Answers are on page 407.

Finding a Number When a Percent of It Is Given

Think about this problem: 20% of what number is 9? This is the *opposite* of finding a percent of a number. To find a percent of a number, you multiply. To find the opposite, divide by the percent.

--- RULE ---

To find a number when a percent of it is given, follow these steps:
1. Change the percent to either a fraction or a decimal.
2. Then divide the number by that fraction or decimal.

Example 1   20% of what number is 9?

METHOD 1

Step 1   Change 20% to a fraction. $20\% = \frac{1}{5}$

Step 2   Divide 9 by $\frac{1}{5}$. $9 \div \frac{1}{5} = \frac{9}{1} \times \frac{5}{1} = \frac{45}{1} = 45$

The answer is 45.

METHOD 2

Step 1   Change 20% to a decimal. $20\% = 0.2$

Step 2   Divide 9 by 0.2.
The answer is 45.
$$0.2\overline{)9.0}^{\displaystyle 4\,5.}$$

You can use the Casio *fx*-260 calculator to solve the same problem.

Example 2   Use the calculator to find 20% of what number is 20.

First press $\boxed{\text{AC}}$.

Then press $\boxed{9}\ \boxed{\div}\ \boxed{2}\ \boxed{0}\ \boxed{\text{SHIFT}}\ \boxed{\%}$.

The display should read $\boxed{45.}$.

EXERCISE 10

Directions: Solve each problem. Use a calculator to check your answers.

1. 18 is 50% of what number?   25% of what number is 30?

2. 45 is 75% of what number? $33\frac{1}{3}\%$ of what number is 25?

3. 60 is 40% of what number?   10% of what number is 50?

4. 30 is $16\frac{2}{3}\%$ of what number? $37\frac{1}{2}\%$ of what number is 90?

5. 240 is 80% of what number?   150% of what number is 60?

6. Paul and Jane Bidwell pay $150 a month on their car loan. This is 5% of their monthly income. How much do they make each month?

7. Sandra has lost 20 pounds. This is 80% of her goal. How many total pounds does she plan to lose?

Answers are on page 407.

Types of Percent Problems

Think about the statement 25% of 12 is 3. The number 3 is the **part**, 12 is the **whole**, and 25% is the **percent.**

Study the three problems that can be made from the statement 25% of 12 is 3.

Example 1   *Finding the part:* What is 25% of 12?

This is the most common type of percent problem.

Change the percent to a fraction or a decimal and multiply.

$25\% = \frac{1}{4}$

$\frac{1}{4} \times 12 = 3$

Or $0.25 \times 12 = 3.00$
The answer is 3.

Example 2   *Finding the percent:* 3 is what percent of 12?

This type of percent problem is easiest to recognize. The percent is missing.

Make a fraction with the part over the whole. Reduce.

$\frac{3}{12} = \frac{1}{4}$

Change the fraction to a percent.
The answer is 25%.

$\frac{1}{4} \times 100\% = 25\%$

Example 3   *Finding the whole:* 3 is 25% of what number?

This is the least common type of percent problem.

Change the percent to a fraction or a decimal, and divide into the part.
The answer is 12.

$25\% = \frac{1}{4}$

$3 \div \frac{1}{4} = \frac{3}{1} \times \frac{4}{1} = 12$

EXERCISE 11

Directions: For each problem write *P* if you are looking for the part, write % if you are looking for the percent, or write *W* if you are looking for the whole. Then solve each problem.

1. 16 is what percent of 32?   Find 80% of 90.

2. 30 is 60% of what number?   What is $4\frac{1}{2}$ % of 800?

3. What percent of 50 is 14?   15 is what percent of 45?

4. What is 3.6% of 900?   120 is what percent of 80?

5. $33\frac{1}{3}$% of what number is 45? What is 8.6% of 200?

6. Find 20% of 60. 30 is what percent of 40?

7. Jake bought a mountain bike on sale. He saved $72 on the bike, which originally sold for $480. What percent of the original price did he save?

8. Sue and Tom Yee want to buy a house for $129,000. They plan to make a down payment of 8%. How much is the down payment?

9. The Friends of the Community Center have raised $12,000 for their renovation fund. This is 60% of the amount they hope to raise. What is the total amount they hope to raise?

Answers are on page 407.

The Percent Circle

Think about the statement "4 is 50% of 8." Remember that 4 is the **part,** 8 is the **whole,** and 50 is the **percent.** Three problems can be written from the statement.

1. What is 50% of 8? You are looking for the *part.*

2. 4 is what percent of 8? You are looking for the *percent.*

3. 4 is 50% of what number? You are looking for the *whole.*

To solve the three basic types of percent problems, you must either multiply or divide. The **percent circle** is a tool to help you remember which operation to use.

Percent Circle

P stands for the *part.*

% stands for the *percent.*

W stands for the *whole.*

The horizontal line means *divided by.*

The × means *multiplied by.*

──── RULE ────

To use the percent circle, follow these steps:
1. Cover the symbol of the number you are looking for.
2. Do the math shown by the uncovered symbols.

TIP
Remember to change the percent to either a fraction or a decimal.

Example 1   Find 30% of 80.

Step 1   Since you are looking for the part, cover P.

Step 2   Change 30% to a decimal. $30\% = 0.3$

Step 3   Since the uncovered symbols are $\% \times W$,
            multiply the percent by the whole. $P = \% \times W = 0.3 \times 80 = 24$
            The answer is 24.

Example 2   14 is what percent of 70?

Step 1   Since you are looking for the percent, cover % .

Step 2   Since the uncovered symbols are $\frac{P}{W}$,
            divide the part by the whole. $\% = \frac{P}{W} = \frac{14}{70} = \frac{1}{5}$

Step 3   Change $\frac{1}{5}$ to a percent. $\frac{1}{5} = 20\%$
            The answer is 20%.

Example 3   60% of what number is 45?

Step 1   Since you are looking for the whole, cover W.

Step 2   Change 60% to a decimal. $60\% = 0.6$

Step 3   Since the uncovered symbols are $\frac{P}{\%}$,
            divide 45 by 60%. $W = \frac{P}{\%} = \frac{45}{0.6} = 75$
            The answer is 75.

In Examples 1 and 3, the percent was changed to a decimal. Remember that the percent can also be changed to a fraction.

EXERCISE 12

Directions: For each problem write P if you are looking for the part, write %
            if you are looking for the percent, or write W if you are looking
            for the whole. Then use the percent circle to solve each problem.
            For practice, check your answers with a calculator.

1. Find 25% of 96.   35 is what percent of 56?

2. 15 is 20% of what number?   What is 3.2% of 600?

3. 72 is what percent of 80?   What percent of 68 is 34?

4. What is 18% of 300?   70 is what percent of 210?

5. 75% of what number is 120?   What is 9% of 1600?

6. Find $12\frac{1}{2}$% of 640.   60 is what percent of 75?

Answers are on page 408.

Proportion and Percent

So far in this chapter you have used decimals, fractions, a calculator, a percent circle, and a few shortcuts to solve percent problems. You can also use proportion. Think about the statement "4 is 50% of 8." Remember that 4 is the *part*, 8 is the *whole*, and 50 is the *percent*. These numbers can be written in a proportion.

$$\frac{\text{part}}{\text{whole}} = \frac{\%}{100} \qquad \text{The statement "4 is 50\% of 8" becomes} \qquad \frac{4}{8} = \frac{50}{100}$$

Notice that the cross products are equal. $4 \times 100 = 400$ and $8 \times 50 = 400$. You can use a proportion to find the missing term in a percent problem. Notice that 100 always goes in the denominator of the second ratio. (Review proportion on page 140.)

Example 1   Find 30% of 80.

Step 1   The part is missing. Set up a proportion with x as the part, 80 as the whole, and 30 as the percent.

$$\frac{\text{part}}{\text{whole}} \ \frac{x}{80} = \frac{30}{100}$$

Step 2   Write a statement to show that the cross products are equal.

$$100x = 2400$$

Step 3   Divide both sides of the statement by 100. 30% of 80 is 24.

$$x = 24$$

Example 2   14 is what percent of 70?

Step 1   The percent is missing. Set up a proportion with 14 as the part, 70 as the whole, and x as the percent.

$$\frac{\text{part}}{\text{whole}} \ \frac{14}{70} = \frac{x}{100}$$

Step 2   Write a statement to show that the cross products are equal.

$$70x = 1400$$

Step 3   Divide both sides of the statement by 70. 14 is 20% of 70.

$$x = 20\%$$

Example 3   60% of what number is 45?

Step 1   The whole is missing. Set up a proportion with 45 as the part, x as the whole, and 60 as the percent.

$$\frac{\text{part}}{\text{whole}} \ \frac{45}{x} = \frac{60}{100}$$

Step 2   Write a statement to show that the cross products are equal.

$$60x = 4500$$

Step 3   Divide both sides of the statement by 60.
60% of 75 is 45.

$$x = 75$$

Do not be confused by the different methods of solving percent problems. Practice every method (using fractions, using decimals, using a calculator, using shortcuts when you can, using the percent circle, and using proportion) until you are comfortable with them. Then choose the method or methods you prefer when you solve percent problems.

EXERCISE 13

Directions: For each problem write P if you are looking for the part, write % if you are looking for the percent, or write W if you are looking for the whole. Then write a proportion to solve each problem. For practice, check your answers with a calculator.

1. There are 24 students in Blanca's GED class. Eighteen of the students passed the GED on their first try. What percent of the students passed the first time?

2. A private hauling company gives 10% of their profit each year to charity. One year their profit was $65,000. How much did they give to charity?

3. Gloria spent $120 at the grocery on Friday. The amount she spent was 25% of the total she has to spend for the week. What total amount does Gloria have for the week?

4. In January 70% of the employees at Ace Electronics had the flu. There are 90 employees at Ace. How many of them had the flu?

5. Sean took his family out to eat at a pizzeria. The bill came to approximately $40. He left the waiter a tip of $6. The tip was about what percent of the bill?

6. Of the 90 employees at Ace Electronics, 30% of them filed their tax returns a month or more before the deadline. How many of the employees filed their tax returns a month or more before the deadline?

Answers are on page 408.

Percent Word Problems

To solve a percent word problem, first decide whether you are looking for the **part,** the **percent,** or the **whole.**

Note: The examples in the rest of this chapter generally show only one method of solution. But remember that you can use decimals, fractions, shortcuts, a calculator, the percent circle, or proportion. For practice, solve the examples with methods other than the ones that are illustrated.

Example 1   Mr. Gomez pays his supplier $80 for a jacket. He puts a 30% markup on each jacket for his customers. Find the amount of the markup.

Step 1   Decide whether you are looking for the part, the percent, or the whole. $80 is the whole. 30% is the percent. Find the part by calculating 30% of $80.

Step 2   Change 30% to a decimal. $30\% = 0.3$

Step 3   Multiply. $0.3 \times \$80 = \$24$
The markup is $24.

Example 2   Mrs. Jackson makes $450 a week. She pays $90 a week for food. Money spent for food is what percent of Mrs. Jackson's income?

Step 1   Decide whether you are looking for the part, the percent, or the whole. $90 is the part of her income Mrs. Jackson spends for food. $450 is her whole income. Find the percent.

Step 2   Make a fraction with the part over the whole and reduce. $\dfrac{\text{part}}{\text{whole}} \quad \dfrac{90}{450} = \dfrac{1}{5}$

Step 3   Change the fraction to a percent. Mrs. Jackson spends 20% of her income on food. $\dfrac{1}{5} \times 100\% = 20\%$

Example 3   Lois got a 6% commission for selling a house. Her commission was $7,200. Find the selling price of the house.

Step 1   Decide whether you are looking for the part, the percent, or the whole. 6% is the percent and $7,200 is the part. Find the whole price of the house.

Step 2   Change 6% to a decimal. $6\% = 0.06$

Step 3   Divide 0.06 into $7,200. The selling price of the house was $120,000.

$$0.06\overline{)\$7200.00} = \$1200\,00$$

EXERCISE 14

Directions: Solve each problem. Use a calculator to check your answers.

1. A sweater that originally sold for $40 was on sale for 15% off the original price. How much is saved by buying the sweater on sale?

2. Mr. and Mrs. Shin need $12,000 for a down payment on a house. So far they have saved $9,000. What percent of the down payment have they saved?

3. Alfredo earns $440 a week. His employer deducts 21% of his earnings for taxes and social security. How much is deducted from Alfredo's weekly pay?

4. John now weighs 172 pounds. This is 80% of John's weight one year ago. How much did John weigh a year ago?

5. The sales tax in Muhammed's state is 6%. How much tax does Muhammed pay for a television that costs $240?

6. Eighteen people attended David's evening math class. This represents 75% of the number registered for the class. How many people are registered for his class?

For problems 7–9, choose the correct answer.

7. Fiona makes $2419 a month and pays $595 a month for rent. Rent is approximately what percent of Fiona's income?

    (1) 15%
    (2) 20%
    (3) 25%
    (4) 30%
    (5) 35%

8. Mr. Kee pays $20 to his supplier for each pair of gloves that he sells. He puts a $6 markup on each pair. The markup is what percent of the price Mr. Kee pays?

    (1) 6%
    (2) 10%
    (3) 20%
    (4) 30%
    (5) 40%

9. Eva sells cosmetics for a 9% commission. One week her sales totaled $3840. How much did she make in commissions that week?

   (1) $384.00

   (2) $345.60

   (3) $307.20

   (4) $268.80

   (5) $230.40

Answers are on page 408.

Multistep Percent Problems

Many percent applications require more than one step. For example, if you calculate the markup on an article of clothing, you need to add the markup to the original price to find the price a merchant charges a customer.

Example 1   Vic pays his supplier $75 for a jacket. If he puts a 40% markup on the jacket, how much does he charge a customer for the jacket?

Step 1   First find the markup. Change 40% to a fraction or a decimal, and multiply by $75.

$40\% = 0.4$
$0.4 \times \$75 = \$30$

Step 2   Add the markup, $30, to the original price, $75. Vic charges $105 for the jacket.

$\$30 + \$75 = \$105$

Note: There is another way to solve Example 1. Think of the original price that Vic pays the supplier as 100%, and think of the price he charges a customer as an additional 40%. The customer pays $100\% + 40\% = 140\%$ of the price to the supplier.

140% of $\$75 = 1.4 \times \$75 = \$105$

With sales and discounts, you usually have to subtract.

Example 2   A chair originally sold for $130. It was on sale at a 20% discount. Find the sale price of the chair.

Step 1   First find the amount of the discount. Change 20% to a fraction or a decimal, and multiply by $130.

$20\% = 0.2$
$0.2 \times \$130 = \$26$

Step 2   Subtract the discount, $26, from the original price, $130. The sale price is $104.

$\$130 - \$26 = \$104$

Note: There is also another way to solve Example 2. Think of the original price as 100% and the sale price as 20% less than the original or $100\% - 20\% = 80\%$ of the original price.

80% of $\$130 = 0.8 \times \$130 = \$104$

Be sure you answer the question. Look carefully at the last step in the next example.

Example 3   Max wants to buy a used car. He has saved $1200, which is 40% of the amount he needs. How much more does Max need to save?

Step 1   First find the whole, the price of the used car. Change 40% to a decimal, and divide into the part that Max has saved.

40% = 0.4

$$0.4 \overline{)\$1200.0}$$
$$\$300 \ 0.$$

Step 2 $3000 is the whole, the price of the used car. To find how much more Max needs to save, subtract the amount he has already saved from $3000. Max needs to save $1800 more.

$$\begin{array}{r} \$3000 \\ - \$1200 \\ \hline \$1800 \end{array}$$

EXERCISE 15

Directions: For problems 1–5, solve each problem. Use a calculator to check your answers.

1. The owner of Gordon's Shoes pays his supplier $25 for a pair of boots. He puts a 30% markup on each pair. Find the selling price of a pair of boots at Gordon's.

2. Last year there were 750 members of the Uptown Tenants' Association. This year's membership is 60% greater. How many people belong to the Association this year?

3. The Allens make $31,200 a year. They spend 25% of their combined income on their mortgage payments. How much do they spend on their mortgage each month?

4. During the last election in Central County, 4800 people went to the polls. This represents 60% of the registered voters. How many registered voters in Central County did *not* go to the polls during the last election?

5. The price of Fran's new furniture was $1800. She chose to pay 15% down and $50 a month for 36 months. Find the total amount she paid for the furniture.

For problems 6–10, choose the correct answer to each problem.

6. The population of Pleasant Hill was 2200 in 1990. By 2000 the population was 125% more than in 1990. How many people lived in Pleasant Hill in 2000?

    (1) 2375
    (2) 2750
    (3) 3275
    (4) 3450
    (5) 4950

7. The Spruce Street Block Association wants to raise $2000 to plant trees. Two weeks after starting their campaign, the association had raised 65% of their goal. How much more money do they need to raise to reach their goal?

   (1) $2260
   (2) $2000
   (3) $1300
   (4) $1000
   (5) $ 700

For problems 8–10, refer to the following information.

Fred is starting a new job. For the first three months he will make $2250 per month. Then he will get a 10% raise for the remainder of the year. At the end of one year he will receive an additional 8% raise if he does well on his performance review. Fred's employer will withhold 15% of his gross salary for federal tax, state tax, and social security.

8. How much will Fred make the first year?

   (1) $27,000
   (2) $27,675
   (3) $29,025
   (4) $29,700
   (5) Not enough information is given.

9. Which of the following represents the amount of Fred's monthly take-home pay during the first month on his job?

   (1) $2250 − 0.15 × $2250
   (2) $2250 − 0.1 × $2250
   (3) $2250 − 0.08 × $2250
   (4) $2475 − 0.15 × $2475
   (5) $2475 + 0.15 × $2475

10. How much is withheld for the first year from Fred's gross salary for state tax?

   (1) $4068
   (2) $2700
   (3) $2160
   (4) $1350
   (5) Not enough information is given.

Answers are on page 409.

Rate of Change

A common application of calculating a percent is finding a **rate of change.** If an amount rises over time—like the price of heating fuel—you can calculate the **rate of increase.** If an amount goes down over time—like the weight of someone on a diet—you can calculate the **rate of decrease.**

RULE

To calculate a rate of change, follow these steps:
1. Find the amount of change, the difference between the original amount and the new amount. Remember that the original amount is always the earlier amount.
2. Put the *amount of change* in the numerator and the *original amount* in the denominator.
3. Multiply by 100%.

Example 1 In a few months the price of heating oil went from $1.20 a gallon to $1.80 a gallon. By what percent did the price increase?

Step 1 Find the amount of change, the difference between the old price and the new price.

$1.80 − $1.20 = $0.60

Step 2 Make a fraction with the *change*, $0.60, over the *original*, $1.20.

$\frac{change}{original} \frac{\$0.60}{\$1.20} = \frac{1}{2}$

Step 3 Reduce and multiply by 100%. The rate of increase in the oil price was 50%.

$\frac{1}{2} \times 100\% = 50\%$

Example 2 Sam weighed 200 pounds last year. He went on a diet, and this year he weighs 160 pounds. What percent of his weight did Sam lose?

Step 1 Find the amount of change, the difference between Sam's old weight and his weight this year.

$200 − 160 = 40$

Step 2 Make a fraction with the *change*, 40, over the *original*, 200. Reduce.

$\frac{change}{original} \frac{40}{200} = \frac{1}{5}$

Step 3 Multiply the reduced fraction by 100%. Sam lost 20% of his weight.

$\frac{1}{5} \times 100\% = 20\%$

EXERCISE 16

Directions: Solve each problem.

1. The price of a dozen eggs increased from $0.88 to $0.99. What was the percent of increase in the price of the eggs?

2. Three years ago Sal bought a motorcycle for $1200. This year he can get only $900 if he sells it. By what percent has the value of the motorcycle decreased?

3. From July to December the number of workers at the Midvale Discount Store rose from 50 to 68. By what percent did the number of workers increase?

4. Workers at the Ajax Company have been asked to take a pay cut. An assembly line worker's weekly wages would decrease from $600 to $550. What is the percent of decrease?

5. The Porter family bought their house in 1975 for $50,000. They sold it in 2001 for $120,000. Find the rate of increase in the market value of the house.

6. Tom bought a new lathe for his shop for $3600. One year later the value of the lathe was $3312. By what percent did the value of the lathe depreciate?

7. In ten years the population of Little Lake increased from 1200 to 1500. Which expression represents the rate of increase in the population?

   (1) $\frac{1500 - 1200}{1500} \times 100\%$

   (2) $\frac{1500 - 1200}{1200} \times 100\%$

   (3) $\frac{1500 - 1200}{100\%}$

   (4) $\frac{100\%}{1500 - 1200}$

8. A digital camera originally sold for $298.99. After Christmas the camera was on sale for $239.99. Which of the following is closest to the discount rate on the original price of the camera?

   (1) 50%
   (2) 40%
   (3) 30%
   (4) 20%
   (5) 10%

Answers are on page **409.**

Successive Percent

The word *successive* means "following after another." In **successive percent** problems, you find a percent of a number, calculate a new amount, and then find a percent of the new amount.

Think about buying an item on sale. To find the sale price of the item, you calculate the discount and subtract the discount from the original price. Then, to find the final price, you calculate any sales tax based on the sale price and add the sales tax to the sale price.

Example 1   A sweater originally cost $40. It was on sale for 10% off. What is the sale price of the sweater in a state where the sales tax is 5%?

Step 1	Find the discount. Calculate 10% of $40.	$0.1 \times \$40 = \$4$
Step 2	Find the sale price by subtracting $4 from $40.	$\$40 - \$4 = \$36$
Step 3	Find the sales tax. Calculate 5% of $36.	$0.05 \times \$36 = \$1.80$
Step 4	Add the sales tax to the sale price. The sale price, including tax, is $37.80.	$\$36 + \$1.80 = \$37.80$

Notice, in the last example, that the sales tax is based on the sale price, $36, not the original price.

Example 2   A color TV was listed at $280. For a Presidents' Day sale, a store offered a 10% discount on all appliances. The store offered an additional 5% off the list price for paying cash. How much does a buyer save if she gets the TV on sale and pays cash?

Step 1	The 10% discount and the additional 5% incentive are both based on the list price. Add the percents.	$10\% + 5\% = 15\%$
Step 2	Find 15% of $280. A buyer saves $42 by buying the TV on sale and paying cash.	$0.15 \times \$280 = \$42$

TIP

When two or more percents are given in a problem, read carefully to determine whether you should add the percents together or use successive percents.

EXERCISE 17

Directions: Solve each problem.

1. A total of 25% of the 1500 employees at the Grant Tool Company belong to a union. Of these union members 20% voted in favor of a strike. How many union members at the company voted to strike?

2. Bob's Bargain Barn regularly offers an 18% discount off all marked prices. During a clearance sale, they offered an additional 10% off the discounted price. Find the clearance sale price of a computer game that was marked $50.

3. A small farm with a market value of $120,000 was assessed for 60% of its market value. The farm is taxed at 2% of the assessed value. Find the yearly tax on the farm.

4. Ms. Vitale, an aerobics instructor, reduces her regular fee by 12% for senior citizens. She also takes 5% off her regular rate for students who pay before the 15th of the month. If her regular fee is $15 an hour, how much would a one-hour aerobics class cost a senior citizen who pays before the 15th?

5. There are 40 students in Ms. Vitale's Wednesday night aerobics class. Of the 40 students, 30% are African American, 45% are Caucasian, and the rest are Hispanic. How many of the students in the aerobics class are Hispanic?

6. Arthur's gross salary is $3000 a month. His employer withholds 10% for federal tax, 5% for social security, and 5% for state tax. Find Arthur's net salary for the month.

7. Of the 240 people who were scheduled to visit an electronics factory one day, 20% did not show up. Of these "no-shows," 75% were from the Tri-State Tour Group. How many of the scheduled Tri-State Tour Group did not show up?

8. Twenty-five percent of all household accidents are caused by carelessness. Of these accidents, 35% involve children. Out of 100,000 household accidents in a year, how many are caused by carelessness and also involve children?

Answers are on page 409.

Simple Interest

Interest is money that money makes. You *earn* interest when your money is in a savings account. You *pay* interest when you borrow money. Calculating interest is a common percent problem in which you *find the part*.

The formula for calculating interest is

$$interest = principal \times rate \times time$$

Principal is the amount of money that is saved or borrowed, **rate** is the percent, and **time** is the period (usually measured in years) that the principal is saved or borrowed.

In the following examples the formula for calculating simple interest is abbreviated as $i = prt$, where i is interest, p is principal, r is rate, and t is time.

Example 1 Find the interest on $800 at 6% annual interest for one year.

Step 1	Change 6% to a decimal.	6% = 0.06
Step 2	Substitute $800 for p, 0.06 for r, and 1 for t in the formula $i = prt$.	$i = prt$ $i = \$800 \times 0.06 \times 1$
Step 3	Multiply across. The interest is $48.	$i = \$48$

TIP
When the interest is for one year, you do not have to multiply by 1.

To find interest for *less than one year*, make a fraction that expresses the time as a part of a year. For example, 6 months is $\frac{6}{12}$ or $\frac{1}{2}$ of a year.

Example 2 Find the interest on $500 at 9% annual interest for 8 months.

Step 1	Change 9% to a fraction and 8 months to a fraction of a year and reduce.	$9\% = \frac{9}{100}$ 8 months $= \frac{8}{12} = \frac{2}{3}$ year
Step 2	Substitute $500 for p, $\frac{9}{100}$ for r, and $\frac{2}{3}$ for t in the formula $i = prt$.	$i = 500 \times \frac{9}{100} \times \frac{2}{3}$
Step 3	Cancel and multiply. The interest is $30.	$i = \frac{\overset{5}{\cancel{500}}}{1} \times \frac{\overset{3}{\cancel{9}}}{\underset{1}{\cancel{100}}} \times \frac{2}{\underset{1}{\cancel{3}}} = \$30$

To find interest for more than one year, make a mixed number or improper fraction that expresses the time. For example, 2 years 4 months is $2\frac{4}{12}$ years or $2\frac{1}{3}$ years or $\frac{7}{3}$ years.

To find a new principal at the end of a time period, add the interest to the original principal.

Example 3   Roger borrowed $6000 dollars from his brother to make home improvements. Roger agreed to pay his brother 8% annual interest. How much did Roger owe in 1 year 6 months?

Step 1   Change 8% to a fraction and 1 year 6 months to an improper fraction.

$8\% = \frac{8}{100}$

$1 \text{ yr } 6 \text{ mo} = 1\frac{6}{12} = 1\frac{1}{2} = \frac{3}{2}$

Step 2   Substitute $6000 for p, $\frac{8}{100}$ for r, and $\frac{3}{2}$ for t in the formula $i = prt$.

$i = \$6000 \times \frac{8}{100} \times \frac{3}{2}$

Step 3   Cancel and multiply. The interest is $720.

$i = \frac{\overset{60}{\cancel{\$6000}}}{1} \times \frac{\overset{4}{\cancel{8}}}{\underset{1}{\cancel{100}}} \times \frac{3}{\underset{1}{\cancel{2}}} = \$720$

Step 4   Add the interest to the original principal.
Roger owes his brother $6720.

$\$6000 + \$720 = \$6720$

Note: These examples illustrate *simple interest*—an annual percent of the principal. In fact, most interest is *compound*. For a time period, such as one month, a fraction of the annual interest is calculated and added to the principal. Compound interest is an application of successive percent. You will not need to calculate compound interest on the GED test.

EXERCISE 18

Directions: Solve each problem.

1. Find the interest on $3000 at 12.5% annual interest for 1 year.

2. How much money will Sara have at the end of one year on $800 deposited in a savings account earning $5\frac{1}{4}\%$ annual interest?

3. What is the simple interest on $5000 at 9% annual interest for 2 years?

4. Find the interest on $800 at 6% annual interest for 9 months.

5. How much interest did Emilia pay on $900 at 11.5% annual interest for 6 months?

6. The Millers paid simple interest on $500 borrowed at 14% annual interest for 1 year 6 months. How much interest did they pay?

7. Sally saved $2000 for 2 years 6 months. If she earned simple interest at an annual rate of 6%, how much was in the account at the end of that time?

8. The Lewis family borrowed $900 at 15% annual interest for 1 year 8 months. How much did they have to repay at the end of that time?

9. To the nearest dollar, find the simple interest on $4000 at 10% annual interest for 2 years 4 months.

10. If you borrow $1200 at 13% annual interest for 9 months, how much do you have to repay at the end of that period?

Answers are on page 410.

Percent Review

PART I

Directions: Use a calculator to solve any of the problems in this section. Mark your answers to problems 1 and 2 on each corresponding number grid.

1. Find 6.2% of 30.

2. 7.5 is 20% of what number?

3. What percent of 35 is 21?

4. Adrian wants to buy a used car that costs $2000. He has already saved $1400. What percent of the total price has he saved?

5. The price of a gallon of gasoline dropped from $1.80 to $1.62. By what percent did the price drop?

6. Find the simple interest on $450 at 8% annual interest for 9 months.

Choose the correct answer to problems 7–10.

7. Memorial Auditorium has 1280 seats. At a recent concert, 75% of the seats were occupied. Of the occupied seats, 80% were sold to students. How many students attended the concert?

   (1) 1024
   (2) 960
   (3) 768
   (4) 320
   (5) 256

For problems 8–10, refer to the following information.

Mr. Allen wants to buy a new band saw. He is considering buying the saw from a dealer in his hometown or another dealer in a nearby state. The chart below compares the prices, sales tax, and shipping costs at the two dealers.

Dealer	Price Rate	Sales Tax	Shipping Charge
Hometown	$695	6%	$50
Out-of-state	$749	none	10%

8. What is the total cost of the band saw, including sales tax and shipping, from the dealer in Mr. Allen's hometown?

   (1) $816.70
   (2) $786.70
   (3) $745
   (4) $736.70
   (5) Not enough information is given.

9. To the nearest dollar, what is the shipping charge on the band saw if it is purchased from the out-of-state dealer?

   (1) $80
   (2) $75
   (3) $70
   (4) $65
   (5) $42

10. Mr. Allen decided to borrow a friend's truck and pick up the saw himself from the out-of-state dealer. Gasoline will cost $12 each way. What will be the total cost of the band saw from the out-of-state dealer, including gasoline for the trip?

    (1) $847.90
    (2) $835.90
    (3) $827.90
    (4) $773
    (5) $761

PART II

Directions: Solve the following problems without a calculator. Mark your answers to problems 11 and 12 on each corresponding number grid.

11. Change 35% to a fraction and reduce to lowest terms.

12. Change 4.8% to a decimal.

Choose the correct answer to each of the following problems.

13. Which of the following has a value greater than $\frac{1}{2}$?

(1) 3.2%

(2) 5%

(3) 10%

(4) 49%

(5) 60%

14. Which of the following is a correct method for finding 20% of a number?

(1) Multiply the number by 2.

(2) Divide the number by 2.

(3) Divide the number by $\frac{1}{5}$.

(4) Multiply the number by 5.

(5) Divide the number by 5.

15. Which of the following is *not* equal to $12\frac{1}{2}$% of 56?

(1) $\frac{1}{8} \times 56$

(2) 0.125×56

(3) $\frac{56}{8}$

(4) $\frac{56}{0.125}$

(5) $56 \times \frac{12\frac{1}{2}}{100}$

16. A stereo is on sale for $350. Which expression below equals the price of the stereo, including a 6% sales tax?

(1) $350 + 0.06

(2) $350 - 0.06 \times $350

(3) $350 + 0.06 \times $350

(4) $0.06 \times $350

(5) $0.06 \times $350 - $350

17. A pair of boots that originally sold for $39.95 were on sale for $35.89. Which of the following is the approximate percent of savings?

(1) 4%

(2) 7.5%

(3) 10%

(4) 12.5%

(5) 15%

18. Which of the following represents the simple interest on $2000 at 8% annual interest for 6 months?

(1) $2000 × 0.08 × 6

(2) $2000 × 0.8 × 6

(3) $2000 × 0.8 × $\frac{1}{2}$

(4) $2000 × 8 × $\frac{1}{2}$

(5) $2000 × 0.08 × $\frac{1}{2}$

19. In a recent year the defense expenditures for the U.S. government were $269 billion. The defense expenditures for the following year were projected to be 3% greater. Which expression represents the projected defense expenditures for the next year?

(1) $269 billion − 0.03 × $269 billion

(2) $269 billion + 0.3 × $269 billion

(3) 1.03 × $269 billion

(4) 1.003 × $269 billion

(5) 1.3 × $269 billion

20. The entire U.S. budget for a recent year was $1.7 trillion or $1,700,000,000,000. Which of the following represents the budget in scientific notation?

(1) $1.7 × 10^3

(2) $1.7 × 10^6

(3) $1.7 × 10^9

(4) $1.7 × 10^{12}

(5) $1.7 × 10^{15}

Answers are on page 410.

You should have gotten at least 16 problems right on this exercise. If you did not get 16 right, review your percent skills before you go on. If you got 16 or more right, correct any problem you got wrong. Then go on to the next chapter.

Chapter 7

Measurement

There are two main systems for measuring distance, weight, and liquid capacity. The United States and parts of the former British Empire use **customary**, or **standard**, units of measure. This system includes inches, feet, and miles for distance, and ounces, pounds, and tons for weight. Most countries use the **metric** system. The metric system includes meters and kilometers for distance, and grams and kilograms for weight.

Customary Measures

The table below shows customary units of measure for length, weight, and liquid measure as well as units of time. Take the time to memorize any of the units and equivalents that you do not know.

In the chart the larger unit of measurement is on the left of the = sign. On the right of the = sign is the equivalent in smaller units. Abbreviations are in parentheses. You may see these abbreviations with or without periods at the end.

Customary Units of Measure
Measures of Length
1 foot (ft)   = 12 inches (in.)
1 yard (yd)   = 36 inches
1 yard   = 3 feet
1 mile (mi)   = 5280 feet
1 mile   = 1760 yards
Measures of Weight
1 pound (lb)   = 16 ounces (oz)
1 ton (T)   = 2000 pounds
Liquid Measures
1 pint (pt)   = 16 ounces (oz)
1 cup   = 8 ounces
1 pint   = 2 cups
1 quart (qt)   = 2 pints
1 gallon (gal)   = 4 quarts
Measures of Time
1 minute (min) = 60 seconds (sec)
1 hour (hr)   = 60 minutes
1 day   = 24 hours
1 week (wk)   = 7 days
1 year (yr)   = 365 days

It is often convenient to change, or **convert**, from one unit of measure to another. For example, inches are appropriate units for measuring short distances such as the width of a table. Feet are appropriate for longer distances, such as the dimensions of a room. The distance between cities is usually measured in miles.

R U L E

To change from a smaller unit to a larger unit, you need to divide.

When you change from a smaller unit to a larger unit, you want *fewer* of the larger units.

Example 1   Change 8 ounces to pounds.

Step 1   Remember that the fraction bar means to divide. $\frac{8}{16} = \frac{1}{2}$ lb
Write 8 as the numerator and 16, the number of ounces in one pound, as the denominator.

Step 2   Reduce. 8 ounces = $\frac{1}{2}$ pound

R U L E

To change from a larger unit to a smaller unit, you need to multiply.

When you change from a larger unit to a smaller unit, you want *more* of the smaller units.

Example 2   Change 10 feet to inches.

Multiply 10 by 12, the number of inches in one foot. $10 \times 12 = 120$ in.
10 feet = 120 inches

When you **convert** from one unit of measure to another, there is often more than one way to express the answer.

Example 3   Change 6 quarts to gallons.

Step 1   Divide 6 by 4, the number of quarts in one gallon.

Step 2   Express the remainder as a fraction and reduce. $1\frac{2}{4} = 1\frac{1}{2}$ gal
6 quarts = $1\frac{1}{2}$ gallons $4\overline{)6}$

Example 4   Change 6 quarts to gallons and quarts.

Step 1   Divide 6 by 4, the number of quarts in one gallon. 1 gal 2 qt
$4\overline{)6}$

Step 2   Express the remainder as 2 quarts.
6 quarts = 1 gallon 2 quarts

The answers to Examples 3 and 4 are both acceptable.

EXERCISE 1

Directions: For problems 1–6, change each measurement to a fraction of the new unit that follows.

1. 18 inches = _____ yard   8 hours = _____ day

2. 40 minutes = _____ hour   12 ounces = _____ pound

3. 9 inches = _____ foot   2 quarts = _____ gallon

4. 500 pounds = _____ ton   528 feet = _____ mile

5. 1 cup = _____ pint   5 minutes = _____ hour

6. 5 days = _____ week   8 inches = _____ foot

For problems 7–10, change each measurement to the smaller unit that follows.

7. 3 pounds = _____ ounces   4 feet = _____ inches

8. 5 minutes = _____ seconds   2 yards = _____ feet

9. 3 tons = _____ pounds   4 days = _____ hours

10. $1\frac{1}{2}$ miles = _____ feet   5 gallons = _____ quarts

Solve problems 11–15.

11. A group of neighbors cooked 130 quarts of tomatoes. They wanted to can them in gallon jars. How many gallon jars did they need for canning?

12. Pieter and his son went camping for 3 whole days. Altogether, how many hours did they camp?

13. Latisha's car was double-parked for 45 minutes. For what fraction of an hour was her car double-parked?

14. Kwan climbed a mountain that is 10,560 feet high. Find the mountain's height in miles.

15. Frank has to carry 3 tons of cement. If his truck carries a maximum of 500 pounds at a time, how many trips will Frank have to make?

Answers are on page 411.

Metric Measures

In the metric system, units of measure are multiples of 10, 100, and 1000. In other words, metric units of measure rely on decimals.

In the metric system, the basic unit length is the **meter**. A meter is a little longer than one yard. The basic unit of liquid measure is the **liter**. A liter is about the same size as a quart. The basic unit of weight is the **gram**. A gram is a very small unit of weight such as the weight of a couple of aspirin tablets. A **kilogram**, which is the metric unit used to weigh people, is a little more than 2 pounds.

These prefixes are used in metric measurements. Learn their meanings before you go on.

kilo-	hecto-	deca-	base unit	deci-	centi-	milli-
1000×	100×	10×	liter meter gram	0.1×	0.01×	0.001×

Examples   one kilometer = 1000 meters

one milliliter = 0.001 liter or $\frac{1}{1000}$ liter

one deciliter = 0.1 liter or $\frac{1}{10}$ liter

one centimeter = 0.01 meter or $\frac{1}{100}$ meter

Below are the most common metric measures and their abbreviations. Take the time now to learn these units before you go on.

Metric Units of Measure	
Measures of Length	
1 meter (m)	= 1000 millimeters (mm)
1 meter	= 100 centimeters (cm)
1 kilometer (km)	= 1000 meters
1 decimeter (dm)	= $\frac{1}{10}$ meter
Measures of Weight	
1 gram (g)	= 1000 milligrams (mg)
1 kilogram (kg)	= 1000 grams
Liquid Measures	
1 liter (L)	= 1000 milliliters (mL)
1 deciliter (dL)	= $\frac{1}{10}$ liter

To change from one unit to another, simply move the decimal point.

───────────────── R U L E ─────────────────

To change from a larger unit to a smaller unit, you need to multiply. You will be moving the decimal point to the right.

Example 1   Change 1.5 meters to centimeters.

Multiply 1.5 by 100. Move the decimal $1.5 \times 100 = 150$
point two places to the right.
1.5 meters = 150 cm

───────────────── R U L E ─────────────────

To change from a smaller unit to a larger unit, you need to divide. You will be moving the decimal point to the left.

Example 2   Change 165 milliliters to liters.

Divide 165 by 1000. Move the decimal $165 \div 1000 = 0.165 L$
point three places to the left.
165 mL = 0.165 L

Review the shortcuts for multiplying and dividing by 10, 100, and 1000 on pages 86 and 89.

EXERCISE 2

Directions: For problems 1–3, answer each question.

1. One kilogram is equal to how many grams?

2. One centimeter is equal to what fraction of a meter?

3. One milliliter is equal to what fraction of a liter?

For problems 4–8, change each metric measurement to the unit that follows.

4. 1.65 kilograms = _____ grams   9 meters = _____ centimeters

5. 3.2 liters = _____ milliliters   4 kilometers = _____ meters

6. 0.6 kilograms = _____ grams   0.25 liter = _____ milliliters

7. 80 centimeters = _____ meter   795 grams = _____ kilogram

8. 500 meters = _____ kilometer   380 milliliters = _____ liter

Answers are on page 412.

Converting Measurements

Using Proportion to Convert Measurements

You can use proportion to change one unit of measure to another. Remember that the parts of a proportion must correspond.

Example 1   Use a proportion to change 3 pounds to ounces.

Step 1   Write a proportion with the ratio of 1 pound to 16 ounces on the left. Write 3 in the pound position. Let x represent the missing ounces.

$$\frac{1 \text{ lb}}{16 \text{ oz}} = \frac{3}{x}$$

Step 2   Find the cross products.

$$1x = 48$$

Step 3   Divide by 1.
3 pounds = 48 ounces

$$x = 48$$

Example 2   Use a proportion to change 10 quarts to gallons.

Step 1   Write a proportion with the ratio of 1 gallon to 4 quarts on the left. Write 10 in the quart position. Let x represent the missing gallons.

$$\frac{1 \text{ gal}}{4 \text{ qt}} = \frac{x}{10}$$

Step 2   Find the cross products.

$$4x = 10$$

Step 3   Divide by 4.
10 quarts = $2\frac{1}{2}$ gallons

$$x = 2\frac{1}{2}$$

Example 3   Use a proportion to change 9.6 meters to centimeters.

Step 1   Write a proportion with the ratio of 1 meter to 100 centimeters on the left. Write 9.6 in the meter position. Let x represent the missing centimeters.

$$\frac{1 \text{ m}}{100 \text{ cm}} = \frac{9.6}{x}$$

Step 2   Find the cross products.

$$1x = 960$$

Step 3   Divide by 1.
9.6 meters = 960 centimeters

$$x = 960$$

EXERCISE 3

Directions: Use a proportion to solve each of the following problems.

1. Change 20 ounces to pounds.

2. Change 35 centimeters to meters.

3. Change 150 minutes to hours.

4. Change 75 inches to feet.

5. Change 850 milliliters to liters.

6. Change 9 quarts to pints.

7. Change $1\frac{3}{4}$ pounds to ounces.

8. Change 400 pounds to tons.

For more practice, use proportion to solve the measures in Exercises 1 and 2.

Answers are on page 412.

Interchanging Measures

On the GED Mathematics Test you will not have to convert between customary units of measure and metric units. However, to get an idea of how the systems compare, use the following chart.

Units of Length	
1 inch = 2.54 centimeters	1 centimeter = 0.3937 inch
1 foot = 0.3048 meter	1 meter = 39.37 inches
1 mile ≈ 1.6 kilometers	1 kilometer ≈ 0.62 mile
Units of Weight	
1 pound ≈ 0.453 kilogram	1 kilogram ≈ 2.2 pounds

Example   Max drives 6 miles to work every weekday morning. What is his driving distance in kilometers?

Multiply 6 miles by 1.6, the approximate $6 \times 1.6 = 9.6$ km
equivalent in kilometers.
Max drives 9.6 kilometers to work.

EXERCISE 4

Directions: Use the chart of equivalents on page 189 to solve each problem. Round each answer to the nearest unit.

1. Sam weighs 180 pounds. What is his weight in kilograms?

2. Maria weighs 55 kilograms. What is her weight in pounds?

3. Mary is 5 feet 6 inches tall. What is her height in centimeters? (Hint: First change her height to inches.)

4. The driving distance between Cleveland and Boston is 632 miles. What is this distance in kilometers?

5. The air travel distance between Paris and Berlin is 540 kilometers. What is this distance in miles?

6. A standard sheet of copy paper in the U.S. is $8\frac{1}{2}$ inches wide and 11 inches high. What are these measurements in centimeters?

Answers are on page 412.

Scales, Meters, and Gauges

A ruler is a tool for measuring short distances. With customary measures, rulers are marked in inches and feet. With metric measures, rulers are marked in centimeters and meters. Gauges are tools for measuring mileage, temperature, speed, electrical current, blood pressure, and so on.

Below is a 6-inch ruler.

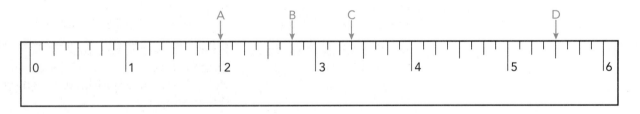

The longest lines on the ruler are inch lines. They are numbered 1, 2, 3, and so on. The second-longest lines are $\frac{1}{2}$-inch lines. The next longest lines are $\frac{1}{4}$-inch lines. The shortest lines are $\frac{1}{8}$-inch lines. Many rulers include even smaller $\frac{1}{16}$-inch lines.

To read a length on a ruler, decide how far a point is to the right of zero.

Example 1   Tell how far to the right of zero the points labeled A, B, C, and D on the ruler are.

Point A is 2 inches.
    Point A is at the line labeled 2.

Point B is $2\frac{3}{4}$ inches.
    Point B is between 2 and 3 inches. Point B is at the third $\frac{1}{4}$-inch line between 2 and 3.

Point C is $3\frac{3}{8}$ inches.
    Point C is between 3 and 4 inches. Point C is at the third $\frac{1}{8}$-inch line between 3 and 4.

Point D is $5\frac{1}{2}$ inches.
    Point D is between 5 and 6 inches. Point D is at the $\frac{1}{2}$-inch line between 5 and 6.

Notice that distances on the 6-inch ruler were given in fractions.

The next illustration shows a metric scale that is 15 centimeters long. The longest lines on the metric scale are the centimeter lines, labeled 1, 2, 3, and so on. The next longest lines are the $\frac{1}{2}$-centimeter lines, or 0.5-centimeter lines. The shortest lines are millimeter lines, or 0.1-centimeter lines.

Notice in the next example that all distances on the metric scale are given in decimals.

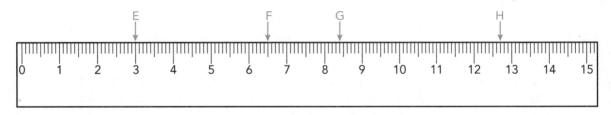

Example 2   Tell how far to the right of zero the points labeled E, F, G, and H on the ruler are.

Point E is 3 centimeters.
    Point E is at the line labeled 3.

Point F is 6.5 centimeters.
    Point F is between 6 and 7 centimeters. Point F is at the middle line, which is 0.5 centimeter.

Point G is 8.4 centimeters.
    Point G is between 8 and 9 centimeters. Point G is at the fourth millimeter, or 0.4-centimeter line.

Point H is 12.7 centimeters.
    Point H is between 12 and 13 centimeters. Point H is at the seventh millimeter, or 0.7-centimeter line.

Example 3   What is the distance from point F to point G?

Point G (the farther point) is 8.4 centimeters.

Point F (the point closer to zero) is 6.5 centimeters.

Subtract to find the difference.   8.4 − 6.5 = 1.9 centimeters

The diagram at the right shows the dial of an instrument that measures **amperes**. An ampere is a unit of electric current. The dial is labeled from 0 to 50 with a small mark halfway between each number.

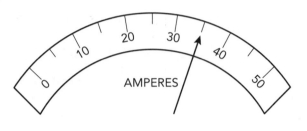

Example 4   What is the reading, in amperes, on the gauge shown above?

The arrow is halfway between 30 and 40.
The reading on the gauge is 35 amperes.

EXERCISE 5

Directions: For problems 1–5, tell the distance in inches from 0 of each labeled point on the ruler below.

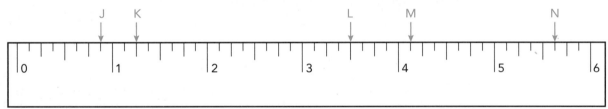

1. Point J

2. Point K

3. Point L

4. Point M

5. Point N

6. What is the distance from point K to point N?

For problems 7–11, tell the distance in centimeters from 0 of each labeled point on the ruler below.

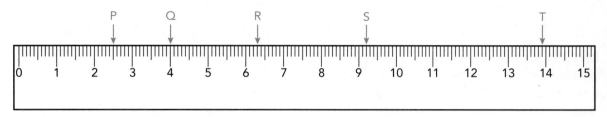

7. Point P

8. Point Q

9. Point R

10. Point S

11. Point T

12. What is the distance from point P to point S?

For problems 13–15, use the diagram to the right of each question.

13. What is the approximate reading, in amperes, of the meter shown at the right?

14. The diagram at the right shows a voltmeter. Volts are a measure of electromotive force. What is the approximate reading, in volts, on the meter?

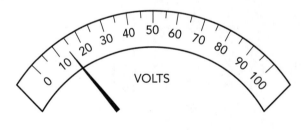

15. The voltmeter pictured at the right takes $\frac{1}{10}$ of a second to rise one volt. How many seconds has it taken to rise to the amount shown?

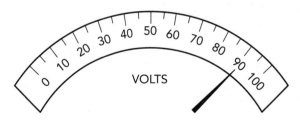

Answers are on page 413.

Measurement Review

PART I

Directions: Use a calculator to solve any of the problems in this section. For problems 1 and 2, mark each answer on the corresponding number grid.

1. 22 inches are what fraction of a yard?

2. 115 centimeters are the same as how many meters?

Choose the correct answer for the following problems.

3. At a price of $4.80 per pound, what is the cost of 2 lb 4 oz of cheese?

   (1) $ 9.60
   (2) $10.80
   (3) $12.60
   (4) $14.40
   (5) $19.20

4. From a cable 4 meters long, Carlo cut a piece 2.15 meters long. Find the length, in *centimeters*, of the remaining piece.

   (1) 285
   (2) 215
   (3) 185
   (4) 115
   (5) 85

5. Gianni needs 3 yd 18 in. of material to make a suit. What is the greatest number of suits that he can make from 15 yards of material?

   (1) 5
   (2) 4
   (3) 3
   (4) 2
   (5) 1

6. For a blood drive at Heather's office, the workers donated 36.5 liters on Wednesday, 42.2 liters on Thursday, and 50.1 liters on Friday. To the nearest tenth of a liter, what was the average amount donated each day?

   (1) 42.9
   (2) 50.1
   (3) 58.8
   (4) 64.4
   (5) 128.8

PART II

Directions: Solve the problems below without using a calculator.

Use the 3-inch ruler pictured below to answer problems 7 and 8.

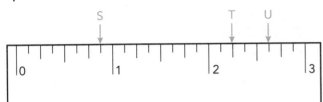

7. What is the distance, in inches, from zero to point U?

(1) $2\frac{1}{2}$

(2) $2\frac{3}{8}$

(3) $2\frac{1}{2}$

(4) $2\frac{5}{8}$

(5) $2\frac{7}{8}$

8. What is the distance, in inches, between points S and T?

(1) $\frac{3}{4}$

(2) $\frac{7}{8}$

(3) $1\frac{1}{8}$

(4) $1\frac{5}{8}$

(5) $1\frac{3}{8}$

9. Which of the following represents the average weight of three boxes that weigh 2.5 kg, 0.96 kg, and 1.2 kg respectively?

(1) $2.5 + 0.96 + 1.2$

(2) $2(2.5 + 0.96 + 1.2)$

(3) $2.5 \times 0.96 \times 1.2$

(4) $\frac{2.5 + 0.96 + 1.2}{3}$

(5) $\frac{2.5 + 0.96 + 1.2}{2}$

Use the 8-centimeter ruler pictured below to answer problems 10 and 11. Mark each answer on the corresponding number grid.

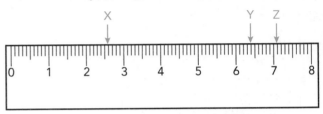

10. What is the distance, in centimeters, from zero to point Z?

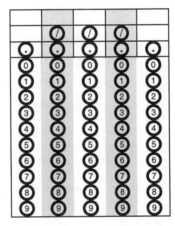

11. What is the distance, in centimeters, between points X and Y?

12. Fred bought 5 cans of tomato paste. Each can weighed 14 ounces. Which of the following represents the total weight of the cans in pounds?

   (1) $5 \times 14 \times 16$

   (2) $\dfrac{5 + 14}{16}$

   (3) $\dfrac{14 \times 16}{5}$

   (4) $\dfrac{5 \times 16}{14}$

   (5) $\dfrac{5 \times 14}{16}$

13. What is the reading, in amperes, on the meter below?

   (1) 29

   (2) 31

   (3) 34

   (4) 37

   (5) 41

14. What is the reading, in volts, on the meter below?

   (1) 76

   (2) 79

   (3) 84

   (4) 89

   (5) 91

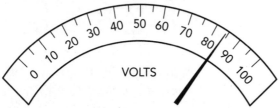

Answers are on page 413.

You should have gotten at least 11 problems right on this exercise. If you did not get 11 right, review your measurements skills before you go on. If you got 11 or more right, correct any problem you got wrong. Then go on to the next chapter.

Chapter 8

Data Analysis, Statistics, and Probability

This chapter is about numerical information, or **data**. A **graph** is a diagram that shows relationships among numbers. A **table** is an organized chart or list of numbers. **Statistics** is a name for organizing and interpreting data. **Probability** is a number that expresses the likelihood that a specific event will take place.

Graphs and Tables

Circle Graphs

A **circle graph** is one way to show data visually. Each pie-shaped piece represents a different part of the whole. When the parts of a circle graph are expressed in percent, the parts add up to 100%, or one whole.

Below is a budget for the Johnson family. To the right of the list of items in the budget is a circle graph that represents each category in the Johnsons' budget.

clothes = 20%

food = 30%

rent = 25%

savings = 10%

other = 15%

---

total = 100%

JOHNSON FAMILY BUDGET

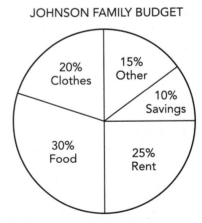

To understand a graph, read the title and each label carefully.

Example 1   What percent of the Johnson family budget is for food and rent?

Add the percents for food and rent.   30% + 25% = 55%
Food and rent represent 55% of the budget.

Example 2   What fraction of the Johnson family budget is for clothes?

Clothes are 20% of the budget.   clothes = 20% = $\frac{20}{100} = \frac{1}{5}$
Change 20% to a fraction.
Clothes are $\frac{1}{5}$ of the budget.

Example 3   The Johnsons take home $3000 a month. According to the budget, how much do the Johnsons pay each month for rent?

Rent is 25% of the budget.   25% = 0.25
Find 25% of $3000.   0.25 × $3000 = $750
The Johnsons pay $750 for rent.

EXERCISE 1

Directions: Use the graph below to answer problems 1–5. Use a calculator whenever needed.

1. The graph divides GED recipients into how many age groups?

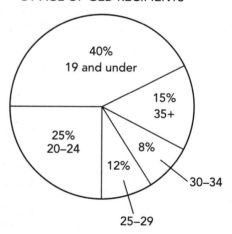

PERCENTAGE DISTRIBUTION BY AGE OF GED RECIPIENTS

40%
19 and under

15%
35+

25%
20–24

8%

12%

30–34

25–29

Source: U.S. Census Bureau

2. GED recipients who were 35 or older represent what percent of the total number of people who received a GED?

3. Which age category represents the greatest number of GED recipients?

4. The age category 20–24 represents what fraction of total GED recipients?

5. In a recent year approximately 500,000 people received GEDs. Use the information in the graph to calculate the number of GED recipients who were 35 or older.

Use the graph below to answer problems 6–11.

6. For every dollar in the federal budget, how many cents are from individual income taxes?

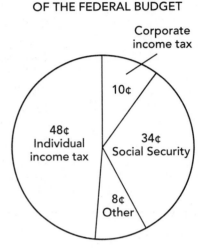

SOURCE OF A DOLLAR
OF THE FEDERAL BUDGET

Corporate
income tax

10¢

48¢
Individual
income tax

34¢
Social Security

8¢
Other

Source: U.S. Census Bureau

7. Corporate income tax is what percent of the source of the federal budget?

8. Receipts from social security insurance represent about what fraction of the source of the federal budget?

9. In a recent year the federal budget was $1.8 trillion or $1,800,000,000,000. What dollar amount of that budget came from corporate income tax?

10. Express your answer to the last problem in scientific notation.

11. According to the federal budget graph, which of the following statements is true?

    (1) Individual income tax and social security make up more than 80% of the budget.

    (2) Corporate income tax is the single greatest source of federal funds.

    (3) Social security insurance is more than half of the federal budget.

    (4) Individual income tax is about one-fourth of the federal budget.

    (5) Corporate income tax is about one-third of the federal budget.

Use the two circle graphs below to choose the best answer to problems 12–15.

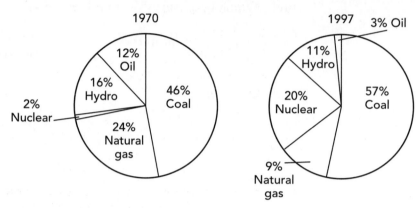

SOURCES OF ENERGY FOR ELECTRIC UTILITY INDUSTRY

Source: U.S. Census Bureau

12. In 1970 natural gas was about what fraction of the energy source for electric utilities?

(1) $\frac{1}{4}$

(2) $\frac{1}{3}$

(3) $\frac{1}{2}$

(4) $\frac{3}{4}$

(5) Not enough information is given.

13. For the years shown on the graphs, which two sources increased as a percent of the total energy source for electric utilities?

(1) hydro and oil

(2) natural gas and oil

(3) coal and nuclear

(4) nuclear and hydro

(5) natural gas and hydro

14. Together nuclear energy and natural gas made up about what fraction of the energy source for electric utilities in 1997?

(1) $\frac{9}{10}$

(2) $\frac{4}{5}$

(3) $\frac{1}{2}$

(4) $\frac{2}{5}$

(5) $\frac{3}{10}$

15. The percent of energy for electric utilities that came from nuclear energy in 1997 was how many times the percent that came from nuclear energy in 1970?

(1) 20 times

(2) 18 times

(3) 12 times

(4) 10 times

(5) 5 times

Answers are on page 414.

Bar Graphs

A **bar graph** organizes information along a **vertical axis**, which runs up and down one side, and a **horizontal axis**, which usually runs along the bottom.

Below is a bar graph that shows noon temperatures for 5 days. The vertical axis running along the left side measures temperature in degrees. The horizontal axis, across the bottom of the graph, lists days of the week. Each vertical bar represents the noon temperature for a different day.

Notice the broken line below 56°. This indicates that there are no temperatures on the graph below 56° so those lower temperatures are not included on the graph.

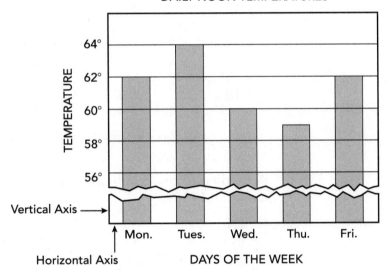

DAILY NOON TEMPERATURES

Example 1   According to the graph, what was the noon temperature on Wednesday?

Find Wednesday on the horizontal axis. Follow the bar labeled "Wed." to the top. Read the temperature at the left on the vertical axis. The bar stops at the line labeled 60°. The temperature at noon on Wednesday was 60°.

<u>Example 2</u>   On what day was the noon temperature 59°?

Look halfway between 58° and 60° to estimate 59° on the vertical axis. Look across until you find a bar that rises to this point. The bar labeled "Thu." ends halfway between 58° and 60°. The noon temperature was 59° on Thursday.

EXERCISE 2

Directions: Use the bar graph below to answer problems 1–6. Use a calculator whenever needed.

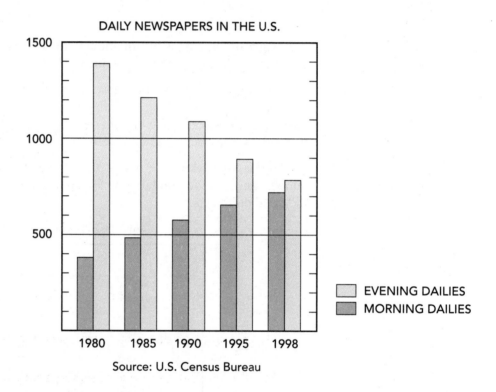

DAILY NEWSPAPERS IN THE U.S.

Source: U.S. Census Bureau

1. According to the graph, the U.S. had about how many morning dailies in 1980?

    (1) 300
    (2) 400
    (3) 500
    (4) 600
    (5) 700

2. About how many evening dailies were there in 1995?

    (1) 900
    (2) 750
    (3) 600
    (4) 550
    (5) 400

3. The number of morning dailies and the number of evening dailies were both between 700 and 800 for which year shown on the graph?

   (1) 1980
   (2) 1985
   (3) 1990
   (4) 1995
   (5) 1998

4. Which of the following is closest to the combined number of morning and evening dailies in 1980?

   (1) 700
   (2) 900
   (3) 1200
   (4) 1500
   (5) 1800

5. From 1980 to 1998 the number of evening dailies in the U.S. dropped by how much?

   (1) 1000
   (2) 750
   (3) 600
   (4) 400
   (5) 200

6. Which of the following best describes the pattern shown on the graph?

   (1) The number of morning and evening dailies has steadily increased.
   (2) The number of morning and evening dailies has steadily decreased.
   (3) The number of morning dailies has increased while the number of evening dailies has decreased.
   (4) The number of morning dailies has stayed about the same while the number of evening dailies has decreased.
   (5) The number of morning dailies has increased while the number of evening dailies has stayed about the same.

Use the bar graph below to answer questions 7–12.

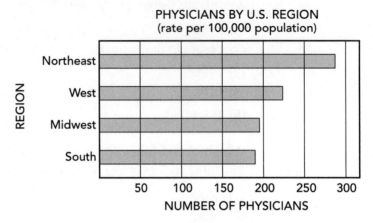

PHYSICIANS BY U.S. REGION
(rate per 100,000 population)

Source: U.S. Census Bureau

7. Which region has about 225 physicians per 100,000 people?

8. Which region has the most physicians per population?

9. Which two regions have fewer than 200 physicians per 100,000 people?

10. The population of Jasper County is 300,000. Jasper County is in the West. If Jasper County is typical of the region, approximately how many physicians are there in the county?

    (1) 200
    (2) 225
    (3) 450
    (4) 675
    (5) 900

11. A typical town of 50,000 in the Midwest has about how many physicians?

    (1) 190
    (2) 95
    (3) 75
    (4) 50
    (5) 25

12. A typical city of 1,000,000 people in the Northeast has about how many physicians?

    (1) 56,000
    (2) 28,000
    (3) 14,000
    (4) 5,600
    (5) 2,800

Answers are on page 414.

Line Graphs

A **line graph**, like a bar graph, has information on both a vertical axis and a horizontal axis. The changing data is shown on a continuous line rather than on a set of bars. Line graphs are useful for showing trends or patterns over a period of time.

The line graph below shows the net income from a farm.

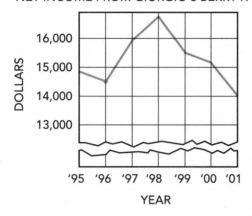

NET INCOME FROM GIORGIO'S BERRY FARM

Example 1   What was the net income from the farm in 1996?

Find '96 on the horizontal axis. Follow the line labeled '96 up until it meets the continuous blue line. Read the dollar amount on the vertical axis directly to the left. The point on the vertical axis is halfway between $14,000 and $15,000. The net income in 1996 was $14,500.

Example 2   In what year was the net income above $16,000?

Find $16,000 on the vertical axis. Look across to the point where the blue line is above $16,000. Read the year on the horizontal axis below the high point. The net income was above $16,000 in 1998.

A **trend** in numbers can help you make a projection. A **projection** is a prediction based on past and current patterns. The graph in the last exercise showed a trend in the number of newspapers in the U.S. The number of morning dailies has increased while the number of evening dailies has decreased.

Look again at the graph of the net income from the berry farm.

Example 3   If the trend for Giorgio's farm continues as it did from 1998 to 2001, which of the following best expresses the projection for 2002 income?

(1) 2002 income will be above $14,000.

(2) 2002 income will be exactly $14,000.

(3) 2002 income will be below $14,000.

According to the graph, income from the farm has been dropping each year since 1998. The 2001 income was about $14,000. The trend suggests that the income for 2002 will be less than $14,000. Choice (3) is correct.

EXERCISE 3

Directions: Use the line graph below to answer problems 1–5.

FARM WORKERS
AS A PERCENTAGE OF U.S. WORKERS

Source: U.S. Bureau of Labor Statistics

1. In 1820 farm workers were about what percent of U.S. workers?

   (1) more than 70%
   (2) about 60%
   (3) about 50%
   (4) less than 40%
   (5) less than 25%

2. For what year were farm workers about 60% of U.S. workers?

    (1) 1960
    (2) 1920
    (3) 1900
    (4) 1880
    (5) 1860

3. For which of the following 20-year periods does the graph show the greatest drop in farm workers as a percent of U.S. workers?

    (1) 1820–1840
    (2) 1860–1880
    (3) 1880–1900
    (4) 1920–1940
    (5) 1960–1980

4. For which of the following 20-year periods did farm workers as a percent of U.S. workers first drop below 10%?

    (1) 1840–1860
    (2) 1880–1900
    (3) 1900–1920
    (4) 1940–1960
    (5) 1960–1980

5. If the trend shown on the graph continues, the percent of farm workers as a percent of U.S. workers in 2000 is likely to be which of the following?

    (1) about the same as 1960
    (2) about 20%
    (3) about 15%
    (4) about 10%
    (5) less than 5%

Use the line graph below to answer problems 6–10.

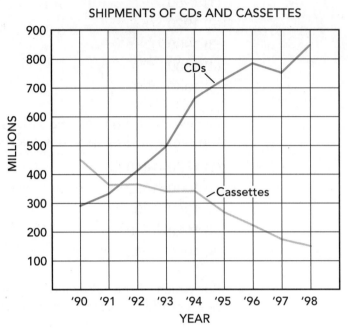

SHIPMENTS OF CDs AND CASSETTES

Source: U.S. Census Bureau

6. In what year shown on the graph were cassette shipments about 150 million more than CD shipments?

(1) 1990
(2) 1991
(3) 1992
(4) 1994
(5) 1995

7. Approximately how many CDs were shipped in 1993?

(1) 250 million
(2) 500 million
(3) 600 million
(4) 750 million
(5) 800 million

8. Between what 2 years did cassette shipments first drop below 200 million?

(1) 1990–1991
(2) 1992–1993
(3) 1994–1995
(4) 1995–1996
(5) 1996–1997

9. According to the graph, between what 2 years did shipments of CDs drop?

   (1) 1991–1992
   (2) 1993–1994
   (3) 1995–1996
   (4) 1996–1997
   (5) 1997–1998

10. Which of the following best describes the trend shown on the graph?

    (1) Shipments of CDs have increased while shipments of cassettes have decreased.
    (2) Shipments of CDs and cassettes have both steadily increased.
    (3) Shipments of CDs and cassettes have remained about the same.
    (4) Shipments of CDs and cassettes have both steadily decreased.
    (5) Shipments of CDs have increased because of decreased competition.

Answers are on page 415.

Tables

A **table** is a list of numbers displayed in columns and rows. Newspapers and magazines frequently use tables to compare data. Although graphs make it easy to compare numbers quickly, tables allow for greater accuracy because they provide actual values.

The table below compares the populations of the three largest metropolitan areas in the U.S. for three different years.

Populations of the Three Largest U.S. Metropolitan Areas (rounded to the nearest thousand)			
	1980	**1990**	**1997**
New York City	17,540,000	18,087,000	19,876,000
Los Angeles	11,498,000	14,532,000	15,609,000
Chicago	7,937,000	8,066,000	8,642,000

Source: U.S. Census Bureau

Example 1   What was the population of metropolitan Chicago in 1980?

Find Chicago in the list. Look to the right in the column labeled 1980.
The population of metropolitan Chicago in 1980 was 7,937,000.

Example 2   By how much did the population of metropolitan Los Angeles increase from 1990 to 1997?

Subtract the 1990 population of Los Angeles from the 1997 population.	15,609,000
	−14,532,000
The increase was 1,077,000 people.	1,077,000

EXERCISE 4

Directions: Use the table below to answer problems 1–5.

Gasoline Prices and Taxes		
Country	Cost per gallon of gas	Percent to taxes
England	$4.37	76.2%
France	3.76	69.1
Germany	3.52	67.9
Italy	3.75	63.5
U.S.	1.71	22.8

Source: Energy Information Administration

1. Which country shown in the table has the highest gasoline price?

2. What percent of the price of gasoline goes for taxes in France?

3. How much more does one gallon of gasoline cost in Italy than in the U.S.?

4. Use your calculator to find how much money, to the nearest penny, goes for taxes for a gallon of gasoline in England.

5. Which expression represents the amount paid in taxes for 15 gallons of gasoline purchased in Germany?

    (1) $15 \times \$3.52$
    (2) $\$3.52 \times 0.679$
    (3) $15 + \$3.52 + 0.679$
    (4) $15 \times \$3.52 \times 0.679$
    (5) $\$3.52 \times 0.679 \div 15$

Use the following table to answer problems 6–10.

Characteristics of College Freshmen (in percent)				
	1970	**1980**	**1990**	**1998**
Sex:				
Male	55	49	46	46
Female	45	51	54	54
Political orientation:				
Liberal	34	20	23	21
Middle of the road	45	60	55	57
Conservative	17	17	20	19

Source: U.S. Census Bureau

6. What was the first year in which females represented more than half of college freshmen?

7. In 1980 what fraction of college freshmen said that their political orientation was liberal?

8. In 1970 what was the ratio of college freshmen who said that they were conservative to those who said that they were liberal?

9. There were 1200 incoming freshmen at Central County State College in 1998. If they followed the characteristics described in the table, how many of them said that they were middle of the road?

10. Which of the following conclusions about college freshmen *cannot* be drawn from the information given in the table?

    (1) The percent of women has increased since 1970.
    (2) The percent who are conservative has changed little since 1970.
    (3) The percent who are liberal has stayed about the same since 1980.
    (4) The percent of men who are liberal has decreased since 1970.
    (5) Most freshmen think of themselves as middle of the road.

Answers are on page 415.

Probability

Probability is the chance of something happening. Probability can be expressed as a fraction, as a decimal, as a percent, or as a ratio. Most often probability is written as a fraction. The probability of an event is the ratio of the number of favorable outcomes to the total number of possible outcomes.

$$\text{probability of an event} = \frac{\text{number of favorable outcomes}}{\text{number of possible outcomes}}$$

A **favorable outcome** is an outcome that you are looking for.

Think about the following situations:

If you toss a coin, there are two possible results. You can get heads or tails.

The probability of getting tails on one toss is $\frac{\text{favorable}}{\text{possible}} = \frac{1}{2}$.

A number cube is a small, six-sided block. Each side is printed with 1, 2, 3, 4, 5, or 6 dots. If you roll a number cube, there are 6 possible results.

The probability of rolling a 6 on the first roll is $\frac{\text{favorable}}{\text{possible}} = \frac{1}{6}$.

The probability of rolling a 5 or higher has 2 favorable outcomes—either 5 or 6—so the probability of rolling a 5 or higher is $\frac{\text{favorable}}{\text{possible}} = \frac{2}{6} = \frac{1}{3}$.

In a typical deck of cards there are 13 hearts, 13 diamonds, 13 spades, and 13 clubs for a total of 52 cards. Of these 52 cards, there are 4 jacks, 4 queens, 4 kings, and 4 aces.

The probability of picking a diamond is $\frac{\text{favorable}}{\text{possible}} = \frac{13}{52} = \frac{1}{4}$.

The probability of picking a jack is $\frac{\text{favorable}}{\text{possible}} = \frac{4}{52} = \frac{1}{13}$.

The probability of picking an ace of spades is $\frac{\text{favorable}}{\text{possible}} = \frac{1}{52}$.

TIP

Notice that whenever possible, a probability should be reduced.

Use the diagram at the right to solve the next three examples.

The picture shows a circle divided into four sections: one yellow, one blue, and two red. Imagine that the arrow spins freely. Each time the arrow spins, it stops on one of the sections of the circle.

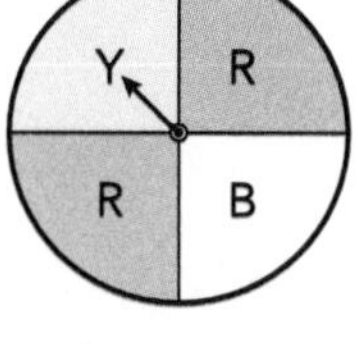

Assume that the arrow never stops on a line.

Example 1   What is the probability that the arrow will land on yellow (Y)?

Step 1   Count the possible outcomes: red, yellow, red, or blue.
There are four possible outcomes.
4 is the denominator.

Step 2   Find the number of favorable outcomes. In this case count the number of times yellow appears on the circle.

$$\frac{\text{favorable}}{\text{possible}} \quad \frac{1}{4}$$

Yellow appears only once. 1 is the numerator.
The probability that the arrow will land on yellow is $\frac{1}{4}$.

Example 2   What is the probability that the arrow will land on red?

Step 1   There are 4 possible outcomes.
4 is the denominator.

Step 2   Since red appears twice, there are 2 favorable outcomes.

$$\frac{\text{favorable}}{\text{possible}} \quad \frac{2}{4} = \frac{1}{2}$$

2 is the numerator. Reduce the fraction.
The probability that the arrow will land on red is $\frac{1}{2}$.

Example 3   What is the probability that the arrow will land on green?

Step 1   Again there are 4 possible outcomes.
4 is the denominator.

Step 2   Since green never appears, 0 is the numerator.

$$\frac{\text{favorable}}{\text{possible}} \quad \frac{0}{4} = 0$$

The probability that the arrow will land on green is 0.

TIP
Remember to reduce a probability to lowest terms.

In some probability problems you may have to find the total number of possible outcomes to complete the problem.

Example 4 A box contains 6 nickels, 4 dimes, and 2 quarters. What is the probability of picking a nickel from the box?

Step 1 Find the total number of possible outcomes—the total number of coins in the box. Add 6, 4, and 2. 12 is the denominator.

$$6 + 4 + 2 = 12 \text{ coins}$$

Step 2 Since there are 6 nickels, 6 is the numerator. Reduce the fraction. The probability of picking a nickel is $\frac{1}{2}$.

$$\frac{\text{favorable}}{\text{possible}} \quad \frac{6}{12} = \frac{1}{2}$$

EXERCISE 5

Directions: For problems 1–4, refer to the diagram below. The arrow is free to spin and stop on any one of the numbered sections.

1. What is the probability that the arrow will land on 1?

2. What is the probability that the arrow will land on 2?

3. What is the probability that the arrow will land on 1 or 5?

4. What is the probability that the arrow will land on an odd number?

Use the following information to answer problems 5–7.

A number cube has 6 sides. Each side has a different number of dots ranging from 1 to 6.

5. What is the probability of rolling a 6?

6. Find the probability of rolling an odd number.

7. What is the probability of rolling either a 1 or a 2?

8. There are 20 marbles in a bag. 16 of them are black. What is the probability of picking a black marble from the bag?

9. Jane's school sold 300 raffle tickets. Jane decided to buy 6 tickets. What is the probability that Jane won the grand prize?

10. The diagram shows a tabletop made of white and colored tiles. What is the probability that a mosquito will land on one of the colored tiles?

Answers are on page 415.

Dependent Probability

The box in Example 4 in the last lesson contained 6 nickels, 4 dimes, and 2 quarters. Suppose the first coin you picked from the box was a dime. You did not put the dime back in the box. Now you would like to find the probability that the next coin you pick will be a nickel. Since you removed one dime from the box, the total number of possible outcomes has changed. The probability of picking a nickel is **dependent** on the fact that you have changed the number of possible outcomes.

Step 1 Find the total number of possible outcomes. $6 + 3 + 2 = 11$ coins
There are now only 3 dimes. Add 6, 3, and 2.
The denominator is 11.

Step 2 Since there are still 6 nickels, 6 is the numerator. $\dfrac{\text{favorable}}{\text{possible}} \quad \dfrac{6}{11}$
The probability that the next coin will be a nickel is $\dfrac{6}{11}$.

Remember that not all situations are dependent on earlier situations. When you toss a coin, the probability of getting tails is $\dfrac{1}{2}$. When you toss a coin a second time, the probability of getting tails is still $\dfrac{1}{2}$. The second toss is not dependent on the outcome of the first toss.

EXERCISE 6

Directions: Use the cards pictured below to answer problems 1–3. Assume that the cards are lying face down.

1. What is the probability of picking a king?

2. The first card Maria picked was a jack. If Maria does not put the jack back among the cards, what is the probability that the next card she picks will be a king?

3. In fact, the second card Maria picked was a 9. If she does not put the two cards back, what is the probability that the next card she picks will be a king?

Use the following information to answer problems 4–6.

Ted's sock drawer contains 6 pairs of blue socks, 3 pairs of black socks, 1 pair of white socks, and 2 pairs of gray socks. Each pair is rolled together.

4. If Ted chooses one pair of socks without looking, what is the probability that he will pick a pair of black socks?

5. The first pair of socks that Ted picked was gray. If he does not return the socks to the drawer, what is the probability that the next pair of socks he picks will be gray?

6. The second pair of socks that Ted picked was blue. If he doesn't return either pair of socks to the drawer, what is the probability that the next pair that he picks will be white?

Use the following information to answer problems 7–9.

Luba bought 1 can of white paint, 3 cans of gray paint, and 4 cans of green paint. When she got home, she realized that the cans had not been labeled.

7. What is the probability that the paint in the first can she opens will be white?

8. The first can Luba opened was gray. What is the probability that the second can she opens will be white?

9. The second can turned out to be gray as well. What is the probability that the paint in the third can will be green?

For problems 10–12, solve each problem.

10. Mr. Robinson bought two raffle tickets. His wife bought three tickets, and his daughter bought one. Altogether, 1000 tickets were sold. What is the probability that Mr. Robinson bought the ticket for the grand prize?

11. What is the probability that someone in the Robinson family will win the grand prize?

12. What is the probability that a person who was born in April was born after April 20th?

Answers are on page 415.

Statistical Analysis

One way to analyze a set of numbers is to find the **mean**, or **average**. You have already learned that the mean is a total divided by the number of items that make up that total.

Another way to analyze a set of numbers is to find the **median**. You have learned that the median is the middle value of an odd number of numbers and halfway between the two middle values of an even set of numbers.

Yet another way to analyze a set of number is to find the **mode**. The mode is the most frequently occurring number in a set.

Example 1   Eight students were asked to pick a number from 1 to 10. Below are the results. What is the mean of the set of numbers?

6 2 5 9 1 7 3 7

Step 1   Find the sum by adding the numbers. $\frac{6+2+5+9+1+7+3+7}{8} = \frac{40}{8} = 5$

Step 2   Divide the sum by 8, the total number of numbers.
The mean is 5.

Example 2   Find the median of the set of numbers above.

Step 1   Arrange the numbers in order   1 2 3 $\underline{5}$ $\underline{6}$ 7 7 9
from smallest to largest.

Step 2   The middle values are 5 and 6.
Find the mean of 5 and 6. $\frac{5+6}{2} = \frac{11}{2} = 5.5$
The median is 5.5.

Example 3   Find the mode of the set of numbers above.

The most frequently occurring number is 7.
The mode is 7.

EXERCISE 7

Directions: Use the table below to answer problems 1–7. Use a calculator whenever needed.

The list below tells the family name and the number of members of each household on one block of Elm Street.

Name	Persons per household	Name	Persons per household
Smith	4	Elliot	3
Miller	5	Starr	2
Gomez	3	Lane	1
Brown	1	Chan	4
Randolph	2	Douglas	2

1. Which family has the highest number of persons per household?

2. Which families have one person per household?

3. How many families are listed in the table?

4. What is the total number of persons on the list?

5. Find the mean household size for the families on Elm Street.

6. Find the median household size for the families.

7. What is the mode for the households listed on the table?

Use the table below to answer problems 8–12. The table shows the range of scores on a math test and the number of students who scored in each range.

Range	No. of scores
90–100	6
80–89	12
70–79	10
60–69	4
0–59	3

8. How many scores were from 90–100?

9. What was the total number of scores?

10. Which range had the most scores? (This is the mode.)

11. How many scores were below 80?

12. How many scores were above 79?

Answers are on page 415.

Data Analysis, Statistics, and Probability Review

PART I

Directions: Use a calculator whenever possible to solve the problems in this section.

Use the line graph and circle graph below to answer problems 1–6.

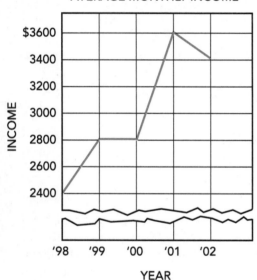

MAYNARD FAMILY
AVERAGE MONTHLY INCOME

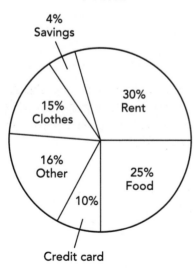

MAYNARD FAMILY
MONTHLY EXPENSES
FOR 2002

1. What was the Maynard family's average monthly income in 2001?

2. In what year did the Maynards' average monthly income first reach $2800?

3. Together the categories of Clothes and Credit Card make up what fraction of the Maynards' monthly expenses for 2002?

4. How much did the Maynards save each month in 2002?

   (1) $ 96
   (2) $112
   (3) $136
   (4) $150
   (5) $340

5. How much did the Maynards spend each month for rent in 2002?

   (1) $ 720
   (2) $ 840
   (3) $ 960
   (4) $1020
   (5) $1200

6. If the income trend from 2001 to 2002 continues, which of the following best predicts the Maynards' approximate monthly income for 2003?

   (1) about $4000
   (2) about $3600
   (3) about $3400
   (4) about $3200
   (5) about $3000

Use the following bar graph and two circle graphs to answer problems 7–12.

TOTAL U.S. POPULATION

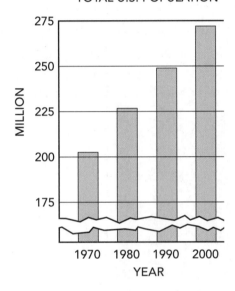

PROJECTIONS OF TOTAL U.S. POPULATION BY AGE

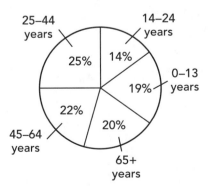

Source: Bureau of the Census

7. What was the approximate population of the U.S. in 1990?

8. For what year shown on the bar graph was the population of the U.S. about 275 million?

9. For each 10-year period shown on the bar graph, the population of the U.S. increased by approximately how much?

10. Approximately how many Americans were 25 to 44 years old in 2000?

    (1) 50 million
    (2) 55 million
    (3) 68 million
    (4) 75 million
    (5) 83 million

11. Some experts think the population of the U.S. will be 380,000,000 in the year 2050. According to the projections on the circle graph, how many Americans will be 65 and older in 2050?

    (1) 38 million
    (2) 46 million
    (3) 58 million
    (4) 76 million
    (5) 88 million

12. According to the projections shown on the circle graphs, which age group will increase most as a percent of the population from 2000 to 2050?

    (1) 0–13
    (2) 14–24
    (3) 25–44
    (4) 45–64
    (5) 65+

PART II

Directions: Solve the following problems without a calculator.

13. A box contains 6 blue marbles and 3 red ones. What is the probability that a marble drawn from the box will be red?

14. When Carl took a marble from the box in the last problem he picked a blue one. If he does not put the first marble he picked back into the box, what is the probability that the next marble he picks will be blue?

For problems 15–18, refer to the table below.

The table shows the range of the heights of students in Mr. Chin's martial arts class as well as the number of students in each range.

Height range	No. of students
6 ft 2 in. and over	1
5 ft 10 in. to 6 ft 1 in.	5
5 ft 6 in. to 5 ft 9 in.	9
5 ft 2 in. to 5 ft 5 in.	3
5 ft 1 in. and under	2

15. According to the chart, how many students are there in Mr. Chin's class?

    (1) 9
    (2) 12
    (3) 15
    (4) 20
    (5) 24

16. Which height range has the greatest number of students (the mode)?

Mark your answer to problems 17 and 18 on the corresponding number grid.

17. What fraction of the students in Mr. Chin's class are 5 ft 10 in. or taller?

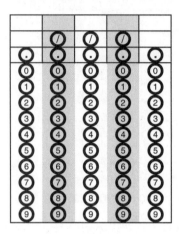

18. What fraction of Mr. Chin's students are under 5 ft 6 in.?

Answers are on page 416.

You should have gotten at least 14 problems right on this exercise. If you did not get 14 right, review your skills in this chapter before you go on. If you got 14 or more right, correct any problem you got wrong. Then go on to the next chapter.

Chapter 9

Basic Geometry

The word **_geometry_** comes from Greek words that mean "to measure land." Geometry is the branch of mathematics that studies points, lines, angles, surfaces, and solid figures. Every built object—from a simple shelf to a satellite—is constructed using the principles of geometry.

Geometry uses special terms. Many geometric terms are words that are used in everyday speech. However, in geometry these words have exact meanings. In this chapter, watch for words such as _plane_ and _closed_ or _opposite_ and _right_. These ordinary words have special mathematical meanings.

You do not have to memorize every new term in this chapter, but you should become familiar with them.

Common Geometric Shapes

Points, Lines, and Angles

Following are several terms used to describe geometric figures.

A **point** has a position in space.

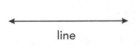

A **ray** is a straight path of points that begins at one point and continues in one direction.

A **line** is a straight path of points that continues in two directions. In the illustration the arrows suggest that the line continues.

A **line segment** has definite length. Every line segment has two **endpoints.**

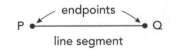

A line is **horizontal** when it runs from left to right.

A line is **vertical** when it runs up and down.

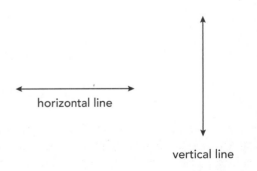

Two lines are **parallel** when they run in the same direction. Parallel lines never cross, no matter how far they are extended.

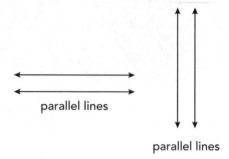

parallel lines

parallel lines

Two lines or line segments meet at a point of **intersection**.

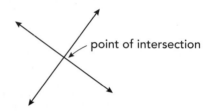

point of intersection

Perpendicular lines are lines that meet or intersect to form right angles. (See *right angle* on the next page.)

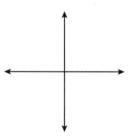

An **angle** is a figure formed by two rays extending from the same point. The point from which the lines extend is called the **vertex**. The size of an angle is measured in degrees (°). The symbol ∠ stands for the word *angle*. The curve drawn inside the angle refers to the opening.

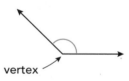

vertex

The size of an angle depends on the amount of **rotation** of the sides. Rotation refers to the "openness" of the sides. One complete rotation is 360°.

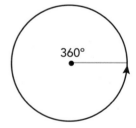

360°

Compare the angles labeled a and b. ∠*a* is greater than ∠*b* because the rotation of the sides in ∠*a* is greater. Notice that the length of the sides that form an angle has nothing to do with the size of the angle.

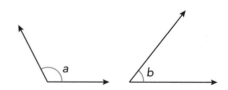

a   b

Take the time now to memorize the names of the angles in the chart you do not already know. Notice that the names depend on the number of degrees in each angle.

Angle Name	Size in Degrees	Examples
acute angle	less than 90°	
right angle	exactly 90°	Small square is a symbol for a right angle.
obtuse angle	greater than 90° and less than 180°	
straight angle	exactly 180°	
reflex angle	greater than 180°	

A **protractor** is a tool for measuring angles. A protractor is usually a half circle made of clear plastic. At the bottom of the protractor are a baseline and crosshairs for lining up the vertex. Two scales, measured in degrees, run along the curved edge of the protractor. One scale goes from 0° to 180°. The other scale goes from 180° to 0°. The protractor in the illustration shows an angle of 135°.

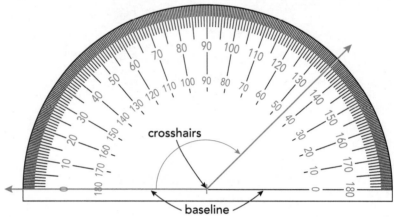

EXERCISE 1

Directions: For problems 1–5, choose the letter that matches the description of each pair of lines.

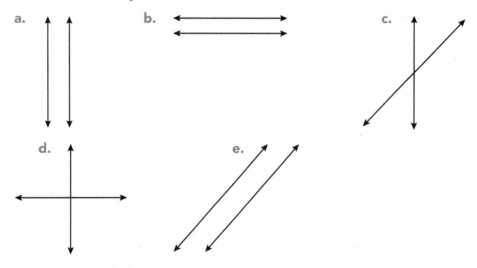

_C_ 1. intersecting but not perpendicular

_e_ 2. vertical and parallel

_b_ 3. parallel but neither vertical nor horizontal

_a_ 4. horizontal and parallel

_D_ 5. perpendicular

For problems 6–12, identify each angle by name—acute, right, obtuse, straight, or reflex.

6. a.   b.   c.

7. a.    b.   c.

8. a.   b.    c.

9. a.    b.   c.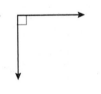

10.	40°	90°	100°
11.	83°	180°	175°
12.	220°	300°	50°

For problems 13–15, solve each problem.

13. An instrument for measuring the number of degrees in an angle is called what?

14. Tell the number of degrees formed by the hands of a clock at each of these times.
    1:00   2:00   3:00   4:00

15. About how many degrees are formed by the hands of a clock at 2:30?

Angle Relationships

The last lesson used lowercase letters such as *a* and *b* to refer to angles. The lowercase letters were in the opening of each angle. Uppercase letters such as *A* and *B* can also refer to angles. Uppercase letters refer to the vertex and a point on each side of an angle.

∠*AOB* refers to the straight angle in the illustration. The angle can also be called ∠*BOA*. In both cases the vertex *O* is in the middle.

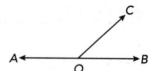

Ray *OC* forms two more angles, ∠*AOC* and ∠*BOC*. ∠*AOC* is obtuse, and ∠*BOC* is acute. If you know the number of degrees in one of these angles, you can find the measurement of the other angle by subtracting the measure of the known angle from 180°.

RULE

Two angles that add up to 180° are called **supplementary angles**.

Example 1 In the illustration above, ∠*BOC* measures 50°. How many degrees are in ∠*AOC*?

Subtract 50° from 180°.   ∠*AOC* = 180° − 50° = 130°
∠*AOC* measures 130°.

In the illustration at the right, ∠*DEF* is a right angle. Ray *EG* forms two more angles, ∠*DEG* and ∠*FEG*. ∠*DEG* and ∠*FEG* are both acute. If you know the number of degrees in one of these angles, you can find the measurement of the other angle by subtracting the measure of the known angle from 90°.

RULE

Two angles that add to 90° are called **complementary angles**.

Example 2 In the illustration above ∠*FEG* measures 35°. How many degrees are in ∠*DEG*?

Subtract 35° from 90°.   ∠*DEG* = 90° − 35° = 55°
∠*DEG* measures 55°.

In the illustration at the right, line WX intersects line YZ at point O. Suppose ∠WOZ measures 70°. ∠WOY measures 180° − 70° = 110° because ∠WOY and ∠WOZ are supplementary.

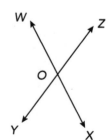

RULE

Adjacent angles are two angles that share a side.

Because ∠WOZ and ∠WOY share a side, they are called adjacent angles. ∠WOZ and ∠WOY share side WO.

∠WOY and ∠ZOX, which both measure 110°, are called vertical angles.

∠WOZ and ∠YOX, which both measure 70°, are also called vertical angles.

RULE

Vertical angles are two angles opposite (across from) each other when two lines intersect. Vertical angles are equal.

Remember that uppercase letters (such as *A*, *B*, and *C*) refer to the vertex and points on the sides of an angle. Lowercase letters (such as *a*, *b*, and *c*) are used to refer to the opening of an angle.

Example 3   Which angle is vertical to ∠*u* in the illustration at the right?
∠*s* is vertical to ∠*u* because ∠*s* is opposite ∠*u*.

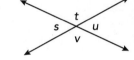

In the illustration at the right, lines *m* and *n* are parallel. Both lines are intersected by a third line *t*, called a **transversal**. The transversal creates four angles at each point of intersection.

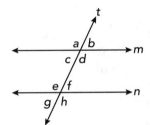

For parallel lines with a transversal, the following statements are true:

- The four acute angles (*b*, *c*, *f*, and *g*) are equal.

- The four obtuse angles (*a*, *d*, *e*, and *h*) are equal.

- Each acute angle is supplementary to each obtuse angle.

Example 4   In the illustration at the right, lines *a* and *b* are parallel. What is the measure of ∠*x*?

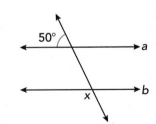

Each acute angle is equal to 50°. ∠x is a supplementary obtuse angle. Subtract 50° from 180°. 180° − 50° = 130°
∠x measures 130°.

EXERCISE 2

Directions: For problems 1–4, solve each problem. Use a calculator whenever necessary.

1. How many degrees are in the *complement* of a 48° angle?

2. How many degrees are in the *supplement* of a 48° angle?

3. Find the *complement* of an angle measuring 25°.

4. Find the *supplement* of an angle measuring 63°.

Use the illustration at the right to solve problems 5–8.

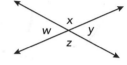

5. Which angle is *vertical* to ∠y?

6. What is the sum of ∠w, ∠x, ∠y, and ∠z?

7. If ∠w measures 75°, what is the measure of ∠x?

8. If ∠x measures 119°, what is the measure of ∠w?

For problems 9–15, solve each problem.

9. The supplement of an acute angle is always what kind of angle?

10. What is the measure of ∠m in the illustration?

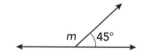

11. If an angle measures 37°, an angle vertical to it will measure how many degrees?

12. In the illustration at the right, ∠XOZ measures 110.5°. What is the measure of ∠YOZ?

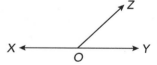

13. In the illustration at the right, ∠AOC measures 138° and ∠AOB measures 47°. What is the measure of ∠BOC?

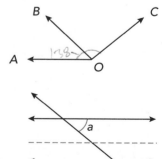

14. A surveyor stretched a wire across a street as shown. If ∠a is 30°, what is the measure of ∠b?

15. In the illustration at the right, line *m* and line *n* are parallel. If ∠*s* measures 120°, which other angles measure 120°?

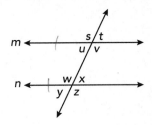

Answers are on page 416.

Plane Figures

Plane geometry is the study of flat surfaces. The most common shapes are rectangles, squares, triangles, and circles. These figures are **2-dimensional**. These figures extend in two directions, but they do not have thickness or depth.

A **polygon** is a closed figure composed of three or more line segments. In the last sentence, the word *closed* means that all the line segments meet.

Look at the three figures below. The first figure is not a polygon because it is open. The second figure is closed, and it is a polygon. The third figure is not a polygon because it is not composed of line segments (straight sides).

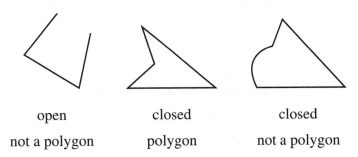

| open | closed | closed |
| not a polygon | polygon | not a polygon |

A **triangle** is a closed, plane figure with three sides.

Examples

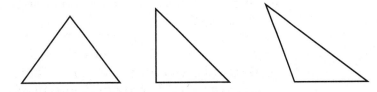

A **quadrilateral** is a polygon with four sides. The chart below lists five quadrilaterals and describes their characteristics.

Quadrilaterals	Examples
A **rectangle** has four right angles. The sides across from each other are parallel and equal in length.	
A **square** has four right angles and four equal sides. The sides across from each other are parallel.	
A **rhombus** has four equal sides.	
A **parallelogram** has two pairs of opposite, parallel sides.	
A **trapezoid** has one pair of parallel sides.	

In a quadrilateral, **opposite** sides are across from each other, and **adjacent** sides share a **vertex** (corner).

Two uppercase letters (the endpoints) refer to one side of a polygon.

In rectangle *ABCD*, sides *AB* and *CD* are opposite each other. Sides *AB* and *AD* are adjacent.

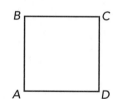

A **circle** is a figure in which every point is the same distance from the center. The distance around a circle is called the **circumference**. The distance from the center to a point on the circle is called the **radius**. The distance across the circle through its center is called the **diameter**. The diameter is exactly two times the radius.

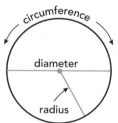

The ratio of the circumference of a circle to its diameter is called **pi**, which is represented by the Greek letter π. The value of π is approximately 3.14 or $\frac{22}{7}$. For any circle, however large or small, the circumference divided by the diameter is always approximately 3.14.

EXERCISE 3

Directions: For problems 1–5, fill in each blank.

1. A closed, plane figure with three sides is called a _____ .

2. A four-sided figure with four right angles and four equal sides is called a _____ .

3. The measure of the distance across a circle through its center is called the _____ .

4. The distance around a circle is called the _____ .

5. To calculate the value of π for any circle, divide the measurement of the circumference by the measurement of its _____ .

For problems 6 and 7, identify each figure.

6.

5 ft
5 ft

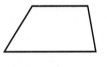

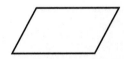

7.

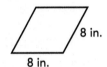
8 in.
8 in.

Use rectangle *EFGH* to answer problems 8–11.

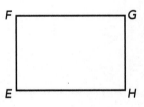

8. Which side is opposite side *EH*?

9. Which side is opposite side *EF*?

10. Name two sides that are adjacent to side *EF*.

11. What is the measure of ∠*FEH*?

For problems 12 and 13, find each measurement.

12. If a circle has a diameter of 36 inches, what is its radius?

13. If a circle has a radius of 7.5 feet, what is its diameter?

Answers are on page **417.**

Perimeter and Circumference

Perimeter is the measure of distance around a plane (flat) figure. Perimeter is measured in units such as inches, feet, yards, centimeters, and meters. To find the perimeter of a figure whose sides are all line segments, add the length of each side. The perimeter of a circle is called the **circumference**.

Below are the perimeter and circumference formulas that will appear on the GED test.

Perimeter of a:

square	Perimeter = 4 × side
rectangle	Perimeter = 2 × length + 2 × width
triangle	Perimeter = $side_1$ + $side_2$ + $side_3$

Circumference of a:

circle	Circumference = π × diameter; π is approximately equal to 3.14.

--- RULE ---

To find the perimeter or circumference of a figure, replace the words *side*, *length*, *width*, or *diameter* in each formula with the values given in a problem.

Example 1 Find the perimeter of the rectangle pictured at the right.

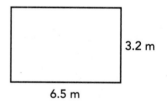

3.2 m

6.5 m

Step 1 Replace *length* with 6.5 m and *width* with 3.2 m in the formula for the perimeter of a rectangle.

P = 2 × length + 2 × width
P = 2 × 6.5 m + 2 × 3.2 m

Step 2 Evaluate the formula by following the order of operations.
The perimeter of the rectangle is 19.4 meters.

P = 13.0 m + 6.4 m
P = 19.4 m

Notice the letter *P* in the last example. Formulas can be written with words or letters that represent words. The formula for the perimeter of a rectangle can be written as $P = 2l + 2w$, where *P* is the perimeter, *l* is the length, and *w* is the width.

You can solve Example 1 using the Casio *fx*-260 calculator, which uses the order of operations.

Press (AC).

Press (2) (×) (6) (·) (5) (+) (2) (×) (3) (·) (2) (=).

The display should read [19.4].

Example 2   Find the perimeter of the square shown at the right.

3 ft

Step 1   Replace *side* with 3 ft in the formula for the perimeter of a square.

$P = 4 \times side$
$P = 4 \times 3$ ft

Step 2   Evaluate the formula.
The perimeter is 12 feet.

$P = 12$ ft

The formula for the perimeter of a square can also be written as $P = 4s$, where P is the perimeter and s is the measure of one side.

Example 3   Find the perimeter of the triangle pictured at the right.

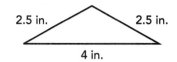
2.5 in.   2.5 in.
4 in.

Step 1   Replace *side*$_1$ with 2.5, *side*$_2$ with 2.5, and *side*$_3$ with 4 in the formula for the perimeter of a triangle.

$P = side_1 + side_2 + side_3$

$P = 2.5$ in. $+ 2.5$ in. $+ 4$ in.

Step 2   Evaluate the formula.
The perimeter is 9 inches.

$P = 9$ in.

The formula for the perimeter of a triangle can also be written as $P = s_1 + s_2 + s_3$, where P is the perimeter and s_1, s_2, and s_3 are the three sides.

Example 4   Find the circumference of the circle pictured at the right.

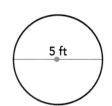
5 ft

Step 1   Replace π with 3.14 and *diameter* with 5 ft in the formula for the circumference of a circle.

$C = \pi \times diameter$
$C = 3.14 \times 5$ ft

Step 2   Evaluate the formula.
The circumference is 15.7 feet.

$C = 15.7$ ft

Remember that the diameter of a circle is two times the radius. To find the circumference of a circle when the radius is given, first multiply the radius by 2. Then substitute values into the formula for the circumference.

Using the Casio *fx*-260 calculator makes solving Example 4 easy.

Press .

Press ⟨ 3 ⟩ ⟨ · ⟩ ⟨ 1 ⟩ ⟨ 4 ⟩ ⟨ × ⟩ ⟨ 5 ⟩ ⟨ = ⟩ .

The display should read [15.7] .

EXERCISE 4

Directions: For problems 1–4, identify each figure. Then use your calculator to find the perimeter or the circumference of the figure. Use 3.14 for π unless told to do otherwise.

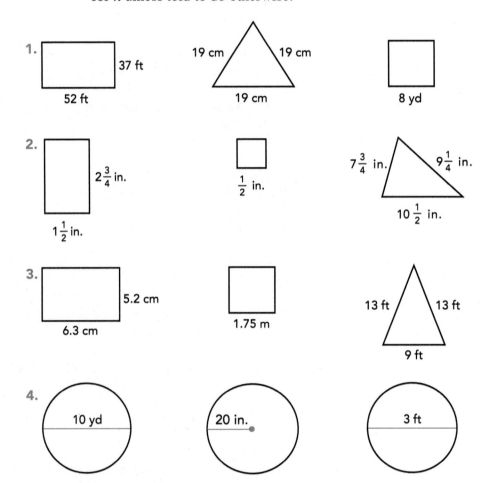

For problems 5–8, solve each problem.

5. What is the circumference of a circle with a *radius* of 7 inches? Use $\frac{22}{7}$ for π.

6. Which expression does *not* equal the perimeter of a rectangle that is 20 feet long and 15 feet wide?

   (1) 20 ft + 15 ft + 20 ft + 15 ft
   (2) 2 × 20 ft + 2 × 15 ft
   (3) 2 × (20 ft + 15 ft)
   (4) 4 × 20 ft
   (5) 70 ft

7. A regular hexagon is a 6-sided figure in which all 6 sides are equal. Which expression is the perimeter (*P*) of a regular hexagon for which each side measures s?

   (1) $P = 3s$
   (2) $P = 4s$
   (3) $P = 6s$
   (4) $P = \frac{s}{4}$
   (5) $P = \frac{s}{6}$

8. Which expression represents the perimeter of the figure at the right?

   (1) 2(1.6) + 2.4
   (2) 1.6 + 2.4
   (3) 1.6 + 2(2.4)
   (4) 2(1.6) + 2(2.4)
   (5) 4(1.6)

Answers are on page 417.

Estimating Pi

In the last lesson you solved perimeter problems by using either 3.14 as the decimal value for π or $\frac{22}{7}$ as the improper fraction value for π. Notice that both of these values are slightly greater than 3.

TIP
To estimate the answer to a circumference problem, use the whole number 3 for π. Use the sign ≈, which means "is approximately equal to." π ≈ 3

Example: Which of the following is closest to the circumference of a circle with a diameter of 15 feet?
(1) 30 ft   (2) 35.3 ft   (3) 47.1 ft   (4) 52.9 ft

Step 1 Replace π with 3 and *diameter* with 15 ft in the formula for the circumference of a circle.

$C = \pi \times \text{diameter}$
$C \approx 3 \times 15 \text{ ft}$

Step 2 Evaluate the formula. The approximate circumference is 45 feet. Choice (3) 47.1 ft is the closest answer to 45 feet.

$C \approx 45 \text{ ft}$

EXERCISE 5

Directions: Estimate an answer to each problem by using the whole number 3 for π. Then use your estimate to choose the best answer to each problem. For more practice, check your answers with a calculator.

1. Find the circumference of the circle at the right.

   (1) 13 ft (2) 15.7 ft (3) 23.6 ft (4) 31.4 ft

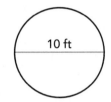

10 ft

2. What is the circumference of a circle with a diameter of 4 yards?

   (1) 20.2 yd (2) 16.4 yd (3) 12.6 yd (4) 10.8 yd

3. Find the circumference of the circle at the right.

   (1) 4.8 m (2) 6.9 m (3) 9.8 m (4) 13.2 m

2.2 m

4. What is the circumference of a circle with a *radius* of 6 inches?

   (1) 6.7 in. (2) 18.9 in. (3) 37.7 in. (4) 49.4 in.

5. Find the circumference of the circle at the right.

   (1) 314 in. (2) 157 in. (3) 78.5 in. (4) 39.3 in.

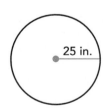

25 in.

6. Find the circumference of a circle with a *radius* of $\frac{1}{2}$ foot.

   (1) 3.1 ft (2) 6.2 ft (3) 9.3 ft (4) 12.4 ft

7. Which of the following is closest to the circumference of a circle with a diameter of 96 inches?

   (1) 300 in. (2) 600 in. (3) 3000 in. (4) 6000 in.

Answers are on page 417.

Perimeter and Circumference Word Problems

Remember that perimeter is the measure of distance around a flat figure. The phrase *find the distance around* means to find the perimeter. Constructing a fence around a garden and building a frame for a picture are practical applications of perimeter.

Watch out for problems where the units of measurement change. Remember to include labels—such as meters, feet, or inches—with the numbers you use in perimeter and circumference formulas.

Example   How many feet of picture framing are required to go around a square picture with a side of 30 inches?

Step 1   Write the formula for the perimeter of a square. $P = 4 \times \text{side}$

Step 2   Replace *side* with 30 in. in the formula. The perimeter is 120 inches. $P = 4 \times 30 \text{ in.}$
$P = 120 \text{ in.}$

Step 3   Change 120 inches to feet. Divide 120 by 12. The picture requires 10 feet of framing. $\frac{120}{12} = 10 \text{ ft}$

EXERCISE 6

Directions: Use your calculator to solve each problem. Draw a picture if it will help you visualize a problem.

1. Mark wants to put a frame around an 8-inch by 10-inch photograph. How many inches of framing does he need?

2. The garden in Hailey's yard is 26 meters long and half as wide. How many meters of fencing does she need to enclose the garden?

3. Find the measurement of the side of the largest square frame that can be made from 100 inches of framing. Express your answer in feet and inches.

For problems 4–6, refer to the following situation.

There are 6 windows on the second floor of Mrs. Jackson's house. Each window has a base of 36 inches and a height of 42 inches. Around each window Mrs. Jackson wants to put weather stripping that costs $0.60 a foot.

4. What is the distance, in inches, around one window on the second floor of Mrs. Jackson's house?

5. Find the measurement, in *feet*, around all the windows on the second floor.

6. What is the total cost of weather stripping for the 6 windows?

Use your calculator to solve problems 7–10.

7. Workers are putting brick trim around the edge of a circular pool in the park in Central City. The diameter of the pool is 50 feet. How many 9-inch-long bricks are needed to go around the edge of the pool?

8. Paul wants to put oak trim around a worktable in his kitchen. The top of the table is 30 inches wide and 72 inches long. How many *feet* of trim does he need to put around the table?

9. The illustration at the right shows a mirror. The top of the mirror is a half circle. The bottom is a rectangle. Rounded up to the nearest inch, how many inches of framing are required to go around the mirror?

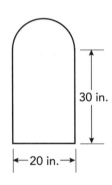

30 in.

←— 20 in. —→

10. Which expression represents the perimeter of the rectangle at the right?

    (1) 25×15

    (2) $2(25) + 2(15)$

    (3) $\frac{4(25)}{12}$

    (4) $\frac{2(25) + 2(15)}{12}$

    (5) $\frac{25 + 15}{12}$

15 ft

25 ft

Answers are on page 418.

Area

Area is a measure of the amount of surface within the perimeter of a flat figure. Area is measured in **square units,** such as square inches, square feet, and square meters.

The rectangle at the right has a length of 5 inches and a width of 3 inches. The surface of the rectangle is covered with 15 small squares. Each square is one square inch. The area of the rectangle is 15 square inches.

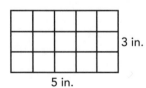

3 in.

5 in.

Following are the formulas for area that you will use in this lesson.

Area of a:	
square	Area = side²
rectangle	Area = length × width
parallelogram	Area = base × height
triangle	Area = $\frac{1}{2}$ × base × height
trapezoid	Area = $\frac{1}{2}$ × (base$_1$ + base$_2$) × height
circle	Area = π × radius²; π is approximately equal to 3.14.

——————————————— R U L E ———————————————

To find the area of a figure, replace the words *side, length, height,* or *radius* in each formula with the values given in a problem.

Example 1 Find the area of the square pictured at the right.

Step 1 Replace *side* with 6 m in the formula for the area of a square.

A = side²
A = (6 m)²   6 m

Step 2 Evaluate the formula. The area of the square is 36 square meters.

A = 6 m × 6 m

A = 36 sq m, or 36 m²

Notice that the label square meters can be abbreviated as sq m or written with an exponent, m².

Example 2 Find the area of the rectangle pictured at the right.

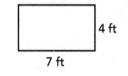

4 ft

7 ft

Step 1 Replace *length* with 7 ft and *width* with 4 ft in the formula for the area of a rectangle.

A = length × width
A = 7 ft × 4 ft

Step 2 Evaluate the formula. The area of the rectangle is 28 square feet.

A = 28 sq ft, or 28 ft²

The length and width of a rectangle are perpendicular to each other. The base and height of a parallelogram, a triangle, and a trapezoid are also perpendicular to each other.

Example 3   Find the area of the parallelogram pictured at the right.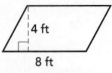

Step 1   Replace *base* with 8 ft and *height* with 4 ft in the formula for the area of a parallelogram.

$A = \text{base} \times \text{height}$
$A = 8 \text{ ft} \times 4 \text{ ft}$

Step 2   Evaluate the formula. The area of the parallelogram is 32 square feet.

$A = 32 \text{ sq ft, or } 32 \text{ ft}^2$

Look at the position of the base and height in each triangle below.

For the triangle at the left, the height is inside the triangle. For the middle

 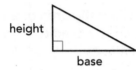 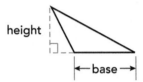

triangle, the height is the left side. For the triangle at the right, the height is a perpendicular distance outside the triangle.

You can think of the area of a triangle as half the area of some 4-sided figure. The figure at the right is a rectangle with a length (base) of 9 meters and a width (height) of 6 meters. The shaded part of the rectangle is a triangle with a base of 9 meters and a height of 6 meters. You can use this idea to remember that the area of a triangle is half the area of a rectangle.

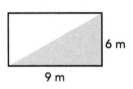

Example 4   Find the area of a triangle with a base of 9 meters and a height of 6 meters.

Step 1   Replace *base* with 9 m and *height* with 6 m in the formula for the area of a triangle.

$A = \frac{1}{2} \times \text{base} \times \text{height}$

$A = \frac{1}{2} \times 9 \text{ m} \times 6 \text{ m}$

Step 2   Evaluate the formula. The area of the triangle is 27 square meters, which is half the area of the rectangle.

$A = 27 \text{ sq m, or } 27 \text{ m}$

Use the Casio *fx*-260 calculator to find the answer quickly in Example 4.

Press [AC].

Press [.] [5] [×] [9] [×] [6] [=].

The display should read [27.].

In the formula for the area of a trapezoid, you calculate the mean or average of the two parallel sides (bases). Then you multiply the average by the height.

Example 5 Find the area of the trapezoid pictured at the right.

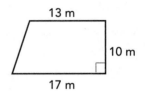

Step 1 Replace *base*₁ with 17 m, *base*₂ with 13 m, and *height* with 10 m in the formula for the area of a trapezoid.

$A = \frac{1}{2} \times (base_1 + base_2) \times height$

$A = \frac{1}{2} \times (17\ m + 13\ m) \times 10\ m$

$A = \frac{1}{2} \times (30\ m) \times 10\ m$

Step 2 Evaluate the formula. The area of the trapezoid is 150 square meters.

$A = 15\ m \times 10\ m$

$A = 150$ sq m, or 150 m²

Use the Casio *fx*-260 calculator to complete Example 5 in one step.

Press AC.

Press

1 0 =.

The display should read [150.].

Example 6 What is the area of a circle whose radius is 3 inches?

Step 1 Replace π with 3.14 and *radius* with 3 in the formula for the area of a circle.

$A = \pi \times radius^2$

$A = 3.14 \times 3^2$

Step 2 Evaluate the formula. The area of the circle is 28.26 square inches.

$A = 3.14 \times 9$

$A = 28.26$ sq in., or 28.26 in.²

Use the Casio *fx*-260 calculator to save time in working Example 6.

Press AC.

Press 3 . 1 4 × 3 x² =.

The display should read [28.26].

EXERCISE 7

Directions: For problems 1–6, identify each figure. Then use your calculator to find the area of each figure. Use 3.14 for π. Use any formulas on page 439 that you need.

1.
12 ft
15 ft

14 ft

6 in.
11 in.

2.
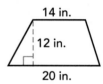
10 yd

12 in.
20 in.

14 in.
12 in.
20 in.

3.
3 ½ in.
8 in.

4 yd

6.5 m

4.
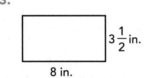
9 cm
← 7 cm →

14 ft
10 ft
12 ft

0.5 m

5.

6 in.
11 in.

8 yd
12.5 yd

20 ft
15 ft
30 ft

6.
1.5 m

10 in.
28 in.

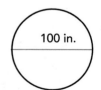
100 in.

For problems 7–10, choose the correct answer.

7. Which expression represents the area, in square inches, of a square whose sides measure $\frac{5}{8}$ inch?

   (1) $\frac{5}{8} + \frac{5}{8}$

   (2) $4\left(\frac{5}{8}\right)$

   (3) $\left(\frac{5}{8}\right)^2$

   (4) $\sqrt{5/8}$

   (5) $\frac{5}{8} \div 4$

8. Which of the following correctly describes the method for finding the area of the figure shown at the right?

   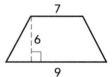

   (1) Find the average of 7, 6, and 9.

   (2) Multiply 9 by 6. Then divide by 2.

   (3) Find the sum of 7 and 9. Then multiply by 6.

   (4) Find the average of 7 and 9. Then multiply by 6.

   (5) Find the sum of 7, 6, and 9. Then divide by 2.

9. Which expression represents the area, in square yards, of the shaded portion of the figure shown at the right?

   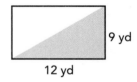

   (1) 12×9

   (2) $12 + 9$

   (3) $\frac{1}{2}(12 + 9)$

   (4) $\frac{1}{2}(12 + 12 + 9 + 9)$

   (5) $\frac{1}{2}(12 \times 9)$

10. What is the area, in square feet, of a square whose sides measure 1 yard?

   (1) 1

   (2) 3

   (3) 9

   (4) 10

   (5) 12

Answers are on page 418.

Area Word Problems

The word *area* does not always appear in problems in which you need to calculate area. Remember that area is a measure of the amount of surface on a flat figure. Finding how much carpet is needed to cover a floor or the amount of paint needed to cover a wall are applications of area.

Read the problems carefully to be sure that your answer uses the correct unit of measurement.

Example 1 How many square yards of carpet does Luba need to cover the floor of her bedroom which is 12 feet long and 9 feet wide?

Step 1 Change both the length and the width to yards. Divide 12 and 9 by 3.

$l = \frac{12}{3} = 4$ yd

$w = \frac{9}{3} = 3$ yd

Step 2 Replace *length* with 4 yd and *width* with 3 yd in the formula for the area of a rectangle.

$A = lw$
$A = 4$ yd $\times$ 3 yd

Step 3 Evaluate the formula.
Luba needs 12 square yards of carpet.

$A = 12$ sq yd

Note: In the last example, you can first find the area of the room in square feet: $A = lw = 12 \times 9 = 108$ square feet. Then divide the answer by 9, the number of square feet in one square yard, $\frac{108}{9} = 12$ square yards.

Watch out for problems that ask you to combine areas.

Example 2 The figure at the right shows the back wall of Jack's garage. How many square feet of siding does Jack need to cover the back wall of the garage?

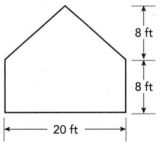

8 ft

8 ft

20 ft

Step 1 The wall is a triangle and a rectangle. Find the area of both shapes.

$A = \frac{1}{2} bh$ $A = lw$

$A = \frac{1}{2}(20)(8)$ $A = (20)(8)$

$A = 80$ sq ft $A = 160$ sq ft

Step 2 Add the two areas.
Jack needs 240 square feet of siding.

$80 + 160 = 240$ sq ft

EXERCISE 8

Directions: Solve each problem. Use any formulas on page 439 that you need.

1. How many square inches of glass are required to cover a photograph that is 8 inches wide and 10 inches long?

2. How many square feet of floor tiles are required to cover the hall shown in the diagram at the right?

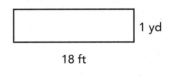

1 yd

18 ft

3. The drawing at the right shows the living room of the Miller family's house. How many square yards of carpet do they need to cover the floor of the living room?

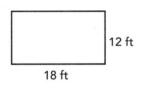

12 ft

18 ft

4. The illustration at the right shows the plan of a deck at the back of the Millers' house. How many square feet of boards do they need to cover the deck?

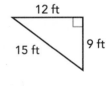

12 ft

10 ft

16 ft

5. A gallon of floor paint will cover about 200 square feet of concrete. The floor of Harold's basement is 25 feet wide and 40 feet long. How many gallons of paint does he need to put one coat of paint on the basement floor?

6. The picture at the right shows the garden in Roberta's yard. She wants to cover the garden with plastic because a weather report predicts frost. How many square yards of plastic does Roberta need to cover the garden?

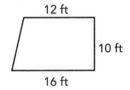

12 ft

9 ft

15 ft

7. Mary wants to make curtains for the three windows in her living room. For each pair of curtains she needs material measuring 6 feet by 8 feet. Altogether, how many square yards of material does she need?

8. Roman wants to repave a circular patio. The radius of the patio is 20 feet. What is the total square footage of the patio?

9. The shaded part of the figure at the right shows the walkway around the pool at the local community center. The pool is a rectangle that measures 34 feet by 18 feet. Find the number of square feet of the walkway around the pool.

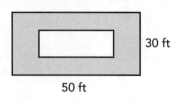

30 ft

50 ft

10. The diagram at the right shows the plan of the dining area and kitchen of a restaurant. Which expression represents the number of square feet of floor of the dining area?

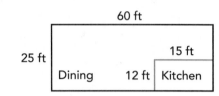

60 ft

25 ft

15 ft

Dining   12 ft   Kitchen

(1) $60^2 - 15^2$

(2) $2(60) + 2(25)$

(3) 60×25

(4) $60 \times 25 + 15 \times 12$

(5) $60 \times 25 - 15 \times 12$

11. Which of the following expresses the number of square feet of the shaded part of the figure shown at the right?

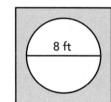

8 ft

12 ft

(1) $12^2 + \pi(8^2)$

(2) $(12 + 1) + 8$

(3) $12^2 - 4^2$

(4) $12^2 - \pi(4^2)$

(5) $12^2 - \pi(8^2)$

12. The diagram at the right shows the front wall of Hal's Hardware. Which expression gives the number of square feet of the wall not including the door and window?

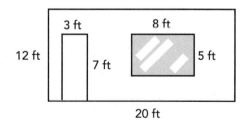

3 ft   8 ft

12 ft   7 ft   5 ft

20 ft

(1) $20 \times 12 - 7 \times 3 - 8 \times 5$

(2) $20 \times 12 + 7 \times 3 + 8 \times 5$

(3) $20 \times 12 - 7 \times 3$

(4) $20 \times 12 - 8 \times 5$

(5) $20 \times 12 + 7 \times 3 - 8 \times 5$

13. Skip and his brother have a business installing carpet. Skip uses a spreadsheet program on his computer to help him estimate jobs. Skip first enters the length of a room (A5) and the width of the room (B5).

Length of room in feet	Width of room in feet	Area of room in square yards	Cost per square yard	Cost of carpet
A5	B5	C5	D5	

Which of the following formulas should Skip enter in the third column to calculate the area of a room in square yards?

(1) $2 \times A5 + 2 \times B5$

(2) $A5 \times B5$

(3) $\frac{A5}{3} \times \frac{B5}{3}$

(4) $(A5 + B5)^2$

(5) $\frac{1}{2}(A5 + B5)$

14. C5 represents the area of a room in square yards (the third column), and D5 represents the cost of carpet per square yard (the fourth column). Which of the following formulas should Skip use to calculate the cost of the carpet in the fifth column?

(1) $\frac{C5}{D5}$

(2) $0.01(C5 \times D5)$

(3) $C5 + D5$

(4) $\frac{C5 + D5}{2}$

(5) $C5 \times D5$

Answers are on page 419.

Solid Figures

Solid geometry is the study of 3-dimensional figures. Remember that plane figures are flat. Solid figures have thickness or depth. A shoebox and a baseball are solid figures. The shapes may be hollow like an empty tin can or solid like a child's building block.

Below are descriptions and examples of six common solid figures.

A **cube** is a box whose dimensions are all the same. Each pair of adjacent sides forms a right angle. Each of the six **faces** is a square.

<u>Examples</u>

A **rectangular solid** is a box each of whose corners is a right angle. Each of the six faces is a rectangle.

Examples

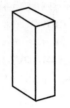

A **square pyramid** is a solid figure whose base is a square and whose four triangular faces meet at a common point called the **vertex**. The height of a square pyramid is a vertical line from the vertex to the center of the square base.

Examples

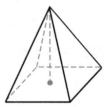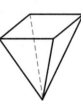

A **cylinder** is a solid figure whose top and bottom are parallel circles. The height of a cylinder is the perpendicular distance between the top and bottom.

Examples

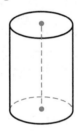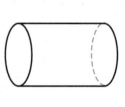

A **cone** is a solid figure with a circular base and a **vertex**. The perpendicular distance from the vertex to the center of the circular base is the **height** of the cone.

Examples

A **sphere** is a solid figure of which every point is the same distance from the center. The distance from any point on the surface of a sphere to the center is called the **radius**.

Examples

EXERCISE 9

Directions: For problems 1 and 2, identify each figure.

1.
 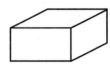

2.

For problems 3–8, use your calculator to solve each problem.

3. For the rectangular solid at the right, find the surface area of the shaded face.

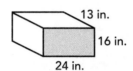

13 in.

16 in.

24 in.

4. For the cylinder at the right, what is the area of the circular base?

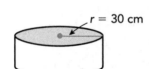

r = 30 cm

5. What is the area of the base of the square pyramid shown at the right?

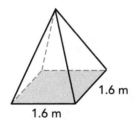

1.6 m

1.6 m

6. For the cube shown at the right, what is the area of one face?

9 in.

7. For the cube in the last problem, what is the surface area of all the faces?

8. The diagram below shows a rectangular solid that is 10 feet long, 8 feet wide, and 5 feet high. It also shows what the figure would look like if it were flattened so that each face is visible. Which expression gives the surface area of the entire figure?

(1) 2(5 + 8) + 2(5 + 10) + 2(8 + 10)

(2) 2(5 × 8) + 2(5 × 10) + 2(8 × 10)

(3) 2(5 + 8 + 10)

(4) 2(5 × 8 × 10)

(5) 2(5)² + 2(8)² + 2(10)²

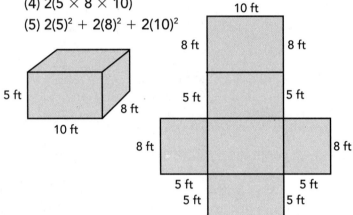

Answers are on page 420.

Volume

Volume is a measure of the amount of space inside a 3-dimensional, or solid, figure.

Volume is measured in **cubic units**, such as cubic inches or cubic meters. The drawing at the right shows one cubic inch. A cubic inch is a 3-dimensional figure that is 1 inch long, 1 inch wide, and 1 inch high.

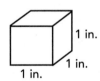

Following are the formulas for volume that you will use in this lesson.

Volume of a:

cube	Volume = edge³
rectangular solid	Volume = length × width × height
square pyramid	Volume = $\frac{1}{3}$ × (base edge)² × height
cylinder	Volume = π × radius² × height; π ≈ 3.14
cone	Volume = $\frac{1}{3}$ × π × radius² × height; π ≈ 3.14

───────────────── R U L E ─────────────────

To find the volume of a figure, replace the words *side*, *length*, *height*, and *radius* in each formula with the values given in a problem.

───

Example 1   Find the volume of the cube at the right.

6 in.

Step 1   Replace *edge* with 6 in. in the formula for the volume of a cube.

$V = \text{edge}^3$
$V = (6 \text{ in.})^3$

Step 2   Evaluate the formula. The volume is 216 cubic inches.

$V = 6 \text{ in.} \times 6 \text{ in.} \times 6 \text{ in.}$
$V = 216 \text{ cu in., or } 216 \text{ in.}^3$

Notice that the label *cubic inches* can be abbreviated as *cu in.* or written with an exponent, *in.*^{3}

Example 2   Find the volume of the rectangular solid at the right.

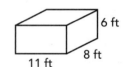

6 ft
8 ft
11 ft

Step 1   Replace *length* with 11 ft, *width* with 8 ft, and *height* with 6 ft in the formula.

$V = \text{length} \times \text{width} \times \text{height}$
$V = 11 \text{ ft} \times 8 \text{ ft} \times 6 \text{ ft}$

Step 2   Evaluate the formula. The volume is 528 cubic feet.

$V = 528 \text{ cu ft, or } 528 \text{ ft}^3$

Example 3   What is the volume of the cylinder at the right?

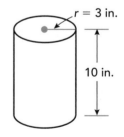

$r = 3$ in.

10 in.

Step 1   Replace π with 3.14, *radius* with 3, and *height* with 10 in the formula for the volume of a cylinder.

$V = \pi \times \text{radius}^2 \times \text{height}$

$V = 3.14 \times 3^2 \times 10$

Step 2   Evaluate the formula. The volume is 282.6 cubic inches.

$V = 282.6 \text{ cu in., or } 282.6 \text{ in.}^3$

Use the Casio *fx*-260 calculator to find the volume in Example 3.

Press AC .

Press 3 · 1 4 × 3 x² × 1 0 = .

The display should read [282.6].

Directions: For problems 1–4, identify each figure. Then use a calculator to find the volume of the figure. Use any formulas on page 439 that you need.

1.

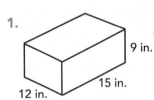

9 in.

15 in.

12 in.

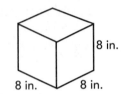

8 in.

8 in.   8 in.

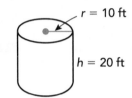

r = 10 ft

h = 20 ft

2.

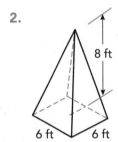

8 ft

6 ft   6 ft

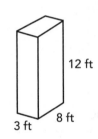

12 ft

3 ft   8 ft

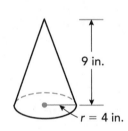

9 in.

r = 4 in.

3.

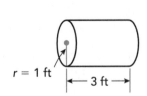

r = 1 ft

← 3 ft →

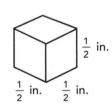

$\frac{1}{2}$ in.

$\frac{1}{2}$ in. $\frac{1}{2}$ in.

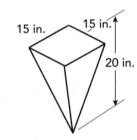

15 in.   15 in.

20 in.

4.

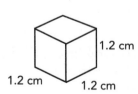

1.2 cm

1.2 cm   1.2 cm

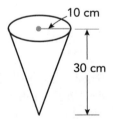

10 cm

30 cm

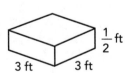

$\frac{1}{2}$ ft

3 ft   3 ft

Solve each problem.

5. What is the volume of the barrel at the right?

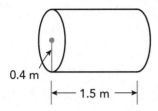

0.4 m

1.5 m

6. The formula for the volume of a sphere is $V = \frac{4}{3}\pi r^3$, where V is the volume and r is the radius. To the nearest cubic inch, what is the volume of a sphere with a radius of 3 inches. Use 3.14 for π.

7. Which expression represents the volume, in cubic inches, of a cube that measures $1\frac{1}{4}$ inches on each edge?

(1) $4 \times 1\frac{1}{4}$

(2) $\frac{1}{2} \times 1\frac{1}{4} \times 1\frac{1}{4}$

(3) $2(1\frac{1}{4}) + 2(1\frac{1}{4})$

(4) $1\frac{1}{4} \times 1\frac{1}{4} \times 1\frac{1}{4}$

(5) $(1\frac{1}{4})^2$

Answers are on page 420.

More Perimeter, Area, and Volume Problems

In some problems you may be asked to find the perimeter or area of complex figures. These figures are often made up of two or more simple figures. To solve these problems, you may first have to calculate a dimension such as a missing length or width.

Example 1   What is the area of the figure at the right?

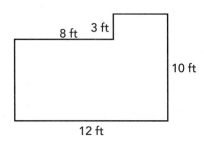

Step 1   Separate the figure into two rectangles. Then decide what dimensions are missing. In the second drawing the two missing dimensions are labeled x and y.

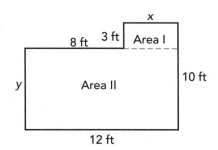

Step 2   Find the missing dimensions by subtracting the sides that you know.

Side x = 12 ft − 8 ft = 4 ft

Side y = 10 ft − 3 ft = 7 ft

Step 3   Find the two areas.

Area I = 4 × 3 = 12 sq ft
Area II = 12 × 7 = 84 sq ft
Total   = 96 sq ft

Step 4   Add the two areas.
The total area is 96 square feet.

Use a shortcut to find how many of one shape fit in another. Study the next example carefully.

Example 2   How many ceramic tiles each measuring 2 inches by 2 inches are needed to cover a countertop that is 80 inches long and 24 inches wide?

Step 1   Divide the area of the countertop by the area of one tile.

$$\frac{\text{area of countertop}}{\text{area of one tile}} \quad \frac{\overset{40}{\cancel{80}} \times \overset{12}{\cancel{24}}}{\underset{1}{\cancel{2}} \times \underset{1}{\cancel{2}}} = 480$$

Step 2   Cancel and multiply across.
The countertop needs 480 tiles.

In the last example you could find the area of the countertop and the area of each tile separately. Then divide the area of one tile into the area of the countertop. However, the method shown in the example is quicker.

EXERCISE 11

Directions: Solve each problem. Use any formulas on page 439 that will help you.

1. Find the perimeter, in inches, of the figure shown at the right.

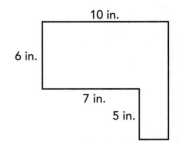

10 in.

6 in.

7 in.

5 in.

2. How many square inches are on the surface of the figure in the last example?

3. Find the area of the figure shown at the right.

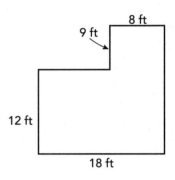

8 ft

9 ft

12 ft

18 ft

4. What is the minimum number of 4-inch by 4-inch square tiles that are needed to cover the top of a square coffee table that measures 5 feet on each side?

5. A 3-pound box of grass seed is enough for 400 square feet of lawn. How many boxes of seed does Carlos need to grow grass on a lawn that is 100 feet long and 80 feet wide?

6. Bill wants to put 2-foot by 2-foot carpet tiles on the floor of his living room, which is shown at the right. Find the least number of carpet tiles he needs to completely cover the floor.

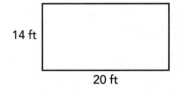

14 ft

20 ft

7. The illustration below shows the dimensions of the bed of a truck. Find the capacity (the total volume), in cubic meters, of the truck bed if it is filled to the top.

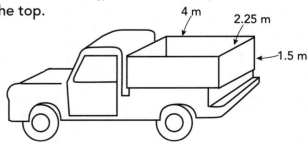

4 m

2.25 m

1.5 m

8. What is the volume, in cubic inches, of the carton shown at the right?

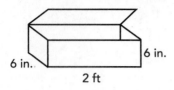

9. How many boxes like the one at the right can fit into the carton in the last problem?

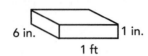

10. For the construction of a new building, a hole was dug 4 yards deep, 20 yards wide, and 30 yards long. Which of the following do you need to know to find out how many truckloads were needed to carry away all the dirt from the hole?

   (1) the diameter of the hole
   (2) the amount of dirt in each truckload
   (3) the number of hours the job required
   (4) the length of the truck
   (5) the amount of dirt left over at the site

11. The diagram at the right shows a large rectangular block with a cylindrical hole through it. Which of the following expresses the volume, in cubic feet, of the concrete that is required to construct the block?

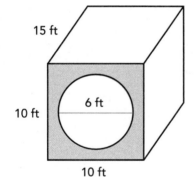

   (1) $15 \times 10 \times 10 - \pi \times 3^2 \times 15$
   (2) $10 \times 10 - \pi \times 3^2$
   (3) $15 \times 10 - \pi \times 3^2 \times 15$
   (4) $15 \times 10 - 3^2 \times 15$
   (5) $\pi \times 3^2 \times 15$

12. Which of the following represents the area of a circle with a diameter of 30 inches?

   (1) 30π
   (2) 60π
   (3) 90π
   (4) 225π
   (5) 900π

Answers are on page 421.

Triangles

You have already learned that a **triangle** is a plane (flat) figure with three sides. Each of the three points where the sides meet is called a **vertex**.

The sum of the three angles in a triangle is 180°.

The angles of a triangle are easy to understand if you start with a square. Each angle of a square is 90°. In the diagram at the right, a diagonal line cuts a square into two triangles. Each triangle has angles of 90° + 45° + 45° = 180°.

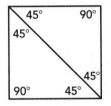

Following are descriptions and examples of the four most common triangles.

An **equilateral triangle** has three equal sides. Each angle is $\frac{1}{3}$ of 180°, or 60°.

Examples

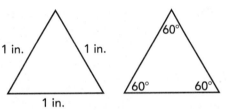

An **isosceles triangle** has two equal sides and two equal angles (called **base angles**). The angle with a different measurement from the base angles is called the **vertex angle**. The third side may be longer or shorter than either of the two equal sides.

Examples

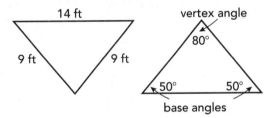

A **scalene triangle** has no equal sides and no equal angles.

Examples

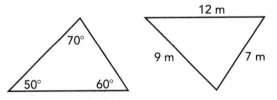

A **right triangle** has one right angle. The side opposite the right angle is called the **hypotenuse**. The other two sides are called **legs**.

Examples

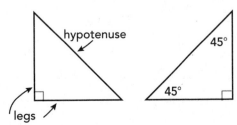

The symbol $\triangle$ stands for the word *triangle*. A side of a triangle is sometimes referred to by the two letters that form the endpoints of each side. For $\triangle ABC$, side BC is the hypotenuse. Sides AB and AC are the legs of this right triangle.

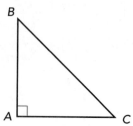

An angle of a triangle is sometimes referred to by the letter at the vertex of the angle. For triangle ABC, $\angle A$ is the right angle. Sometimes three letters refer to an angle. The letter of the vertex must be in the middle. For the triangle above, $\angle A$ is the same as $\angle BAC$ or $\angle CAB$.

Example 1   In triangle PQR, $\angle P = 35°$ and $\angle Q = 65°$. Find the measure of $\angle R$.

Step 1   Add the measure of $\angle P$ and $\angle Q$. $35° + 65° = 100°$

Step 2   Subtract the sum from $180°$. $180° - 100° = 80°$
The measure of $\angle R$ is equal to $80°$.

Use the memory key on the Casio *fx*-260 calculator to solve Example 1 easily.

Press [AC].

Press [3] [5] [+] [6] [5] [=].

The display should read [⎯⎯⎯⎯ 100.].

Press [M+] to save the number 100 into memory.

Then press [1] [8] [0] [−] [MR] [=].

[MR] stands for "memory recall." In this problem [MR] recalls "100," the sum of the two known angles, and subtracts that sum from 180.

The display should read [⎯⎯⎯⎯ 80.].

Press [ON] to clear the memory for the next problem.

Example 2   In triangle STU, $\angle S = 60°$ and $\angle T = 30°$. What kind of triangle is STU?

Step 1   Add the measure of $\angle S$ and $\angle T$. $60° + 30° = 90°$

Step 2   Subtract the sum from $180°$. The $180° - 90° = 90°$
measure of $\angle U = 90°$. A triangle STU is a right triangle.
with one right angle is a right triangle.

<u>Example 3</u>   What is the measure of ∠x in
the drawing at the right?

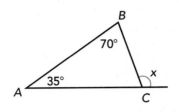

Step 1   Add the measure of ∠A and ∠B.   35° + 70° = 105°

Step 2   Subtract the sum from 180°.   180° − 105° = 75°
The measure of ∠C = 75°.

Step 3   Since ∠C and ∠x form a straight angle,   180° − 75° = 105°
subtract ∠C from 180°.
The measure of ∠x equals 105°.

Memorize the names of the four common types of triangles before you try
the next exercise.

TIP
If a triangle problem does not have a diagram, take the time to draw one.

EXERCISE 12

Directions: For problems 1–3, identify each triangle as equilateral, isosceles,
scalene, or right.

1.

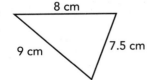

2.

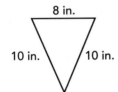

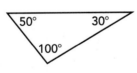

3.

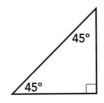

For problems 4–6, refer to △KLH at the right.

4. Find the measurement of ∠L.

5. What kind of triangle is △KLH?

6. Side KH is called the _____.

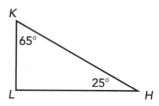

For problems 7 and 8, refer to △WXY at the right.

7. If ∠W = 65° and ∠X = 50°, what is the measurement of ∠Y?

8. What kind of triangle is △WXY?

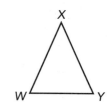

Solve each problem.

9. In triangle ABC, ∠A = 30° and ∠B = 60°. How many degrees are in ∠C?

10. What kind of triangle is △ABC in the last problem?

11. The vertex angle of an isosceles triangle measures 82°. How many degrees are there in each base angle?

12. Each base angle of an isosceles triangle measures 63°. How many degrees are there in the vertex angle?

13. In the triangle at the right, side DE measures 8 inches and side DF measures 5 inches. The perimeter of the triangle is 21 inches. What kind of triangle is DEF?

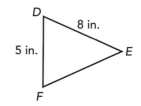

14. In triangle PQR, ∠P = 25° and ∠Q = 35°. What kind of triangle is △PQR?

15. In triangle XYZ, side XY is 4 inches long and side YZ is 5 inches long. The perimeter of the triangle is 16 inches. What kind of triangle is △XYZ?

16. What is the sum of the two acute angles in a right triangle?

17. Find the number of degrees in ∠x in the diagram at the right.

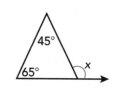

Answers are on page 421.

Similarity and Congruence

Similarity

When you say that two things are similar, you mean that they are alike in some ways, but they are not identical. In geometry **similar** figures have the same shape but different sizes. For example, the two triangles at the right are similar because their angles are the same size.

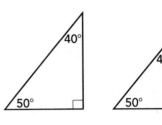

The **corresponding** (matching) sides of similar figures can be written as a proportion. The drawing at the right shows two similar rectangles.

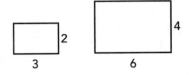

$$\frac{\text{length}}{\text{width}} \quad \frac{3}{2} = \frac{6}{4}$$

For the small rectangle, the ratio of the length to the width is 3:2. For the large rectangle, the ratio of the length to the width is 6:4, which reduces to 3:2. These two rectangles are similar because the ratios of their corresponding sides are equal.

--- **R U L E** ---

Two triangles are similar if
1. any two angles of one triangle are equal to two angles of the other triangle, or if
2. the sides of one triangle are proportional to the sides of the other triangle

---

Example 1   In triangle *DEF*, $\angle D = 50°$ and $\angle E = 75°$. In triangle *GHI*, $\angle G = 55°$ and $\angle I = 50°$. Are these triangles similar? Why, or why not?

Step 1   Find $\angle F$. Subtract the sum of $\angle D$ and $\angle E$ from 180°.

$$\begin{array}{r} 50° \\ +75° \\ \hline 125° \end{array} \qquad \begin{array}{r} 180° \\ -125° \\ \hline 55° = \angle F \end{array}$$

Step 2   Find $\angle H$. Subtract the sum of $\angle G$ and $\angle I$ from 180°.

$$\begin{array}{r} 55° \\ +50° \\ \hline 105° \end{array} \qquad \begin{array}{r} 180° \\ -105° \\ \hline 75° = \angle H \end{array}$$

Each triangle has angles of 50°, 55°, and 75°.
The triangles are similar because they have equal angles.

Example 2 Are the two triangles at the right similar? Tell why or why not.

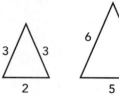

Step 1 Find the ratio of one long side to the short side of the small triangle.

long:short = 3:2

Step 2 Find the ratio of one long side to the short side of the large triangle. The triangles are *not* similar because the corresponding sides are not proportional.

long:short = 6:5

Remember: In similar triangles, *corresponding sides are opposite equal angles.*

Look at these two triangles.

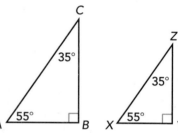

Side *AB* corresponds to side *XY* because both sides are across from 35° angles.

Side *BC* corresponds to side *YZ* because both sides are across from 55° angles.

Side *AC* corresponds to side *XZ* because both sides are across from 90° angles.

You can use the proportional relationship between corresponding sides to find a missing measurement in similar figures.

Example 3 In triangle *ABC*, *AB* = 9 ft and *BC* = 18 ft. In triangle *GHI*, *GH* = 5 ft. Find the length of *HI*.

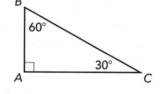
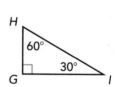

Step 1 The triangles are similar because each has angles of 30°, 60°, and 90°. Write a proportion with the corresponding sides of each triangle. Let *x* stand for the missing hypotenuse *HI*.

$$\frac{\text{short leg}}{\text{hypotenuse}} \quad \frac{9}{18} = \frac{5}{x}$$

Step 2 Write a statement that the cross products are equal.

$9x = 90$

Step 3 Divide both sides by 9. The length of *HI* is 10 feet.

$x = 10$

Example 4   A vertical yardstick casts
a 2-foot shadow. At the
same time a building
casts a 48-foot shadow.
How tall is the building?

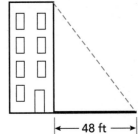

Step 1   Draw a picture that
shows the height and
shadow of each figure.

3 ft
|← 2 ft →|
|←—— 48 ft ——→|

Step 2   The triangles are similar because the angles
are equal. Each triangle has a 90° angle. The
other angles are equal because the sun casts
a shadow at the same angle on both the
yardstick and the building. Write a proportion
with the height of each figure and the length
of its shadow. Since the other measurements
are in feet, write the height of the yardstick as
3 feet.

Let x stand for the height of the building. $\dfrac{\text{height}}{\text{shadow}} \quad \dfrac{3}{2} = \dfrac{x}{48}$

Step 3   Write a statement that the cross products are equal. $2x = 144$

Step 4   Divide both sides by 2. The building is 72 feet tall. $x = 72$

EXERCISE 13

Directions: Solve each problem.

1. Are the rectangles at the
right similar? Tell why or
why not.

    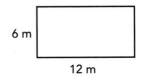

    6 m
    12 m
    1 m
    3 m

2. Are the rectangles at the
right similar? Tell why or
why not.

    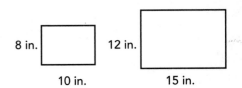

    8 in.
    10 in.
    12 in.
    15 in.

3. In triangle *MNO*, ∠*M* = 45° and ∠*N* = 85°. In triangle *PQR*,
    ∠*P* = 50° and ∠*Q* = 45°. Are these triangles similar? Tell
    why or why not.

4. In triangle *ABC*, ∠*A* = 60° and ∠*B* = 50°. In triangle *DEF*, ∠*D* = 50°
    and ∠*E* = 80°. Are these triangles similar? Tell why or why not.

5. Are the triangles at the right similar? Tell why or why not.

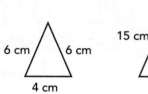
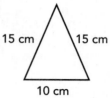

6. Are the triangles at the right similar? Tell why or why not.

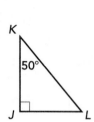
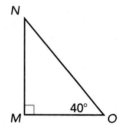

7. In triangle *JKL* above, side *JK* = 8 inches and side *JL* = 12 inches. In triangle *MNO*, side *MN* = 14 inches. Find the length of side *MO*.

8. In the diagram at the right, ∠*S* and ∠*W* are both right angles. Are the two triangles similar?

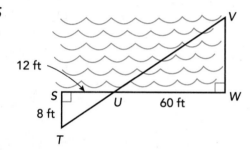

9. In problem 8, side *VW* is the distance across a river. Find the measure of *VW*.

10. In the diagram at the right, ∠*CDE* and ∠*CAB* are both right angles. Are triangles *CAB* and *CDE* similar? Tell why or why not.

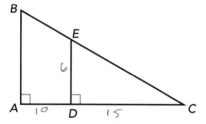

11. In problem 10, side *CD* = 15 inches, side *AD* = 10 inches, and side *DE* = 6 inches. Find the length of side *AB*.

12. The diagram at the right shows a 6-foot post with a 5-foot shadow as well as a tree with a 65-foot shadow. Which proportion below can be used to find height x of the tree?

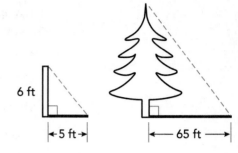

(1) $5:6 = x:65$
(2) $6:5 = x:65$
(3) $6:65 = x:5$
(4) $5:x = 6:65$
(5) Not enough information is given.

Answers are on page 421.

Congruence

Geometric figures are **congruent** if they have the same shape *and* the same size. If you place one figure on top of the other and they fit exactly, they are congruent.

The symbol $\cong$ means "is congruent to."

- The statement $AB \cong CD$ means that line segment AB and line segment CD have the same length.

- The statement $\angle A \cong \angle B$ means that $\angle A$ and $\angle B$ each have the same number of degrees.

The corresponding angles of congruent figures are equal, and the corresponding sides are equal. Remember that *corresponding* means "in the same position." For two congruent triangles there are six corresponding parts—three sides and three angles.

Triangle *ABC* and triangle *DEF* pictured below are congruent. The triangles have three pairs of congruent sides and three pairs of congruent angles.

congruent sides	congruent angles
$AB \cong DE$	$\angle A \cong \angle D$
$BC \cong EF$	$\angle B \cong \angle E$
$AC \cong DF$	$\angle C \cong \angle F$

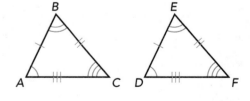

Notice the small curves at each angle and the small lines in the middle of each side. These marks indicate congruent parts.

Triangles are congruent if they meet any one of the three following conditions:

- **Angle Side Angle**
- **Side Angle Side**
- **Side Side Side**

ANGLE SIDE ANGLE (ASA) REQUIREMENT

Two triangles are congruent if two angles and a corresponding side of one triangle are the same as two angles and a corresponding side of the other triangle.

Example 1 The two triangles at the right are congruent because two angles and a corresponding side are the same.

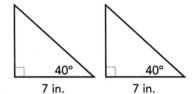

Example 2 The two triangles at the right are *not* congruent because the equal sides are not corresponding. The 5-foot side in the first triangle is opposite a 90° angle. The 5-foot side in the other triangle is opposite a 45° angle.

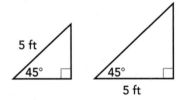

SIDE ANGLE SIDE (SAS) REQUIREMENT

Two triangles are congruent if two sides and a corresponding angle of one triangle are the same as two sides and a corresponding angle of the other triangle.

Example 3 The two triangles at the right are congruent because two sides and a corresponding angle are the same.

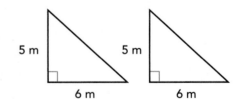

Example 4 The triangles at the right are *not* congruent because the equal sides are not corresponding.

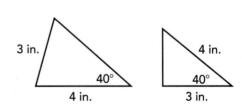

SIDE SIDE SIDE (SSS) REQUIREMENT

Two triangles are congruent if the three sides of one triangle equal the three sides of the other triangle.

Example 5   The two triangles at the right are congruent because the three sides in each triangle are the same.

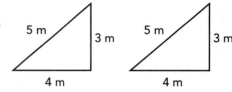

Example 6   The triangles at the right are *not* congruent because the three sides in one triangle are not the same as the three sides in the other triangle.

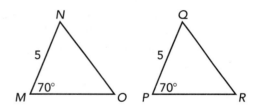

EXERCISE 14

Directions: Use the two triangles pictured below to answer problems 1–6.

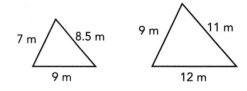

1. What side corresponds to *MN*?

2. What angle corresponds to ∠*O*?

3. What side corresponds to *PR*?

4. What angle corresponds to ∠*Q*?

5. In addition to the information given in the drawing, which of the following would be enough to satisfy the Side Angle Side (SAS) requirement for congruence?

    (1) ∠*N* ≅ ∠*R*
    (2) *MO* ≅ *PR*
    (3) *NO* ≅ *PR*

6. In addition to the information given in the drawing, which of the following would be enough to satisfy the Angle Side Angle (ASA) requirement for congruence?

    (1) *MN* ≅ *PR*
    (2) ∠*M* ≅ ∠*O*
    (3) ∠*N* ≅ ∠*Q*

Solve each problem.

7. In △DEF, ∠D = 90°, ∠E = 60°, and ∠F = 30°. In △GHI, ∠G = 90°, ∠H = 60°, and ∠I = 30°. Are these two triangles necessarily congruent? Tell why or why not.

8. Are the triangles at the right congruent? Tell why or why not.

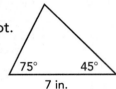 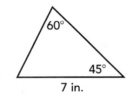

9. Are the triangles at the right congruent? Tell why or why not.

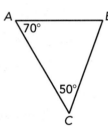 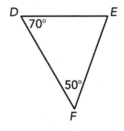

10. For the triangles at the right, which of the following conditions, along with the information given, is enough to guarantee that the triangles are congruent?

 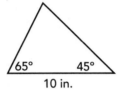

(1) AC ≅ DF

(2) ∠B ≅ ∠E

(3) AB ≅ EF

11. For the triangles at the right, which of the following conditions, along with the information given, is enough to guarantee that the triangles are congruent?

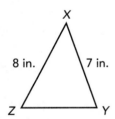 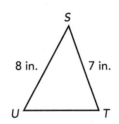

(1) ∠Y ≅ ∠U

(2) ∠X ≅ ∠S

(3) ∠Z ≅ ∠T

12. For the triangles at the right, which of the following conditions, along with the information given, is enough to guarantee that the triangles are congruent?

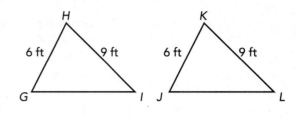

(1) $GI \cong JL$

(2) $GI \cong KL$

(3) $HI \cong JL$

Answers are on page 422.

Pythagorean Relationship

A Greek mathematician named Pythagoras discovered a special relationship among the sides of a right triangle. We call his discovery the **Pythagorean theorem**, or the **Pythagorean relationship**. With this relationship, you can find the length of any side of a right triangle if you know the lengths of the other two sides.

─────── **RULE** ───────

The Pythagorean relationship states:
The square of the hypotenuse of a right triangle is equal to the sum of the squares of the other two sides.

As a formula, the Pythagorean relationship is $a^2 + b^2 = c^2$, where a and b are the legs of a right triangle and c is the hypotenuse.

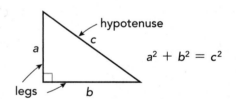

The diagram at the right shows a right triangle with legs of 3 and 4 and a hypotenuse of 5. The sum of the squares of the legs ($3^2 + 4^2 = 9 + 16 = 25$) equals the square of the hypotenuse ($5^2 = 25$).

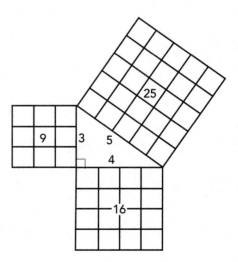

Example 1   Find the length of the hypotenuse of the triangle at the right.

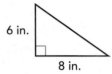

6 in.

8 in.

Step 1   Replace *a* with 6 and *b* with 8 in the formula for the Pythagorean relationship.

$a^2 + b^2 = c^2$
$6^2 + 8^2 = c^2$

Step 2   Evaluate the formula.

$36 + 64 = c^2$
$100 = c^2$

Step 3   The formula gives the hypotenuse squared. To find the hypotenuse, find the square root of 100. The hypotenuse is 10 inches.

$\sqrt{100} = c$
$10 = c$

To review finding a square root, see page 34.

You can use the Casio *fx*-260 calculator to find the hypotenuse in Example 1.

Press `AC`.

Press `6` `x²` `+` `8` `x²` `=`.

The display should read ☐ 100. ☐.

To find the square root of 100, press `SHIFT` `x²`.

The display should read ☐ 10. ☐.

If you know the length of the hypotenuse and the length of one leg of a right triangle, *subtract* the squares of the sides that are given. (You will learn more about solving equations in the next chapter.)

Example 2   Find the length of the missing leg in the right triangle at the right.

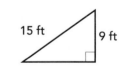

15 ft   9 ft

Step 1   Replace *b* with 9 and *c* with 15 in the formula for the Pythagorean relationship.

$a^2 + b^2 = c^2$
$a^2 + 9^2 = 15^2$

Step 2   Evaluate the formula.

$a^2 + 81 = 225$

Step 3   Subtract 81 from both sides of the equation.

$a^2 = 144$

Step 4   The formula gives the leg squared. To find the missing leg, find the square root of 144. The missing leg is 12 feet.

$a = \sqrt{144}$
$a = 12$

TIP
In some problems you will have to recognize that a figure is a right triangle. For example, problems that mention north, south, east, or west refer to the directions that are usually shown on a map. *North* means up, and *south* means down. *East* means to the right, and *west* means to the left. Drawing a picture may help you see that the problem involves a right triangle.

Example 3 A boat sails 20 miles east of the port and then 15 miles south to an island. How far is the boat from the port if you measure the distance in a straight line?

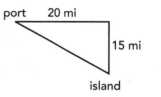

Step 1 Make a drawing. East is to the right, and south is down. Notice that the distance from the island to the port is the hypotenuse of a right triangle.

Step 2 Replace *a* with 20 and *b* with 15 in the formula for the Pythagorean relationship.

$$a^2 + b^2 = c^2$$
$$20^2 + 15^2 = c^2$$

Step 3 Evaluate the formula.

$$400 + 225 = c^2$$
$$625 = c^2$$

Step 4 The formula gives the hypotenuse squared. To find the hypotenuse, find the square root of 625. The boat is 25 miles from the port.

$$\sqrt{625} = c$$
$$25 = c$$

EXERCISE 15

Directions: Use your calculator to solve each problem.

1. Find the hypotenuse of the triangle at the right.

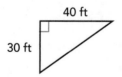

2. One leg of a right triangle measures 10 inches. The other leg measures 24 inches. Find the length of the hypotenuse.

3. In triangle *XYZ* at the right, side *XY* = 12 inches and side *YZ* = 5 inches. Find the length of *XZ*.

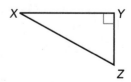

4. What is the length of the hypotenuse of a right triangle whose legs measures 12 yards and 16 yards?

5. Marita drove 60 miles west from Belleville to Mactown and then 45 miles south to Shreveport. She returned to Belleville on Route 3. How far is it from Shreveport to Belleville along Route 3?

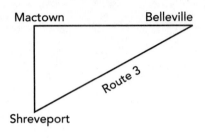

For problems 6–10, choose the correct answer.

6. One leg of a right triangle measures 18 yards. The hypotenuse measures 30 yards. Which expression gives the length of the other leg?

   (1) $\sqrt{18 + 30}$
   (2) $\sqrt{30 - 18}$
   (3) $18^2 + 30^2$
   (4) $30^2 - 18^2$
   (5) $\sqrt{30^2 - 18^2}$

7. In triangle *ABC* at the right, *AB* = 16 feet and *AC* = 34 feet. Find the length in feet of side *BC*.

   (1) 20
   (2) 25
   (3) 30
   (4) 32
   (5) 40

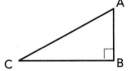

8. A 17-foot ladder just touches the bottom of a window. The bottom of the ladder is 8 feet from the base of the building. Find the distance, in feet, from the ground to the bottom of the window.

   (1) 12
   (2) 15
   (3) 18
   (4) 20
   (5) 25

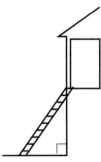

9. Louie drove 48 miles directly north and then 36 miles directly west. Find the shortest distance in miles from the point where he ended up to his starting point.

(1) 24

(2) 36

(3) 48

(4) 60

(5) 72

10. On a bike trip Manny rode 15 miles directly west and then 36 miles directly south. Which of the following expresses the shortest distance in miles from the point where he started to the point where he ended his trip?

(1) $2(15) + 2(36)$

(2) 15×36

(3) $\sqrt{15^2 + 36^2}$

(4) $\sqrt{15 + 36}$

(5) $\frac{15 + 36}{2}$

Answers are on page 422.

Basic Geometry Review

PART I

Directions: Use a calculator to solve any of the problems in this section, and use any formulas on page 439 that will help you.

For problems 1–8, solve each problem.

1. The length of a rectangle is 12 inches, and the width is $4\frac{1}{4}$ inches. Find the perimeter of the rectangle.

2. Find the number of degrees in $\angle AOB$.

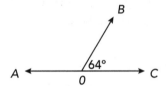

3. Find the perimeter of the triangle at the right.

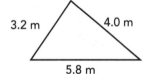

3.2 m   4.0 m
5.8 m

4. To the nearest foot, what is the circumference of a circle with a diameter of 30 feet?

5. Find the volume of a rectangular container that is 15 inches long, $3\frac{1}{2}$ inches wide, and 10 inches high.

6. To the nearest square inch, what is the area of a circle with a radius of 7 inches?

7. A side of a square measures 3.2 meters. What is the perimeter of the square?

8. What is the area of a rectangle with a length of 12.5 cm and a width of 7.4 cm?

For problems 9 and 10, fill in each answer on the corresponding number grid.

9. Find the area in square inches of a square that measures $\frac{3}{4}$ inch on each side.

10. What is the area of the triangle at the right?

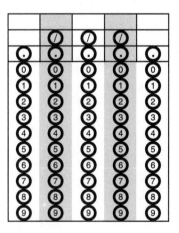

2.7 cm
4.0 cm

For problems 11–13, refer to the following information.

The diagram below shows the plan of a new pool at the Uptown Community Center. The depth of the pool will be 6 feet throughout. The edge of the pool will be surrounded by ceramic tile strips that are each 6 inches long.

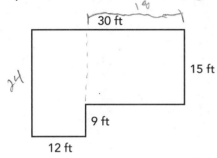

11. What is the minimum number of ceramic tile strips that are required to completely surround the edge of the pool?

(1) 96

(2) 108

(3) 216

(4) 432

(5) Not enough information is given.

12. Find the area, in square yards, of the bottom of the pool.

(1) 31

(2) 62

(3) 124

(4) 186

(5) 532

13. If the pool is filled to its limit, how many cubic feet of water will it hold?

(1) 3348

(2) 2232

(3) 1674

(4) 1116

(5) Not enough information is given.

For problems 14 and 15, choose the correct answer.

14. The sails of the two boats below are similar triangles. Find the height, in feet, of the small sail.

(1) 7.2

(2) 3.6

(3) 2.5

(4) 1.8

(5) 0.9

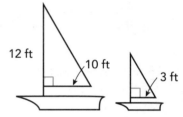

15. In the rectangle below, side *BC* measures 36 inches and diagonal line *AC* measures 39 inches. Find the length, in inches, of side *AB*.

(1) 15

(2) 18

(3) 30

(4) 33

(5) 42

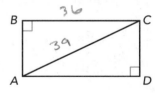

PART II

Directions: Solve the following problems without a calculator.

16. The distance around a circle is called the _____.

17. If a circle has a diameter of 30 inches, what is the radius?

Use the illustration below to answer problems 18–20.

18. Which angle is vertical to ∠e?

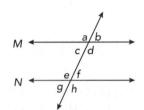

Lines M and N are parallel.

19. If ∠b = 62°, what is the measure of ∠d?

20. List all the acute angles in the diagram.

For problems 21–28, choose the correct answer to each problem.

21. Which of the following describes the pair of lines at the right?

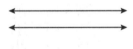

(1) perpendicular
(2) horizontal and parallel
(3) parallel but neither vertical nor horizontal
(4) vertical and parallel
(5) intersecting but not perpendicular

22. What type of angle is ∠x shown in the diagram at the right?

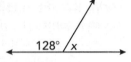

(1) acute
(2) right
(3) obtuse
(4) straight
(5) reflex

23. Which of the following represents the perimeter of the rectangle at the right?

(1) 3.5×1.8
(2) $4(3.5)$
(3) $\frac{3.5 + 1.8}{2}$
(4) $2(3.5) + 2(1.8)$
(5) $(3.5)^2 + (1.8)^2$

24. Sharon wants to put fencing around the rectangular garden in her yard. The garden measures 20 feet by 8 feet. She wants to leave a 4-foot opening for a walkway into the garden. Which of the following expressions gives the number of feet of fencing that she needs?

(1) $20 + 8$
(2) $(2 \times 20) + (2 \times 8)$
(3) $(2 \times 20) + (2 \times 8) - 4$
(4) $(20 \times 8) - 4$
(5) $2(20 - 8)$

25. Which of the following represents the area, in square inches, of the figure shown?

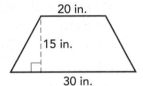

(1) 15 + 20 + 30

(2) 2(15 + 20 + 30)

(3) $\frac{1}{2}$ (15 + 20) × 30

(4) $\frac{1}{2}$ (20 + 30) × 15

(5) 15(20² + 30²)

26. Which of the following represents the volume, in cubic centimeters, of the cylinder?.

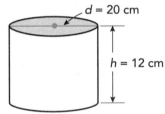

(1)   600π

(2) 1200π

(3) 2400π

(4) 3600π

(5) 4200π

27. In triangle XYZ, $\angle X = 33°$ and $\angle Y = 57°$. What kind of triangle is $\triangle XYZ$?

(1) equilateral

(2) isosceles

(3) obtuse

(4) right

(5) both isosceles and right

28. For the triangles below, $\angle G \cong \angle J$ and $\angle I \cong \angle L$. Which of the conditions listed below, together with the given information, is enough to guarantee that the triangles are congruent?

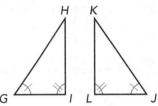

(1) $\angle H \cong \angle K$

(2) $\angle G \cong \angle K$

(3) $GI \cong JL$

(4) $GI \cong HI$

(5) Not enough information is given.

For problems 29 and 30, fill in each answer on the corresponding number grid.

29. In the illustration at the right, $\angle a = 65.5°$. How many degrees are there in $\angle d$?

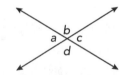

30. What is the minimum number of 2-inch by 2-inch square tiles that are required to cover a rectangular tabletop that is 30 inches wide and 40 inches long?

Answers are on page 423.

You should have gotten at least 24 problems right on this exercise. If you did not get 24 right, review your geometry skills before you go on. If you got 24 or more right, correct any problem you got wrong. Then go on to the next chapter.

Chapter 10

The Basics of Algebra

Algebra extends the skills you have mastered in arithmetic. Algebra uses negative as well as positive numbers. Algebra also uses letters or symbols to represent unknown numbers called **variables.**

In this chapter you will learn to perform basic operations with signed numbers, to solve equations and inequalities, to write algebraic expressions, and to use equations to solve word problems.

Working with Signed Numbers

The Number Line

The number line pictured at the right represents all the numbers you have worked with in arithmetic. Proper fractions are between 0 and 1. Mixed numbers fit between the whole numbers. Points on this number line represent the numbers $1\frac{1}{2}$ and 4.8. Except for zero, all the numbers on this line are **positive numbers.** Positive numbers are numbers greater than zero. The arrow at the right end means that the numbers go on and on.

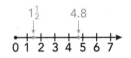

Algebra extends the set of numbers to include numbers less than zero. These are called **negative numbers.** The number line below shows both positive and negative numbers.

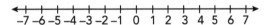

The arrows at both ends of the number line mean that the positive and negative numbers go on and on. Positive numbers are to the right of zero, and negative numbers are to the left. Zero is neither positive nor negative.

- A number on the number line is *greater than* any number to its left.

- A number on the number line is *less than* any number to its right.

TIP
Positive numbers do not have to be written with a plus sign (+). The number 8 is understood to be +8. Negative numbers, however, must have a minus sign (−).

<u>Example</u>   Which is greater, –5 or +3?

Since +3 is to the right of –5, the number +3 is greater.

Remember that the symbol < means "is less than." The symbol > means "is greater than." And the symbol = means "is equal to."

Think about the following examples:

– 6 < +3 because – 6 is to the left of +3 on a horizontal number line.

+10 > −12 because +10 is to the right of −12 on a horizontal number line.

Absolute value is the distance from a number to zero on the number line. Absolute value is neither positive nor negative. The absolute value of −5 is 5. The symbol for absolute value is | |. The statement |−5| = 5 means "the absolute value of negative 5 is 5." The statement |+5| = 5 means "the absolute value of positive 5 is 5."

EXERCISE 1

Directions: Use the number line below to tell which letter corresponds to each of the following numbers. The first problem is done as an example.

1. +6 = J   −3 $-6\frac{1}{2}$ −8 $+\frac{2}{3}$

2. $\frac{5}{4}$ $+\frac{16}{3}$ 2.75   −3.5   −0.2

For problems 3–5, fill in each blank with the symbol < for "is less than," the symbol > for "is greater than," or the symbol = for "is equal to."

3. −9 ____ −2   +3 ____ −5   −1 ____ +1

4.   5 ____ +5   12 ____ −3   −1 ____ −2

5. +8 ____ −8   −7 ____ −10   2 ____ −3

6. Which has the greater value, |− 6| or |−8| ?

7. Which has the greater value, +3 or −4?

Answers are on page 424.

Adding Signed Numbers

On a horizontal number line, a positive sign (+) means moving to the right. A negative sign (−) means moving to the left.

Example 1 What is (+3) + (+2)?

Start at +3 and move 2 units to the right on the number line. The sum is +5.

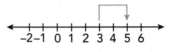

Example 2 What is −4 +(−1)?

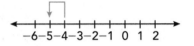

Start at −4 and move 1 unit to the left on the number line. The sum is −5.

Example 3 Find the sum of +2 +(−5).

Start at +2 and move 5 units to the left on the number line. The sum is −3.

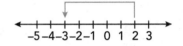

──────── R U L E ────────

To add two signed numbers, follow these steps:
1. If the signs are the same, add and give the total the sign of the numbers.
2. If the signs are different, subtract and give the total the sign of the number with the greater absolute value.

Example 4 Find (−16) + (−8).

Step 1 Since the numbers have the same signs, find their sum.   (−16) + (−8) = −24

Step 2 Since they are both negative numbers, the answer is negative.

Notice the use of signs in the last example. The + sign between (−16) and (−8) means to add. The problem could also be written as −16 − 8. This is also an addition problem.

<u>Example 5</u> $+8 + (-15) =$

Step 1   Since the numbers have different signs, subtract. $+8 + (-15) = -7$

Step 2   Since -15 has a greater absolute value than $+8$, make the answer negative.

RULE

To add more than two signed numbers, follow these steps:
1. Add the positive numbers and make the sum positive.
2. Add the negative numbers and make the sum negative.
3. Find the difference between the two sums and give the answer the sign of the sum with the greater absolute value.

<u>Example 6</u> $(-9) + (10) + (-8) + (+4) =$

Step 1   Add the positive numbers. $+10 + 4 = +14$

Step 2   Add the negative numbers. $-9 - 8 = -17$

Step 3   Find the difference between the two sums. Since -17 has a greater absolute value than $+14$, the answer is negative. $+14 - 17 = -3$

EXERCISE 2

Directions: Solve each addition problem.

1. $-9 - 3 =$	$+7 - 15 =$	$-32 + 15 =$
2. $+8 - 6 =$	$+12 + 1 =$	$-7 - 13 =$
3. $+11 - 24 =$	$+16 - 5 =$	$-13 - 14 =$
4. $+6 + (-11) =$	$+14 + (-14) =$	$-8 + (-7) =$
5. $(-12) + (-13) =$	$(+8) + (-7) =$	$(-9) + (+8) =$
6. $+5 - 8 + 9 =$	$+8 - 6 - 5 =$	
7. $-18 - 2 + 6 =$	$-3 - 9 - 4 =$	
8. $(-9) + (-4) + (+8) =$	$(-1) + (-8) + (+6) =$	
9. $(-10) + (-3) + (-8) =$	$(+7) + (+11) + (-2) =$	

10. At 5:00 P.M. the temperature was −10°. By 8:00 P.M. the temperature had dropped another 4 degrees. Which of the following represents the 8:00 P.M. temperature as a signed numbers problem?

(1) $+10 - 4 = +6$

(2) $+10 + 4 = +14$

(3) $-10 - 4 = -14$

Answers are on page 424.

Subtracting Signed Numbers

Subtracting a number means adding its opposite. On a number line **opposite** means "on the other side of zero." For example, the opposite of 5 is −5. Subtracting 5 from a number is the same as adding −5.

--- R U L E ---

To subtract signed numbers, follow these steps:
1. Change the sign of the number being subtracted and drop the subtraction sign.
2. Follow the rules for adding signed numbers.

Example 1   What is $(-8) - (+3)$?

Step 1   The minus sign before $(+3)$ means that $+3$ is being subtracted. Change $+3$ to -3 and drop the subtraction sign. $(-8) - (+3)$

Step 2   Since both signs are now the same, add the numbers and make the sum negative. $-8 - 3 = -11$

Example 2   Find $(-10) - (-2)$.

Step 1   The minus sign before (-2) means that -2 is being subtracted. Change -2 to $+2$ and drop the subtraction sign. $(-10) - (-2)$

Step 2   Since the signs are now different, find the difference between the two numbers. Make the answer negative since -10 has a greater absolute value than $+2$. $-10 + 2 = -8$

Example 3   Simplify $(+6) - (-4) + (-2) - (+5)$.

Step 1   The minus signs before (-4) and $(+5)$ mean that -4 and $+5$ are being subtracted. Change -4 to $+4$ and change $+5$ to -5. Then drop the subtraction signs.

$(+6) - (-4) + (-2) - (+5) =$
$+ 6 + 4 - 2 - 5$

Step 2   Find the sum of the positive numbers. $+6 + 4 = +10$

Step 3   Find the sum of the negative numbers. $-2 - 5 = -7$

Step 4   Since the signs are now different, find the difference between the two numbers. Make the answer positive since $+10$ has the greater absolute value.

$+10 - 7 = +3$

EXERCISE 3

Directions: Solve each problem.

1. $(+6) - (+4) =$ $(-8) - (+7) =$ $(-9) - (-8) =$

2. $(+10) - (-9) =$ $(+8) - (7) =$ $(-9) - (-9) =$

3. $(-10) - (+12) =$ $(+6) - (-7) =$ $(-11) - (-8) =$

4. $(+20) - (-3) =$ $(-18) - (+4) =$ $(+5) - (-1) =$

5. $(-11) + (-3) - (-6) =$ $(+6) - (-3) + (-2) =$

6. $(-9) - (+4) - (+10) =$ $(-15) - (20) + (+6) =$

7. $(-8) + (-13) - (+6) =$ $(-3) + (-4) - (-5) - (-6) =$

8. At dawn the temperature was 7° above zero. By dusk the temperature had dropped to $-17°$. Which of the following represents the temperature drop from dawn to dusk as a signed numbers problem?

   (1) $-17 + 7 = -10$
   (2) $(-17) - (+7) = -17 - 7 = -24$
   (3) $(-17) - (-7) = -17 + 7 = -10$

9. In March Andy owed his brother Luis $120. In April Andy borrowed another $50 from Luis. As a signed numbers problem, which of the following represents the amount that Andy owed his brother in April?

   (1) $(-\$120) - (-\$50) = -\$120 + \$50 = -\$70$
   (2) $(-\$120) + (-\$50) = -\$120 - \$50 = -\$170$
   (3) $(-\$120) + (+\$50) = -\$120 + \$50 = -\$70$

10. In May Mary owed her sister Martha $200. In June Mary paid Martha $75. As a signed numbers problem, which of the following represents the amount that Mary owed her sister in June?

    (1) $(-\$200) + (+\$75) = -\$200 + \$75 = -\$125$
    (2) $(-\$200) - (+\$75) = -\$200 - \$75 = -\$275$
    (3) $(+\$200) - (+\$75) = +\$200 - \$75 = +\$125$

Answers are on page 425.

Multiplying Signed Numbers

Before learning the rules for multiplying signed numbers, study the following applications of multiplying signed numbers.

If you gain 2 pounds a week for 5 weeks, you will weigh 10 pounds *more* than you weigh now. In algebra this is $(+2)(+5) = +10$.

If you lose 2 pounds a week for 5 weeks, you will weigh 10 pounds *less* than you weigh now. In algebra this is $(-2)(+5) = -10$.

If you have been gaining 2 pounds a week for 5 weeks, you weighed 10 pounds less five weeks ago. In algebra this is $(+2)(-5) = -10$.

If you have been losing 2 pounds a week for 5 weeks, you weighed 10 pounds more 5 weeks ago. In algebra this is $(-2)(-5) = +10$.

The pattern to these examples is simple.

─── **RULE** ───

To multiply two signed numbers, follow these steps:
1. Multiply the two numbers.
2. If the signs of the two numbers are alike, make the product positive.
3. If the signs of the two numbers are different, make the product negative.

<u>Example 1</u>   What is the product of (-8) and (-7)?

Since the signs are the same, the answer is positive. $(-8)(-7) = +56$

Example 2   What is $(12)(-3)$?

Since the signs are different, the answer is negative.

$(12)(-3) = -36$

Example 3   Find $-3 \cdot 10$.

Since the signs are different, the answer is negative.

$-3 \cdot 10 = -30$

——————————————— R U L E ———————————————

To find the product of more than two signed numbers, follow these steps:
1.   Multiply all the numbers together.
2.   If the problem has an even number of negative signs, the final product is positive.
3.   If the problem has an odd number of negative signs, the final product is negative.

Example 4   What is $(-6)(+2)(-4)$?

Step 1   Multiply $6 \times 2 = 12$. Then multiply $12 \times 4 = 48$. $(-6)(+2)(-4) = +48$

Step 2   Since there is an even number of negative signs (two), the answer is positive.

Example 5   Find $(-2)(-3)(-7)$.

Step 1   Multiply $2 \times 3 = 6$. Then multiply $6 \times 7 = 42$. $(-2)(-3)(-7) = -42$

Step 2   Since there is an odd number of negative signs (three), the answer is negative.

EXERCISE 4

Directions: Solve each problem. Use a calculator whenever needed.

1. $(-2)(+9) =$ $(-6)(-6) =$ $(+5)(-9) =$

2. $(+8)(3) =$ $(-10)(7) =$ $(+18)(-2) =$

3. $-7 \cdot -4 =$ $24 \cdot -\frac{1}{2} =$ $-0.1 \cdot -6 =$

4. $-\frac{3}{4} \cdot 12 =$ $18 \cdot \frac{2}{3} =$ $-11 \cdot -5 =$

5. $(-7)(6)(-2) =$ $(+5)(+4)(-2) =$

6. $(4)(-2)(-1)(-6) =$ $(10)(-\frac{1}{2})(3)(-1) =$

7. $(2)(-3)(5)(-\frac{1}{3}) =$ $8(-3)(5)(\frac{1}{4}) =$

8. $(-6)^2 =$ $(-5)^3 =$

9. The Sunshine Daycare Center has been enrolling 3 new children every month. As a signed numbers problem, which expression below represents how many fewer children were in the school 6 months ago?

    (1) $(+3)(+6) = +18$
    (2) $(-3)(-6) = +18$
    (3) $(+3)(-6) = -18$

10. Calvin spent $20 a week on lottery tickets for 6 weeks. As a signed numbers problem, which of the following represents the amount that Calvin spent on lottery tickets?

    (1) $(-6)(-\$20) = +\$120$
    (2) $(6)(-\$20) = -\$120$
    (3) $(-6)(\$20) = -\$120$

Answers are on page 425.

Dividing Signed Numbers

The rule for dividing signed numbers is similar to the rules for multiplying signed numbers.

──────────────── R U L E ────────────────

To divide two signed numbers, follow these steps:
1. Divide or reduce the numbers.
2. If the signs are alike, make the quotient positive.
3. If the signs are different, make the quotient negative.

──

Example 1   What is $+30/-6$?

Divide 30 by 6. Since the signs are different, $+30/-6 = -5$
the quotient is negative.

Example 2   What is $\frac{-8}{-12}$?

Divide 8 and 12 by 4. Since the signs are alike, $\frac{-8}{-12} = \frac{2}{3}$
the quotient is positive.

When a problem does not divide evenly, the answer can be either a mixed number or an improper fraction.

Example 3   What is $\frac{-28}{-12}$?

Divide 28 by 12. Since the signs are alike, the quotient is positive. $\frac{-28}{-12} = 2\frac{4}{12} = 2\frac{1}{3}$ or $\frac{7}{3}$

For the last problem, you could first reduce $\frac{-28}{-12}$ by dividing the numerator and denominator by 4.

EXERCISE 5

Directions: Solve each problem. Use a calculator whenever needed.

1. $\frac{-40}{-20} =$ $\frac{-12}{+6} =$ $\frac{72}{-9} =$

2. $\frac{+16}{-24} =$ $\frac{-15}{+5} =$ $\frac{30}{-36} =$

3. $\frac{-108}{-9} =$ $\frac{-48}{-60} =$ $\frac{+65}{-5} =$

4. $\frac{-63}{+35} =$ $\frac{75}{-100} =$ $\frac{-15}{-150} =$

5. The temperature has dropped 20 degrees in the last 5 hours. As a signed numbers problem, which expression represents the average drop in temperature each hour?

   (1) $\frac{-20}{5} = -4$

   (2) $\frac{-20}{-5} = +4$

   (3) $\frac{+20}{+5} = +4$

6. Dewayne lost 15 pounds over a 5-week period. As a signed numbers problem, which of the following represents his average weekly weight loss?

   (1) $\frac{15}{5} = 3$

   (2) $\frac{-15}{5} = -3$

   (3) $\frac{-15}{-5} = +3$

7. Holly owns shares of Acme Electronics stock. In the last quarter of the year the value of her stock dropped $450. Each share of stock dropped $1.50. As a signed numbers problem, which of the following represents a calculation of the number of shares Holly owns?

   (1) $\frac{\$450}{-\$1.50} = -300$

   (2) $\frac{-\$450}{\$1.50} = -300$

   (3) $\frac{-\$450}{-\$1.50} = 300$

Answers are on page 425.

Mixed Signed Numbers Problems

When you worked with whole numbers, you learned to solve problems according to an **order of operations** (page 43). Signed numbers can be combined in the same order.

ORDER OF OPERATIONS

When solving a problem, follow these steps in order:

1. operations in grouping symbols, such as parentheses or the fraction bar
2. powers and roots, from left to right
3. multiplication and division, from left to right
4. addition and subtraction, from left to right

Remember the acronym: <u>P</u>lease <u>E</u>xcuse <u>M</u>y <u>D</u>ear <u>A</u>unt <u>S</u>ally.

Example 1 Simplify the expression $(-4)(-2) - (5)(-3)$.

Step 1 Do the two multiplications first.

$$(-4)(-2) - (5)(-3) = \\ +8 - (-15)$$

Step 2 Change -15 to $+15$ and add.

$$+8 + 15 = +23$$

Example 2 Simplify $3(5 - 12)$.

Step 1 Combine the numbers inside parentheses.

$$3(5 - 12) \\ 3(-7)$$

Step 2 Multiply 3 and -7.

$$3(-7) = -21$$

EXERCISE 6

Directions: Simplify each expression. Use a calculator whenever needed.

1. $-4(13 - 8) =$ $\qquad$ $-5 + (-8)(-6) =$

2. $(12)(-2) + (-1)(-15) =$ $\qquad$ $(-8)^2 - (-5)^2 =$

3. $\frac{-8}{4} + \frac{15}{-3} =$ $\qquad$ $(-3)(5) + \frac{6}{-2} =$

4. $-6 + \frac{30}{5} =$ $\qquad$ $\frac{-36}{9} - (-10) =$

5. $(-2)(-8) + (-9)(7) =$ $\qquad$ $(15)(-1) - 9 =$

6. $(-7)(+20) + (10)^2 =$ $\qquad$ $2(-4 + 3 - 7) =$

7. $9(8 - 12) =$ $\qquad$ $\frac{24 - 6}{-2} =$

8. $\sqrt{29 - 4} - (-3) =$ $\qquad$ $\frac{15 - 3}{-4 - 2} =$

9. $\dfrac{(-20) - (-21)}{5 - 7} =$

$\dfrac{-96}{-8} + (-3)^2 =$

10. $\dfrac{+9 - 7 - 5}{-3} =$

$(8 - 14)^2 - (-6)^2 =$

Answers are on page 426.

Simplifying Algebraic Expressions

In algebra, letters often stand for numbers you want to find. These letters are called **variables,** or **unknowns.**

The illustration at the right shows a triangle with sides of $x + 3$, $2x$, and $2x + 4$. The perimeter of the triangle can be represented by the following expression:

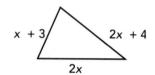

$x + 3 + 2x + 2x + 4$

The expression above has five **terms.** There are three x-terms, or terms using variables, and two numerical terms. To **simplify** the expression, combine the *like* terms according to the rules for combining signed numbers. In other words, combine x-terms with x-terms and numerical terms with numerical terms.

Remember that x is the same as $1x$.

Example 1   Simplify the expression $x + 3 + 2x + 2x + 4$.

Step 1   Combine all the x-terms. $x + 2x + 2x = 5x$

Step 2   Combine all the numerical terms. $3 + 4 = 7$

The simplified expression is $5x + 7$. $5x + 7$

To **evaluate** an expression, first substitute a value for the unknown. Evaluating an expression is like using a formula.

Example 2   What is the perimeter of the triangle pictured above if $x = 9$?

Substitute 9 for x in the expression $5x + 7$. $5(9) + 7 =$
The perimeter of the triangle is 52. $45 + 7 = 52$

For the last example, you can also substitute $x = 9$ into the original expression for the perimeter.

$x + 3 + 2x + 2x + 4 =$

$9 + 3 + 2(9) + 2(9) + 4 =$

$9 + 3 + 18 + 18 + 4 = 52$

Again, the perimeter is 52. The expression $x + 3 + 2x + 2x + 4$ and the expression $5x + 7$ have the same value when $x = 9$. The two expressions are called **equivalent expressions.**

EXERCISE 7

Directions: For problems 1–4, simplify each expression.

1. $6m + m =$ $5y - y =$ $7p - 6p =$

2. $4a - 3 + 7a - 1 =$ $x + 5x - 3x =$ $8z - 5 + 2z - 9 =$

3. $8 + 3y - 2 + 7y =$ $7c - 4 + 5 - c =$ $6k + 7 - 5k =$

4. $10s + 4s - 6s =$ $4n + 3 + n - 1 =$ $6 + 8x + 5 - 9x =$

For problems 5–8, solve each problem.

5. Write and simplify an expression for the length from *A* to *B* of the line segment at the right.

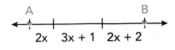

6. If the value of *x* is 4, what is the length from *A* to *B* in the last problem?

7. Write and simplify an expression for the perimeter of the rectangle pictured at the right.

8. If the value of *y* is 6, what is the perimeter of the rectangle in the last problem?

Answers are on page 426.

Simplifying Expressions with Parentheses

The illustration at the right shows two squares. Each side of the smaller square is *x*. The perimeter of the smaller square is 4*x*. Each side of the larger square is *x* + 2. The perimeter of the larger square is 4(*x* + 2).

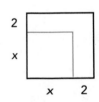

According to the **distributive property** (page 41), multiplication is distributive over addition and subtraction. In symbols, $a(b + c) = ab + ac$, and $a(b - c) = ab - ac$.

Remember that a number standing next to a letter means to multiply: $3a$ means 3 times a.

Example 1   Simplify the expression 4(*x* + 2).

Multiply both *x* and 2 by 4. $4(x + 2) = \mathbf{4x + 8}$

Example 2   What is the value of 4*x* + 8 when *x* = 3?

Substitute 3 for *x*. $4(3) + 8 = 12 + \mathbf{8} = 20$

Example 3   Simplify the expression $3(2y - 1) + 5$.

Step 1   Multiply both $2y$ and -1 by 3. $6y - 3 + 5$

Step 2   Combine the like (numerical) terms. $6y + 2$

EXERCISE 8

Directions: For problems 1–5, simplify each expression.

1. $5(m + 2) =$ $3(a - 1) + 4 =$

2. $2y + 3(y - 5) =$ $2x + 1 + 5(x - 1) =$

3. $9 + 7(2a + 3) =$ $6(5a - 1) + 11 =$

4. $3c + 5(2c + 1) =$ $8n - 2(3n + 1) =$

5. $10(p + 3) - 8p =$ $s + 6(2s - 3) =$

Solve each problem.

6. Which expression represents the area
    of the rectangle pictured at the right?

    (1) $x + 2$
    (2) $x + 3$
    (3) $x + 6$
    (4) $3x + 2$
    (5) $3x + 6$

7. What is the area of the rectangle in the last problem when $x = 9$?

Answers are on page 426.

Solving One–Step Equations

An equation is a statement that says two amounts
are equal. The equals sign ($=$) separates the two sides
of an equation. Think of an equation as an old-fashioned
balance with weights on one side and apples on the other.
If you remove an apple from one side, you must remove
an equivalent weight on the other side in order to keep
the scale balanced.

Look at the equation $m + 43 = 74$. The equation means "Some number called m plus 43 is equal to 74." The goal in solving this equation is to get the unknown m alone on one side of the equation. In an equation with one operation (in this case, addition), you can get the unknown to stand alone by subtracting 43. But to keep the equation balanced, you must subtract 43 from both sides.

To solve an equation with one operation, perform the **inverse,** or **opposite,** operation on both sides of the equation. You will get a statement that says "unknown = value" or "value = unknown."

- The inverse of addition is subtraction.

- The inverse of subtraction is addition.

- The inverse of multiplication is division.

- The inverse of division is multiplication.

Example 1   Solve for the unknown in $m + 43 = 74$.

Step 1   43 is added to the unknown.
The inverse of addition is subtraction.
Subtract 43 from both sides of the equation. The solution is $m = 31$.

$$m + 43 = 74$$
$$\underline{\;\; -43 \;\; -43}$$
$$m \quad\quad = 31$$

Step 2   To check, substitute the value of the unknown into the original equation. Substitute 31 for m. Since both sides of the equation equal 74, the answer $m = 31$ is correct.

$$31 + 43 = 74$$

Example 2   Solve and check the equation $39 = y - 15$.

Step 1   15 is subtracted from the unknown.
The inverse of subtraction is addition.
Add 15 to both sides of the equation.
The solution is $54 = y$.

$$39 = y - 15$$
$$\underline{+15 \quad\quad + 15}$$
$$54 = y$$

Step 2   To check, substitute 54 for y in the original equation.

$$39 = 54 - 15$$

Example 3   Solve and check the equation $6x = 132$.

Step 1   The unknown is multiplied by 6.
The inverse of multiplication is division.
Divide both sides of the equation by 6.
The solution is $x = 22$.

$$6x = 132$$
$$\frac{6x}{6} = \frac{132}{6}$$
$$x = 22$$

Step 2   To check, substitute 22 for x.

$$6(22) = 132$$

Example 4   Solve and check the equation $10 = \frac{w}{7}$.

Step 1   The unknown is divided by 7. $10 = \frac{w}{7}$
The inverse of division is multiplication.
Multiply both sides of the equation by 7. $7(10) = \frac{w}{7}(7)$

The solution is $70 = w$. $70 = w$

Step 2   To check, substitute 70 for w. $10 = \frac{70}{7}$

TIP

With one–step equations, it is often easy to guess an answer, but it is important to develop good habits of carefully writing each step. In longer equations, the answers will not be so obvious.

EXERCISE 9

Directions: Solve and check each equation.

1. $f + 20 = 57$ $8y = 96$ $b - 19 = 28$

2. $\frac{x}{3} = 9$ $33 = k - 8$ $11 = 2d$

3. $15p = 75$ $42 = t + 7$ $18 = d - 6$

4. $9 = \frac{m}{4}$ $25z = 100$ $n + 36 = 60$

5. $56 = 8x$ $43 = r - 7$ $\frac{a}{5} = 8$

6. $c - 4 = 27$ $m + 16 = 200$ $\frac{c}{9} = -2$

7. $12y = 6$ $-3 = a + 19$ $15r = 9$

8. Which of the following best describes the way to solve for x in $1.5x = 6$?

    (1) Add 1.5 to both sides of the equation.
    (2) Subtract 1.5 from both sides of the equation.
    (3) Multiply both sides of the equation by 1.5.
    (4) Divide both sides of the equation by 1.5.

9. Which of the following describes the method for solving for y in the equation $y + 2.3 = 8$?

    (1) Multiply both sides of the equation by 2.3.
    (2) Divide both sides of the equation by 2.3.
    (3) Add 2.3 to both sides of the equation.
    (4) Subtract 2.3 from both sides of the equation.

Answers are on page 426.

Solving Longer Equations

Solving Equations with More than One Operation

Look at the equation $4m + 2 = 26$. You need to get the unknown value by itself on one side of the equation. To do this, you will need to perform *two* inverse operations. Mathematicians have agreed on the correct order for solving multistep equations.

--- RULE ---

To solve an equation with more than one operation, follow these steps:
1. Add or subtract first.
2. Then multiply or divide.

Example 1   Solve for m in $4m + 2 = 26$.

Step 1   Subtract 2 from both sides of the equation.
The equation is now $4m = 24$.

$$\begin{aligned} 4m + 2 &= 26 \\ -2 &\quad -2 \end{aligned}$$

Step 2   Divide both sides of the equation by 4.

The solution is $m = 6$.

$$\frac{4m}{4} = \frac{24}{4}$$
$$m = 6$$

To check the last example, substitute 6 for m into the original equation.
$$4m + 2 = 26$$
$$4(6) + 2 = 26$$

Since both sides of the equation equal 26, $m = 6$ is the correct solution.

Example 2   Solve for s in $5 = \frac{s}{3} - 7$.

Step 1   Add 7 to both sides of the equation.
The equation is now $12 = \frac{s}{3}$.

$$\begin{aligned} 5 &= \frac{s}{3} - 7 \\ +7 &\quad\quad +7 \\ \hline 12 &= \frac{s}{3} \end{aligned}$$

Step 2   Multiply both sides of the equation by 3.
The solution is $36 = s$.

$$3 \cdot 12 = \frac{s}{3} \cdot 3$$
$$36 = s$$

Example 3   Find the value of r in $\frac{2}{3}r + 5 = 23$.

Step 1   Subtract 5 from both sides of the equation.
The equation is now $\frac{2}{3}r = 18$.

$$\begin{aligned} \frac{2}{3}r + 5 &= 23 \\ -5 &\quad -5 \\ \hline \frac{2}{3}r &= 18 \end{aligned}$$

Step 2   Since r is multiplied by $\frac{2}{3}$, divide both sides of the equation by $\frac{2}{3}$. Remember: to divide by a fraction means to multiply by the reciprocal. Multiply both sides of the equation by $\frac{3}{2}$. The solution is $r = 27$.

$$\frac{3}{2} \times \frac{2}{3}r = \frac{18}{1} \times \frac{3}{2}$$
$$r = 27$$

EXERCISE 10

Directions: Solve and check each equation.

1. $7m - 2 = 54$ $\frac{1}{3}p + 8 = 11$

2. $\frac{a}{3} + 5 = 9$ $40 = 13z + 14$

3. $7 = \frac{c}{2} + 3$ $2n + 3 = 11$

4. $82 = 9d + 10$ $\frac{3}{4}y - 3 = 12$

5. $25c - 17 = 183$ $39 = 16k - 9$

6. $\frac{w}{2} - 7 = 3$ $10 = 6a + 7$

7. $2 = 6x - 10$ $9r + 15 = 18$

8. $3y + 4 = 25$ $7 = 4n + 5$

Answers are on page 427.

Solving Equations with Separated Unknowns

Sometimes the unknowns are separated in an equation. You need to combine the unknowns as you did when you learned to simplify expressions (page 292). Remember that the unknown x is understood to be $1x$. Look at the following examples carefully.

$$5x + 2x = 7x \qquad 4a + a = 5a \qquad 6c - 5c = c \qquad m + m = 2m$$

In the second example, a means $1a$. In the third example, c means $1c$. In the last example, $m + m$ means $1m + 1m$.

Example 1   Solve for x in $5x - 2x + 8 = 26$.

Step 1   Combine the unknowns, $5x - 2x = 3x$.

Step 2   Subtract 8 from both sides of the equation.

$$\begin{aligned} 3x + 8 &= 26 \\ -8 &{-8} \\ \hline 3x &= 18 \end{aligned}$$

Step 3   Divide both sides of the equation by 3.

$$\frac{3x}{3} = \frac{18}{3}$$

The solution is $x = 6$.

$$x = 6$$

--- R U L E ---

To solve an equation with separated unknowns, follow these steps:
1. Combine the unknowns.
    a. If the unknowns are on the *same* side of the equals sign, follow the rules for adding and subtracting.
    b. If the unknowns are on *different* sides of the equals sign, combine them by using inverse operations.
2. Use inverse operations to solve the equation.

In the next example, the unknowns are on different sides of the equals sign. Use inverse operations to combine them.

Example 2   Solve for *a* in $9a - 3 = 2a + 11$.

Step 1   To combine the *a*'s, use the inverse of addition. Subtract 2*a* from both sides of the equation.

$$9a - 3 = 2a + 11$$
$$\underline{-2a \qquad -2a \qquad}$$
$$7a - 3 = \qquad 11$$

Step 2   Add 3 to both sides of the equation.

$$\underline{+ 3 \qquad\quad +3\;}$$
$$7a \qquad = \qquad 14$$

Step 3   Divide both sides of the equation by 7. The solution is *a* = 2.

$$\frac{7a}{7} = \frac{14}{7}$$
$$a = 2$$

You can also solve the equation by first subtracting 9*a* from both sides.

Step 1   Subtract 9*a* from both sides of the equation.

$$9a - 3 = \quad 2a + 11$$
$$\underline{-9a \qquad\quad -9a \qquad}$$
$$-3 = -7a + 11$$

Step 2   Subtract 11 from both sides of the equation.

$$\underline{-11 \qquad\quad -11\;}$$
$$-14 = -7a$$

Step 3   Divide both sides of the equation by −7. The solution is 2 = *a*.

$$\frac{-14}{-7} = \frac{-7a}{-7}$$
$$2 = a$$

The solution is the same with both methods. However, to avoid using signed numbers, combine the unknowns on the side of the equation with more unknowns.

Example 3   Solve for y in $20 - 2y = 3y$.

Step 1   Combine the unknowns on the side with the greater unknown value.
$3y$ is more than $2y$.
Add $2y$ to both sides of the equation.

$$\begin{array}{rcl} 20 - 2y &=& 3y \\ +2y & & +2y \\ \hline 20 & = & 5y \end{array}$$

Step 2   Divide both sides of the equation by 5.
The solution is $4 = y$.

$$\frac{20}{5} = \frac{5y}{5}$$

$$4 = y$$

There is a shorter way of writing the solutions to equations. Below are the three examples from this lesson. Each new line shows the *result* of performing each step rather than the actual work. Look at these examples carefully. Be sure that you understand how to get from line to line.

Example 1   Solve for x in $5x - 2x + 8 = 26$.

Step 1   Combine the unknowns.

$$5x - 2x + 8 = 26$$
$$3x + 8 = 26$$

Step 2   Subtract 8 from both sides.

$$3x = 18$$

Step 3   Divide both sides by 3.
The solution is $x = 6$.

$$x = 6$$

Example 2   Solve for a in $9a - 3 = 2a + 11$.

Step 1   Subtract $2a$ from both sides.

$$9a - 3 = 2a + 11$$
$$7a - 3 = 11$$

Step 2   Add 3 to both sides.

$$7a = 14$$

Step 3   Divide both sides by 7.
The solution is $a = 2$.

$$a = 2$$

Example 3   Solve for y in $20 - 2y = 3y$.

Step 1 $3y$ is more than $2y$. Add $2y$ to both sides.

$$20 - 2y = 3y$$
$$20 = 5y$$

Step 2   Divide both sides by 5.
The solution is $4 = y$.

$$4 = y$$

EXERCISE 11

Directions: Solve and check each equation.

1. $5y - y = 19 + 9$ $6f = 14 - f$

2. $6t + 8 + 4t = 58$ $3 = y + 8y$

3. $9c = 44 - 2c$ $8r + 17 = 5r + 32$

4. $8m = 2m + 30$ $7n - 9 = 3n + 7$

5. $4a + 55 = 9a$ $6z + 11 = 5z + 20$

6. $4p = p + 18$ $5y - 4 = 2y + 77$

Answers are on page 427.

Solving Equations with Parentheses

Part of the information in an equation may be contained in parentheses.

--- **R U L E** ---

To solve an equation with parentheses, follow these steps:
1. Multiply each term inside the parentheses by the number outside the parentheses. (You can review this operation on page 293.)
2. Then combine the unknowns and the numbers as you did in the last exercise.

Example 1   Solve for x in $6(x + 1) = 20 - x$.

Step 1   Multiply $x + 1$ by 6. $6(x + 1) = 20 - x$
                                           $6x + 6 = 20 - x$

Step 2   Add x to each side. $7x + 6 = 20$

Step 3   Subtract 6 from both sides. $7x = 14$

Step 4   Divide both sides by 7. $x = 2$
The solution is $x = 2$.

Example 2   Solve for y in $3(y + 4) + 2 = 29$.

Step 1	Multiply $y + 4$ by 3.	$3(y + 4) + 2 = 29$ $3y + 12 + 2 = 29$
Step 2	Add 12 and 2.	$3y + 14 \quad = 29$
Step 3	Subtract 14 from both sides.	$3y \qquad\quad = 15$
Step 4	Divide both sides by 3. The solution is $y = 5$.	$y \qquad\quad = 5$

EXERCISE 12

Directions: Solve each equation.

1. $4(x - 2) + x = 27$ $3(y - 2) + 4 = 16$

2. $2a + 5(a + 3) = 99$ $8(s + 7) = 100 - 3s$

3. $4(c + 4) = 61 + c$ $3(t + 10) = t + 90$

4. $7(m - 8) = 2m + 4$ $5(m + 3) - 8 = 37$

5. $2(x + 6) - 3 = 11$ $9(y - 1) - 4y = 1$

Answers are on page 428.

Substituting to Solve Equations

On a multiple-choice test such as the GED, you can use answer choices to solve equations. Remember that an equation is a statement that two amounts are equal. When you substitute the correct solution into an equation, you will get two equal amounts.

Example 1   Choose the correct solution to $5m - 1 = 49$.

(1) 8   (2) 9   (3) 10   (4) 12

Step 1   Substitute each answer choice into the equation and solve.
$5(8) - 1 = 40 - 1 = 39$, which does not equal 49.
$5(9) - 1 = 45 - 1 = 44$, which does not equal 49.
$5(10) - 1 = 50 - 1 = 49$, which equals 49.

Step 2   Choose answer choice (3). The solution is $m = 10$.

Example 2   Choose the correct solution to $2(x + 3) - 1 = 23$.

(1) 8 (2) 9 (3) 10 (4) 11

Step 1   Substitute each answer choice into the equation and solve.
$2(8 + 3) - 1 = 2(11) - 1 = 22 - 1 = 21$, which does not equal 23.
$2(9 + 3) - 1 = 2(12) - 1 = 24 - 1 = 23$, which equals 23.

Step 2   Choose answer choice (2). The solution is $x = 9$.

EXERCISE 13

Directions: Substitute answer choices to solve each equation.

1. $6x - 3 = 45$

    (1) 6   (2) 7   (3) 8   (4) 9

2. $2y + 1 = 27$

    (1) 12   (2) 13   (3) 14   (4) 15

3. $\frac{w}{5} + 6 = 10$

    (1) 4   (2) 5   (3) 10   (4) 20

4. $25 = 3z - 2$

    (1) 7   (2) 9   (3) 11   (4) 13

5. $18 = m + 11$

    (1) 7   (2) 9   (3) 10   (4) 14

6. $50 = 4n + 2$

    (1) 12   (2) 20   (3) 36   (4) 48

7. $2(r - 3) + 5 = 15$

    (1) 4   (2) 5   (3) 8   (4) 9

8. $6(p + 1) - 7 = 53$

    (1) 15   (2) 12   (3) 10   (4) 9

9. $70 = 8(c + 4) - 2$

    (1) 12   (2) 10   (3) 9   (4) 5

10. $34 = 3(f - 2) + 4$

    (1) 10   (2) 12   (3) 14   (4) 20

Answers are on page 428.

Solving Inequalities

You learned that an equation is a statement that says two amounts are equal. An **inequality** is a statement that two amounts are not equal. Below are four symbols used to write inequalities.

Symbol Meaning	Example
$<$ is less than	$3 < 4$ "3 is less than 4"
$>$ is greater than	$5 > 2$ "5 is greater than 2"
$\leq$ is less than or equal to	$m \leq 6$ "m is less than or equal to 6"
$\geq$ is greater than or equal to	$x \geq 8$ "x is greater than or equal to 8"

The expression $m \leq 6$ means that m can be 6 or any number less than 6, including negative numbers.

The expression $x \geq 8$ means that x can be 8 or any number greater than 8.

Solving inequalities is very much like solving equations. You can perform inverse operations on both sides of inequalities to find the value of the unknown.

Example 1   Solve for m in $6m - 2 \leq 40$.

Step 1   Add 2 to both sides of the inequality. $6m \leq 42$

Step 2   Divide both sides of the inequality by 6. $m \leq 7$
The solution is $m \leq 7$. This inequality is true
for 7 and every number less than 7.

Example 2   Which of the following is *not* a solution to the inequality
$6m - 2 \leq 40$?

(1) -5 (2) 0   (3) 4   (4) 7   (5) 9

From the last example, you know that $m \leq 7$.
Among the answer choices, -5, 0, 4, and 7 are all less than or equal to 7. Only choice (5) 9 is *not* less than or equal to 7.

Inequalities are different from equations when they are multiplied or divided by negative numbers. If you multiply or divide both sides of an inequality by a negative number, the direction of the inequality symbol changes.

Think about the inequality $7 > 5$.

If you add the same number to both sides, the inequality will be true.

$7 + 3 > 5 + 3$ or $10 > 8$, which is true.

If you subtract the same number from both sides, the inequality will be true.

$$7 - 11 > 5 - 11 \text{ or } -4 > -6, \text{ which is true.}$$

If you multiply both sides by the same positive number, the inequality will be true.

$$2(7) > 2(5) \text{ or } 14 > 10, \text{ which is true.}$$

If you multiply both sides by the same negative number, the inequality is *not* true.

$$-2(7) > -2(5) \text{ or } -14 > -10, \text{ which is not true.}$$

—————————————————————— **R U L E** ——————————————————————

If you multiply or divide both sides of an inequality by a negative number, the inequality symbol changes direction.

For the last problem, $-14 < -10$.

Example 3   What is the solution to $-3x + 4 \leq 19$?

Step 1   Subtract 4 from both sides of the inequality.

$$-3x + 4 \leq 19$$
$$-3x \quad\ \leq 15$$

Step 2   Divide both sides of the inequality by -3 and change the direction of the inequality symbol. The solution is $x \geq -5$.

$$x \quad\ \geq -5$$

EXERCISE 14

Directions: For problems 1–5, answer each question.

1. For the inequality $m - 6 > 1$, could m be equal to 7?

2. For the inequality $8r \leq 16$, could r equal 2?

3. For the inequality $d + 7 \geq 2$, could d equal -5?

4. For the inequality $2f < 12$, could f equal 4?

5. Which of the following is *not* a solution to $9c \leq 27$?
   (1) 4   (2) 3   (3) 1   (4) 0   (5) -2

For problems 6–8, solve each inequality.

6. $5m - 4 \leq 26$ $3n + 2 > 14$ $4p - 3 < 15$

7. $7c - 3 \leq 5c + 15$ $8y + 1 < y + 22$ $3(s - 2) \geq 2s + 10$

8. $\frac{x}{3} + 5 \geq 7$ $5(a + 3) < 2(a - 6)$ $4w - 5 \leq 3w + 6$

For problems 9 and 10, choose the correct answer.

9. Which of the following is the solution to $-2x < 6$?

(1) $x < 3$ (2) $x < -3$ (3) $x > 3$ (4) $x > -3$ (5) $x > 6$

10. Which of the following is the solution to $-4a + 3 \geq 31$?

(1) $a \leq -7$ (2) $a \geq 7$ (3) $a \geq -7$ (4) $a \geq 28$ (5) $a \leq 28$

Answers are on page 428.

Writing Algebraic Expressions

To use algebra, you must learn to translate mathematical relationships into **algebraic expressions.** Below are several examples of algebraic expressions using the four basic arithmetic operations of addition, subtraction, multiplication, and division, as well as powers and roots. Read each example carefully. Watch for the words that suggest which mathematical operation to write. Remember that any letter can be used to represent an unknown number.

Example	Expression	Explanation
a number increased by four	$x + 4$ or $4 + x$	*Increased by* means to add.
nine more than a number	$r + 9$ or $9 + r$	*More than* means to add.
eight less than a number	$y - 8$	*Less than* means to subtract.
eight decreased by a number	$8 - y$	*Decreased by* means to subtract. (Compare the order of this example to that of the last one.)
four times a number	$4e$	*Times* means to multiply. (Notice that there is no sign between a number and the unknown in multiplication expressions.)
the product of ten and a number	$10p$	A *product* is the answer to multiplication.
a number divided by five	$m/5$ or $\frac{m}{5}$	Notice that the divisor goes on the bottom.
five divided by a number	$5/n$ or $\frac{5}{n}$	The unknown is the divisor.
one-fourth of a number	$\frac{1}{4}s$ or $\frac{s}{4}$	Remember that $\frac{1}{4}$ of a number is the same as the number divided by 4.
a number raised to the second power	r^2	A second power is an exponent of 2.
the square root of a number	$\sqrt{c}$	The symbol for square root is $\sqrt{}$.

Notice that the order of numbers and variables is important with subtraction and division. The expression $d - 8$ is *not* the same as $8 - d$. Similarly, $\frac{x}{5}$ is *not* the same as $\frac{5}{x}$.

EXERCISE 15

Directions: Write an algebraic expression for each of the following. Use the letter x to represent each unknown.

1. a number increased by nine

2. the product of seven and a number

3. five times a number

4. the sum of a number and eight

5. a number minus ten

6. one less than a number

7. three divided by a number

8. a number decreased by twenty

9. a number divided by fifteen

10. a number plus one-half

11. a number divided by two

12. four more than a number

13. the square root of a number

14. a number raised to the third power

15. three-fifths of a number

Answers are on page 429.

Using Variables in Word Problems

As a first step in solving some word problems, it is helpful to express number relationships with variables. Pay close attention to the words that suggest mathematical relationships in the following examples.

<u>Example 1</u>   Let *r* represent the amount of rent that Max pays each month. Next year Max will have to pay $40 more each month. Write an algebraic expression that tells Max's monthly rent next year.

The phrase "$40 more" means to add. If his monthly rent this year is *r*, his monthly rent next year will be $r + 40$. $r + 40$

<u>Example 2</u>   Four friends won *w* dollars in a lottery. They decided to share the money equally. Write an expression for the amount each friend will get.

"To share equally" means to divide. The total amount they won is *w*. $\frac{w}{4}$

The amount each friend will get is *w* divided by 4 or $\frac{w}{4}$.

EXERCISE 16

Directions: For problems 1–6, write an algebraic expression for each situation described.

1. Jack makes *d* dollars per hour. His boss offered him a raise of $2 an hour. Write an expression for his new hourly wage.

2. Normally there are *s* students in John's GED class. Because of bad weather, five students were absent one night. Write an expression for the number of students who came to class that night.

3. Beef costs *c* per pound. Write an expression for the cost of $2\frac{1}{4}$ pounds of beef.

4. Let *i* stand for Ellen's gross income. Of her income, $\frac{1}{5}$ goes for taxes and social security. Write an expression for the amount of Ellen's income that is withheld for taxes and social security.

5. The total town budget for summer programs is *x*. Six programs share the money equally. Write an expression for the amount each program gets.

6. The Smiths take home *t* dollars each month. They spend 80% of their take-home pay for basic expenses. Write an expression for the amount of their basic expenses.

For problems 7—10, choose the correct answer to each problem.

7. The length of a rectangle is ℓ. The width is two inches less than the length. Write an expression for the width of the rectangle.

   (1) 2ℓ

   (2) $2 - \ell$

   (3) $\ell + 2$

   (4) $\ell - 2$

   (5) $\frac{\ell}{2}$

8. The sales tax rate in Bill's state is 6%. Write an expression for the amount of sales tax Bill needs to pay on an item that costs m dollars.

   (1) $m - 6$

   (2) $m + 6$

   (3) $\frac{m}{6}$

   (4) $6m$

   (5) $0.06m$

9. Frank is y years old. Write an expression for his age 10 years ago.

   (1) $y + 10$

   (2) $y - 10$

   (3) $10y$

   (4) $\frac{y}{10}$

   (5) $10 - y$

10. Beverly weighs p pounds. Write an expression for her weight after she loses 15 pounds.

   (1) $p + 15$

   (2) $p - 15$

   (3) $\frac{p}{15}$

   (4) $15p$

   (5) $15 - p$

Answers are on page 429.

Writing and Solving One–Step Equations

To write equations from word problems, watch for verbs such as *is* or *equals*. These verbs suggest where to put the equals sign.

Example 1   A number increased by twelve is twenty. Find the number.

Step 1   Let x stand for the number. $x + 12 = 20$
The phrase *increased by* means to add.
Replace "is twenty" with "$= 20$."

Step 2   Subtract 12 from both sides. $x = 8$
The solution is $x = 8$.

Example 2   Andy's gross pay minus the $125 his employer deducts each week is his net pay. Andy's net pay is $625 a week. What is his gross pay?

Step 1   Let x stand for Andy's gross pay. $x - 125 = 625$
Minus means to subtract.
Replace "is $625" with "$= 625$."

Step 2   Add 125 to both sides. $x = 750$
Andy's gross pay is $750.

The last two examples are easy to solve without writing equations. Later, when word problems are more complex, equations can make your work easier. Take the time now to write and solve one–step equations.

EXERCISE 17

Directions: For problems 1–6, choose the equation that correctly matches the verbal description.

1. A number increased by nine is fifteen.

    (1) $a - 9 = 15$ (2) $a + 9 = 15$ (3) $9a = 15$

2. Two-thirds of a number is twelve.

    (1) $2c = 12$ (2) $3c = 12$ (3) $\frac{2}{3}c = 12$

3. A number divided by three is twenty.

    (1) $\frac{x}{3} = 20$ (2) $\frac{3}{x} = 20$ (3) $\frac{3}{20} = x$

4. When you subtract sixteen from a number, the result is ten.

    (1) $16 - y = 10$ (2) $y - 16 = 10$ (3) $\frac{y}{16} = 10$

5. Twenty is the same as the product of three and a number.

    (1) $20 = m - 3$ (2) $20 = m + 3$ (3) $20 = 3m$

6. When a number is divided by seven, the result is four.

   (1) $\frac{7}{r} = 4$ (2) $\frac{r}{7} = 4$ (3) $r = \frac{4}{7}$

For problems $7-12$, write and solve an equation for each statement. Let x represent the unknown number.

7. Nine less than a number is fifteen.

8. The product of six and a number is twenty-seven.

9. A number divided by five equals fifty.

10. Three is equal to a number decreased by five.

11. Sixty is equal to three-fourths of a number.

12. The product of seven and a number is eighty-four.

Write and solve an equation for each of the following problems.

13. The original price minus a $40 discount is the sale price of a new color TV. The sale price is $290. What was the original price?

14. The total payroll at Acme, Inc., divided by 15 is the amount each employee takes home every week. Every worker takes home $600 a week. Find the total weekly payroll.

15. Sandy pays one-fourth of her monthly income for rent. Her monthly rent is $640. What is her monthly income?

16. At the last meeting of a block association, 75% of the members attended. Altogether, there were 90 people at the meeting. How many people belong to the association?

Answers are on page 429.

Writing Longer Algebraic Expressions

Earlier you learned to write algebraic expressions using the four basic operations of addition, subtraction, multiplication, and division, as well as powers and roots.

On the next page are examples of algebraic expressions, each of which has more than one operation. Read each example carefully. Watch for the words that suggest which mathematical operation to write.

Example	Expression	Explanation
twice a number increased by four	$2x + 4$ or $4 + 2x$	*Twice* means to multiply, and *increased by* means to add.
twice the sum of a number and four	$2(x + 4)$	*Twice* means to multiply, and the parentheses group the sum together.
five less than three times a number	$3a - 5$	*Times* means to multiply, and *less than* means to subtract.
the sum of a number and one-third of the same number	$c + \frac{1}{3}c$ or $c + \frac{c}{3}$	*Sum* means to add, and *one-third of* means to divide.
five divided into the sum of three and a number	$\frac{x+3}{5}$ or $(x + 3)/5$	The fraction bar groups $x + 3$ together. First find the sum. Then divide by 5.
three more than half a number	$\frac{1}{2}r + 3$ or $\frac{r}{2} + 3$	*More than* means to add, and *half* means to multiply by $\frac{1}{2}$ or to divide by 2.

EXERCISE 18

Directions: For problems 1–8, choose the algebraic expression that correctly matches the written description.

1. two less than seven times a number

   (1) $2m - 7$ (2) $7m - 2$ (3) $2(m - 7)$

2. the sum of a number and five all divided by four

   (1) $\frac{x + 5}{4}$ (2) $4(x + 5)$ 3) $\frac{x + 4}{5}$

3. a number increased by eight times itself

   (1) $a + 8$ (2) $8a$ (3) $a + 8a$

4. twice the sum of a number and six

   (1) $2(y + 6)$ (2) $6(y + 2)$ (3) $2y + 6y$

5. three more than one-half of a number

   (1) $n + 3n$ (2) $\frac{n}{2 + 3}$ (3) $\frac{3 - n}{2}$

6. twice a number subtracted from seven times the same number

   (1) $7s - 2$ (2) $7 - 2s$ (3) $7s - 2s$

7. six more than twice a number

   (1) 6w + 2   (2) 2w + 6   (3) 2(w + 6)

8. nine less than three times a number

   (1) 3p − 9   (2) 9p − 3   (3) 3(p − 9)

For problems 9–16, write an algebraic expression for each verbal expression. Use *x* to represent the unknown number.

9. twice a number increased by six

10. five less than the product of eight and a number

11. the sum of two times a number and four times the same number

12. eight more than half a number

13. subtract one from one-third of a number

14. take three times a number from fifteen

15. the sum of a number and seven, all divided by four

16. the sum of twelve and a number, all multiplied by ten

Answers are on page 429.

Writing and Solving Longer Equations

You learned to write one–step equations from words. To write longer equations, follow the same procedure. Watch for verbs, such as *is* and *equals*. These verbs tell you where to put the equals sign.

Example 1   Eight more than three times a number is twenty. Find the number.

Step 1   Let *x* stand for the unknown in the phrase "8 more than 3 times a number." Replace "is twenty" with "= 20." $3x + 8 = 20$

Step 2   Solve the equation. First subtract 8 from both sides. $3x = 12$

Step 3   To get the unknown alone, divide both sides by 3. The solution is *x* = 4. $x = 4$

Example 2   One-third of a number decreased by seven equals four. Find the number.

Step 1   Let x stand for the unknown in the phrase $\frac{x}{3} - 7 = 4$
"7 less than $\frac{1}{3}$ of a number."
Replace "equals 4" with "= 4."

Step 2   Add 7 to both sides. $\frac{x}{3} = 11$

Step 3   Multiply both sides by 3.
The solution is x = 33. $x = 33$

EXERCISE 19

Directions: Write and solve an equation for each problem.

1. Half a number decreased by five is six.

2. Three times a number plus four equals nineteen.

3. Four times a number increased by one is twenty-one.

4. Twice a number decreased by nine equals seven.

5. Three more than six times a number is twelve.

6. Five times a number decreased by two equals nine.

7. One less than three times a number is five.

8. Four times a number decreased by two equals eighteen.

9. When twice a number is increased by one, the result is thirteen.

10. Ten more than six times a number equals thirty-four.

11. Eight less than half a number is twelve.

12. Three less than a number divided by eight is six.

13. Seven less than twice a number equals the same number increased by three.

Answers are on page 429.

Using Algebra to Solve Word Problems

The key to solving algebra word problems is to organize the given information carefully. Look at the next examples carefully and be sure that you understand each step.

Example 1   The sum of three *consecutive* numbers is 57. Find the numbers.

Step 1   The word *consecutive* means "one following another." Let x represent the first number. The next number is 1 more than x, or $x + 1$. The third number is 2 more than x, or $x + 2$.

x = first number
$x + 1$ = second number
$x + 2$ = third number

Step 2   Write an equation that shows that the sum of the three numbers is 57.

$x + x + 1 + x + 2 = 57$

Step 3   Combine like terms and solve the equation. The first number is 18.

$3x + 3 = 57$
$3x = 54$
$x = 18$

Step 4   To find the other two numbers, substitute 18 for x in the expressions $x + 1$ and $x + 2$.

first number $= 18$
second number $= 18 + 1 = 19$
third number $= 18 + 2 = 20$

Algebra is a convenient tool for solving ratio problems.

Example 2   There are twice as many women as there are men in Juanita's Spanish class. There are 24 students in the class. How many of the students are women?

Step 1   Let x represent the number of men, and let $2x$ represent the number of women.

men $= x$
women $= 2x$

Step 2   Write an equation that shows that the total number of students is 24.

$x + 2x = 24$

Step 3   Combine like terms and solve the equation.

$3x = 24$
$x = 8$

Step 4   To find the number of women, substitute 8 for x in the expression $2x$.

women $= 2(8) = 16$

EXERCISE 20

Directions: Solve each problem.

1. The sum of two consecutive whole numbers is 27. Find the numbers.

2. The sum of three numbers is 60. The second number is two more than the first. The third number is two more than the second. Find the three numbers.

3. There are six times as many union workers as there are nonunion workers at the Acme Dye plant. Eight fewer than the number of union workers is equal to four times the number of nonunion workers. How many union workers are there at the plant?

4. There are three times as many women in a GED class as there are men. When the number of women is decreased by two, the result is the same as when the number of men is increased by ten. Find the number of men and women in the class.

5. Juan and his boss Felipe are house painters. For every dollar that Juan gets, Felipe gets $3. They made $3600 for painting a house. How much did Felipe make on the job?

6. Paul, Jeff, and Jerry worked together repairing Paul's car. Jeff worked twice as many hours as Jerry, and Paul worked six hours more than Jeff. Altogether, they worked 51 hours. How many hours did Paul work?

7. The Millers, the Rigbys, and the Smiths went on a camping trip. The Millers spent $100 more than the Rigbys, and the Smiths spent twice as much as the Millers. If the cost of the trip was $580 altogether, how much did the Smiths spend?

8. Steve is 24 years older than his son Jed. Steve's age now is 8 years less than three times his son's age. How old is Steve now?

9. Altogether, Tim, Laura, and Eric worked 210 hours campaigning for their friend Jake who was running for the senate. Laura worked 10 hours more than Tim, and Eric worked twice as many hours as Laura. How many hours did Laura work on the campaign?

10. For taxes, social security, and a savings plan, Jane's employer deducts one dollar for every six dollars that she takes home. Jane's gross salary each week is $644. How much does Jane take home each week?

Answers are on page 430.

Using Algebra to Solve Geometry Problems

Study the next examples carefully to see how to substitute algebraic expressions into geometry formulas.

Example 1   The perimeter of a rectangle is 74 inches. The length of the rectangle is 5 inches more than the width. Find the length of the rectangle.

Step 1   Let x represent the width and $x + 5$ the length.

width $= x$
length $= x + 5$

Step 2   Substitute 74 for P, $x + 5$ for the length, and x for the width in the formula for the perimeter of a rectangle.

$P = 2l + 2w$
$74 = 2(x + 5) + 2x$

Step 3   Solve the equation. The solution is $x = 16$.

$74 = 2x + 10 + 2x$
$74 = 4x + 10$
$64 = 4x$
$16 = x$

Step 4   Substitute 16 for x in the expression $x + 5$ to find the length. The length is 21 inches.

length $= x + 5$
$= 16 + 5 = 21$

Example 2   In the illustration at the right, $\angle AOC$ is a right angle. What is the measure of $\angle AOB$?

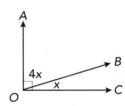

Step 1   Write an equation that shows the sum of the angles equal 90°.

$4x + x = 90$

Step 2   Solve the equation. The solution is $x = 18$.

$5x = 90$
$x = 18$

Step 3   Substitute 18 for x in the expression for $\angle AOB$. $4x = 4(18) = 72°$
The measure of $\angle AOB$ is 72°.

Directions: Solve each problem.

1. Find the measure, in degrees, of the smallest angle in the triangle pictured at the right.

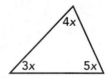

2. A rectangle has a perimeter of 48 feet. The length is twice the width. Find the measure of the width of the rectangle.

3. In the illustration at the right, ∠AOC measures 90°. Find the measure of ∠AOB.

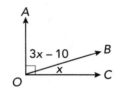

4. A rectangle has a perimeter of 60 inches. The ratio of the width to the length is 2:3. Find the length of the rectangle in inches.

5. Find the measure of ∠AOD in the illustration at the right.

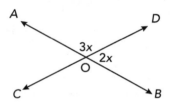

6. For the rectangle at the right, the ratio of WX to WZ is 5:6. The perimeter of the rectangle is 110 feet. Find the length of WZ in feet.

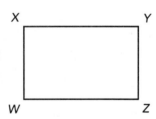

7. Find the measure of ∠AOD in the illustration at the right.

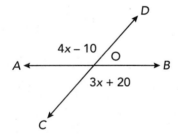

8. The perimeter of the rectangle pictured at the right is 34 feet. *MP* is 3 feet longer than *MN*. Find the measure of *MN* in feet.

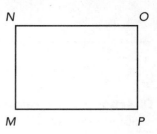

9. How many degrees are there in ∠*W* in the illustration at the right?

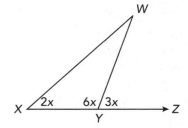

10. The perimeter of the square pictured at the right is equal to the perimeter of the rectangle. Solve for *x*.

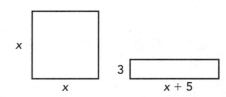

Answers are on page 431.

Basics of Algebra Review

PART I

Directions: Use a calculator to solve any of the problems below.

1. $+18 - 12 - 7 =$

2. $(-8)(-3)(-\frac{1}{2}) =$

3. $(-6)^3 =$

4. $+9 - (-3) + (-6) - (+8) =$

5. Simplify the expression $8x + 7 - 5x - 3$.

6. What is the value of the expression in problem 5 when $x = -7$?

7. Simplify $\frac{14-9}{8-3}$.

8. Simplify the expression $7(a + 2) - 3 + a$.

9. What is the value of the expression in problem 8 when $a = -2$?

For problems 10 and 11, solve for each unknown. Mark each answer on the corresponding number grid.

10. $\frac{m}{3} + 1 = 8$

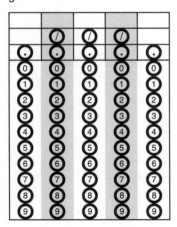

11. $3(c - 8) = c + 4$

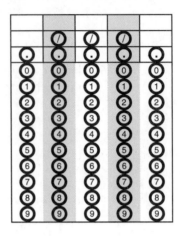

For problems 12–15, solve for each unknown.

12. $12.5 = n + 1.5$

13. $96 + 2a = a + 101$

14. $20 - 4z = 5z - 25$

15. $9x - 5 \leq 7x + 11$

PART II

Directions: Solve the following problems without a calculator.

16. Which of the following is *not* equal to $\frac{-15}{-12}$?

   (1) $1\frac{1}{4}$

   (2) $\frac{5}{4}$

   (3) $-1\frac{3}{12}$

   (4) 1.25

   (5) $+\frac{15}{12}$

17. Which of the following is *not* a solution to $4m - 3 > 17$?

(1) 11

(2) 9

(3) 7

(4) 6

(5) 4

18. Which of the following represents the perimeter of the rectangle below?

(1) $4x + 2$

(2) $5x + 1$

(3) $6x + 1$

(4) $10x + 2$

(5) $12x + 1$

2x

3x + 1

19. Write an equation for "nine times a number decreased by five equals six times the same number increased by seven."

(1) $9x + 5 = 6x$

(2) $9x - 5 = 7$

(3) $9x - 6x = 7$

(4) $9x - 6x = 5$

(5) $9x - 5 = 6x + 7$

20. Ten times a number decreased by seven equals 101 plus that number. Find the number.

(1) 12

(2) 13

(3) 18

(4) 20

(5) 23

21. Sam and Joe are house painters. Sam makes $5 an hour less than Joe. On a job that took them both 40 hours to complete, they made $1400. How much does Sam make in one hour?

(1) $10

(2) $15

(3) $18

(4) $20

(5) $25

22. Kate makes $320 more each month than her husband Tim. Together they make $2840 each month. How much does Kate make in a month?

(1) $ 640

(2) $1260

(3) $1580

(4) $1740

(5) $1900

23. In isosceles triangle *ABC* below, vertex angle *B* is twice each base angle. Find the measurement of each base angle.

(1) 25°

(2) 30°

(3) 40°

(4) 45°

(5) 60°

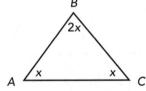

For problems 24 and 25, mark each answer on the corresponding number grid.

24. There are 25 more women than men in the night school that Maria attends. Altogether, there are 115 students in the night school. How many women attend the night school?

25. The rectangle below has a perimeter of 168 centimeters. Find the measurement, in centimeters, of the length of the rectangle.

$2x$

$3x - 1$

Answers are on page 431.

You should have gotten at least 20 problems right on the last exercise. If you did not get 20 right, review your algebra skills before you go on. If you got 20 or more right, correct any problem you got wrong. Then go on to the next chapter.

Chapter 11

Advanced Topics in Algebra and Geometry

This chapter builds on the skills you learned in algebra and geometry. You will learn to graph algebraic relationships and to manipulate powers and roots in algebraic expressions. You will also learn to use the ratios of the right-triangle relationships of trigonometry.

The Coordinate Plane

The **coordinate plane** is a tool for graphing algebraic relationships. The flat surface, or plane, is divided by a horizontal line called the **x-axis** and a vertical line called the **y-axis**. Each of these lines is simply a number line with positive and negative values and zero in the middle. The two lines intersect at 0, which is called the **origin**. The x-axis and y-axis divide the coordinate plane into four sections called **quadrants**.

A point anywhere on the graph can be identified by a pair of numbers called the **coordinates** of the point. The coordinates are written inside parentheses in the order (x, y). This set of numbers is called an **ordered pair**. The x-coordinate has a positive value for points to the right of the y-axis and a negative value for points to the left of the y-axis. The y-coordinate has a positive value for points above the x-axis and a negative value for points below the x-axis.

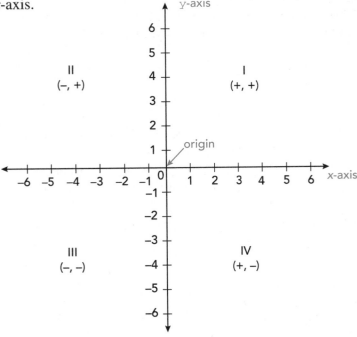

Notice the four quadrants labeled I, II, III, and IV. The signs in parentheses below each Roman numeral tell the signs of any point in each quadrant. Remember that the first number in an order pair tells the distance to the right or the left of the vertical axis. The second number tells the distance above or below the horizontal axis.

Use the coordinate plane grid below for Examples 1 and 2.

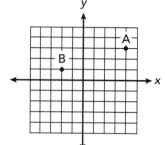

Example 1   What are the coordinates of point A?
Point A is 4 units to the right of the y-axis, or +4, and 3 units above the x-axis, or +3. The coordinates of point A are (4, 3).

Example 2   What are the coordinates of point B?

Point B is 2 units to the left of the y-axis, or –2, and 1 unit above the x-axis, or +1. The coordinates of point B are (−2, 1).

Use the coordinate plane grid below for examples 3, 4, and 5.

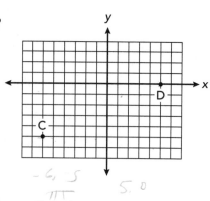

Example 3   What are the coordinates of point C?

Point C is 6 units to the left of the y-axis, or −6, and 5 units below the x-axis, or −5. The coordinates of point C are (−6, −5).

Example 4   In which quadrant is point C?

Point C is in quadrant III.

Example 5   What are the coordinates of point D?

Point D is 5 units to the right of the y-axis, or +5. Point D is neither above nor below the x-axis. The coordinates of point D are (5, 0).

On the GED test you will see coordinate plane grids with small circles where you can mark the position of a point. In the grid at the right, the circle that is marked corresponds to the point (5, −3).

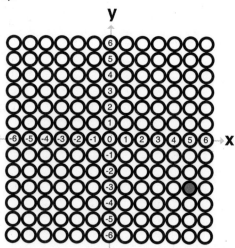

EXERCISE 1

Directions: Solve each problem.

1. Write the coordinates for each point shown on the coordinate plane grid below.

   Point A = (9 ,5)
   Point B = (4 ,10)
   Point C = (-2 , 4)
   Point D = (-6 , 10)
   Point E = (-11 , 3)
   Point F = (-13 , 0)
   Point G = (-7 , -2)
   Point H = (-3 , -7)
   Point I = (0 , -6)
   Point J = (6 , -7)
   Point K = (10 , -3)
   Point L = (12 , 0)

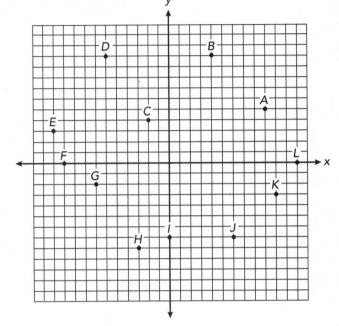

2. Which points above lie on the x-axis?

   F, L

3. Which points above lie in quadrant II?

   D, C, E

4. Which points above lie in quadrant IV?

   J, K

5. Mark the following points on the coordinate plane grid at the right.

   Point A = (6, 4)
   Point B = (−5, 3)
   Point C = (−2, −7)
   Point D = (1, −6)
   Point E = (−8, 0)
   Point F = (3, 0)
   Point G = (0, −4)
   Point H = (0, 7)

6. Which points in problem 5 lie on the y-axis? −4, 7

7. Which point in problem 5 lies in quadrant III?

   C

Answers are on page 433.

Distances on the Coordinate Plane

The distance between points on the coordinate plane is not measured in inches, feet, or meters. Instead, distance between points is measured in units of whole numbers as you will see in this section.

To find the distance between two points, you may be able to count spaces.

Example 1   What is the distance from point A to point B on the graph at the right?

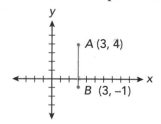

Point *A* is 4 units above the *x*-axis, and point *B* is 1 unit below. The distance between points *A* and *B* is $4 + 1 = 5$.

Example 2   What is the distance from point *C* to point *D* on the graph at the right?

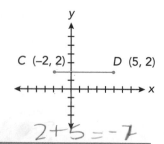

Point *C* is 2 units to the left of the *y*-axis, and point *D* is 5 units to the right. The distance between points *C* and *D* is $2 + 5 = 7$.

$2 + 5 = -7$

TIP
Distance is always positive regardless of the signs of the coordinates.

Example 3   What is the area of rectangle *EFGH*?

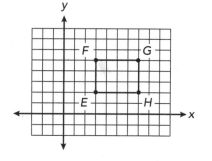

Step 1   Use the formula for the area of a rectangle. $A = lw$

Step 2   Multiply the length (4) by the width (3). $A = 4 \times 3$

Step 3   The area of the rectangle is 12. $A = 12$

The distance between point *S* and point *T* in the figure at the right is more complicated. The distance between points *S* and *T* is the hypotenuse of a right triangle, where the legs of the triangle are shown with dotted lines.

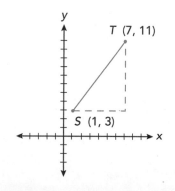

There is a special formula for finding the distance between any two points on the coordinate plane. The formula is based on the Pythagorean relationship.

RULE

The distance d between two points on the coordinate plane is $d = \sqrt{(x_2 - x_1)^2 + (y_2 - y_1)^2}$, where (x_1, y_1) and (x_2, y_2) are two points in the plane.

Point S on the last graph has the coordinates $(1, 3)$. Point S is (x_1, y_1) in the formula. Point T has the coordinates $(7, 11)$. Point T is (x_2, y_2) in the formula. When you subtract the x-values, $7 - 1$, you find the horizontal leg of the right triangle. When you subtract the y-values, $11 - 3$, you find the vertical leg of the right triangle.

Remember that the small numbers 1 and 2 immediately after each x and y are not used in computations. These small numbers are used only to identify different points.

Example 3   Find the distance from point S to point T in the preceding figure.

Step 1   Substitute 7 for x_2, 1 for x_1, 11 for y_2, and 3 for y_1.

$$d = \sqrt{(x_2 - x_1)^2 + (y_2 - y_1)^2}$$
$$= \sqrt{(7 - 1)^2 + (11 - 3)^2}$$

Step 2   Solve the formula.

$$= \sqrt{(6)^2 + (8)^2}$$

Step 3   The distance from points S to T is 10.

$$= \sqrt{36 + 64}$$
$$= \sqrt{100}$$
$$= 10$$

EXERCISE 2

Directions: Solve each problem. Use the formula $d = \sqrt{(x_2 - x_1)^2 + (y_2 - y_1)^2}$ for the distance between two points on a plane when necessary. For problems 1–4, use the graph below.

1. What is the distance from point A to point B?

2. What is the distance from point B to point C?

3. What are the coordinates of point D that forms the fourth corner of rectangle $ABCD$?

4. What is the area of rectangle $ABCD$?

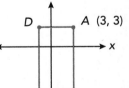

For problems 5–8, use the graph below.

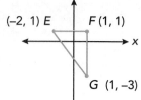

5. Find the distance from point *E* to point *F*.

6. What is the distance from point *F* to point *G*?

7. What is the distance from point *E* to point *G*?

8. What is the area of triangle *EFG*?

Solve each problem.

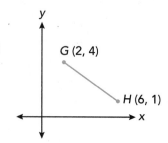

9. What is the distance from point *G* to point *H* in the graph at the right?

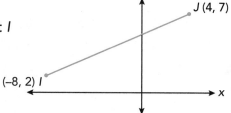

10. Find the distance between point *I* and point *J*.

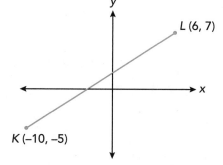

11. Find the distance between points *K* and *L*.

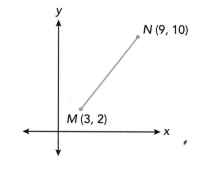

12. Which of the following represents the distance between points *M* and *N*?

    (1) $\sqrt{(9 + 3)^2 + (10 + 2)^2}$

    (2) $\sqrt{(3 - 2)^2 + (10 - 9)^2}$

    (3) $\sqrt{(3 + 2)^2 + (10 + 9)^2}$

    (4) $\sqrt{(9 - 3)^2 + (10 - 2)^2}$

    (5) $\sqrt{(9 - 2)^2 + (10 - 3)^2}$

Answers are on page 433.

Linear Equations

Think about the equation $y = x + 2$. For every value of x, you can find a corresponding value of y by substituting and solving the equation.

Suppose you let $x = 1, 3,$ and -2 for the equation $y = x + 2$.

If $x = 1$, then $y = 1 + 2 = 3$.
If $x = 3$, then $y = 3 + 2 = 5$.
If $x = -2$, then $y = -2 + 2 = 0$.

The three values of x and their corresponding values of y are the coordinates for three points on the coordinate plane: $(1, 3)$, $(3, 5)$, and $(-2, 0)$.

The graph at the right shows these three points. Notice that the points lie in a straight line. The coordinates of any point on the line are solutions to the equation $y = x + 2$. This type of equation is called a **linear equation** because its graph forms a straight line.

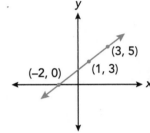

------- R U L E -------

To make a graph of a linear equation, follow these steps:
1. Substitute each value of x into the equation to find the corresponding value of y.
2. Make a table of the x and y values.
3. Put these points on the coordinate plane and connect them with a straight line.

Example 1   Make a graph of the equation $y = 2x - 1$. Let $x = 2, 5,$ and -1.

Step 1   Substitute each value of x into the equation to find the corresponding value of y.

If $x = 2$, then $y = 2(2) - 1 = 4 - 1 = 3$.
If $x = 5$, then $y = 2(5) - 1 = 10 - 1 = 9$.
If $x = -1$, then $y = 2(-1) - 1 = -2 - 1 = -3$.

Step 2   Make a table of the x and y values.

x	y
2	3
5	9
−1	−3

Step 3   Put these points on the coordinate plane and connect them with a straight line.

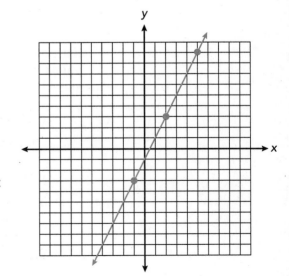

On the GED test you will not have to make a graph of an equation, but you may need to know whether a point lies on the graph of an equation.

To find out whether a point is on the graph of an equation, substitute the *x*-coordinate of the point into the equation. If the solution to the equation is the same as the *y*-coordinate, then the point is on the graph of the equation.

Example 2   Is the point (4, 7) on the graph of $y = 2x - 1$?

Substitute 4 for *x* in $y = 2x - 1$. $y = 2x - 1$
This gives *y* the value of 7. $y = 2(4) - 1 = 8 - 1 = 7$
Therefore, point (4, 7) is on the
graph of $y = 2x - 1$.

Example 3   Is the point (−2, −4) on the graph of $y = 2x - 1$?

Substitute −2 for *x* in $y = 2x - 1$. $y = 2x - 1$
This gives *y* the value of −5. $y = 2(-2) - 1 = -4 - 1 = -5$
Therefore, point (−2, −4) is *not* on
the graph of $y = 2x - 1$.

EXERCISE 3

Directions: For problems 1–6, answer each question.

1. Is the point (2, 5) on the graph of the equation $y = 3x - 1$?

2. Is the point (3, 4) on the graph of the equation $y = 4x - 5$?

3. Is the point (6, 7) on the graph of the equation $y = \frac{x}{2} + 4$?

4. Is the point (3, 2) on the graph of the equation $y = \frac{2}{3}x + 1$?

5. Is the point (8, −5) on the graph of the equation $y = -x + 3$?

6. Is the point (6, −2) on the graph of the equation $y = -\frac{x}{2} + 1$?

For problems 7–10, fill in the table for each given value of *x*. Then put the points for each problem on the grid, connect the points with a straight line and label the line with the problem number.

7. $y = x + 3$

x	y
1	
4	
−3	

8. $y = 2x - 3$

x	y
5	
3	
0	

9. $y = \frac{x}{3} + 1$

x	y
6	
3	
-3	

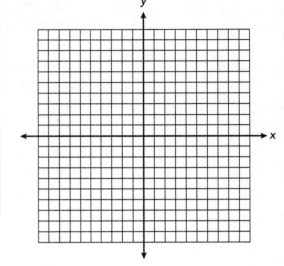

10. $y = -x + 5$

x	y
8	
5	
1	

Answers are on page 434.

Slope and Intercepts

In the last lesson you learned that the graph of a linear equation is a straight line. To describe the graph of a linear equation, mathematicians talk about the *slope* and the *intercepts* of a graph.

The **slope** is a measure of how "steep" a line is. Slope tells something about what a linear equation looks like.

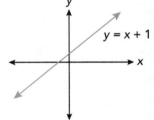

- A line that rises from left to right has a **positive slope.** The graph at the right shows the equation $y = x + 1$. The slope of the graph is positive. When the value of x gets greater, the value of y also gets greater. For example, when $x = 5$, $y = 6$, and when $x = 7$, $y = 8$.

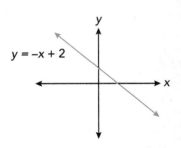

- A line that goes down from left to right has a **negative slope.** The graph at the right shows the equation $y = -x + 2$. The slope of the graph is negative. When the value of x gets greater, the value of y gets smaller. For example, when $x = -3$, $y = -1$, and when $x = -8$, $y = -6$.

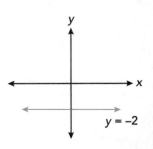

- A horizontal line has a **zero slope.** The graph at the right shows the equation $y = -2$. The slope of the graph is 0. There are no corresponding values for x.

• A vertical line has an **undefined slope.** The graph at the right shows the equation $x = 3$. The slope of the graph is undefined. There are no corresponding values for y.

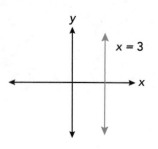

RULE

The slope of a line $= \frac{y_2 - y_1}{x_2 - x_1}$ where (x_1, y_1) and (x_2, y_2) are two points on the line.

The formula for the slope of a line is simply the ratio of the vertical leg of a right triangle to the horizontal leg of the right triangle.

Look at the graph at the right. The expression $y_2 - y_1$ represents the vertical leg, and the expression $x_2 - x_1$ represents the horizontal leg.

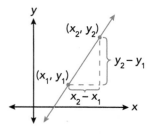

Example 1   What is the slope of a line that passes through the points (2, 5) and (6, 13)?

Step 1   Insert coordinates into the equation to find the slope.

Step 2   Subtract the y-values of the two points. $13 - 5 = 8$

slope $= \frac{13 - 5}{6 - 2} = \frac{8}{4} = 2$

Step 3   Subtract the x-values of the two points. $6 - 2 = 4$

Step 4   Divide 8 by 4. The slope is $+2$.

An **intercept** tells where a line crosses an axis. In the graph at the right, the line labeled m crosses the y-axis at $+3$. The coordinates of the y-intercept are (0, 3). The line crosses the x-axis at -2. The coordinates of the x-intercept are $(-2, 0)$.

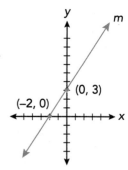

—————————————— R U L E ——————————————

To find the *y*-intercept of a linear equation, substitute 0 for *x* and solve for *y*.

Example 2 What is the *y*-intercept of the equation $y = 3x - 6$?

Replace *x* with 0 and solve for *y*.
$$y = 3x - 6$$
$$y = 3(0) - 6$$
$$y = 0 - 6$$

The coordinates of the *y*-intercept are (0, −6). $y = -6$

—————————————— R U L E ——————————————

To find the *x*-intercept of a linear equation, substitute 0 for *y* and solve for *x*.

Example 3 What is the *x*-intercept of the equation $y = 3x - 6$?
Replace *y* with 0 and solve for *x*.
$$y = 3x - 6$$
$$0 = 3x - 6$$
$$6 = 3x$$

The coordinates of the *x*-intercept are (2, 0). $2 = x$

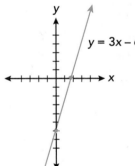

The graph at the right shows the equation $y = 3x - 6$. Notice that the graph crosses the *y*-axis at (0, −6) and that the graph crosses the *x*-axis at (2, 0).

The slope of $y = 3x - 6$ is $\frac{-6 - 0}{0 - 2} = \frac{-6}{-2} = +3$

In the equation above, notice that the slope, 3, equals the number multiplied by *x*. Notice also that the *y*-intercept, −6, is the last term in the equation.

—————————————— R U L E ——————————————

For a linear equation in the form $y = mx + b$, *m* represents the slope and *b* represents the *y*-intercept.

Example 4   What are the slope and y-intercept of the equation $y = 4x + 1$?

   Step 1   Since m represents the slope of the equation $y = mx + b$, the slope of $y = 4x + 1$ is 4.

   Step 2   Since b represents the y-intercept of $y = mx + b$, the y-intercept of $y = 4x + 1$ is $+1$, or $(0, 1)$.

EXERCISE 4

Directions: Solve each problem.

1. What is the slope of a straight line that passes through the points $(3, 2)$ and $(5, 8)$?

2. What is the slope of a straight line that passes through the points $(2, 5)$ and $(10, 9)$?

3. What is the slope of a straight line that passes through the points $(2, 4)$ and $(-7, 10)$?

4. What is the slope of a straight line that passes through the two points shown in the graph at the right?

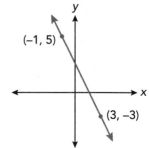

5. Which of the following best represents an equation for the vertical line labeled v in the diagram at the right?
   (1) $x = -4$
   (2) $x = +4$
   (3) $y = -4$
   (4) $y = +4$
   (5) $x = y$

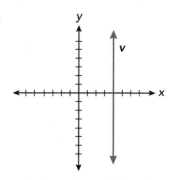

6. Which of the following best describes the slope of a straight-line graph that rises from left to right?

   (1) zero
   (2) undefined
   (3) positive
   (4) negative
   (5) none of the above

7. What is the slope of the equation $y = 2x - 4$?

8. On the coordinate plane grid at the right, mark the *y*-intercept of the equation $y = 2x - 4$.

9. Which of the following equations has a *y*-intercept with the coordinates (0, 5)?

   (1) $y = 5x - 1$
   (2) $y = 2x - 5$
   (3) $y = 5x + 1$
   (4) $y = 2x + 5$
   (5) $y = 5x - 2$

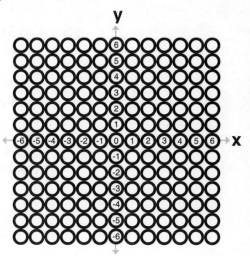

10. What are the coordinates of the *x*-intercept of the equation $y = \frac{x}{2} + 4$?

Use the information in the table and the corresponding graph for problems 11 and 12.

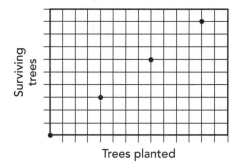

trees planted	surviving trees
0	0
4	3
8	6
12	9

11. Find the slope of the line that connects the points in the graph.

12. What are the coordinates of the *y*-intercept of the graph?

Answers are on page 434.

Multiplying and Dividing Monomials

Multiplying Monomials

You know that a number multiplied by itself is the same as a number raised to the second power. For example, $4 \times 4 = 4^2 = 16$. From working with formulas, you know that a variable multiplied by itself is that variable raised to the second power. For example, $x \cdot x = x^2$. Variables such as x^2, $-5x$, and $64y^2$ are called **monomials**. A monomial is an algebraic expression with only one letter, number, or group of letters and numbers not separated by plus or minus signs.

----------------- RULE -----------------

To multiply monomials, follow the rules for multiplying signed numbers and add the exponents of like variables.

Remember that a variable with no exponent is understood to be to the first power. Study the next examples carefully.

Example 1   Find $5x \cdot 3x$.
Multiply the numbers, $5 \times 3 = 15$, and $5x \cdot 3x = 15x^2$
add the exponents of the variables, $x^{1+1=2}$

Example 2   What is $y(3y - 8)$?
Multiply y by each term in the parentheses. $y(3y - 8) = 3y^2 - 8y$

Example 3   Find $4mn^2 \cdot 5m^2n^3$.
Multiply the numbers, $4 \times 5 = 20$, and $4mn^2 \cdot 5m^2n^3 = 20m^3n^5$
add the exponents of each variable.

Example 4   Write an expression for the area of
the rectangle at the right.

Step 1   Replace l with $3x$ and w with $2x$ in the $A = lw$
formula for the area of a rectangle. $A = 3x \cdot 2x$

Step 2   Multiply the numbers and add the $A = 6x^2$
exponents of the variables.
The area of the rectangle is $6x^2$.

<u>Example 5</u>   If the area of the rectangle in the last example is 150, what is the value of x?

Step 1	Substitute 150 for A.	$A = 6x^2$
		$150 = 6x^2$
Step 2	Divide both sides by 6.	$25 = x^2$
Step 3	Find the square root of 25. The value of x is 5.	$\sqrt{25} = x$
		$5 = x$

EXERCISE 5

Directions: Multiply each monomial.

1. $4x \cdot 3x =$ $2c(c - 5) =$ $(-4a^2)(-6a^3) =$

2. $m^3 \cdot m^4 =$ $n(7n + 4) =$ $3s(s^2 - 2s) =$

3. $5t(6t - 1) =$ $10x \cdot \frac{1}{2}x =$ $4d(d + 12) =$

4. Which of the following is an expression for the area of the rectangle at the right?

   (1) $2x + 4$
   (2) $2x + 8$
   (3) $x^2 + 4x$
   (4) $x^2 + 8$
   (5) $x^2 + 8x$

5. What is the area of the rectangle in problem 4 if $x = 3$?

6. Which of the following is an expression for the area of the triangle at the right?

   (1) $\frac{1}{3}$
   (2) $2x$
   (3) $3x$
   (4) x^2
   (5) $\frac{x^2}{2}$

7. If the area of the triangle in problem 6 is 32, what is the value of x?

Answers are on page 435.

Dividing Monomials

Think about the problem $\dfrac{x^5}{x^2}$.

The problem can be written as $\dfrac{x \cdot x \cdot x \cdot x \cdot x}{x \cdot x}$. After canceling, the result is $x \cdot x \cdot x$, or x^3.

The shortcut is to subtract the exponents. $x^{5-2=3} = x^3$

RULE

To divide monomials, follow the rules for dividing signed numbers and subtract the exponents of like variables.

Example 1 Simplify $\dfrac{20a^3}{4a}$.

Divide the numbers, $\dfrac{20}{4} = 5$, and subtract the exponents of the variables, $a^{3-1=2}$.

$\dfrac{20a^3}{4a} = 5a^2$

Example 2 Simplify $\dfrac{6a^4b^5}{8a^2b^2}$.

Reduce the numbers, $\dfrac{6}{8} = \dfrac{3}{4}$, and subtract the exponents of like variables, $a^{4-2=2}$ and $b^{5-2=3}$.

$\dfrac{6a^4b^5}{8a^2b^2} = \dfrac{3a^2b^3}{4}$, or $\dfrac{3}{4}a^2b^3$

Notice the two ways of writing the last answer. Both are correct.

EXERCISE 6

Directions: Divide each monomial.

1. $\dfrac{x^4}{x} =$ $\qquad$ $\dfrac{25y}{20y} =$ $\qquad$ $\dfrac{8c^2}{2c} =$

2. $\dfrac{6a^4}{3a} =$ $\qquad$ $\dfrac{8x^5}{2x^3} =$ $\qquad$ $\dfrac{x^2y}{xy} =$

3. $\dfrac{15mn}{5n} =$ $\qquad$ $\dfrac{6a^3b^4}{9ab} =$ $\qquad$ $\dfrac{12s^4}{16s} =$

4. The area of the rectangle below is $20x^2$.
   Which of the following is an expression for the length?

   (1) x

   (2) 2x

   (3) 4x

   (4) 5x

   (5) 10x

   [rectangle with side labeled $4x$ and $A = 20x^2$ inside]

5. If the area of the rectangle in problem 4 is 180 square centimeters, what is the value of x?

Answers are on page 435.

Factoring

In the Whole Numbers chapter of this book, you learned that a **factor** is a number that divides evenly into another number. For example, the numbers 1, 2, 4, and 8 are all factors of 16.

A **prime number** is a number that can be divided evenly only by itself and 1. For example, 5 is a prime number because it can be divided evenly only by 5 and 1. 6 is *not* a prime number because it can be divided evenly by 2 and 3 as well as 6 and 1.

Factoring means writing a number or expression as a product of other numbers or terms.

Example 1 Write 12 as a product of prime factors.

Step 1 Find two whole numbers that multiply together to give 12. $12 = 3 \times 4$

Step 2 Check both numbers to see whether there are prime factors of either 3 or 4. 3 is a prime number, but $4 = 2 \times 2$. $12 = 2 \times 2 \times 3$

For the last example, you could start with 6×2. 2 is a prime factor, but 6 is a product of 3×2. The result is the same. The prime factors of 12 are $2 \times 2 \times 3$.

Think about the algebraic expression $10x + 6$. The expression has two **terms**, $10x$ and 6. Both terms can be divided by the whole number 2.

Example 2 Factor the expression $10x + 6$.

Step 1 Find a whole number that divides evenly into both $10x$ and 6. 2 divides evenly into $10x$ and 6. $\frac{10x}{2} = 5x$ and $\frac{6}{2} = 3$

Step 2 Write 2 outside a set of parentheses. Write the result of dividing $10x$ and 6 by 2 inside the parentheses. $2(5x + 3)$

The factored expression of $10x + 6$ is $2(5x + 3)$.

Look at the expression $x^2 - 4x$. There is no whole number other than 1 that divides evenly into both terms. However, you can divide both terms by x.

Example 3   Factor the expression $x^2 - 4x$.

  Step 1   Divide each term by the letter that is in each term, x. $\frac{x^2}{x} = x$ and $\frac{4x}{x} = 4$

  Step 2   Write x outside a set of parentheses. Write the result of dividing both terms by x inside the parentheses. The factored expression of $x^2 - 4x$ is $x(x - 4)$. $x(x - 4)$

EXERCISE 7

Directions: For problems 1–4, write each whole number as a product of prime factors.

1. 9 =   10 =   15 =

2. 18 =   20 =   24 =

3. 25 =   30 =   36 =

4. 40 =   50 =   81 =

For problems 5–8, factor a whole number out of each expression. Then write the factored expression.

5. $4n + 4 =$ $3p - 6 =$

6. $15a - 10 =$ $14c + 35 =$

7. $6b + 8 =$ $6f - 30 =$

8. $36y - 9 =$ $16k + 56 =$

For problems 9–12, factor out a variable from each expression. Then write the factored expression.

9. $c^2 + 8c =$ $d^2 + 4d =$

10. $y^2 - 5y =$ $n^2 - 8n =$

11. $m^2 + 3m =$ $p^2 - 2p =$

12. $a^2 - 8a =$ $s^2 + 9s =$

Answers are on page 435.

Simplifying and Finding Square Roots

Earlier in this book you found the square root of **perfect squares**, numbers that have exact square roots. For example, $\sqrt{81} = 9$ and $\sqrt{144} = 12$. Most numbers do not have exact square roots. For some numbers, however, you can find a factor that has an exact square root.

--- **R U L E** ---

To simplify a square root, follow these steps:
1. Find a factor that is a perfect square.
2. Write the square root of the perfect square outside the $\sqrt{}$ sign and leave the other factor inside the $\sqrt{}$ sign.

Example 1   Simplify $\sqrt{75}$.

Step 1   Think about the factors of 75: 1, 3, 5, 15, and 25. Besides 1, the other perfect square is 25. Write 75 as a multiple of 25 and 3.

$$\sqrt{75} = \sqrt{25 \cdot 3}$$

Step 2   Write 5, the square root of 25, outside the $\sqrt{}$ sign. Leave 3 inside the $\sqrt{}$ sign.

$$\sqrt{75} = 5\sqrt{3}$$

Think about the answer $5\sqrt{3}$. The square root of 3 is approximately 1.73. (You can check this on a calculator.) The answer $5\sqrt{3}$ is approximately $5(1.73) = 8.65$.

To check the square root of 75, find $(8.65)^2$. The answer should be close to 75.

$(8.65)^2 = (8.65)(8.65) = 74.8225$, which is approximately 75.

Example 2   Simplify $\sqrt{18}$.

Step 1   Think about the factors of 18: 1, 2, 3, 6, and 9. Besides 1, the other perfect square is 9. Write 18 as a multiple of 9 and 2.

$$\sqrt{18} = \sqrt{9 \cdot 2}$$

Step 2   Write 3, the square root of 9 outside the $\sqrt{}$ sign. Leave 2 inside the $\sqrt{}$ sign.

$$\sqrt{18} = 3\sqrt{2}$$

Again, think about the answer $3\sqrt{2}$. The square root of 2 is approximately 1.41. (Check this on a calculator.) The answer $3\sqrt{2}$ is approximately 3(1.41), or 4.23.

To check the square root of 18, find $(4.23)^2$. The answer should be close to 18. $(4.23)^2 = (4.23)(4.23) = 17.8929$, which is approximately 18.

However, you can use the Casio *fx*–260 calculator to find the square of a number that does not have a whole number square root.

<u>Example 3</u>   Simplify $\sqrt{145}$.

Press $\boxed{\text{AC}}$.

Press $\boxed{1}$ $\boxed{4}$ $\boxed{5}$ $\boxed{\text{SHIFT}}$ $\boxed{x^2}$.

The display should read $\boxed{12.04159458}$.

Rounded to the nearest hundredth, $\sqrt{145} = 12.04$.

<u>Example 4</u>   Use the Pythagorean relationship to find the length of the hypotenuse of the triangle at the right. Round your answer to the nearest hundredth.

Step 1   Substitute 3 for both a and b in the formula $a^2 + b^2 = c^2$.

$$3^2 + 3^2 = c^2$$

Step 2   Solve for c and use the calculator to find $\sqrt{18}$. The length of the hypotenuse is 4.242640687. Rounded to the nearest hundredth, the answer is 4.24.

$$9 + 9 = c^2$$
$$18 = c^2$$
$$\sqrt{18} = c$$
$$4.24 = c$$

EXERCISE 8

Directions: For problems 1–2, simplify each square root.

1. $\sqrt{27} =$ $\sqrt{8} =$ $\sqrt{20} =$

2. $\sqrt{150} =$ $\sqrt{48} =$ $\sqrt{50} =$

For problem 3, use the calculator to find the square root. Round your answers to the nearest tenth.

3. $\sqrt{12} \approx$ $\sqrt{32} \approx$ $\sqrt{200} \approx$

4. For the right triangles below, use the Pythagorean relationship to calculate the length of each hypotenuse. Express the length to the nearest tenth.

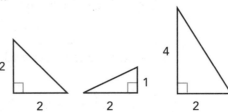

Answers are on page 435.

Trigonometric Ratios

The word **trigonometry** comes from Greek words that mean "measuring triangles." Trigonometry is the study of the relationship between pairs of sides in right triangles.

The three most common ratios in trigonometry are the **sine**, the **cosine**, and the **tangent**. The abbreviations for these ratios are *sin*, *cos*, and *tan*.

In the triangle at the right, angle *A* is one of the two acute angles in a right triangle. Side *AC* is the hypotenuse. Side *BC*, which is across from ∠*A*, is labeled *opposite*. And side *AB*, which forms one side of ∠*A*, is labeled *adjacent*.

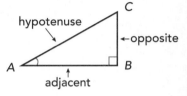

Below are the definitions of the sine, the cosine and the tangent.

$$\sin = \frac{\text{opposite side}}{\text{hypotenuse}} \qquad \cos = \frac{\text{adjacent side}}{\text{hypotenuse}} \qquad \tan = \frac{\text{opposite side}}{\text{adjacent side}}$$

For the triangle at the right, the legs measure 3 and 4, and the hypotenuse is 5. Following are the three trigonometric ratios for angle *X*:

$$\sin X = \frac{\text{opposite}}{\text{hypotenuse}} = \frac{3}{5} = 0.6$$

$$\cos X = \frac{\text{adjacent}}{\text{hypotenuse}} = \frac{4}{5} = 0.8$$

$$\tan X = \frac{\text{opposite}}{\text{adjacent}} = \frac{3}{4} = 0.75$$

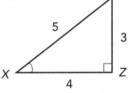

Example 1   For the triangle at the right, what is the tangent of ∠*M* to the nearest thousandth?

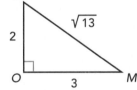

The tangent is $\frac{\text{opposite}}{\text{adjacent}}$.

2 is opposite and 3 is adjacent.

The tangent of ∠*M* is $\frac{2}{3}$ or 0.667.

A scientific calculator is a convenient tool for finding the trigonometric ratios of an angle when you know the number of degrees in the angle.

You can use the Casio *fx–260* to find a trigonometric ratio for an angle.

Press ⏺AC⏺.

Then press the number of degrees in the angle followed by ⏺SIN⏺, ⏺COS⏺, or ⏺TAN⏺.

Example 2   Use a calculator to find the sine of 25°.

Press ⏺AC⏺.

Press ⏺2⏺ ⏺5⏺ ⏺SIN⏺.

The display should read ⏹0.422618261⏹.

To the nearest thousandth, the sine of 25° is 0.423.

Example 3   Use a calculator to find the cosine of 50°.

Press `AC`.

Press `5` `0` `COS`.

The display should read `0.642787609`.

To the nearest thousandth, the cosine of 50° is 0.643.

Example 4   Write an equation with a trigonometric ratio to express the height x of triangle ABC at the right.

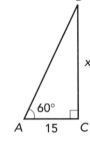

Side AB is the hypotenuse. Height BC is opposite the 60° angle and base AC is adjacent. The ratio of the height x to the base 15 is the tangent of 60°.

$$\tan 60° = \frac{x}{15}$$

Example 5   To the nearest tenth, what is the height of the triangle in the previous example?

Step 1   Find tan 60° on a calculator.

Press `AC`.

Press `6` `0` `TAN`.

The display should read `1.732050808`.

Round to the nearest thousandth. $\tan 60° = 1.732$

Step 2   Multiply both sides of the equation by 15 to solve for x. $1.732 = \frac{x}{15}$

Step 3   Round 25.98 to the nearest tenth. $25.98 = x$
The height of the triangle is 26.0. $25.98 \rightarrow 26.0$

EXERCISE 9

Directions: For problems 1–3, use the triangle below.

1. Which side, XY, XZ, or YZ is opposite ∠X?

2. Which side in triangle XYZ is the hypotenuse?

3. Does the ratio of $\frac{YZ}{XZ}$ represent the sine, the cosine, or the tangent of ∠X?

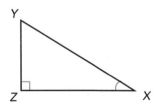

For problems 4–6, use the triangle below. Tell what each of the following ratios represents for ∠M: the sine, the cosine, or the tangent.

4. $\frac{12}{13}$ =

5. $\frac{5}{12}$ =

6. $\frac{5}{13}$ =

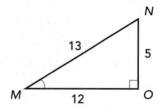

For problems 7–9, use triangle EFG below. Write a ratio for each of the following.

7. sin *E* =

8. cos *E* =

9. tan *E* =

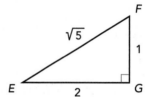

Use a calculator to fill in the following chart. Where necessary, round each answer to the nearest thousandth.

	angle	sin	cos	tan
10.	30°			
11.	45°			
12.	60°			
13.	75°			

14. The diagram below shows a building that casts a shadow 44 feet long. The angle created by the shadow and an imaginary line from the top of the building to the end of the shadow is 65°.

Which of the following equations can be used to calculate the height of the building?

(1) $\sin 65° = \frac{x}{44}$

(2) $\cos 65° = \frac{x}{44}$

(3) $\tan 65° = \frac{x}{44}$

(4) $\sin 65° = \frac{44}{x}$

(5) $\tan 65° = \frac{44}{x}$

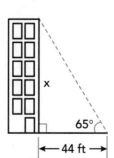

15. Use a calculator to find the height of the building to the nearest tenth of a foot.

16. Which of the following equations can be used to calculate the length of y in the triangle at the right?

    (1) $\cos 45° = \frac{y}{7}$

    (2) $\sin 45° = \frac{y}{7}$

    (3) $\tan 45° = \frac{y}{7}$

    (4) $\cos 45° = \frac{7}{y}$

    (5) $\tan 45° = \frac{7}{y}$

17. Use a calculator to find the length, to the nearest tenth, of *y* in problem 16.

Answers are on page 435.

Quadratic Equations

The equation $y = x^2 + 1$ is called a **quadratic equation**. The name *quadratic* comes from the Latin word for squared. In a quadratic equation at least one variable is raised to the second power. Remember that *x squared* means "*x* raised to the second power."

You already have used quadratic equations in this book. The Pythagorean relationship and the formula for the distance between two points on the rectangular coordinate plane are quadratic equations.

Remember that the graph of a linear equation is a straight line. The graph of a quadratic equation looks very different.

Suppose you let $x = 2, 1, 0, -1$, and -2 for the equation $y = x^2 + 1$.

If $x = 2$, then $y = (2)^2 + 1 = 4 + 1 = 5$.

If $x = 1$, then $y = (1)^2 + 1 = 1 + 1 = 2$.

If $x = 0$, then $y = (0)^2 + 1 = 0 + 1 = 1$.

If $x = -1$, then $y = (-1)^2 + 1 = 1 + 1 = 2$.

If $x = -2$, then $y = (-2)^2 + 1 = 4 + 1 = 5$.

The five values of *x* and their corresponding values of *y* are the coordinates for five points on the rectangular coordinate plane: $(2, 5)$, $(1, 2)$, $(0, 1)$, $(-1, 2)$, and $(-2, 5)$.

The graph at the right shows these five points. Notice that the points lie on a curve called a **parabola**. The coordinates of any point on the parabola are solutions to the equation $y = x^2 + 1$.

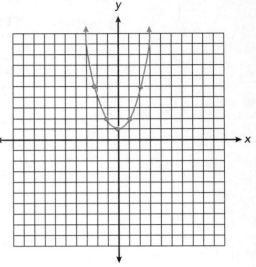

To find out whether a point is on the graph of an equation, substitute the x-value of the point into the equation. If the solution to the equation is the same as the y-value, then the point is on the graph.

Example 1   Does the point (3, 6) lie on the graph of the equation $y = x^2 - x$?

Substitute 3 for x in $y = x^2 - x$.
This gives y the value of 6.
Therefore, point (3, 6) is on the graph.

$y = x^2 - x$
$y = 3^2 - 3 = 9 - 3$
$y = 6$

Example 2   Does the point (4, 28) lie on the graph of the equation $y = 2x^2 + 3$?

Substitute 4 for x in $y = 2x^2 + 3$.
This gives y the value of 35.
Therefore, point (4, 28) is *not* on the graph.

$y = 2x^2 + 3$
$y = 2(4)^2 + 3 = 2(16) + 3$
$y = 35$

--- R U L E ---

To solve and graph a quadratic equation, follow these steps:
1. Substitute each value of x into the equation to find the corresponding value of y.
2. Make a table of the x and y values.
3. Put these points on the coordinate plane and connect them with a curved line.

Example 3   Make a graph of the equation $y = x^2 - 3$. Let $x = 2, 1, 0, -1,$ and -2.

Step 1   Substitute each value of x into the equation to find the corresponding value of y.

When $x = 2$, $y = 2^2 - 3 = 4 - 3 = 1$

When $x = 1$, $y = 1^2 - 3 = 1 - 3 = -2$

When $x = 0$, $y = 0^2 - 3 = 0 - 3 = -3$

When $x = -1$, $y = (-1)^2 - 3 = 1 - 3 = -2$

When $x = -2$, $y = (-2)^2 - 3 = 4 - 3 = 1$

Step 2 Make a table of the x and y values.

Step 3 Put these points on the coordinate plane and connect them with a curved line.

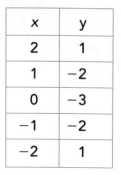

x	y
2	1
1	−2
0	−3
−1	−2
−2	1

Think about the quadratic equation $x^2 = 16$. This equation has two solutions. You know that the square root of 16 is 4. However, the square root of 16 can also be −4 since $(-4)(-4) = 16$. To solve a quadratic equation, substitute answer choices into the equation. Remember that there must be *two* solutions.

<u>Example 4</u> Which of the following are the solutions to $x^2 - 8x + 12 = 0$?

(1) $x = 3$ and $x = 4$
(2) $x = 6$ and $x = 2$
(3) $x = -3$ and $x = 4$
(4) $x = 6$ and $x = -2$
(5) $x = -6$ and $x = -2$

Step 1 Try the solutions in choice (1). Substitute 3 for x. Since $-24 + 21$ does not equal 0, choice (1) is incorrect.

$x^2 - 8x + 12 = 0$
$3^2 - 8(3) + 12 = 0$
$9 - 24 + 12 = 0$
$-24 + 21 \neq 0$ **incorrect**

Step 2 Try the first solution in choice (2). Substitute 6 for x. Since $-48 + 48$ does equal 0, $x = 6$ is a correct solution.

$x^2 - 8x + 12 = 0$
$6^2 - 8(6) + 12 = 0$
$36 - 48 + 12 = 0$
$-48 + 48 = 0$ **correct**

Step 3 Try the second solution in choice (2). Substitute 2 for x. Since $-16 + 16$ does equal 0, $x = 2$ is also a correct solution.

$x^2 - 8x + 12 = 0$
$2^2 - 8(2) + 12 = 0$
$4 - 16 + 12 = 0$
$-16 + 16 = 0$ **correct**

Since both solutions in choice (2) are correct, choice (2) is the answer.

For more practice, try substituting answer choices (3), (4), and (5) in the last example. Remember that *both* values in each solution must be correct.

EXERCISE 10

Directions: For problems 1–3, use the equation $y = 2x^2 - 5$.

1. What is the value of y when $x = 2$?

2. What is the value of y when $x = -3$?

3. What is the value of y when $x = 0$?

For problems 4–6, answer each question.

4. Is the point (3, 12) a solution to the equation $y = x^2 + x$?

5. Is the point (0, 2) a solution to the equation $y = x^2 - 3x + 2$?

6. Does the point (−4, 10) lie on the graph of the equation $y = x^2 - x - 6$?

For each equation, fill in the table for each given value of x.

7. $y = x^2 + x + 1$

x	y
2	
1	
0	
−1	
−2	
−3	

8. $y = x^2 - x + 3$

x	y
3	
2	
1	
0	
−1	
−2	

For problems 9–12, choose the correct solution to each quadratic equation.

9. $x^2 - 14x + 48 = 0$
    (1) $x = 4$ and $x = 12$
    (2) $x = 3$ and $x = -16$
    (3) $x = 6$ and $x = 8$
    (4) $x = 2$ and $x = -24$

10. $x^2 - 3x - 10 = 0$
    (1) $x = 5$ and $x = -2$
    (2) $x = 10$ and $x = 1$
    (3) $x = 2$ and $x = -5$
    (4) $x = -10$ and $x = -1$

11. $x^2 - x - 12 = 0$
    (1) $x = 2$ and $x = 6$
    (2) $x = 12$ and $x = -1$
    (3) $x = -4$ and $x = 3$
    (4) $x = 4$ and $x = -3$

12. $x^2 - 9x + 8 = 0$
    (1) $x = 8$ and $x = 1$
    (2) $x = 4$ and $x = -2$
    (3) $x = -4$ and $x = 2$
    (4) $x = -8$ and $x = 1$

Answers are on page 436.

Advanced Algebra and Geometry Review

PART I

Directions: Use a calculator to solve any of the problems in this section. For problems 1 and 2, mark each answer on the corresponding number grid.

1. What is the area of triangle *ABC*?

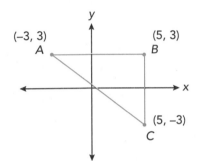

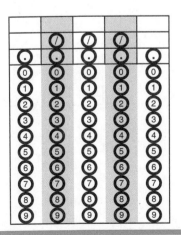

2. When $x = -4$, what is the value of y in the equation $y = -3x + 2$?

3. Does the point (2, 5) lie on the graph of the equation $y = \frac{x}{2} + 4$?

4. What is the slope of a straight line that passes through points (8, 6) and (4, 2) on the coordinate plane?

5. Does the point (2, 2) lie on the graph of the equation $y = x^2 - 3x + 4$?

Use the illustration below to answer questions 6 and 7.

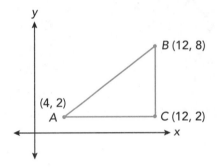

6. What is the distance from point *A* to point *C*?

7. What is the distance from point *A* to point *B*?

PART II

Directions: Solve the following problems without using a calculator.

8. Mark the point $(-4, -2)$ on the coordinate plane grid.

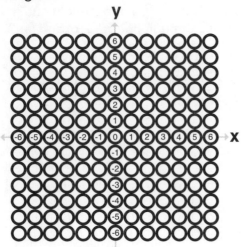

9. Simplify the expression $\frac{14xy^3}{7xy}$.

10. Write 40 as a product of prime factors.

11. Factor the expression $12m - 16$.

12. Factor the expression $a^2 + 9a$.

13. Simplify $\sqrt{45}$.

14. Mark the coordinates of the y-intercept for the equation $y = -4x + 6$ on the coordinate plane grid.

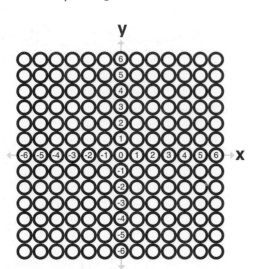

Choose the correct answer to each problem.

15. What are the coordinates of a point on the rectangular coordinate plane that lies 3 units to the right of the vertical axis and 7 units below the horizontal axis?

   (1) $(3, 7)$
   (2) $(3, -7)$
   (3) $(3, 0)$
   (4) $(-3, 7)$
   (5) $(-3, -7)$

16. Which expression represents the area of the rectangle below?

   (1) $x^2 - 3$
   (2) $x - 3x$
   (3) $2x - 3x$
   (4) $2x^2 - 6$
   (5) $x^2 - 3x$

17. Which of the following represents the cosine of $\angle A$ in the triangle below?

   (1) $\frac{3}{5}$
   (2) $\frac{4}{5}$
   (3) $\frac{3}{4}$
   (4) $\frac{5}{4}$
   (5) $\frac{5}{3}$

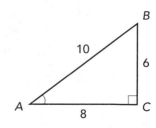

18. Which of the following represents sin X for the diagram below?

   (1) $\frac{YZ}{XZ}$
   (2) $\frac{XZ}{YZ}$
   (3) $\frac{XY}{YZ}$
   (4) $\frac{YZ}{XY}$
   (5) $\frac{YZ}{XZ}$

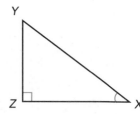

19. The diagram shows a pole that casts a shadow 20 feet long. The angle created by the shadow and an imaginary line to the top of the pole measures 75°. Which of the following represents an equation for finding the height x of the pole?

   (1) $\tan 75° = \dfrac{x}{20}$

   (2) $\sin 75° = \dfrac{x}{20}$

   (3) $\cos 75° = \dfrac{x}{20}$

   (4) $\tan 75° = \dfrac{20}{x}$

   (5) $\sin 75° = \dfrac{20}{x}$

75°

20 ft

x

20. What are the correct solutions for $x^2 - 15x + 44 = 0$?

   (1) $x = 2$ and $x = 22$

   (2) $x = 4$ and $x = 11$

   (3) $x = -4$ and $x = 11$

   (4) $x = 44$ and $x = -1$

   (5) $x = -44$ and $x = 1$

Answers are on page 437.

You should have gotten at least 16 problems right on this last exercise. If you did not get 16 right, review this chapter before you go on. If you got 16 or more right, correct any problem you got wrong. Then go on to the Posttest.

Mathematics

Directions: The test that follows is similar to the GED Mathematics Test. The test has two parts. On the first part, you will be permitted the use of a calculator. On the second part, no calculator use is allowed. Each part of this Posttest should take no longer than 45 minutes to complete.

At the end of 45 minutes, if you have not completed Part I, mark your place and finish the test. Do the same with Part II. This will give you an idea of whether you can finish the real test in 90 minutes. Mark each answer on the answer grid. Answer as many questions as you can. A blank will be a wrong answer, so make a reasonable guess if you are not sure. Use any formulas on page 439 that you need.

When you finish, check your answers. The evaluation chart at the end of the answers will help you determine which areas to review before you are ready for the actual GED Mathematics Test.

POSTTEST

Posttest Answer Grid, Part I

1 ① ② ③ ④ ⑤

2 ① ② ③ ④ ⑤

3 ① ② ③ ④ ⑤

4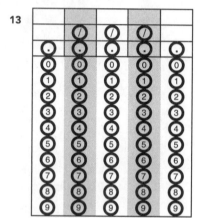

5

6 ① ② ③ ④ ⑤

7 ① ② ③ ④ ⑤

8 ① ② ③ ④ ⑤

9 ① ② ③ ④ ⑤

10 ① ② ③ ④ ⑤

11 ① ② ③ ④ ⑤

12

13

14 ① ② ③ ④ ⑤

15 ① ② ③ ④ ⑤

16 ① ② ③ ④ ⑤

17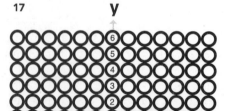

18 ① ② ③ ④ ⑤

19 ① ② ③ ④ ⑤

20 ① ② ③ ④ ⑤

21

22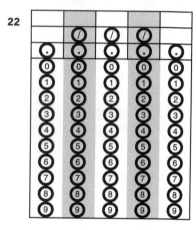

23 ① ② ③ ④ ⑤

24 ① ② ③ ④ ⑤

25 ① ② ③ ④ ⑤

POSTTEST

Part I

Directions: Solve each problem. You may use a calculator on any of these problems. Use the formulas on page 439 as needed.

For problems 1 and 2, refer to the following passage.

Sam is building a cabinet. The materials that he needs will cost $480. To determine the price of the cabinet for his customer, Sam charges 30% more than the cost of the materials. Sam asks for a down payment of 40% of the total before the work begins. The customer pays the balance when the job is finished.

1. Find the total price Sam will charge for the cabinet.

   (1) $780
   (2) $672
   (3) $624
   (4) $584
   (5) $504

2. What is the down payment the customer must pay?

   (1) $374.40
   (2) $249.60
   (3) $230.40
   (4) $192.00
   (5) $176.00

3. To the nearest square foot, what is the area of the shaded part of the figure?

   (1) 1000
   (2) 886
   (3) 686
   (4) 569
   (5) 77

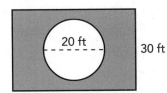
20 ft / 30 ft / 40 ft

Directions: For problems 4 and 5, mark each answer on the corresponding number grid on the answer page.

4. Eighteen railroad ties, each 2.9 meters long, are laid end to end. Find the total length, in meters, of the eighteen ties.

5. Ellen drove 220 miles in 3.5 hours. To the nearest tenth, find Ellen's average speed in miles per hour.

Directions: For problems 6 and 7, refer to the following passage.

Mr. and Mrs. Allen are planning to buy a house that is listed at $146,000. When they sign the contract, they must make a down payment of 10% of the listed price. They also have to pay $2000 to their lawyer, $8760 as a commission to their real estate agent, and $900 for other expenses involved with the purchase.

6. Find the total amount the Allens must pay the day they sign the contract.

   (1) $18,760
   (2) $21,360
   (3) $24,260
   (4) $25,360
   (5) $26,260

7. The commission the real estate agent receives is what percent of the list price of the house?

   (1) 3%
   (2) 5%
   (3) 6%
   (4) 8%
   (5) 10%

8. In the diagram below, *MN* = 10, *NO* = 3, and *QO* = 48. Find *PQ*.

   (1) 480
   (2) 360
   (3) 320
   (4) 240
   (5) 160

   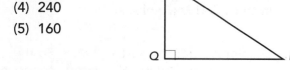

9. At a factory the ratio of male employees to female employees is 5:3. Altogether, there are 96 employees. How many women work at the factory?

   (1) 64
   (2) 60
   (3) 36
   (4) 32
   (5) 28

10. The height of this triangle is three times the base. The area of the triangle is 96. Find the height of the triangle.

    (1) 4
    (2) 8
    (3) 16
    (4) 24
    (5) 48

    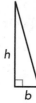

11. To build a bookcase, Paul needs 8 pieces of lumber, each $38\frac{1}{2}$ inches long. What is the minimum number of 10-foot boards that he should buy?

    (1) 1
    (2) 2
    (3) 3
    (4) 4
    (5) 5

Directions: For problems 12 and 13, mark each answer on the corresponding number grid on the answer page.

12. Find the perimeter, in meters, of this figure.

    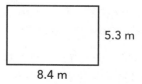

    8.4 m

13. A butcher sliced 4.56 pounds of meat from a leg of lamb that weighed 7 pounds. Find the weight, in pounds, of the remaining leg of lamb.

14. These two figures have equal areas. Find the side of the square.

    (1) 20
    (2) 40
    (3) 50
    (4) 75
    (5) 100

    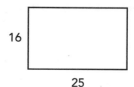

    16

    25   s

15. Jack sells used cars at his garage. The four cars he has for sale now are priced at $2380, $4950, $8265, and $5790 respectively. Find the median price of the cars.

    (1) $5320
    (2) $5346
    (3) $5370
    (4) $5400
    (5) $5790

16. The area of this triangle is 147. The ratio of side *AB* to side *AC* is 2:3. Find the length of side *AB*.

    (1) 3.5
    (2) 7
    (3) 14
    (4) 21
    (5) 28

    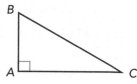

POSTTEST

17. Mark the point $(-3, +4)$ on the coordinate plane grid on the answer page.

Directions: For problems 18–20, refer to the table below.

Corn Production of Four Farmers				
	A	B	C	D
Yield (bushels/acre)	135	167	148	112
Cost ($/bushel)	$3.40	$2.20	$1.90	$1.40
Net ($/acre*)	−$135	$33.40	$74	$112

*based on a price of $2.40/bushel

18. Which farmer had the highest yield?

(1) A

(2) B

(3) C

(4) D

(5) Not enough information is given.

19. If farmers C and D each have 200 acres of corn, how much more does farmer D net than farmer C?

(1) $ 4,600

(2) $ 7,600

(3) $ 8,120

(4) $20,320

(5) Not enough information is given.

20. Based on the information in the table, which of the following statements is true?

(1) The lower the cost, the higher the profit.

(2) The higher the yield, the higher the profit.

(3) A higher yield results in lower profits.

(4) Higher profits come from higher costs.

(5) Higher profits come from lower yields.

Directions: For problems 21 and 22, mark each answer on the corresponding number grid on the answer page.

21. Find the volume, rounded to the nearest cubic foot, of the cylindrical tank.

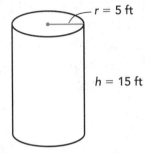

22. Alfredo drove 2 miles north and then 4.8 miles east. Find the shortest distance, to the nearest tenth of a mile, from Alfredo's current location to his starting point.

23. $\angle AOB$ is a right angle. Find the measurement of $\angle COD$.

(1) 42°

(2) 48°

(3) 52°

(4) 122°

(5) 132°

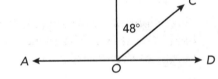

24. AB is parallel to CD, and $\angle b = 119°$. Find $\angle h$.

(1) 71°

(2) 61°

(3) 29°

(4) 19°

(5) 9°

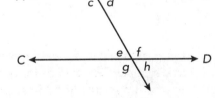

25. For the equation $y = 3x - 2$, what are the coordinates of the point on the graph of the equation when $x = 2$?

(1) (2, 4)

(2) (3, 2)

(3) (6, 2)

(4) (4, 2)

(5) (2, 3)

POSTTEST

Posttest Answer Grid, Part II

26 ① ② ③ ④ ⑤

27 ① ② ③ ④ ⑤

28 ① ② ③ ④ ⑤

29 ① ② ③ ④ ⑤

30 ① ② ③ ④ ⑤

31

32 ① ② ③ ④ ⑤

33 ① ② ③ ④ ⑤

34 ① ② ③ ④ ⑤

35 ① ② ③ ④ ⑤

36 ① ② ③ ④ ⑤

37

38 ① ② ③ ④ ⑤

39 ① ② ③ ④ ⑤

40 ① ② ③ ④ ⑤

41 ① ② ③ ④ ⑤

42 ① ② ③ ④ ⑤

43

44 ① ② ③ ④ ⑤

45 ① ② ③ ④ ⑤

46 ① ② ③ ④ ⑤

47 ① ② ③ ④ ⑤

48 ① ② ③ ④ ⑤

49 ① ② ③ ④ ⑤

50 ① ② ③ ④ ⑤

POSTTEST

Part II

Directions: Solve the following problems without a calculator. Use the formulas on page 439 as needed.

26. At the Acme tool shop 35 employees work 40 hours a week at an average wage of $12 an hour. Which of the following expresses the total weekly payroll for the employees at Acme?

    (1) $\frac{35 \times 40}{12}$

    (2) $35 \times 40 \times 12$

    (3) $35 + 40 \times 12$

    (4) $35(40 + 12)$

    (5) $12(35 + 40)$

27. In $\triangle XYZ$, $\angle X = 65°$ and $\angle Y = 50°$. What kind of triangle is $\triangle XYZ$?

    (1) right

    (2) scalene

    (3) isosceles

    (4) equilateral

    (5) Not enough information is given.

28. Grace has to type a 2500-word report and a 500-word letter. She can type 65 words per minute. Which of the following expresses the number of minutes she will need to type both the report and the letter?

    (1) $\frac{2500 + 500}{65}$

    (2) $65(2000) + 65(500)$

    (3) $65(2500 + 500)$

    (4) $\frac{2500 \times 500}{65}$

    (5) $\frac{2500}{65} + 500$

29. Solve for r in the equation $9r - 8 = 6r + 7$.

    (1) $\frac{1}{3}$

    (2) 1

    (3) 3

    (4) 5

    (5) 15

30. James, Steve, and Charlie worked together to build a garage. Steve worked twice as many hours as James. Charlie worked 10 hours more than Steve. Altogether, they worked 100 hours. How many hours did Charlie work?

    (1) 18

    (2) 33

    (3) 36

    (4) 46

    (5) 50

Directions: For problem 31, mark the answer on the corresponding number grid on the answer page.

31. What is the value of $(\frac{2}{3})^2$?

32. Solve for w in $3w + 1 \le 7(3 - w)$.

    (1) $w \le 2$

    (2) $w \le 4$

    (3) $w \le 5$

    (4) $w \le 10$

    (5) $w \le 20$

33. Which of the following is the same as $x^2 - 8x$?

    (1) $x(-8)$

    (2) $(x - 8)(x + 8)$

    (3) $x^2 + 8x$

    (4) $x(1 - 8)$

    (5) $x(x - 8)$

POSTTEST

34. Which of the following is the same as $6a + 24b - 18$?

    (1) $(6a + 4b)(4a - 3)$
    (2) $6a(1 + 4b - 3)$
    (3) $6(a + 4b - 3)$
    (4) $(a + b)(6 + 4 - 18)$
    (5) $6(1 + 4b - 3a)$

Directions: For problems 35 and 36, refer to the table below.

Unemployment Rates			
	1994	1996	1998
Total	6.1%	5.4%	4.5%
16–19 years	17.6	16.7	14.6
20–24 years	9.7	9.3	7.9
25–44 years	5.3	4.6	3.6
45–64 years	4.0	3.3	2.7
65 years +	4.0	3.6	3.2

35. Based on the information in the table, the 1998 unemployment rate for 16- to 19-year-olds was about how many times the unemployment rate for 25- to 44-year-olds?

    (1) half
    (2) the same
    (3) twice
    (4) three times
    (5) four times

36. For what year was the total unemployment rate less than 5%?

    (1) 1994
    (2) 1996
    (3) 1998
    (4) 1994 and 1996
    (5) 1996 and 1998

37. Mark the y-intercept of the equation $y = 3x + 4$ on the coordinate plane grid on the answer page.

38. What is the slope of the line that passes through points A and B?

    (1) $\frac{5}{2}$
    (2) $-\frac{5}{2}$
    (3) $-\frac{4}{3}$
    (4) $\frac{3}{4}$
    (5) $-\frac{2}{5}$

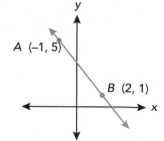

39. What is the distance between points A and B in the illustration above?

    (1) 5
    (2) 7
    (3) 8
    (4) 9
    (5) 11

40. These two figures have the same area. What is the measurement, in feet, of the base of the triangle?

    (1) 4
    (2) 6
    (3) 8
    (4) 12
    (5) 16

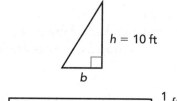

. POSTTEST

41. Arrange the following lengths of 2-inch by 4-inch lumber in order from shortest to longest.

 A: $2\frac{1}{2}$ feet

 B: $33\frac{1}{3}$ inches

 C: 3 feet $3\frac{1}{3}$ inches

 D: 29 inches

 E: 3 feet

 (1) A, B, D, E, C
 (2) B, D, A, E, C
 (3) C, D, A, B, E
 (4) D, A, B, E, C
 (5) C, B, D, A, E

42. Which of the following expresses 67,500,000 in scientific notation?

 (1) 6.75×10^{-7}
 (2) 6.75×10^{6}
 (3) 6.75×10^{7}
 (4) 6.75×10^{-6}
 (5) 6.75×10^{-8}

Directions: For problem 43, mark the answer on the corresponding number grid on the answer page.

43. A square has an area of 2.25 square meters. Find the measurement, in meters, of each side.

44. For these two triangles, $DE \cong GH$ and $EF \cong HI$. Which of the following, along with the information given, is enough to make the triangles congruent?

 (1) $\angle D \cong \angle F$
 (2) $\angle E \cong \angle H$
 (3) $\angle D \cong \angle I$
 (4) $EF \cong GI$
 (5) $DF \cong GH$

45. Marlene spends $\frac{1}{3}$ of her income on rent, $\frac{1}{5}$ on food, and $\frac{3}{10}$ on loan payments. What total fraction of her income does she pay for these expenses?

 (1) $\frac{2}{3}$
 (2) $\frac{3}{4}$
 (3) $\frac{4}{5}$
 (4) $\frac{5}{6}$
 (5) $\frac{9}{10}$

46. At a sale Ruth bought 4 cans of pea soup, 6 cans of tomato soup, and 10 cans of chicken soup. There were no labels on the cans. The first can she opened turned out to be tomato soup. The second can she opened was chicken soup. What is the probability that the third can she opens will be pea soup?

 (1) $\frac{1}{4}$
 (2) $\frac{1}{5}$
 (3) $\frac{4}{9}$
 (4) $\frac{2}{9}$
 (5) $\frac{1}{9}$

47. What is the value of $\frac{x^2}{4}$ when $x = -10$?

(1) $\frac{2}{5}$

(2) $\frac{5}{2}$

(3)   25

(4) -25

(5)   50

48. This illustration shows three points on a coordinate plane. What are the coordinates of the fourth point that will form, along with the other three points, a rectangle with an area of 24?

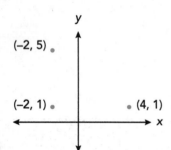

(1) (5, 4)

(2) (4, 6)

(3) (4, 4)

(4) (5, 5)

(5) (4, 5)

49. Riley cut a 25-inch wire into 40 equal pieces. Assuming no waste, what was the length, in inches, of each piece?

(1) $1\frac{3}{5}$

(2) $1\frac{2}{5}$

(3) $\frac{7}{8}$

(4) $\frac{5}{8}$

(5) $\frac{3}{8}$

50. Last year the Capello family paid $720 a month rent from January through September. Then from October through December they paid $792 a month. Which expression represents their mean monthly rent for the year?

(1) $\frac{\$720 + \$792}{2}$

(2) $\frac{\$720 + \$792}{12}$

(3) $\frac{6 \times \$720 + 6 \times \$792}{12}$

(4) $9 \times \$720 + 3 \times \$792$

(5) $\frac{9 \times \$720 + 3 \times \$792}{12}$

Answers start on page 365.

POSTTEST

Answer Key

Part I

1. (3) $624   30% = 0.3   0.3 × $480 = $144
$144 + $480 = $624

2. (2) $249.60   40% = 0.4
0.4 × $624 = $249.60

3. (2) 886   Area = $lw - \pi r^2$
= 40 × 30 − 3.14 × 10²
= 1200 − 314
= 886

4. 52.2   18 × 2.9 = 52.2 meters

5. 62.9 $\frac{220}{3.5} = 62.857 \rightarrow 62.9$

6. (5) $26,260 10% = 0.1
0.1 × $146,000 = $14,600
$14,600 + $2,000 + $8,760 + $900 = $26,260

7. (3) 6% $\frac{\$8,760}{\$146,000} = 0.06 = 6\%$

8. (5) 160 $\frac{3}{10} = \frac{48}{x}$
3x = 480
x = 160

9. (3) 36   5 + 3 = 8 total $\frac{women}{total} \frac{3}{8} = \frac{x}{96}$
8x = 288
x = 36

10. (4) 24   b = x and h = 3x
Area = $\frac{1}{2} \cdot x \cdot 3x = \frac{3x^2}{2}$
$96 = \frac{3x^2}{2}$
$192 = 3x^2$
$64 = x^2$
8 = x
24 = 3x

11. (3) 3   Each board makes $\frac{10 \times 12}{38.5} =$
3 pieces + a remainder.
To get 8 pieces, Paul needs 3 boards.

12. 27.4   P = 2l + 2w
P = 2(8.4) + 2(5.3)
P = 16.8 + 10.6
P = 27.4

13. 2.44   7.00 − 4.56 = 2.44

14. (1) 20 $lw = s^2$
$25 \times 16 = s^2$
$400 = s^2$
$20 = s$

15. (3) $5370 $2380 $4950 $5790 $8265
$\frac{\$4950 + \$5790}{2} = \frac{\$10,740}{2} = \$5370$

16. (3) 14   b = 3x and h = 2x
Area = $\frac{1}{2} \cdot 3x \cdot 2x$
$147 = \frac{6x^2}{2}$
$294 = 6x^2$
$49 = x^2$
7 = x
14 = 2x

17. (−3, 4)

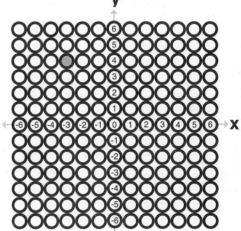

18. (2) B

19. (2) $7,600 D = 200 × $112 = $22,400
C = 200 × $74 = $14,800
$22,400 − $14,800 = $7,600

20. (1) The lower the cost, the higher the profit.

21. 1178   V = $\pi r^2 h$
V = 3.14 × 5² × 15
V = 3.14 × 25 × 15 = 1177.5→1178

POSTTEST

22. 5.2

$$a^2 + b^2 = c^2$$
$$2^2 + (4.8)^2 = c^2$$
$$4 + 23.04 = c^2$$
$$27.04 = c^2$$
$$5.2 = c$$

23. (1) 42°   90° − 48° = 42°

24. (2) 61°   180° − 119° = 61°

25. (1) (2, 4)   When $x = 2$, $y = 3(2) − 2 = 6 − 2 = 4$.

Part II

26. (2) 35 × 40 × 12

27. (3) isosceles 180° − 65° − 50° = 65°
Since two angles are equal, the triangle is isosceles.

28. (1) $\dfrac{2500 + 500}{65}$

29. (4) 5

$$9r − 8 = 6r + 7$$
$$3r = 15$$
$$r = 5$$

30. (4) 46

James's hours = x
Steve's hours = $2x$
Charlie's hours = $2x + 10$
$x + 2x + 2x + 10 = 100$
$5x = 90$
$x = 18$
$2(18) + 10 = 36 + 10 = 46$

31. $\dfrac{4}{9}$ $(\dfrac{2}{3})^2 = \dfrac{2}{3} \times \dfrac{2}{3} = \dfrac{4}{9}$

32. (1) $w \le 2$

$$3w + 1 \le 7(3 − w)$$
$$3w + 1 \le 21 − 7w$$
$$10w \le 20$$
$$w \le 2$$

33. (5) $x(x − 8)$ $x^2 − 8x = x(x − 8)$

34. (3) $6(a + 4b − 3)$ $6a + 24b − 18 = 6(a + 4b − 3)$

35. (5) four times
3.6 × 4 = 14.4, which is close to 14.6.

36. (3) 1998   The unemployment rate for 1998 was 4.5%.

37. (0, 4)   When $x = 0$, $y = 3(0) + 4 = +4$

38. (3) $−\dfrac{4}{3}$ slope $= \dfrac{5 − 1}{−1 − 2} = \dfrac{4}{−3} = −\dfrac{4}{3}$

39. (1) 5   distance $= \sqrt{(−1 − 2)^2 + (5 − 1)^2}$
$= \sqrt{(−3)^2 + (4)^2}$
$= \sqrt{9 + 16}$
$= \sqrt{25}$
$= 5$

40. (3) 8

$$lw = \dfrac{1}{2}bh$$
$$80 \cdot \dfrac{1}{2} = \dfrac{1}{2}b \cdot 10$$
$$40 = 5b$$
$$8 = b$$

41. (4) D, A, B, E, C

A: $2\dfrac{1}{2}$ ft $= 2\dfrac{1}{2} \times 12 = 30$ in.

B: $33\dfrac{1}{3}$ in.

C: 3 feet $3\dfrac{1}{3}$ in. $= 36 + 3\dfrac{1}{3} = 39\dfrac{1}{3}$ in.

D: 29 in.

E: 3 ft = 36 in.

42. (3) 6.75×10^7
The decimal point moves 7 places to the left.

POSTTEST

43. 1.5
$$Area = s^2$$
$$2.25 = s^2$$
$$\sqrt{2.25} = s$$
$$1.5 = s$$

44. (2) $\angle E \cong \angle H$ This satisfies the side angle side requirement.

45. (4) $\dfrac{5}{6}$
$$\dfrac{1}{3} = \dfrac{10}{30}$$
$$\dfrac{1}{5} = \dfrac{6}{30}$$
$$+ \dfrac{3}{10} = \dfrac{9}{30}$$
$$\overline{\phantom{+ \dfrac{3}{10} = }\dfrac{25}{30} = \dfrac{5}{6}}$$

46. (4) $\dfrac{2}{9}$ $\dfrac{\text{favorable outcomes}}{\text{total}}$ $\dfrac{4}{18} = \dfrac{2}{9}$

47. (3) 25 $\dfrac{x^2}{4} = \dfrac{(-10)^2}{4} = \dfrac{100}{4} = 25$

48. (5) (4, 5)

49. (4) $\dfrac{5}{8}$ $\dfrac{25}{40} = \dfrac{5}{8}$

50. (5) $\dfrac{9 \times \$720 + 3 \times \$792}{12}$

They paid \$720 for 9 months + \$792 for 3 months. To find the mean, divide by 12 months.

Evaluation Chart

On the chart below, circle the numbers of the problems you got wrong. To the right of the problem numbers, you will find the section and starting pages that cover the skills you need to solve the problems. Use this chart to determine the skills on which you need more practice.

	Problem	Section	Starting Page
Number Operations	5, 26, 28, 30	Word Problems	51
	13, 42	Decimals	75
	31, 45, 49	Fractions	103
	9	Ratio and Proportion	137
	1, 2, 6, 7	Percent	149
Data Analysis, Statistics, and Probability	18, 19, 20, 35, 36, 46	Data Analysis, Statistics, and Probability	197
	15, 50	Mean and Median	30, 217
Measurement and Geometry	11, 41	Customary Measures	183
	4	Metric Measures	186
	3, 12, 14, 16, 21, 40, 43	Perimeter, Circumference, Area, and Volume	234
	23, 24	Angles	223
	8, 10, 27	Triangles	259
	44	Congruence	267
	22	Pythagorean Relationship	271
	38	Slope	331
Algebra	47	Expressions	292
	29	Equations	294
	32	Inequalities	304
	33, 34	Factoring	339
	17, 25, 37, 39, 48	Coordinate Plane	323

Mathematics

Directions: Following is another test similar to the GED Mathematics Test. The test has two parts. On the first part, you will be permitted the use of a calculator. On the second part, no calculator use is allowed. Each part of the Practice Test should take no longer than 45 minutes to complete.

At the end of 45 minutes, if you have not completed Part I, mark your place and finish the test. Do the same with Part II. This will give you an idea of whether you can finish the real test in 90 minutes. Mark each answer on the answer grid. Answer as many questions as you can. A blank will be a wrong answer, so make a reasonable guess if you are not sure. Use any formulas on page 439 that you need.

When you finish, check your answers. The evaluation chart at the end of the answer key will help you determine which areas you may need to review before you are ready for the actual GED Mathematics Test.

PRACTICE TEST

Practice Test Answer Grid, Part I

1 ① ② ③ ④ ⑤

2 ① ② ③ ④ ⑤

3 ① ② ③ ④ ⑤

4 [grid-in answer box: / . 0–9]

5 [grid-in answer box: / . 0–9]

6 ① ② ③ ④ ⑤

7 ① ② ③ ④ ⑤

8 ① ② ③ ④ ⑤

9 ① ② ③ ④ ⑤

10 ① ② ③ ④ ⑤

11 ① ② ③ ④ ⑤

12 [grid-in answer box: / . 0–9]

13 [grid-in answer box: / . 0–9]

14 ① ② ③ ④ ⑤

15 ① ② ③ ④ ⑤

16 ① ② ③ ④ ⑤

17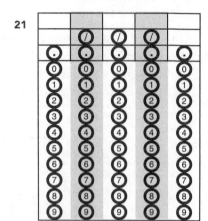

18 ① ② ③ ④ ⑤

19 ① ② ③ ④ ⑤

20 ① ② ③ ④ ⑤

21 [grid-in answer box: / . 0–9]

22 [grid-in answer box: / . 0–9]

23 ① ② ③ ④ ⑤

24 ① ② ③ ④ ⑤

25 ① ② ③ ④ ⑤

PRACTICE TEST

Part I

Directions: Solve each problem. You may use a calculator on any of these problems. Use the formulas on page 439 as needed.

1. How many degrees are there in angle x in the diagram?

   (1) 175°
   (2) 165°
   (3) 155°
   (4) 75°
   (5) 65°

   25° x

2. A high-speed train can travel as fast as 155 miles per hour. To the nearest ten miles, how many miles can this train travel in 1 hour and 45 minutes?

   (1) 260
   (2) 270
   (3) 280
   (4) 290
   (5) 300

3. For this figure, $AD = 30$. What is the length of DE?

   (1) 9
   (2) 12
   (3) 15
   (4) 18
   (5) 27

   A 5 B   D
        3
       C
             E

Directions: For problems 4 and 5, mark each answer on the corresponding number grid on the answer page.

4. Find the volume, in cubic inches, of the square pyramid shown below.

   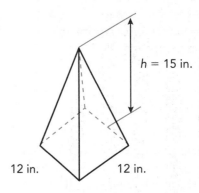

   $h = 15$ in.

   12 in.   12 in.

5. Simplify the expression $10^3 - 10^2$.

6. The list shows the prices of navel oranges at five different stores. Which store's price is the lowest?

   Store A: 5 for $0.99
   Store B: $0.25 each
   Store C: 3 for $1
   Store D: $2 a dozen
   Store E: 2 for $0.40

   (1) Store A
   (2) Store B
   (3) Store C
   (4) Store D
   (5) Store E

7. The diagram shows the wooden form for pouring a concrete patio. Find the volume, in cubic feet, of the poured concrete.

   (1) 40
   (2) 50
   (3) 60
   (4) 75
   (5) 90

   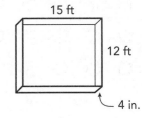

   15 ft

   12 ft

   4 in.

PRACTICE TEST

Directions: For problems 8–10, refer to the following information.

Steve is a carpenter. He charges his customers for time and materials. This means that he bills for each hour that he and his assistant work. Steve also bills for the exact cost of the materials that he uses on the job. Below is a list of the time and materials for the renovation of an enclosed porch.

Time:
Steve—40 hours at $30 per hour
Assistant—40 hours at $12 per hour

Materials:
10 sheets of gypsum board—$14 each
5 boxes of ceramic tiles—$20 each
assorted lumber and hardware—$115

8. Which of the following expresses the combined cost, in dollars, of Steve's and his assistant's time?

    (1) 40(30) + 40(12)
    (2) 40 × 30 + 12
    (3) 40 × 30 × 12
    (4) 30(40 + 12)
    (5) 12(40 + 30)

9. Steve had to pay 6% sales tax on all the materials he used for the job. What was the total sales tax for the materials?

    (1) $12.90
    (2) $14.40
    (3) $17.90
    (4) $21.30
    (5) $27.30

10. Steve deducts 20% of his assistant's wages for taxes and social security. What was the assistant's take-home pay for the renovation job?

    (1) $384
    (2) $396
    (3) $408
    (4) $440
    (5) $460

11. The diagram shows the dimensions of the city block where José lives. Which of the following is the best estimate of the total distance José must walk around the block if he starts and stops at the same point?

    (1) 600 × 200
    (2) 2(600) + 2(200)
    (3) 600 + 200
    (4) 600 × 400
    (5) $\frac{(600 + 200)}{2}$

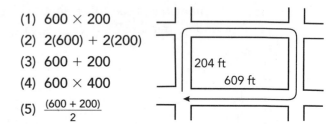

Directions: For problems 12 and 13, mark each answer on the corresponding number grid on the answer page.

12. Laura bought 5 raffle tickets to help support her son's school. The school sold a total of 1000 tickets. What is the probability that Laura will win the grand prize?

13. What is the positive number solution to the equation $x^2 = 1.44$?

Directions: For problems 14 and 15, refer to the table below.

Comparative Price of Souvenir Sweatshirts		
	Wholesale	Retail
Store A	$10	$20
Store B	$12	$18
Store C	$15	$20
Store D	$16	$28
Store E	$20	$28

14. For which store does the retail price of a sweatshirt show a 50% markup over the wholesale price?

(1) A
(2) B
(3) C
(4) D
(5) E

15. The owner of Store A decided to reduce the retail price of a sweatshirt by 20%. Find the new price of the sweatshirt.

(1) $20
(2) $18
(3) $17
(4) $16
(5) $15

16. At the farthest point in its orbit, the moon is 253,000 miles from Earth. Which of the following represents this number of miles in scientific notation?

(1) 253×10
(2) 2.53×10^3
(3) 2.53×10^4
(4) 2.53×10^5
(5) 2.53×10^6

17. Mark the coordinates of the y-intercept of the equation $y = 5x + 1$ on the corresponding coordinate plane grid on the answer page.

18. The map shows the distances between towns. Westport is directly west of Middletown, and Southport is directly south of Westport. What is the shortest distance in miles between Middletown and Southport?

(1) 160
(2) 140
(3) 120
(4) 100
(5) 90

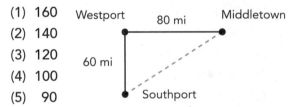

19. Miguel borrowed $2000 interest free from his brother to buy a used car. So far Miguel has paid back $1200. What fraction of the total does he still have to pay?

(1) $\frac{3}{20}$
(2) $\frac{1}{5}$
(3) $\frac{2}{5}$
(4) $\frac{3}{5}$
(5) $\frac{3}{4}$

20. For the equation $y = 2x - 3$, find the value of y when $x = 4$.

   (1) $y = 3$
   (2) $y = 4$
   (3) $y = 5$
   (4) $y = 7$
   (5) $y = 8$

Directions: For problems 21 and 22, mark each answer on the corresponding number grid on the answer page.

21. The rectangular solid below has a volume of 24 cubic meters. What is the height of the figure in meters?

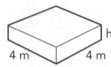

4 m   4 m

22. A baseball batting average is the number of hits a player gets divided by the number of times the player was at bat. To the nearest thousandth, find the batting average of a player who got 35 hits for 90 times at bat.

Directions: For problems 23–25, refer to the graph below.

VOLUME OF BUSINESS
FOR THREE HOTELS

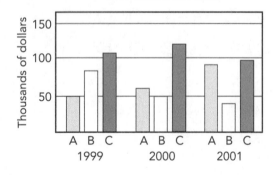

23. In 2000 the volume of business for Hotel C was approximately how many times that of Hotel A?

   (1) 4 times
   (2) 3 times
   (3) twice
   (4) one-half
   (5) the same

24. For the three years shown on the graph, which of the following best estimates the *mean* amount of yearly business for Hotel A?

   (1) about $30,000
   (2) about $40,000
   (3) a little less than $50,000
   (4) a little more than $60,000
   (5) about $80,000

25. For the periods shown on the graph, which of the following is true?

   (1) Only Hotel A showed a steady increase in business.
   (2) Only Hotel B showed a steady increase in business.
   (3) Hotel A consistently had the lowest volume of business.
   (4) Hotel C had the lowest volume of business.
   (5) Hotel A and Hotel C had nearly the same amount of business.

PRACTICE TEST

Practice Test Answer Grid, Part II

26 ① ② ③ ④ ⑤

27 ① ② ③ ④ ⑤

28 ① ② ③ ④ ⑤

29 ① ② ③ ④ ⑤

30 ① ② ③ ④ ⑤

31

32 ① ② ③ ④ ⑤

33 ① ② ③ ④ ⑤

34 ① ② ③ ④ ⑤

35 ① ② ③ ④ ⑤

36 ① ② ③ ④ ⑤

37

38 ① ② ③ ④ ⑤

39 ① ② ③ ④ ⑤

40 ① ② ③ ④ ⑤

41 ① ② ③ ④ ⑤

42 ① ② ③ ④ ⑤

43

44 ① ② ③ ④ ⑤

45 ① ② ③ ④ ⑤

46 ① ② ③ ④ ⑤

47 ① ② ③ ④ ⑤

48 ① ② ③ ④ ⑤

49 ① ② ③ ④ ⑤

50 ① ② ③ ④ ⑤

PRACTICE TEST

Part II

Directions: Solve the following problems without a calculator. Use the formulas on page 439 as needed.

26. Elena is one year more than twice her daughter's age. If x represents her daughter's age, which expression represents Elena's age?

    (1) $2x$
    (2) $x + 2$
    (3) $2x + 2$
    (4) $2(x + 1)$
    (5) $2x + 1$

27. The list below shows the weight of five friends two months ago. Each of them went on a diet and lost 10% of his or her weight. Who now weighs 135 pounds?

    Carlos 180 lb
    Reggie 160 lb
    Mike   150 lb
    Silvia 140 lb
    Anna   130 lb

    (1) Carlos
    (2) Reggie
    (3) Mike
    (4) Silvia
    (5) Anna

28. According to the information in the figure, what is the relationship between segments AB and CD? They are

    (1) equal
    (2) parallel
    (3) perpendicular
    (4) intersecting
    (5) corresponding

    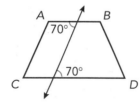

29. If $2x - 3 = 17$, then what is the value of x?

    (1) 5
    (2) 10
    (3) 15
    (4) 20
    (5) 25

30. What is the measurement of $\angle B$?

    (1) 100°
    (2) 80°
    (3) 60°
    (4) 40°
    (5) 20°

    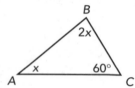

Directions: For problem 31, mark your answer on the corresponding number grid on the answer page.

31. The steepness of a ramp is the ratio of the rise to the run. What is the steepness, in fraction form, of a ramp that rises 4 feet over a run of 36 feet?

    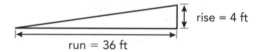

32. Which of the following represents the distance between points A and C?

    (1) 4
    (2) 6
    (3) 4^2
    (4) 6^2
    (5) $\sqrt{4^2 + 6^2}$

    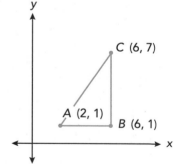

PRACTICE TEST

33. If $9m + 5 = 2m + 26$, what is the value of m?

(1) 2
(2) 3
(3) 5
(4) 7
(5) 14

34. All five members of the Perez family bought new sneakers. The adult sizes for Mr. and Mrs. Perez cost $69 each. The shoes for their children cost $49 each. Which expression represents the total cost, in dollars, for the shoes?

(1) $\frac{69 + 49}{5}$
(2) $5(69 + 49)$
(3) $5(69)(49)$
(4) $3(69) + 2(49)$
(5) $2(69) + 3(49)$

35. Juan is now 25 years older than his daughter Sue. In three years the sum of their ages will be 99. If x represents Sue's age now, which equation expresses the sum of their ages in three years?

(1) $2x + 25 = 99$
(2) $2x + 28 = 99$
(3) $x + 25 = 99$
(4) $2x + 31 = 99$
(5) $x + 28 = 99$

36. What is the slope of the line that passes through points P and Q?

(1) $\frac{6 - 1}{4 - 1}$
(2) $\frac{4 - 1}{6 - 1}$
(3) $\frac{6}{4 - 1}$
(4) $\frac{6 - 1}{4}$
(5) $\frac{6}{4}$

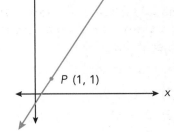

37. Mark the y-intercept of the equation $y = -8x + 3$ on the corresponding coordinate plane grid on the answer page.

38. When $x = 4$, what is the value of $\frac{6}{x^2}$?

(1) $\frac{1}{16}$
(2) $\frac{3}{8}$
(3) $\frac{1}{2}$
(4) $\frac{3}{4}$
(5) 3

39. A triangular area in a parking lot has been set aside for landscaping. It measures 25 feet on one side, 35 feet on another, and 40 feet on a third. Which of the following expresses the total feet of concrete curbing required to surround the landscaped space?

(1) $2(25) + 2(35)$
(2) $0.5(25)(40)$
(3) $25 + 35 + 40$
(4) $0.5(35)(40)$
(5) $25^2 + 35^2$

40. The expression $c^2 + 3c$ is the same as which of the following?

(1) $c(2 + 3)$
(2) $c(c + 3)$
(3) $2(3 + c)$
(4) $3(2 + c)$
(5) $c(2 + c)$

41. Which expression represents the number of degrees in vertex angle B?

(1) $180 - 2x$
(2) x
(3) $3x$
(4) $180 + x$
(5) $180 - x$

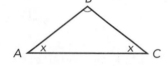

42. According to the information in the diagram below, which statement is true?

(1) AB is the longest side.
(2) BC is the longest side.
(3) AC is the longest side.
(4) All three sides are equal.
(5) Sides AB and BC are equal.

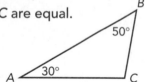

Directions: For problem 43, mark your answer on the corresponding number grid on the answer page.

43. Pete drove 328 miles on 10 gallons of gasoline. To the nearest tenth, what average distance did he drive on one gallon of gasoline?

44. For what values of a is the equation $a^2 + 5a - 24 = 0$ true?

(1) $+12$ and -2
(2) -12 and $+2$
(3) $+6$ and -4
(4) $+8$ and -3
(5) -8 and $+3$

45. The table shows the coordinates of two points on the graph of a linear function. What is the missing value of y?

(1) 14
(2) 15
(3) 16
(4) 18
(5) 21

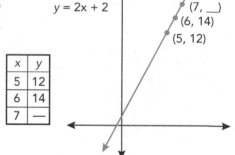

x	y
5	12
6	14
7	—

46. Which of the following represents the area of the shaded part of the figure?

(1) $2(20) + 2(12)$
(2) $\dfrac{20 + 12}{2}$
(3) $20^2 + 12^2$
(4) $0.5(20)(12)$
(5) $0.5 + 20 + 12$

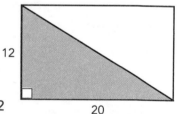

47. What is the approximate reading in volts on the meter below?

(1) 21

(2) 26

(3) 32

(4) 38

(5) 41

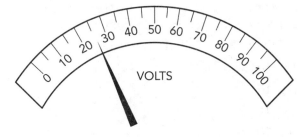

48. Sally makes $650 a week, and she tries to save $65 each week. What fraction of her income does she save?

(1) $\frac{1}{10}$

(2) $\frac{1}{6}$

(3) $\frac{1}{5}$

(4) $\frac{1}{4}$

(5) $\frac{1}{3}$

49. One side of square B is twice the measurement of one side of square A. The area of square A is what fraction of the area of square B?

(1) $\frac{1}{2}$

(2) $\frac{1}{3}$

(3) $\frac{1}{4}$

(4) $\frac{1}{5}$

(5) $\frac{1}{8}$

50. For the equation $y = -8x + 3$, find the value of y when $x = 1$.

(1) $y = 5$

(2) $y = -5$

(3) $y = 8$

(4) $y = 11$

(5) $y = -11$

Answers start on page 380.

PRACTICE TEST
Answer Key

Part I

1. (3) 155°   180° − 25° = 155°

2. (2) 270   1 hr 45 min = $1\frac{3}{4}$ hr = 1.75 hr
      155 × 1.75 = 271.25→270 miles

3. (4) 18   DE = x
      $\frac{3}{5} = \frac{x}{30}$
      5x = 90
      x = 18

4. 720 $V = \frac{1}{3} \times (\text{edge})^2 \times h$
      $V = \frac{1}{3} \times 12^2 \times 15$
      $V = 720$

5. 900 $10^3 − 10^2 = (10)(10)(10) − (10)(10) =$
            1000 − 100 = 900

6. (4) Store D   A = $\frac{\$0.99}{5}$ = $0.198 each
      B = $0.25 each
      C = $1 ÷ 3 = $0.333 each
      D = $2 ÷ 12 = $0.167 each
      E = $0.40 ÷ 2 = $0.20 each

7. (3) 60   4 inches = $\frac{4}{12} = \frac{1}{3}$ ft
      $V = 15 \times 12 \times \frac{1}{3} = 60$ cu ft

8. (1) 40(30) + 40(12)

9. (4) $21.30   10 × $14 = $140
            5 × $20 = $100
            $\underline{+115}$
            $355
      $355 × 0.06 = $21.30

10. (1) $384   40 x $12 = $480
            $480 x 0.2 = $96
            $480 − $96 = $384

11. (2) 2(600) + 2(200)   P = 2l + 2w
                  P = 2(600) + 2(200)

12. $\frac{1}{200}$ $\frac{5}{1000} = \frac{1}{200}$

13. 1.2 $x^2 = 1.44$
            x = 1.2

14. (2) B   retail − wholesale = markup
      For store B, 18 − 12 = 6.
      $\frac{6}{12} = \frac{1}{2}$ = 50%

15. (4) $16   20% = 0.2
            0.2 × $20 = $4
            $20 − $4 = $16

16. (4) 2.53×10^5
      The decimal point moves 5 places to the left.

17. (0, 1)   When x = 0, y = 5(0) + 1 = 1.

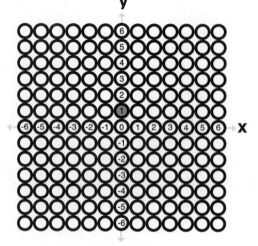

18. (4) 100 $a^2 + b^2 = c^2$
            $60^2 + 80^2 = c^2$
            $3600 + 6400 = c^2$
            $\sqrt{10,000} = c$
            $100 = c$

19. (3) $\frac{2}{5}$
      $2000 − $1200 = $800 left to pay
      $\frac{800}{2000} = \frac{2}{5}$

20. (3) y = 5
      When x = 4, y = 2(4) − 3 = 8 − 3 = 5.

21. 1.5   V = lwh
            24 = 4 × 4 × h
            $\frac{24}{16}$ = h
            1.5 = h

22. 0.389 $\frac{35}{90}$ = 0.388888→0.389

23. (3) twice   In 2000 Hotel C had about $120,000
                  in business.
            In 2000 Hotel A had about $60,000
                  in business.
            $\frac{\$120,000}{\$60,000}$ = 2

PRACTICE TEST

24. (4) a little more than $60,000

1999	$50,000
2000	60,000
2001	80,000
	$190,000 ÷ 3 ≈ $63,000

25. (1) Only Hotel A showed a steady increase in business.

Part II

26. (5) $2x + 1$

27. (3) Mike   10% = 0.1 0.1 × 150 = 15
150 − 15 = 135

28. (2) parallel

29. (2) 10 $2x − 3 = 17$
$2x = 20$
$x = 10$

30. (2) 80° $x + 2x + 60 = 180$
$3x = 120$
$x = 40$
$2x = 2(40) = 80$

31. $\frac{1}{9}$ $\frac{\text{rise}}{\text{run}}$ $\frac{4}{36} = \frac{1}{9}$

32. (5) $\sqrt{4^2 + 6^2}$ distance $= \sqrt{(6 − 2)^2 + (7 − 1)^2}$
$= \sqrt{4^2 + 6^2}$

33. (2) 3 $9m + 5 = 2m + 26$
$7m = 21$
$m = 3$

34. (5) $2(69) + 3(49)$

35. (4) $2x + 31 = 99$
Sue = x now and $x + 3$ in 3 years.
Juan = $x + 25$ now and $x + 25 + 3 = x + 28$
in 3 years.
$x + 3 + x + 28 = 99$
$2x + 31 = 99$

36. (1) $\frac{6 − 1}{4 − 1}$
slope $= \frac{y_2 − y_1}{x_2 − x_1} = \frac{6 − 1}{4 − 1}$

37. (0, 3) When $x = 0$, $y = −8(0) + 3 = 3$.
(See grid at the right.)

38. (2) $\frac{3}{8}$ $\frac{6}{x^2} = \frac{6}{4^2} = \frac{6}{16} = \frac{3}{8}$

39. (3) $25 + 35 + 40$
Perimeter = the sum of the three sides

40. (2) $c(c + 3)$

41. (1) $180 − 2x$
All three angles = 180° so angle B =
180° − the other two angles ($x + x$).

42. (1) AB is the longest side.
$\angle C = 180° − 50° − 30° = 100°$
$\angle C$ is the largest angle.
The side opposite $\angle C$ is the longest.

43. 32.8 $\frac{328}{10} = 32.8$ mpg

44. (5) −8 and +3
When $a = −8$, $(−8)^2 + 5(−8) − 24 =$
$64 − 40 − 24 = 0$.
When $a = +3$, $(+3)^2 + 5(+3) − 24 =$
$9 + 15 − 24 = 0$.

45. (3) 16
When $x = 7$, $y = 2(7) + 2 = 14 + 2 = 16$.

46. (4) 0.5(20)(12) $A = \frac{1}{2}bh = 0.5(20)(12)$

47. (2) 26

48. (1) $\frac{1}{10}$ $\frac{\$65}{\$650} = \frac{1}{10}$

49. (3) $\frac{1}{4}$ Give a value to one side.
If side of A = 3, area A = $3^2 = 9$,
and area B = $6^2 = 36$.
$\frac{9}{36} = \frac{1}{4}$

50. (2) $y = −5$
When $x = 1$, $y = −8(1) + 3 = −8 + 3 = −5$.

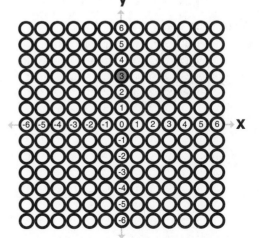

Evaluation Chart

On the chart below, circle the number of the problems you got wrong. To the right of the problem numbers, you will find the sections and starting pages that cover the skills you need to solve the problems. Be sure to review all skills you missed before you take the actual GED Mathematics Test.

	Problem	Section	Starting Page
Number Operations	5	Whole Numbers	17
	8, 34	Word Problems	51
	16, 22, 43	Decimals	75
	19, 48	Fractions	103
	31	Ratio and Proportion	137
	9, 10, 14, 15, 27	Percent	149
Data Analysis, Statistics, and Probability	6, 12, 23, 24, 25	Data Analysis, Statistics, and Probability	197
Measurement and Geometry	2	Customary Measures	183
	47	Scales	190
	4, 7, 11, 39, 46, 49	Perimeter, Circumference, Area, and Volume	234
	1, 28	Angles	223
	30, 41, 42	Triangles	259
	3	Similarity	263
	18	Pythagorean Relationship	271
	36	Slope	331
Algebra	26, 38	Expressions	292
	29, 33, 45, 50	Equations	294
	21, 35	Word Problems	315
	40	Factoring	339
	17, 32, 37	Coordinate Plane	323
	20	Linear Equations	329
	13, 44	Quadratic Equations	346

Answer Key

Chapter 1

Exercise 1, page 17

1. 389   417
2. 2,100   1,456
3. 75,000   32,312
4. 4 1 2 5 0
5. 2 8 9 3 7
6. ten thousands
7. millions
8. 800 or 8 hundred
9. 60,000 or 60 thousand
10. 20 or twenty
11. 900,000 or 9 hundred thousand
12. 4,000,000 or 4 million

Exercise 2, page 18

Addition Facts

	1	3	8	4	6	9	7	10	2	5
8	9	11	16	12	14	17	15	18	10	13
1	2	4	9	5	7	10	8	11	3	6
3	4	6	11	7	9	12	10	13	5	8
6	7	9	14	10	12	15	13	16	8	11
4	5	7	12	8	10	13	11	14	6	9
9	10	12	17	13	15	18	16	19	11	14
5	6	8	13	9	11	14	12	15	7	10
7	8	10	15	11	13	16	14	17	9	12
2	3	5	10	6	8	11	9	12	4	7
10	11	13	18	14	16	19	17	20	12	15

Exercise 3, page 19

Multiplication Facts

	12	3	1	4	10	9	7	5	6	8	11	0	2
9	108	27	9	36	90	81	63	45	54	72	99	0	18
7	84	21	7	28	70	63	49	35	42	56	77	0	14
4	48	12	4	16	40	36	28	20	24	32	44	0	8
5	60	15	5	20	50	45	35	25	30	40	55	0	10
2	24	6	2	8	20	18	14	10	12	16	22	0	4
1	12	3	1	4	10	9	7	5	6	8	11	0	2
8	96	24	8	32	80	72	56	40	48	64	88	0	16
10	120	30	10	40	100	90	70	50	60	80	110	0	20
12	144	36	12	48	120	108	84	60	72	96	132	0	24
0	0	0	0	0	0	0	0	0	0	0	0	0	0
11	132	33	11	44	110	99	77	55	66	88	121	0	22
3	36	9	3	12	30	27	21	15	18	24	33	0	6
6	72	18	6	24	60	54	42	30	36	48	66	0	12

Exercise 4, page 20

1. 12   56   100   1026
2. 9   41   63   241
3. 16 and 17
4. 42, 44, and 46
5. 11, 13, 17, 19, 23, 29
6. 31
7. 16
8. 7
9. 1, 2, 4, and 8
10. 1, 3, and 5

Exercise 5, page 23

1.
$$\begin{array}{r} 25,624 \\ +\,92,183 \\ \hline 117,807 \end{array}$$

2.
$$\begin{array}{r} 60,845 \\ -\,2,926 \\ \hline 57,919 \end{array}$$

3.
$$\begin{array}{r} 49,005 \\ -\,6,774 \\ \hline 42,231 \end{array}$$

4.
$$\begin{array}{r} 83 \\ 2096 \\ +\,194 \\ \hline 2373 \end{array}$$

5.
$$\begin{array}{r} 5708 \\ \times\,6 \\ \hline 34,248 \end{array}$$

6.
$$\begin{array}{r} 349 \\ \times\,74 \\ \hline 1396 \\ 2443 \\ \hline 25,826 \end{array}$$

7.
$$\begin{array}{r} 872 \\ \times\,409 \\ \hline 7848 \\ 34880 \\ \hline 356,648 \end{array}$$

8.
$$\begin{array}{r} 50,000 \\ \times\,65 \\ \hline 3,250,000 \end{array}$$

9.
```
     26 r 4
17)446
   34
   106
   102
     4
```

10.
```
    308
8)2464
```

11.
```
  9,006
6)54,036
```

12.
```
  30,045
− 15,586
  14,459
```

13.
```
   194
     8
  2366
+ 850
  3418
```

14.
```
    96
× 500
48,000
```

15.
```
3,000,000
− 816,000
2,184,000
```

16.
```
  29,058
×      7
 203,406
```

17.
```
        47
800)37,600
    32 00
     5 600
     5 600
         0
```

18.
```
      74
× 8,000
 592,000
```

19.
```
5,040,000
− 264,500
4,775,500
```

20.
```
        306
35)10,710
   105
    21
     0
   210
   210
     0
```

21.
```
  5,090
×     8
 40,720
```

22.
```
     423
12)5076
   48
    27
    24
    36
    36
     0
```

23.
```
  7000
−  88
  6912
```

24.
```
 400,300
−  9,216
 391,084
```

25.
```
     705
4)2820
```

26.
```
    346
× 450
17300
1384
155,700
```

27.
```
  2,900
    857
 11,630
+   405
 15,792
```

28.
```
   8,060 r 3
7)56,423
```

29.
```
1,300,500
− 807,631
  492,869
```

30.
```
      740
19)14,060
   13 3
     76
     76
      0
```

Exercise 6, page 25

1. 80 240 6130 300
2. 13,700 4,300 500 6,000
3. 5,000 50,000 92,000
4. 70,000 410,000 2,700,000
5. $27,000
6. $120

Exercise 7, page 27

1. 200 + 100 + 5,000 = 5,300
   7,000 + 800 + 40,000 = 47,800
   90 + 20 + 300 = 410

2. $40,000 - 9,000 = 31,000$
   $200,000 - 40,000 = 160,000$
   $3,000 - 900 = 2,100$
3. $40 \times 800 = 32,000$
   $70 \times 900 = 63,000$
   $500 \times 70 = 35,000$
4. $7,000 + 500 + 100 = 7,600$
   $90,000 - 10,000 = 80,000$
   $90 \times 1,000 = 90,000$
5. 3 digits
6. 4 digits
7. 2 digits
8. (3) 600 and 700
9. (3) 10 and 20
10. (1) 1000 and 2000
11. (2) 582 because $5400 \div 9 = 600$
12. (1) 721 because $21,000 \div 30 = 700$
13. (2) 63 because $30,000 \div 500 = 60$
14. (3) 212 because $12,000 \div 60 = 200$

Exercise 8, page 29

1. 5044   47,411   385
2. 29,589   153,689   2064
3. 32,103   62,016   37,084
4. 7855   78,958   114,356
5. 260
6. 1213
7. 14
8. 642
9. 12
10. 1372
11. 582
12. 721
13. 63
14. 212

Exercise 9, page 31

1. mean = 193

$$
\begin{array}{r} 353 \\ 19 \\ + 207 \\ \hline 579 \end{array}
\qquad
3\overline{)579} \;\; 193
$$

   median = 207   19   207   353

2. mean = 1995

$$
\begin{array}{r} 2046 \\ 971 \\ 3113 \\ + 1850 \\ \hline 7980 \end{array}
\qquad
4\overline{)7980} \;\; 1995
$$

   median = 1948   971   **1850**   **2046**   3113

$$
\begin{array}{r} 1850 \\ + 2046 \\ \hline 3896 \end{array}
\qquad
2\overline{)3896} \;\; 1948
$$

3. mean = 253

$$
\begin{array}{r} 240 \\ 313 \\ 189 \\ + 270 \\ \hline 1012 \end{array}
\qquad
4\overline{)1012} \;\; 253
$$

   median = 255   189   **240**   **270**   313

$$
\begin{array}{r} 240 \\ + 270 \\ \hline 510 \end{array}
\qquad
2\overline{)510} \;\; 255
$$

4. average = 173 pounds

$$
\begin{array}{r} 187 \\ + 159 \\ \hline 346 \end{array}
\qquad
2\overline{)346} \;\; 173
$$

5. mean = 65°

$$
\begin{array}{r} 69 \\ 71 \\ 56 \\ 63 \\ + 66 \\ \hline 325 \end{array}
\qquad
5\overline{)325} \;\; 65
$$

6. average = $34,800

$$
\begin{array}{r} \$34,700 \\ 33,900 \\ + 35,800 \\ \hline \$104,400 \end{array}
\qquad
3\overline{)\$104,400} \;\; \$34,800
$$

7. average = $2607

$$
\begin{array}{r} \$2566 \\ 3327 \\ + 1928 \\ \hline \$7821 \end{array}
\qquad
3\overline{)\$7821} \;\; \$2607
$$

Exercise 10, page 34

1. $6^2 = 6 \times 6 = 36$
   $1^3 = 1 \times 1 \times 1 = 1$
   $2^4 = 2 \times 2 \times 2 \times 2 = 16$
2. $5^3 = 5 \times 5 \times 5 = 125$
   $3^5 = 3 \times 3 \times 3 \times 3 \times 3 = 243$
   $10^2 = 10 \times 10 = 100$
3. $9^4 = 9 \times 9 \times 9 \times 9 = 6561$
   $15^2 = 15 \times 15 = 225$
   $8^0 = \dfrac{8}{8} = 1$

4. $20^2 = 20 \times 20 = 400$
   $30^5 = 30 \times 30 \times 30 \times 30 \times 30 = 24,300,000$
   $16^1 = 16$

5. $25^2 = 25 \times 25 = 625$
   $8^4 = 8 \times 8 \times 8 \times 8 = 4096$
   $50^2 = 50 \times 50 = 2500$

6. hundreds $= 10^2$
   thousands $= 10^3$
   ten thousands $= 10^4$
   hundred thousands $= 10^5$

Exercise 11, page 36

1. (2) 14 because $14 \times 14 = 196$
2. (3) 21 because $21 \times 21 = 441$
3. (4) 32 because $32 \times 32 = 1024$
4. (4) 39 because $39 \times 39 = 1521$
5. $\sqrt{361} = 19$
   Guess 20 because $20 \times 20 = 400$.

   $$20\overline{)361} \quad\quad \begin{array}{r} 18 \\ +20 \\ \hline 38 \end{array} \quad\quad 2\overline{)38}^{\,19}$$

   $$\begin{array}{r} 18 \\ 20\overline{)361} \\ \underline{20} \\ 161 \\ \underline{160} \end{array}$$

6. $\sqrt{676} = 26$
   Guess 30 because $30 \times 30 = 900$.

   $$\begin{array}{r} 22 \\ 30\overline{)676} \\ \underline{60} \\ 76 \\ \underline{60} \end{array} \quad \begin{array}{r} 22 \\ +30 \\ \hline 52 \end{array} \quad 2\overline{)52}^{\,26}$$

7. $\sqrt{1849} = 43$
   Guess 40 because $40 \times 40 = 1600$.

   $$\begin{array}{r} 46 \\ 40\overline{)1849} \\ \underline{160} \\ 249 \\ \underline{240} \end{array} \quad \begin{array}{r} 46 \\ +40 \\ \hline 86 \end{array} \quad 2\overline{)86}^{\,43}$$

8. $\sqrt{3364} = 58$
   Guess 60 because $60 \times 60 = 3600$

   $$\begin{array}{r} 56 \\ 60\overline{)3364} \\ \underline{300} \\ 364 \\ \underline{360} \end{array} \quad \begin{array}{r} 56 \\ +60 \\ \hline 116 \end{array} \quad 2\overline{)116}^{\,58}$$

9. (2) $s \times s = 6889$
10. $\sqrt{5184} = 72$
11. $\sqrt{2704} = 52$
12. $\sqrt{1089} = 33$

Exercise 12, page 38

1. 6 12 24 48 96
   $\times2$ $\times2$ $\times2$ $\times2$

2. 81 84 87 90 93 96
   $+3$ $+3$ $+3$ $+3$ $+3$

3. 32 29 26 23 20
   -3 -3 -3 -3

4. 13 17 21 25 29 33 37
   $+4$ $+4$ $+4$ $+4$ $+4$ $+4$

5. 10 5 15 10 20 15 25
   -5 $+10$ -5 $+10$ -5 $+10$

6. 100 81 64 49 36 25 16 9
   -19 -17 -15 -13 -11 -9 -7

   or identify these numbers as the squares
   of 10, 9, 8, 7, 6, 5, 4, 3

7. 5 9 17 33 65
   $+4$ $+8$ $+16$ $+32$

8. 2 3 5 8 12 17 23 30
   $+1$ $+2$ $+3$ $+4$ $+5$ $+6$ $+7$

9. 320 160 80 40 20 10
   $\div2$ $\div2$ $\div2$ $\div2$ $\div2$

10. 4 8 7 14 13 26 25 50 49
    $\times2$ -1 $\times2$ -1 $\times2$ -1 $\times2$ -1

11.
Month	March	April	May	June	July	August
Balance	$30,000	$24,000	$18,000	$12,000	$6,000	$0

$-$$6,000$ $-$$6,000$ $-$$6,000$ $-$$6,000$ $-$$6,000$

12.
Year	1910	1930	1950	1970	1990	2010
Population	1,500	3,000	6,000	12,000	24,000	48,000

$\times2$ $\times2$ $\times2$ $\times2$ $\times2$

Exercise 13, page 42

1. (4) $30 + 20$
2. (3) 3×9
3. (2) $9 + (7 + 4)$
4. (4) $7 + 8$
5. (2) $5 \times (2 \times 4)$
6. (3) 12×20
7. (4) $(16 \times 14) + (16 \times 27)$
8. (1) 4×21
9. (2) $3 \times 8 - 2$
10. (4) $3(15 - 6)$

Exercise 14, page 45

1. $\dfrac{5 + 9}{2} = \dfrac{14}{2} = 7$

   $2 \times 6 + 4 \times 3 = 12 + 12 = 24$

   $3(9 + 5) = 3(14) = 42$

2. $\dfrac{11 - 5}{3 - 1} = \dfrac{6}{2} = 3$

   $11 \times 2 - 5 \times 3 = 22 - 15 = 7$

   $7(12 - 3) = 7(9) = 63$

3. $\dfrac{8 + 4 + 9}{3} = \dfrac{21}{3} = 7$

   $3 \cdot 5^2 = 3 \cdot 25 = 75$

   $4 + 6 \times 5 = 4 + 30 = 34$

4. $12(3 + 4) = 12(7) = 84$

   $2(9 - 4) = 2(5) = 10$

   $\dfrac{20 + 10}{20 - 10} = \dfrac{30}{10} = 3$

5. $(4 + 7)(5 - 2) = (11)(3) = 33$

   $\dfrac{20 - 9 + 4}{5} = \dfrac{15}{5} = 3$

   $4 \cdot 3^2 = 4 \cdot 9 = 36$

6. $10^2 - 3 \cdot 7 = 100 - 21 = 79$

   $2(8 - 2)^2 = 2(6)^2 = 2(36) = 72$

   $(6 + 1) - (5 - 4) = 7 - 1 = 6$

Whole Numbers Review, page 47

Part I

1. 416
2. 517,717
3. 131,796
4. 22,112
5. 37
6. 348,000
7. 73,811
8. 17,088
9. 1,722,100

10. 3534

11. 2146 → 2100

12. 47

Part II

13. (4) 72
14. (1) 36,000
15. (5) 10
16. (1) 9

    $2 \underset{\times 2}{\nearrow} 4 \underset{-1}{\searrow} 3 \underset{\times 2}{\nearrow} 6 \underset{-1}{\searrow} 5 \underset{\times 2}{\nearrow} 10 \underset{-1}{\searrow} 9$

17. (5) 500 and 600
18. (5) 1225 $35^2 = 35 \times 35 = 1225$

19. (1) 63

$$1 \quad 3 \quad 7 \quad 15 \quad 31 \quad 63$$
$$+2 \quad +4 \quad +8 \quad +16 \quad +32$$

20. (2) 4(9 + 15)

21. (4) 34 $\quad \dfrac{27 + 36 + 28 + 39 + 40}{5} = \dfrac{170}{5} = 34$

22. (2) 23

23. 1200 $\quad$ 1024 $\quad$ <u>1137</u> $\quad$ <u>1263</u> $\quad$ 1440

$$\dfrac{1137 + 1263}{2} = \dfrac{2400}{2} = 1200$$

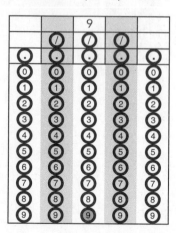

24. 7 $\quad \dfrac{70 \times 2}{50 - 30} = \dfrac{140}{20} = 7$

25. 9 $\quad 30 \div 6 + (8 - 4) = 5 + 4 = 9$

Chapter 2

Exercise 1, page 52

1. (3) Find the difference between the number of votes Mr. Sanders received and the number of votes his opponent received.
2. (3) How much did the TV cost before it was on sale?
3. (2) Find Manny's total car payments for 12 months.
4. (3) Find out how far Pancho drove on 1 gallon of gasoline.
5. (2) How much did Gordon weigh at the end of December?
6. (2) How much do both Marilyn and Calvin take home in a month?
7. (3) Find the distance Carmen can drive with 13 gallons of gas.
8. (1) How much more does Gloria need to save for the TV?

Exercise 2, page 54

1. a. March unemployment of 8,248 and September unemployment of 10,549
   b. $10,549 - 8,248 = 2,301$
2. a. the price of the joists, $134.40, and the number of feet of joists, 64
   b. $\dfrac{\$134.40}{64} = \$2.10$
3. a. the price of a child's ticket, $6, and the number of children who attended, 1230; the price of an adult's ticket, $10, and the number of adults who attended
   b. Not enough information is given. You do not know the number of adults who attended.
4. a. the total number of cars sold, 543, and the number made in the U.S., 387
   b. $543 - 387 = 156$ cars
5. a. the miles driven, 132, and the number of hours, 3
   b. $\dfrac{132}{3} = 44$ mph
6. a. the miles driven, 132, and the number of gallons used
   b. Not enough information is given. You do not know how many gallons were used.
7. a. the total number of adults, 2500, and the number of high school graduates, 1950
   b. $2500 - 1950 = 550$ adults
8. a. the population of California, 32,667,000, and the population of Texas, 19,760,000
   b. $32,667,000 - 19,760,000 = 12,907,000$

9. a. monthly rent, $625, and monthly food cost, $380
   b. $625 − $380 = $245
10. a. the price she charges for shirts, $12; the price for jeans, $16; and the price she pays her supplier for shirts and jeans
    b. Not enough information is given. You do not know how much she pays her supplier for shirts or jeans.

Exercise 3, page 58

Questions may vary, but operations and solutions should not.

1. a. How much older is father than son?
   b. Subtract son's age from father's age.
   c. 37 − 8 = 29 years
2. a. What is Connie's wage per hour?
   b. Divide weekly income by number of hours.
   c. $\frac{\$440}{40} = \$11$
3. a. What are the number of seats in the auditorium?
   b. Multiply number of rows by number of seats per row.
   c. 33 × 28 = 924 seats
4. a. What is the total votes cast for county clerk?
   b. Add opponent's votes and winner's votes.
   c. 92,965 + 72,557 = 165,522 votes
5. a. What are the mortgage payments for 1 year?
   b. Multiply monthly payment by 12 months.
   c. $859 × 12 = $10,308
6. a. What is the total utility bill for the month?
   b. Add the three utility bills.
   c. $42 + $55 + $73 = $170
7. a. In how many minutes can Kim type a 1700-word letter?
   b. Divide number of words in letter by typing rate.
   c. $\frac{1700}{85} = 20$ minutes
8. a. What was Cheryl's net income for the year?
   b. Subtract deductions from gross income.
   c. $28,296 − $6,780 = $21,516
9. a. What are the number of contributors needed to raise $10,000?
   b. Divide $10,000 by average contribution per person.
   c. $\frac{10,000}{25} = 400$ people
10. a. What is the total cost of beef?
    b. Multiply number of pounds by cost per pound.
    c. 15 × $6 = $90

11. a. What amount will each person receive?
    b. Divide winnings by number of people, 4.
    c. $\frac{\$200}{4} = \$50$
12. a. What is the original price?
    b. Add sale price to amount of savings. (The original price is more than the sale price. Here the word *less* is not a clue for subtraction.)
    c. $69 + $20 = $89

Exercise 4, page 60

1. 4,695
$$\begin{array}{r} 67{,}576 \\ -\ 62{,}881 \\ \hline 4{,}695 \end{array}$$

2. $258
$$\begin{array}{r} \$198 \\ +\ 60 \\ \hline \$258 \end{array}$$

3. $3480
$$\begin{array}{r} \$290 \\ \times\ 12 \\ \hline 580 \\ 290 \\ \hline \$3480 \end{array}$$

4. 23 miles
$$\begin{array}{r} 23 \\ 20\overline{)460} \\ 40 \\ \hline 60 \\ 60 \\ \hline \end{array}$$

5. 211 pounds
$$\begin{array}{r} 178 \\ +\ 33 \\ \hline 211 \end{array}$$

6. $1,850
$$\begin{array}{r} \$\ 1{,}850 \\ 12\overline{)\$22{,}200} \\ 12 \\ \hline 102 \\ 96 \\ \hline 60 \\ 60 \\ \hline \end{array}$$

7. 312 miles
$$\begin{array}{r} 24 \\ \times\ 13 \\ \hline 72 \\ 24 \\ \hline 312 \end{array}$$

8. $95
$$\begin{array}{r} \$385 \\ -\ 290 \\ \hline \$95 \end{array}$$

Exercise 5, page 61

In these answers, the first solution shows rounding. The second solution is exact.

1. (2) 310   5 × 60 = 300   5 × 62 = 310
2. (3) 1672   400 + 700 + 500 = 1600
              437 + 739 + 496 = 1672

3. (4) 155 $2000 - 1850 = 150$
               $2002 - 1847 = 155$

4. (2) $256 $200 + $60 = 260
              $198 + $58 = 256

5. (4) $289 $\frac{$1200}{4} = 300 $\frac{$1156}{4} = 289

6. (1) $2840 $\frac{$36,000}{12} = 3000 $\frac{$34,080}{4} = 2840

7. (4) $2016 $100 \times $20 = 2000
               $112 \times $18 = 2016

8. (3) 69 $100 - 30 = 70$ $96 - 27 = 69$

9. (3) $31,260 $\frac{$180,000}{6} = $30,000$

             $\frac{$187,560}{6} = $31,260$

10. (5) Not enough information is given. You do not know Fred's regular hourly wage.

Exercise 6, page 64

1. $7,800 \times 30 = $234,000$
$2,100 \times 30 = $63,000$
$234,000 - $63,000 = $171,000$

2. $4 + 6 + 10 = 20$ cases
$20 \times 20 = 400$ cans

3. $35 \times $10.50 = 367.50
$6 \times $15.75 = 94.50
$367.50 + $94.50 = 462

4. $45 \times 18 = 810
$150 + $810 = 960

5. $1000 + 500 = 1500$ words
$\frac{1500}{75} = 20$ minutes

6. $450 \times 12 = $5,400$
$450 + $24 = 474
$474 \times 12 = $5,688$
$5,400 + $5,688 = $11,088$

7. $100 + 65 = 165$ handles
$165 \times 12 = 1980$ handles

8. $178 + 32 = 210$ miles
$\frac{210}{5} = 42$ mph

Exercise 7, page 65

1. Apt. A $= $480 \times 12 = 5760
Apt. B $= $412 + $84 = 496
          $496 \times 12 = 5952
$5952 - $5760 = 192

2. rent $= $480 + $48 = 528
$2230 - $528 = 1702

3. Family Furniture: $1199 - $100 = 1099
$1279 - $1099 = 180

4. $45 \times 36 = 1620
$1620 + $150 = 1770

5. $54 \times 24 = 1296
$1296 + $200 = 1496

6. $1770 - $1496 = 274

7. $1770 - $1099 = 671

8. $18 \times 80 = 1440

9. $13,500 + $1,440 = $14,940$
$18,000 - $14,940 = $3,060$

10. $\frac{$3060}{90} = 34 per hour

Exercise 8, page 68

1. $c = nr = 3 \times $25 = 75
2. $c = nr = 6 \times $198 = 1188
3. $c = nr = 4 \times $19 = 76
4. $d = rt = 4 \times 55 = 220$ miles
5. $d = rt = 3 \times 64 = 192$ miles
6. $d = rt = 2 \times 415 = 830$ miles
7. $m = \frac{a+b+c}{3} = \frac{82+76+94}{3} = \frac{252}{3} = 84$
8. $F \approx 2 \times C + 30 = 2 \times 11 + 30 = 22 + 30 = 52\,°F$
9. $r = \frac{c}{n} = \frac{$396}{36} = 11
10. $n = \frac{c}{r} = \frac{$50}{$12} = 4$ with a remainder

Maria can buy 4 pairs of children's shorts.

Exercise 9, page 69

1. (2) $6(265 + 304)$
2. (1) $200(5 + 10)$
3. (4) $40 \times 13 - 125$
4. (3) $5(45 + 30)$
5. (4) $(4 \times 55) + (3 \times 40)$
6. (1) $12(50 - 10)$
7. (2) $(3 \times 16) + (2 \times 24)$
8. (1) $\frac{34 + 80 + 65}{3}$

Word Problems Review, page 72

Part I

1. 156 boxes $\frac{7488}{48} = 156$

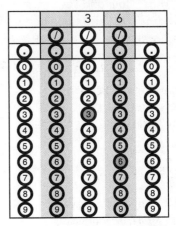

2. 357 employees $420 - 63 = 357$

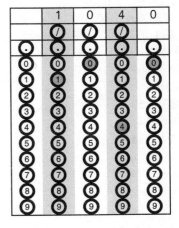

3. (3) 138,109 $259{,}056 - 120{,}947 = 138{,}109$
4. (3) $2605.61
    debits = $658.00 + $49.57 = $707.57
    credits = $2453.18 + $860.00 = $3313.18
    balance = $3313.18 − $707.57 = $2605.61
5. (3) $1215 $525 + 6($115) = $525 + $690 = $1215
6. (5) Not enough information is given. You do not know the amount of discount.

Part II

7. $36 $1.69 × 10 = $16.90
            $16.90 + $19 = $35.90 → $36

8. $1040   15 × $56 = $840
             $840 + $200 = $1040

9. (1) $2,500,000 $\frac{\$12{,}500{,}000}{5} = \$2{,}500{,}000$
10. (1) 12(9 + 6)
11. (3) Divide 81,480 by 84; then add 200.
12. (2) 370   (6 × 55) + (2 × 20) = 330 + 40 = 370

Chapter 3

Exercise 1, page 76

1. 3 9 7 1 6
2. 7 1 6 5 8
3. 8 5 9 7 1
4. 8 3 4 2 5
5. hundredths
6. tenths
7. hundredths
8. thousandths

Exercise 2, page 77

1. nine tenths   eighteen hundredths
2. sixteen thousandths   four and seven tenths
3. two ten-thousandths   ten and three hundredths
4. thirty-one thousandths
5. eighteen hundred-thousandths
6. one and two hundred three thousandths
7. two hundred eight ten-thousandths
8. forty-two and five tenths
9. thirty and eighty hundredths

Exercise 3, page 78

1. 0.067 3.405 8.0906 6.3
2. 80.025 124.009 7.5 0.0023
3. 5 0.3708 29.3 60.0502

Exercise 4, page 79

1. 0.4   6.3
2. 0.18   95.4
3. 0.009   5.015
4. 0.106   8.0029
5. 0.0034   512.07
6. 0.000045   70.306

Exercise 5, page 79

1. 0.7 0.62 0.403
2. 0.0029 0.101 0.9
3. 0.8 5.23 0.4
4. 0.062, 0.26, 0.602, 0.62
5. 0.0034, 0.34, 0.403, 0.43
6. 0.77, 0.701, 0.7, 0.67
7. 0.55, 0.511, 0.505, 0.5
8. (2) C, D, B, A, E
9. (4) E, D, A, C, B

Exercise 6, page 81

1. 0.5 5.7 29.6
2. 0.13 0.07 2.60
3. 0.059 0.127 0.038
4. 13 3 99
5. $1.59 $0.03 $28.70
6. $13 $3 $147
7. $1.60

Exercise 7, page 83

1.
$$\begin{array}{r} 0.6 \\ +\ 0.9 \\ \hline 1.5 \end{array} \qquad \begin{array}{r} 0.57 \\ +0.8 \\ \hline 1.37 \end{array}$$

2.
$$\begin{array}{r} 16. \\ 9.24 \\ +\ 170.3 \\ \hline 195.54 \end{array} \qquad \begin{array}{r} 25.34 \\ 4. \\ +1.816 \\ \hline 31.156 \end{array}$$

3.
$$\begin{array}{r} 12.3 \\ 4.8 \\ +0.625 \\ \hline 17.725 \end{array} \qquad \begin{array}{r} 4.036 \\ 2.19 \\ +18.7 \\ \hline 24.926 \end{array}$$

4.
$$\begin{array}{r} 8.9 \\ 12.66 \\ +0.742 \\ \hline 22.302 \end{array} \qquad \begin{array}{r} 0.73 \\ 0.0094 \\ +0.085 \\ \hline 0.8244 \end{array}$$

5.
$$\begin{array}{r} 4.3 \\ 12.8 \\ +1.9 \\ \hline 19.0 = 19 \end{array}$$

6.
$$\begin{array}{r} 0.20 \\ 4.38 \\ +0.02 \\ \hline 4.60 = 4.6 \end{array}$$

7.
$$\begin{array}{r} 0.017 \\ 0.143 \\ +0.087 \\ \hline 0.247 \end{array}$$

8.
$$\begin{array}{r} 4 \\ 21 \\ +6 \\ \hline 31 \end{array}$$

9. (5) 19.036 (6) 4.5975 (7) 0.2463 (8) 30.92
10. 1.6 + 2.15 + 0.45 = 4.2 pounds
11. 2.8 + 0.12 = 2.92 centimeters
12. 65.5 + 2.5 = 68 inches

Exercise 8, page 84

1.
$$\begin{array}{r} 0.80 \\ -\ 0.26 \\ \hline 0.54 \end{array} \qquad \begin{array}{r} 0.500 \\ -\ 0.345 \\ \hline 0.155 \end{array}$$

2.
$$\begin{array}{r} 18.00 \\ -\ 0.32 \\ \hline 17.68 \end{array} \qquad \begin{array}{r} 4.090 \\ -\ 2.076 \\ \hline 2.014 \end{array}$$

3.
$$\begin{array}{r} 0.300 \\ -\ 0.094 \\ \hline 0.206 \end{array} \qquad \begin{array}{r} 1.0040 \\ -\ 0.0025 \\ \hline 1.0015 \end{array}$$

4.
$$\begin{array}{r} 12.300 \\ -\ 8.094 \\ \hline 4.206 \end{array} \qquad \begin{array}{r} 7.00 \\ -\ 6.93 \\ \hline 0.07 \end{array}$$

5.
$$\begin{array}{r} 4.3 \\ -\ 1.4 \\ \hline 2.9 \end{array}$$

6.
$$\begin{array}{r} 1.37 \\ -\ 0.46 \\ \hline 0.91 \end{array}$$

7.
$$\begin{array}{r} 0.386 \\ -\ 0.094 \\ \hline 0.292 \end{array}$$

8.
$$\begin{array}{r} 15 \\ -\ 10 \\ \hline 5 \end{array}$$

9. (5) 2.905 (6) 0.9078 (7) 0.2919 (8) 5.23
10. 0.36 − 0.012 = 0.348 centimeter
11. 23.15 − 1.6 = 21.55 grams
12. $14.8 − $9.57 = $5.23 million

Exercise 9, page 87

1.

$$\begin{array}{r} 0.8 \\ \times\ 0.7 \\ \hline 0.56 \end{array} \qquad \begin{array}{r} 9.3 \\ \times\ 0.4 \\ \hline 3.72 \end{array}$$

2.

$$\begin{array}{r} 1.6 \\ \times\ 0.03 \\ \hline 0.048 \end{array} \qquad \begin{array}{r} 15 \\ \times\ 0.4 \\ \hline 6.0 = 6 \end{array}$$

3.

$$\begin{array}{r} 2.56 \\ \times\ 0.08 \\ \hline 0.2048 \end{array} \qquad \begin{array}{r} 0.107 \\ \times\ 0.9 \\ \hline 0.0963 \end{array}$$

4.

$$\begin{array}{r} 7.4 \\ \times\ 0.2\,5 \\ \hline 3\,7\,0 \\ 1\,4\,8 \\ \hline 1.8\,5\,0 = 1.85 \end{array} \qquad \begin{array}{r} 6.9 \\ \times\ 0.1\,2 \\ \hline 1\,3\,8 \\ 6\,9 \\ \hline 0.8\,2\,8 \end{array}$$

5. $4.2 \times 10 = 42$
   $10 \times 0.95 = 9.5$
   $2.08 \times 10 = 20.8$
6. $100 \times 3.5 = 350$
   $0.72 \times 100 = 72$
   $100 \times 0.128 = 12.8$
7. $1.97 \times 1000 = 1970$
   $0.685 \times 1000 = 685$
   $1000 \times 0.4 = 400$
8. $13 \times 4 = 52$
9. $0.4 \times 1.8 = 0.72$
10. $300 \times 0.6 = 180$
11. (8) 53.76 (9) 0.7098 (10) 179.18
12. $(0.6)^2 = 0.6 \times 0.6 = 0.36$
    $(1.5)^2 = 1.5 \times 1.5 = 2.25$
    $(0.13)^2 = 0.13 \times 0.13 = 0.0169$
13. $\$1.699 \times 11 = \$18.689 \rightarrow \$18.69$
14. $384 \times 0.75 = 288$ votes

Exercise 10, page 89

1.

$$\begin{array}{r} 0.013 \\ 3\overline{)0.039} \end{array} \qquad \begin{array}{r} 0.0024 \\ 7\overline{)0.0168} \end{array}$$

2.

$$\begin{array}{r} 0.67 \\ 8\overline{)5.36} \end{array} \qquad \begin{array}{r} 8.4 \\ 9\overline{)75.6} \end{array}$$

3.

$$\begin{array}{r} 0.75 \\ 14\overline{)10.50} \\ \underline{9\,8} \\ 70 \\ \underline{70} \end{array} \qquad \begin{array}{r} 43.2 \\ 12\overline{)518.4} \\ \underline{48} \\ 38 \\ \underline{36} \\ 24 \\ \underline{24} \end{array}$$

4.

$$\begin{array}{r} 0.466 \rightarrow 0.47 \\ 9\overline{)4.200} \end{array} \qquad \begin{array}{r} 0.323 \rightarrow 0.32 \\ 8\overline{)2.590} \end{array}$$

5.

$$\begin{array}{r} 1.133 \rightarrow 1.13 \\ 3\overline{)3.400} \end{array} \qquad \begin{array}{r} 0.442 \rightarrow 0.44 \\ 7\overline{)3.100} \end{array}$$

6. $0.04 \div 10 = 0.004$
   $20.6 \div 10 = 2.06$
   $1.9 \div 10 = 0.19$
7. $5.6 \div 100 = 0.056$
   $12.7 \div 100 = 0.127$
   $4.23 \div 100 = 0.0423$
8. $195 \div 1000 = 0.195$
   $4.8 \div 1000 = 0.0048$
   $520.6 \div 1000 = 0.5206$
9. $2.857142857 \rightarrow 2.857$
10. $\sqrt{0.64} = 0.8 \qquad \sqrt{0.0144} = 0.12$
11. $\$1.5 \div 4 = \$0.375$ million
12. $82.5 \div 10 = 8.25$ pounds

Exercise 11, page 92

1.

$$\begin{array}{r} 4\,2. \\ 0.2\overline{)8.4} \end{array} \qquad \begin{array}{r} 1\,0.5 \\ 0.5\overline{)5.2\,5} \end{array}$$

2.

$$\begin{array}{r} 81. \\ 0.04\overline{)3.24} \end{array} \qquad \begin{array}{r} 30\,20. \\ 0.03\overline{)90.60} \end{array}$$

3.

$$\begin{array}{r} 3.8 \\ 2.3\overline{)8.7\,4} \\ \underline{6\,9} \\ 1\,8\,4 \\ \underline{1\,8\,4} \end{array} \qquad \begin{array}{r} 0.76 \\ 3.8\overline{)2.8\,88} \\ \underline{2\,6\,6} \\ 2\,28 \\ \underline{2\,28} \end{array}$$

4.

$$\begin{array}{r} 15. \\ 0.028\overline{)0.420} \\ \underline{28} \\ 140 \\ \underline{140} \end{array} \qquad \begin{array}{r} 50. \\ 0.134\overline{)6.700} \\ \underline{6\,70} \\ 0 \end{array}$$

5.

$$\begin{array}{r} 5.71 \rightarrow 5.7 \\ 0.7\overline{)4.0\,00} \end{array} \qquad \begin{array}{r} 0.88 \rightarrow 0.9 \\ 0.9\overline{)0.8\,00} \end{array}$$

6.

$$\begin{array}{r} 0.065 \rightarrow 0.07 \\ 0.3\overline{)0.0\,195} \end{array} \qquad \begin{array}{r} 1.393 \rightarrow 1.39 \\ 0.6\overline{)0.8\,360} \end{array}$$

7. $2.142857143 \rightarrow 2.143$
8. $18 \div 1.5 = 12$ pieces
9. $\$12.25 \div 2.5 = \$4.90$

Exercise 12, page 94

1. $7.4 \times 10^2 \qquad 1.8 \times 10^4 \qquad 6.93 \times 10^6$
2. $9.5 \times 10^7 \qquad 4.5 \times 10^5 \qquad 2.06 \times 10^8$
3. 274,000   9,300   4,600,000
4. 81,000   63,500,000   120,000
5. 7.24×10^9
6. 2.7×10^7
7. 865,000 miles
8. 3.675×10^9 miles

Exercise 13, page 95

1. $15 \times 1.5 = 22.5$ miles

2	2	.	5	

2. $10.65 + 0.2 = 10.85$ feet
$11.5 - 10.85 = 0.65$ feet

0	.	6	5	

3. $1.3 + 1.12 = 2.42$ million

2	.	4	2	

4. $\dfrac{1300}{8} = 162.5 \rightarrow 163$ pieces per hour

5. $1.15 \times \$6.49 = \$7.4635 \rightarrow \$7.46$

6. $0.45 \times 175 = 78.75 \rightarrow 79$ kilograms

7. $\$1.35 + \$0.85 + \$1.05 = \$3.25$ million
$\$4.0 - \$3.25 = \$0.75$ million

8. $\dfrac{1786}{82} \approx 21.78 \rightarrow 21.8$ points per game

9. $394 \times 1.75 = 689.5 \rightarrow 690$ miles

10. $\dfrac{269.70}{18.60} = 14.5$ hours

11. (1) $2.5(60) + 1.5(48)$

12. (3) $4 - 2(1.45)$

Decimals Review, page 98

Part I

1. 38.995

2. 0.0737

3. 0.016

4. 0.027

5. 200

6. 2.414

7. $5.657 \rightarrow 5.7$

	5	.	7	

8. $2.8 \times 2.8 = 7.84$

	7	.	8	4

9. $\frac{223}{12} \approx 18.58 \rightarrow 18.6$

22. $15.23 + 2.07 = 17.3$ million

10. (5) .293 $\quad \frac{22}{75} \approx 0.2933 \rightarrow 0.293$

11. (3) \$60.00 $\quad (5 \times \$7.80) + (2.5 \times \$8.40) =$
$\$39 + \$21 = \$60$

12. (5) 32.5 $\quad 13 + 4 + 15.5 = 32.5$

13. (4) \$114.80 $\quad 70 \times \$1.64 = \$114.80$

14. (2) 48 $\quad \frac{622}{13} \approx 47.8 \rightarrow 48$

15. (1) \$1.77 $\quad 52 \times \$0.034 = \$1.768 \rightarrow \$1.77$

Part II

16. hundredths

17. 60.043

18. 408.0015

19. 0.06, 0.066, 0.6, 0.606

20. 230,000

21. 7.016

23. $3.00 - 1.75 = 1.25$ yards

24. (4) $5(125) + 3(190)$

25. (4) D, B, E, C, A

Chapter 4

Exercise 1, page 104

1. $\frac{5}{8}$ $\quad \frac{1}{6}$ $\quad \frac{19}{20}$

2. $\frac{2}{2}$ $\quad \frac{7}{4}$ $\quad \frac{8}{3}$

3. $3\frac{1}{2}$ $\quad \frac{9}{8}$

4. $\frac{5}{12}$

5. $\frac{7}{50}$

Exercise 2, page 107

In these answers the number following the phrase "reduce by" tells what number to divide into both the numerator and the denominator in order to reduce each fraction to lowest terms in one step.

1. $\frac{6}{10} = \frac{3}{5}$ $\quad$ $\frac{4}{6} = \frac{2}{3}$ $\quad$ $\frac{14}{20} = \frac{7}{10}$ $\quad$ $\frac{4}{32} = \frac{1}{8}$

   reduce by 2 $\quad$ reduce by 2 $\quad$ reduce by 2 $\quad$ reduce by 4

2. $\frac{18}{36} = \frac{1}{2}$ $\quad$ $\frac{18}{24} = \frac{3}{4}$ $\quad$ $\frac{25}{35} = \frac{5}{7}$ $\quad$ $\frac{45}{50} = \frac{9}{10}$

   reduce by 18 $\quad$ reduce by 6 $\quad$ reduce by 5 $\quad$ reduce by 5

3. $\frac{15}{40} = \frac{3}{8}$ $\quad$ $\frac{45}{60} = \frac{3}{4}$ $\quad$ $\frac{30}{45} = \frac{2}{3}$ $\quad$ $\frac{10}{25} = \frac{2}{5}$

   reduce by 5 $\quad$ reduce by 15 $\quad$ reduce by 15 $\quad$ reduce by 5

4. $\frac{70}{100} = \frac{7}{10}$ $\quad$ $\frac{50}{60} = \frac{5}{6}$ $\quad$ $\frac{80}{160} = \frac{1}{2}$ $\quad$ $\frac{40}{200} = \frac{1}{5}$

   reduce by 10 $\quad$ reduce by 10 $\quad$ reduce by 80 $\quad$ reduce by 40

5. $\frac{30}{200} = \frac{3}{20}$ $\quad$ $\frac{50}{250} = \frac{1}{5}$ $\quad$ $\frac{7}{28} = \frac{1}{4}$ $\quad$ $\frac{9}{30} = \frac{3}{10}$

   reduce by 10 $\quad$ reduce by 50 $\quad$ reduce by 7 $\quad$ reduce by 3

6. $\frac{27}{45} = \frac{3}{5}$ $\quad$ $\frac{22}{33} = \frac{2}{3}$ $\quad$ $\frac{17}{34} = \frac{1}{2}$ $\quad$ $\frac{13}{39} = \frac{1}{3}$

   reduce by 9 $\quad$ reduce by 11 $\quad$ reduce by 17 $\quad$ reduce by 13

Exercise 3, page 108

1. a. $\frac{6}{15} = \frac{2}{5}$ $\quad$ b. $\frac{9}{15} = \frac{3}{5}$ $\quad$ c. $\frac{3}{15} = \frac{1}{5}$

2. a. $\frac{18}{24} = \frac{3}{4}$ $\quad$ b. $\frac{6}{24} = \frac{1}{4}$

3. a. $\$60 + \$30 = \$90$ $\quad$ b. $\frac{30}{90} = \frac{1}{3}$ $\quad$ c. $\frac{60}{90} = \frac{2}{3}$

4. a. $175 + 125 = 300$ miles $\quad$ b. $\frac{175}{300} = \frac{7}{12}$

   c. $\frac{125}{300} = \frac{5}{12}$

5. a. $\frac{600}{2400} = \frac{1}{4}$ $\quad$ b. $\frac{450}{2400} = \frac{3}{16}$

   c. $\frac{150}{2400} = \frac{1}{16}$ $\quad$ d. $\frac{200}{2400} = \frac{1}{12}$

Exercise 4, page 109

1. $\frac{3}{5} = \frac{12}{20}$ $\quad$ $\frac{5}{12} = \frac{10}{24}$ $\quad$ $\frac{7}{8} = \frac{35}{40}$ $\quad$ $\frac{3}{4} = \frac{12}{16}$

2. $\frac{5}{11} = \frac{20}{44}$ $\quad$ $\frac{13}{20} = \frac{26}{40}$ $\quad$ $\frac{7}{10} = \frac{42}{60}$ $\quad$ $\frac{19}{20} = \frac{95}{100}$

3. $\frac{3}{4} = \frac{75}{100}$ $\quad$ $\frac{5}{9} = \frac{20}{36}$ $\quad$ $\frac{1}{8} = \frac{3}{24}$ $\quad$ $\frac{1}{3} = \frac{12}{36}$

Exercise 5, page 111

1. $\frac{15}{9} = 1\frac{2}{3}$ $\quad$ $\frac{36}{8} = 4\frac{1}{2}$

   $\frac{13}{5} = 2\frac{3}{5}$ $\quad$ $\frac{31}{6} = 5\frac{1}{6}$

2. $\frac{6}{2} = 3$ $\quad\quad$ $\frac{28}{16} = 1\frac{3}{4}$

   $\frac{15}{15} = 1$ $\quad\quad$ $\frac{24}{18} = 1\frac{1}{3}$

3. $\frac{7}{4} = 1\frac{3}{4}$ $\quad\quad$ $\frac{21}{3} = 7$

   $\frac{50}{12} = 4\frac{1}{6}$ $\quad$ $\frac{21}{6} = 3\frac{1}{2}$

4. $\frac{12}{5} = 2\frac{2}{5}$ $\quad$ $\frac{28}{9} = 3\frac{1}{9}$

   $\frac{19}{2} = 9\frac{1}{2}$ $\quad$ $\frac{73}{10} = 7\frac{3}{10}$

Exercise 6, page 112

1. $4 = \frac{4}{1}$ $\quad\quad$ $10 = \frac{10}{1}$ $\quad\quad\quad$ $9 = \frac{9}{1}$

   $16 = \frac{16}{1}$ $\quad\quad$ $50 = \frac{50}{1}$

2. $6 = \frac{12}{2}$

3. $5 = \frac{20}{4}$

4. $2\frac{2}{3} = \frac{8}{3}$ $\quad\quad$ $1\frac{5}{8} = \frac{13}{8}$ $\quad\quad$ $8\frac{2}{5} = \frac{42}{5}$

   $3\frac{3}{4} = \frac{15}{4}$ $\quad\quad$ $3\frac{5}{6} = \frac{23}{6}$

5. $5\frac{4}{7} = \frac{39}{7}$ $\quad\quad$ $3\frac{1}{2} = \frac{7}{2}$ $\quad\quad$ $7\frac{1}{3} = \frac{22}{3}$

   $6\frac{2}{9} = \frac{56}{9}$ $\quad\quad$ $10\frac{1}{3} = \frac{31}{3}$

6. $12\frac{3}{4} = \frac{51}{4}$ $\quad\quad$ $9\frac{1}{4} = \frac{37}{4}$ $\quad\quad$ $13\frac{2}{3} = \frac{41}{3}$

   $15\frac{1}{3} = \frac{46}{3}$ $\quad\quad$ $4\frac{3}{8} = \frac{35}{8}$

Exercise 7, page 113

1. $\frac{6}{12}$ $\quad$ $\frac{9}{18}$

2. $\frac{4}{9}$ $\quad$ $\frac{21}{50}$

3. $\frac{2}{3}$ $\quad$ $\frac{23}{40}$

4. 8 $\quad$ 4 $\quad$ 9 $\quad$ 12 $\quad$ 6 $\quad$ 21 $\quad$ 14 $\quad$ 3

Exercise 8, page 115

1. 10 $\quad$ 12 $\quad$ 36 $\quad$ 6

2. 18 $\quad$ 40 $\quad$ 18 $\quad$ 24

3. 24

4. $\frac{7}{12} = \frac{14}{24}$ and $\frac{5}{8} = \frac{15}{24}$

5. $\frac{5}{8}$ is larger

6. 20 $\quad$ 12 $\quad$ 24

7. 18 $\quad$ 40 $\quad$ 36

8. $\frac{5}{8} = \frac{25}{40}$ and $\frac{11}{20} = \frac{22}{40}$ and $\frac{1}{2} = \frac{20}{40}$

9. $\frac{5}{8}$ is largest

10. $\frac{8}{9} = \frac{32}{36}$ and $\frac{7}{12} = \frac{21}{36}$ and $\frac{2}{3} = \frac{24}{36}$

11. $\frac{7}{12}$ is smallest

Exercise 9, page 117

1.
$\begin{array}{r} \frac{2}{9} \\ +\frac{4}{9} \\ \hline \frac{6}{9}=\frac{2}{3} \end{array}$
$\qquad$
$\begin{array}{r} \frac{8}{15} \\ +\frac{11}{15} \\ \hline \frac{19}{15}=1\frac{4}{15} \end{array}$
$\qquad$
$\begin{array}{r} \frac{5}{8} \\ +\frac{5}{8} \\ \hline \frac{10}{8}=1\frac{2}{8}=1\frac{1}{4} \end{array}$

2.
$\begin{array}{r} 6\frac{5}{9} \\ +7\frac{8}{9} \\ \hline 13\frac{13}{9}=14\frac{4}{9} \end{array}$
$\qquad$
$\begin{array}{r} 1\frac{7}{8} \\ +20\frac{3}{8} \\ \hline 21\frac{10}{8}=22\frac{2}{8}=22\frac{1}{4} \end{array}$
$\qquad$
$\begin{array}{r} \frac{5}{16} \\ +\frac{7}{16} \\ \hline \frac{12}{16}=\frac{3}{4} \end{array}$

3.
$\begin{array}{r} \frac{3}{4} \\ \frac{1}{4} \\ +\frac{3}{4} \\ \hline \frac{7}{4}=1\frac{3}{4} \end{array}$
$\qquad$
$\begin{array}{r} 2\frac{7}{12} \\ 4\frac{11}{12} \\ +9\frac{5}{12} \\ \hline 15\frac{23}{12}=16\frac{11}{12} \end{array}$
$\qquad$
$\begin{array}{r} 5\frac{4}{9} \\ 4\frac{5}{9} \\ +3\frac{8}{9} \\ \hline 12\frac{17}{9}=13\frac{8}{9} \end{array}$

4.
$\begin{array}{r} \frac{5}{6}=\frac{10}{12} \\ +\frac{7}{12}=\frac{7}{12} \\ \hline \frac{17}{12}=1\frac{5}{12} \end{array}$
$\qquad$
$\begin{array}{r} \frac{2}{3}=\frac{8}{12} \\ +\frac{3}{4}=\frac{9}{12} \\ \hline \frac{17}{12}=1\frac{5}{12} \end{array}$
$\qquad$
$\begin{array}{r} \frac{2}{5}=\frac{12}{30} \\ +\frac{5}{6}=\frac{25}{30} \\ \hline \frac{37}{30}=1\frac{7}{30} \end{array}$

5. rounded answers:
   10 + 5 = 15   10 + 3 = 13   10 + 9 = 19
   exact answers:

$\begin{array}{r} 9\frac{2}{3}=9\frac{4}{6} \\ +4\frac{1}{2}=4\frac{3}{6} \\ \hline 13\frac{7}{6}=14\frac{1}{6} \end{array}$
$\qquad$
$\begin{array}{r} 10\frac{1}{8}=10\frac{3}{24} \\ +3\frac{1}{3}=3\frac{8}{24} \\ \hline 13\frac{11}{24} \end{array}$
$\qquad$
$\begin{array}{r} 9\frac{1}{2}=9\frac{2}{4} \\ +8\frac{3}{4}=8\frac{3}{4} \\ \hline 17\frac{5}{4}=18\frac{1}{4} \end{array}$

6. rounded answers:
   3 + 5 + 2 = 10
   1 + 0 + 1 = 2
   4 + 2 + 7 = 13
   exact answers:

$\begin{array}{r} 2\frac{5}{6}=2\frac{5}{6} \\ 4\frac{1}{2}=4\frac{3}{6} \\ +1\frac{2}{3}=1\frac{4}{6} \\ \hline 7\frac{12}{6}=9 \end{array}$
$\qquad$
$\begin{array}{r} \frac{1}{2}=\frac{10}{20} \\ \frac{1}{4}=\frac{5}{20} \\ +\frac{3}{5}=\frac{12}{20} \\ \hline \frac{27}{20}=1\frac{7}{20} \end{array}$
$\qquad$
$\begin{array}{r} 4\frac{1}{3}=4\frac{8}{24} \\ 1\frac{5}{6}=1\frac{20}{24} \\ +6\frac{5}{8}=6\frac{15}{24} \\ \hline 11\frac{43}{24}=12\frac{19}{24} \end{array}$

Exercise 10, page 118

1.
$\begin{array}{r} \frac{5}{8} \\ -\frac{1}{8} \\ \hline \frac{4}{8}=\frac{1}{2} \end{array}$
$\qquad$
$\begin{array}{r} 8\frac{5}{6} \\ -2\frac{1}{6} \\ \hline 6\frac{4}{6}=6\frac{2}{3} \end{array}$
$\qquad$
$\begin{array}{r} 4\frac{7}{8} \\ -2\frac{3}{8} \\ \hline 2\frac{4}{8}=2\frac{1}{2} \end{array}$

2.
$\begin{array}{r} 10\frac{4}{5} \\ -8\frac{1}{5} \\ \hline 2\frac{3}{5} \end{array}$
$\qquad$
$\begin{array}{r} \frac{19}{20} \\ -\frac{13}{20} \\ \hline \frac{6}{20}=\frac{3}{10} \end{array}$
$\qquad$
$\begin{array}{r} 6\frac{13}{15} \\ -2\frac{4}{15} \\ \hline 4\frac{9}{15}=4\frac{3}{5} \end{array}$

3.
$\begin{array}{r} \frac{25}{36}=\frac{25}{36} \\ -\frac{4}{9}=\frac{16}{36} \\ \hline \frac{9}{36}=\frac{1}{4} \end{array}$
$\qquad$
$\begin{array}{r} 8\frac{5}{6}=8\frac{5}{6} \\ -1\frac{1}{3}=1\frac{2}{6} \\ \hline 7\frac{3}{6}=7\frac{1}{2} \end{array}$
$\qquad$
$\begin{array}{r} 4\frac{17}{18}=4\frac{17}{18} \\ -4\frac{1}{6}=4\frac{3}{18} \\ \hline \frac{14}{18}=\frac{7}{9} \end{array}$

4. rounded answers:
   8 − 2 = 6   10 − 1 = 9   11 − 6 = 5
   exact answers:

$\begin{array}{r} 7\frac{5}{8} \\ -2 \\ \hline 5\frac{5}{8} \end{array}$
$\qquad$
$\begin{array}{r} 9\frac{3}{4}=9\frac{9}{12} \\ -1\frac{5}{12}=1\frac{5}{12} \\ \hline 8\frac{4}{12}=8\frac{1}{3} \end{array}$
$\qquad$
$\begin{array}{r} 10\frac{1}{2}=10\frac{8}{16} \\ -6\frac{3}{16}=6\frac{3}{16} \\ \hline 4\frac{5}{16} \end{array}$

Exercise 11, page 119

1.
$\begin{array}{r} 9=8\frac{3}{3} \\ -1\frac{2}{3}=1\frac{2}{3} \\ \hline 7\frac{1}{3} \end{array}$
$\qquad$
$\begin{array}{r} 11=10\frac{8}{8} \\ -3\frac{5}{8}=3\frac{5}{8} \\ \hline 7\frac{3}{8} \end{array}$
$\qquad$
$\begin{array}{r} 8=7\frac{12}{12} \\ -5\frac{7}{12}=5\frac{7}{12} \\ \hline 2\frac{5}{12} \end{array}$

2.
$\begin{array}{r} 8\frac{3}{8}=7\frac{3}{8}+\frac{8}{8}=7\frac{11}{8} \\ -4\frac{7}{8}=\qquad\qquad 4\frac{7}{8} \\ \hline 3\frac{4}{8}=3\frac{1}{2} \end{array}$
$\qquad$
$\begin{array}{r} 9\frac{1}{3}=8\frac{1}{3}+\frac{3}{3}=8\frac{4}{3} \\ -7\frac{2}{3}=\qquad\qquad 7\frac{2}{3} \\ \hline 1\frac{2}{3} \end{array}$

$\begin{array}{r} 7\frac{3}{10}=6\frac{3}{10}+\frac{10}{10}=6\frac{13}{10} \\ -4\frac{9}{10}=\qquad\qquad 4\frac{9}{10} \\ \hline 2\frac{4}{10}=2\frac{2}{5} \end{array}$

3.
$\begin{array}{r} 5\frac{7}{12}=4\frac{7}{12}+\frac{12}{12}=4\frac{19}{12} \\ -2\frac{11}{12}=\qquad\qquad 2\frac{11}{12} \\ \hline 2\frac{8}{12}=2\frac{2}{3} \end{array}$

$$15\frac{1}{6} = 14\frac{1}{6} + \frac{6}{6} = 14\frac{7}{6}$$
$$-13\frac{5}{6} = \qquad\qquad 13\frac{5}{6}$$
$$\rule{4cm}{0.4pt}$$
$$1\frac{2}{6} = 1\frac{1}{3}$$

$$20\frac{5}{9} = 19\frac{5}{9} + \frac{9}{9} = 19\frac{14}{9}$$
$$-7\frac{7}{9} = \qquad\qquad 7\frac{7}{9}$$
$$\rule{4cm}{0.4pt}$$
$$12\frac{7}{9}$$

4.
$$\frac{7}{10} = \frac{7}{10}$$
$$-\frac{1}{2} = \frac{5}{10}$$
$$\rule{3cm}{0.4pt}$$
$$\frac{2}{10} = \frac{1}{5}$$

$$3\frac{2}{3} = 3\frac{8}{12} = 2\frac{8}{12} + \frac{12}{12} = 2\frac{20}{12}$$
$$-1\frac{3}{4} = 1\frac{9}{12} = \qquad\qquad 1\frac{9}{12}$$
$$\rule{4cm}{0.4pt}$$
$$1\frac{11}{12}$$

$$\frac{5}{8} = \frac{25}{40}$$
$$-\frac{3}{5} = \frac{24}{40}$$
$$\rule{3cm}{0.4pt}$$
$$\frac{1}{40}$$

5.
$$8\frac{1}{5} = 8\frac{4}{20} = 7\frac{4}{20} + \frac{20}{20} = 7\frac{24}{20}$$
$$-3\frac{3}{4} = 3\frac{15}{20} = \qquad\qquad 3\frac{15}{20}$$
$$\rule{4cm}{0.4pt}$$
$$4\frac{9}{20}$$

$$11\frac{3}{5} = 11\frac{6}{10}$$
$$-9\frac{1}{2} = 9\frac{5}{10}$$
$$\rule{3cm}{0.4pt}$$
$$2\frac{1}{10}$$

$$9\frac{1}{2} = 9\frac{3}{6} = 8\frac{3}{6} + \frac{6}{6} = 8\frac{9}{6}$$
$$-5\frac{2}{3} = 5\frac{4}{6} = \qquad\qquad 5\frac{4}{6}$$
$$\rule{4cm}{0.4pt}$$
$$3\frac{5}{6}$$

6. rounded answers:
$$16 - 8 = 8 \qquad 8 - 4 = 4 \qquad 9 - 3 = 6$$
exact answers:
$$16\frac{1}{4} = 16\frac{2}{8} = 15\frac{2}{8} + \frac{8}{8} = 15\frac{10}{8}$$
$$-7\frac{5}{8} = 7\frac{5}{8} = \qquad\qquad 7\frac{5}{8}$$
$$\rule{4cm}{0.4pt}$$
$$8\frac{5}{8}$$

$$7\frac{11}{12} = 7\frac{22}{24}$$
$$-3\frac{5}{8} = 3\frac{15}{24}$$
$$\rule{3cm}{0.4pt}$$
$$4\frac{7}{24}$$

$$8\frac{9}{10} = 8\frac{18}{20}$$
$$-2\frac{3}{4} = 2\frac{15}{20}$$
$$\rule{3cm}{0.4pt}$$
$$6\frac{3}{20}$$

Exercise 12, page 120

1. $\frac{3}{4} \times \frac{5}{7} = \frac{15}{28}$ $\qquad$ $\frac{2}{3} \times \frac{1}{3} = \frac{2}{9}$ $\qquad$ $\frac{1}{10} \times \frac{3}{8} = \frac{3}{80}$

2. $\frac{7}{8} \times \frac{1}{5} = \frac{7}{40}$ $\qquad$ $\frac{1}{4} \times \frac{5}{16} = \frac{5}{64}$ $\qquad$ $\frac{3}{10} \times \frac{3}{5} = \frac{9}{50}$

3. $\frac{2}{9} \times \frac{4}{5} = \frac{8}{45}$ $\qquad$ $\frac{1}{5} \times \frac{1}{6} = \frac{1}{30}$ $\qquad$ $\frac{3}{5} \times \frac{1}{2} = \frac{3}{10}$

Exercise 13, page 121

1. $\frac{3}{4} \times \frac{6}{7} = \frac{9}{14}$ $\qquad$ $\frac{14}{15} \times \frac{3}{7} = \frac{2}{5}$ $\qquad$ $\frac{4}{5} \times \frac{5}{6} = \frac{2}{3}$

2. $\frac{4}{9} \times \frac{3}{8} = \frac{1}{6}$ $\qquad$ $\frac{5}{8} \times \frac{2}{15} = \frac{1}{12}$ $\qquad$ $\frac{9}{10} \times \frac{2}{3} = \frac{3}{5}$

3. $\frac{3}{20} \times \frac{1}{3} = \frac{1}{20}$ $\qquad$ $\frac{4}{5} \times \frac{5}{24} = \frac{1}{6}$ $\qquad$ $\frac{2}{3} \times \frac{9}{20} = \frac{3}{10}$

4. $\frac{6}{7} \times \frac{7}{8} \times \frac{4}{5} = \frac{3}{5}$ $\qquad$ $\frac{9}{10} \times \frac{1}{4} \times \frac{8}{9} = \frac{1}{5}$ $\qquad$ $\frac{2}{4} \times \frac{2}{9} \times \frac{15}{16} = \frac{5}{32}$

Exercise 14, page 122

1. $\frac{1}{2} \times \frac{16}{1} = \frac{8}{1} = 8$ $\qquad\qquad$ $\frac{10}{1} \times \frac{2}{3} = \frac{20}{3} = 6\frac{2}{3}$

   $\frac{3}{8} \times \frac{12}{1} = \frac{9}{2} = 4\frac{1}{2}$

2. $\frac{8}{1} \times \frac{7}{10} = \frac{28}{5} = 5\frac{3}{5}$ $\qquad\qquad$ $\frac{2}{5} \times \frac{10}{1} = \frac{4}{1} = 4$

   $\frac{9}{1} \times \frac{11}{20} = \frac{99}{20} = 4\frac{19}{20}$

3. $\frac{5}{6} \times \frac{9}{1} = \frac{15}{2} = 7\frac{1}{2}$ $\qquad\qquad$ $\frac{15}{1} \times \frac{7}{100} = \frac{21}{20} = 1\frac{1}{20}$

   $\frac{2}{3} \times \frac{4}{1} = \frac{8}{3} = 2\frac{2}{3}$

4. $4\frac{2}{3} \times \frac{15}{16} = \frac{14}{3} \times \frac{15}{16} = \frac{35}{8} = 4\frac{3}{8}$

   $2\frac{1}{4} \times \frac{8}{9} = \frac{9}{4} \times \frac{8}{9} = \frac{2}{1} = 2$

   $\frac{1}{4} \times 1\frac{1}{2} = \frac{1}{4} \times \frac{3}{2} = \frac{3}{8}$

5. rounded answers:

$4 \times 7 = 28 \qquad 1 \times 2 = 2 \qquad 4 \times 3 = 12$

exact answers:

$3\frac{3}{4} \times 6\frac{2}{3} = \frac{15}{4} \times \frac{20}{3} = \frac{25}{1} = 25$

$1\frac{1}{5} \times 2\frac{1}{3} = \frac{6}{5} \times \frac{7}{3} = \frac{14}{5} = 2\frac{4}{5}$

$4\frac{3}{8} \times 3\frac{3}{7} = \frac{35}{8} \times \frac{24}{7} = \frac{15}{1} = 15$

Exercise 15, page 124

1. $\frac{1}{3} \div \frac{1}{6} = \frac{1}{3} \times \frac{6}{1} = \frac{2}{1} = 2$

$5 \div \frac{5}{6} = \frac{5}{1} \times \frac{6}{5} = \frac{6}{1} = 6$

$4\frac{1}{2} \div \frac{3}{4} = \frac{9}{2} \times \frac{4}{3} = \frac{6}{1} = 6$

2. $\frac{1}{3} \div \frac{2}{3} = \frac{1}{3} \times \frac{3}{2} = \frac{1}{2}$

$4 \div \frac{3}{8} = \frac{4}{1} \times \frac{8}{3} = \frac{32}{3} = 10\frac{2}{3}$

$\frac{5}{9} \div \frac{3}{4} = \frac{5}{9} \times \frac{4}{3} = \frac{20}{27}$

3. $5\frac{5}{6} \div \frac{7}{8} = \frac{35}{6} \times \frac{8}{7} = \frac{20}{3} = 6\frac{2}{3}$

$\frac{9}{10} \div \frac{3}{5} = \frac{9}{10} \times \frac{5}{3} = \frac{3}{2} = 1\frac{1}{2}$

$3\frac{1}{3} \div \frac{1}{3} = \frac{10}{3} \times \frac{3}{1} = \frac{10}{1} = 10$

4. $10 \div 1\frac{1}{2} = \frac{10}{1} \div \frac{3}{2} = \frac{10}{1} \times \frac{2}{3} = \frac{20}{3} = 6\frac{2}{3}$

$1\frac{1}{3} \div 3\frac{1}{5} = \frac{4}{3} \div \frac{16}{5} = \frac{4}{3} \times \frac{5}{16} = \frac{5}{12}$

$6 \div 1\frac{1}{3} = \frac{6}{1} \div \frac{4}{3} = \frac{6}{1} \times \frac{3}{4} = \frac{9}{2} = 4\frac{1}{2}$

5. $21 \div 4\frac{1}{5} = \frac{21}{1} \div \frac{21}{5} = \frac{21}{1} \times \frac{5}{21} = \frac{5}{1} = 5$

$2\frac{2}{9} \div 2 = \frac{20}{9} \div \frac{2}{1} = \frac{20}{9} \times \frac{1}{2} = \frac{10}{9} = 1\frac{1}{9}$

$\frac{9}{10} \div 3 = \frac{9}{10} \div \frac{3}{1} = \frac{9}{10} \times \frac{1}{3} = \frac{3}{10}$

6. $5\frac{5}{6} \div 7 = \frac{35}{6} \div \frac{7}{1} = \frac{35}{6} \times \frac{1}{7} = \frac{5}{6}$

$2\frac{1}{4} \div 1\frac{1}{8} = \frac{9}{4} \div \frac{9}{8} = \frac{9}{4} \times \frac{8}{9} = \frac{2}{1} = 2$

$2\frac{1}{2} \div 4\frac{3}{4} = \frac{5}{2} \div \frac{19}{4} = \frac{5}{2} \times \frac{4}{19} = \frac{10}{19}$

Exercise 16, page 125

1. $0.6 = \frac{6}{10} = \frac{3}{5}$

$0.5 = \frac{5}{10} = \frac{1}{2}$

$0.45 = \frac{45}{100} = \frac{9}{20}$

$0.80 = \frac{80}{100} = \frac{4}{5}$

2. $0.125 = \frac{125}{1000} = \frac{1}{8}$

$0.065 = \frac{65}{1000} = \frac{13}{200}$

$0.15 = \frac{15}{100} = \frac{3}{20}$

$0.96 = \frac{96}{100} = \frac{24}{25}$

3. $0.024 = \frac{24}{1000} = \frac{3}{125}$

$0.0002 = \frac{2}{10,000} = \frac{1}{5,000}$

$0.010 = \frac{10}{1000} = \frac{1}{100}$

$0.34 = \frac{34}{100} = \frac{17}{50}$

4. $2.5 = 2\frac{5}{10} = 2\frac{1}{2}$

$3.75 = 3\frac{75}{100} = 3\frac{3}{4}$

$4.001 = 4\frac{1}{1000}$

$6.05 = 6\frac{5}{100} = 6\frac{1}{20}$

Exercise 17, page 127

1.
$$4\overline{)3.00} = 0.75 \qquad 20\overline{)9.00} = 0.45 \qquad 10\overline{)7.0} = 0.7 \qquad 8\overline{)5.00} = 0.62\frac{1}{2} \text{ or } 0.625$$

2.
$$2\overline{)1.0} = 0.5 \qquad 20\overline{)1.00} = 0.05 \qquad 25\overline{)4.00} = 0.16 \qquad 8\overline{)3.00} = 0.37\frac{1}{2} \text{ or } 0.375$$

3. $\quad 0.83 \qquad 0.44 \qquad 0.08 \qquad 0.67$

4. $\quad 0.29 \qquad 0.17 \qquad 0.42 \qquad 0.31$

5. $\frac{3}{8} = 0.375$ and $\frac{2}{5} = 0.4$ $\frac{2}{5}$ is larger

    $\frac{2}{3} = 0.667$ and $\frac{3}{5} = 0.6$ $\frac{2}{3}$ is larger

    $\frac{13}{20} = 0.65$ and $\frac{7}{10} = 0.7$ $\frac{7}{10}$ is larger

    $\frac{1}{6} = 0.167$ and $\frac{2}{9} = 0.222$ $\frac{2}{9}$ is larger

Exercise 18, page 128

1. 8×10^{-3} 4.46×10^{-2} 9.1×10^{-5}
2. 1.5×10^{-6} 2.7×10^{-2} 3.4×10^{-4}
3. 0.0000198 0.0000011 0.092
4. 0.0051 0.000733 0.0000409
5. 1.9×10^{-3}
6. 0.00000018

Exercise 19, page 131

1. $\frac{1}{8}$ cup $\frac{1}{2} \times \frac{1}{4} = \frac{1}{8}$

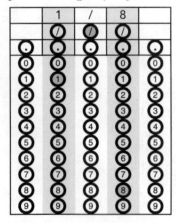

2. $\frac{3}{4}$ mile $\frac{45}{60} = \frac{3}{4}$

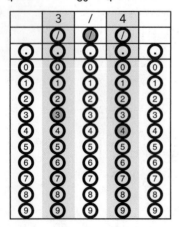

3. $\frac{1}{4}$ mile $60 - 45 = 15$ $\frac{15}{60} = \frac{1}{4}$

    or $1 - \frac{3}{4} = \frac{4}{4} - \frac{3}{4} = \frac{1}{4}$

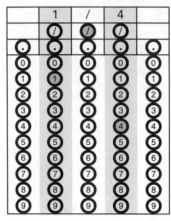

4. $4 $38 \div 9\frac{1}{2} = \frac{38}{1} \div \frac{19}{2} = \frac{38}{1} \times \frac{2}{19} = \frac{4}{1} = 4$

5. $10\frac{1}{8}$ pounds $2\frac{1}{2} = 2\frac{4}{8}$

                  $2\frac{5}{8} = 2\frac{5}{8}$

                  $1\frac{3}{4} = 1\frac{6}{8}$

             $+ 3\frac{1}{4} = 3\frac{2}{8}$

                 $8\frac{17}{8} = 10\frac{1}{8}$

6. Yes. The total weight is $\frac{1}{8}$ pound over her limit.

    $10 + 10\frac{1}{8} = 20\frac{1}{8}$ pounds

7. $187\frac{1}{2}$ pounds $3 \times 62\frac{1}{2} = \frac{3}{1} \times \frac{125}{2} = \frac{375}{2} = 187\frac{1}{2}$

8. 20 lots $90 \div 4\frac{1}{2} = \frac{90}{1} \div \frac{9}{2} = \frac{90}{1} \times \frac{2}{9} = \frac{20}{1} = 20$

9. $\frac{1}{4}$ pound $\frac{3}{4} - \frac{1}{2} = \frac{3}{4} - \frac{2}{4} = \frac{1}{4}$

10. (2) 80 $\frac{1}{6} \times \frac{500}{1} = \frac{250}{3} = 83\frac{1}{3}$

    $83\frac{1}{3}$ to the nearest 10 is 80.

11. (4) $\frac{3}{5}$ 294 to the nearest 100 is 300. $\frac{300}{500} = \frac{3}{5}$

12. (3) 4 $10 \div 2\frac{1}{4} = \frac{10}{1} \div \frac{9}{4} = \frac{10}{1} \times \frac{4}{9} = \frac{40}{9} = 4\frac{4}{9}$

    She can make 4 complete dresses.

13. (4) $\frac{1}{3}$ $\frac{12}{35}$ is close to $\frac{12}{36} = \frac{1}{3}$

Fractions Review, page 133

Part I

1. $\frac{4}{5}$ $\frac{48}{60} = \frac{4}{5}$

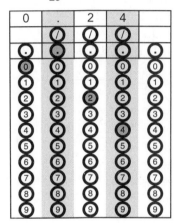

2. 0.24 $\frac{6}{25} = 0.24$

3. (1) $\frac{23}{40}$ $\frac{1}{5} = \frac{8}{40}$ $1 - \frac{17}{40} = \frac{40}{40} - \frac{17}{40} = \frac{23}{40}$

$\frac{1}{8} = \frac{5}{40}$

$+\frac{1}{10} = \frac{4}{40}$

$\frac{17}{40}$

4. (5) $144 $\frac{1}{5} \times \frac{\overset{144}{720}}{1} = \frac{144}{1} = 144$

5. (2) $69   take-home pay: $\frac{23}{40} \times \frac{\overset{18}{720}}{1} = \frac{414}{1} = 414$

$\frac{1}{6}$ of take-home pay: $\frac{1}{6} \times \frac{\overset{69}{414}}{1} = \frac{69}{1} = 69$

6. (4) $9.20

$41.40 \div 4\frac{1}{2} = \frac{41.40}{1} \div \frac{9}{2} = \frac{41.40}{1} \times \frac{2}{9} = \frac{9.20}{1} = 9.20$

7. (3) $8.85 $1\frac{1}{2} \times 5.90 = \frac{3}{2} \times \frac{\overset{2.95}{5.90}}{1} = \frac{8.85}{1} = 8.85$

Part II

8. $\frac{7}{20}$ $0.35 = \frac{35}{100} = \frac{7}{20}$

9. $\frac{23}{3}$ $7\frac{2}{3} = \frac{21}{3} + \frac{2}{3} = \frac{23}{3}$

10. 5.67 $5\frac{2}{3} = \frac{17}{3} = 3\overline{)17.000}^{5.666 \to 5.67}$

11. $6\frac{1}{2}$ $\frac{52}{8} = 6\frac{4}{8} = 6\frac{1}{2}$

12. $\frac{7}{15}$ and $\frac{9}{20}$

   In each fraction the numerator is less than half of the denominator.

13. 4   6   10   12

14. $\frac{5}{9}$ $\frac{2}{3} = \frac{6}{9}$ $\frac{5}{9}$ is smaller.

15. $15\frac{7}{8}$

$$7\frac{3}{8}$$
$$3\frac{5}{8}$$
$$+ 4\frac{7}{8}$$
$$\overline{14\frac{15}{8} = 15\frac{7}{8}}$$

16. $3\frac{2}{5}$

$$12\frac{1}{5} = 11\frac{1}{5} + \frac{5}{5} = 11\frac{6}{5}$$
$$- 8\frac{4}{5} \qquad\qquad = 8\frac{4}{5}$$
$$\overline{\qquad\qquad\qquad 3\frac{2}{5}}$$

17. $20\frac{19}{20}$

$$5\frac{3}{4} = 5\frac{15}{20}$$
$$6\frac{1}{2} = 6\frac{10}{20}$$
$$+ 8\frac{7}{10} = 8\frac{14}{20}$$
$$\overline{19\frac{39}{20} = 20\frac{19}{20}}$$

18. $4\frac{3}{4}$

$$8\frac{5}{12} = 8\frac{5}{12} = 7\frac{5}{12} + \frac{12}{12} = 7\frac{17}{12}$$
$$- 3\frac{2}{3} = 3\frac{8}{12} = \qquad\qquad\qquad 3\frac{8}{12}$$
$$\overline{\qquad\qquad\qquad\qquad 4\frac{9}{12} = 4\frac{3}{4}}$$

19. $\frac{1}{20}$

$$\frac{\cancel{3}^{1}}{\cancel{32}_{2}} \times \frac{1}{\cancel{62}_{2}} \times \frac{\cancel{4}^{1}}{5} = \frac{1}{20}$$

20. $1\frac{1}{2}$

$$\frac{\cancel{5}^{1}}{1} \times \frac{3}{\cancel{102}_{2}} = \frac{3}{2} = 1\frac{1}{2}$$

21. $12\frac{1}{2}$

$$3\frac{3}{4} \times 3\frac{1}{3} = \frac{\cancel{15}^{5}}{\cancel{4}_{2}} \times \frac{\cancel{10}^{5}}{\cancel{3}_{1}} = \frac{25}{2} = 12\frac{1}{2}$$

22. 6

$$\frac{3}{4} \div \frac{1}{8} = \frac{3}{\cancel{4}_{1}} \times \frac{\cancel{8}^{2}}{1} = \frac{6}{1} = 6$$

23. 7

$$24\frac{1}{2} \div 3\frac{1}{2} = \frac{49}{2} \div \frac{7}{2} = \frac{\cancel{49}^{7}}{\cancel{2}_{1}} \times \frac{\cancel{2}^{1}}{\cancel{7}_{1}} = \frac{7}{1} = 7$$

24. (3) $4\frac{3}{4}$

$$8\frac{1}{2} = 8\frac{2}{4} = 7\frac{2}{4} + \frac{4}{4} = 7\frac{6}{4}$$
$$- 3\frac{3}{4} = 3\frac{3}{4} = \qquad\qquad\qquad 3\frac{3}{4}$$
$$\overline{\qquad\qquad\qquad\qquad 4\frac{3}{4}}$$

25. (4) $\frac{1}{3}$ 1189 to the nearest 100 = 1200

   423 to the nearest 100 = 400

$$\frac{400}{1200} = \frac{1}{3}$$

26. (4) $10 - 3.5 - 0.75$ $3\frac{1}{2} = 3.5$ and $\frac{3}{4} = 0.75$

27. (4) 0.00034   Move the decimal point 4 places to the left.

Chapter 5

Exercise 1, page 138

1. $24:30 = 4:5$ $200:125 = 8:5$ $\frac{28}{21} = \frac{4}{3}$

2. $\frac{3.4}{1.7} = \frac{2}{1}$ 4 to 1000 = 1 to 250

   $560 to $320 = 7 to 4

3. makes:saves = $600:$60 = 10:1

4. saves:makes = $60:$600 = 1:10

5. Armenian:total = 4:24 = 1:6

6. distance:gallons = 110:22 = 5:1

Exercise 2, page 139

1. number of men = 20 − 12 = 8
   a. women to total = 12:20 = 3:5
   b. men to total = 8:20 = 2:5
   c. men to women = 8:12 = 2:3
   d. women to men = 12:8 = 3:2

2. 105 union + 45 non-union = 150 total
   a. union:total = 105:150 = 7:10
   b. non-union:total = 45:150 = 3:10
   c. union:non-union = 105:45 = 7:3
   d. total:union = 150:105 = 10:7

3. $18 million − $3 million = $15 million not spent on education
   education:not education =
   $3 million:$15 million = 1:5

4. 15 fractions + 5 decimals = 20 combined
   combined:total = 20:50 = 2:5

5. (3) 3 to 4
   Round each number to the nearest hundred.
   1213 → 1200 and 887 → 900
   voters:registered voters = 900:1200 = 3:4

Exercise 3, page 141

1. $\dfrac{m}{6} = \dfrac{10}{15}$ $15m = 60$ $m = 4$

   $\dfrac{3}{a} = \dfrac{5}{6}$ $5a = 18$ $a = 3\dfrac{3}{5}$

   $\dfrac{4}{9} = \dfrac{y}{3}$ $9y = 12$ $y = 1\dfrac{3}{9} = 1\dfrac{1}{3}$

   $\dfrac{8}{7} = \dfrac{4}{x}$ $8x = 28$ $x = 3\dfrac{4}{8} = 3\dfrac{1}{2}$

2. $\dfrac{1}{3} = \dfrac{s}{5}$ $3s = 5$ $s = 1\dfrac{2}{3}$

   $\dfrac{3}{6} = \dfrac{w}{5}$ $6w = 15$ $w = 2\dfrac{3}{6} = 2\dfrac{1}{2}$

   $\dfrac{2}{11} = \dfrac{4}{p}$ $2p = 44$ $p = 22$

   $\dfrac{2}{8} = \dfrac{9}{x}$ $2x = 72$ $x = 36$

3. $\dfrac{4}{e} = \dfrac{6}{8}$ $6e = 32$ $e = 5\dfrac{2}{6} = 5\dfrac{1}{3}$

   $\dfrac{3}{7} = \dfrac{4}{y}$ $3y = 28$ $y = 9\dfrac{1}{3}$

   $\dfrac{15}{40} = \dfrac{x}{60}$ $40x = 900$ $x = 22\dfrac{2}{4} = 22\dfrac{1}{2}$

   $\dfrac{30}{a} = \dfrac{12}{16}$ $12a = 480$ $a = 40$

4. (1) $\dfrac{4 \times 7}{9}$ $\dfrac{x}{7} = \dfrac{4}{9}$ $9x = 4 \times 7$ $x = \dfrac{4 \times 7}{9}$

5. (3) $\dfrac{5 \times 3}{12}$ $\dfrac{5}{12} = \dfrac{c}{3}$ $12c = 5 \times 3$ $c = \dfrac{5 \times 3}{12}$

Exercise 4, page 143

1. $\$1,500$ $\dfrac{\text{earns}}{\text{takes home}}$ $\dfrac{13}{10} = \dfrac{1950}{x}$

   $13x = 19,500$

   $x = \$1,500$

2. 20 games won

   5 won + 3 lost = 8 played

   $\dfrac{\text{won}}{\text{played}}$ $\dfrac{5}{8} = \dfrac{x}{32}$

   $8x = 160$

   $x = 20$

3. 80 women

   7 men + 2 women = 9 total

   $\dfrac{\text{women}}{\text{total}}$ $\dfrac{2}{9} = \dfrac{x}{360}$

   $9x = 720$

   $x = 80$

4. 500 defective parts

   20 good + 1 defective = 21 total

   $\dfrac{\text{defective}}{\text{total}}$ $\dfrac{1}{21} = \dfrac{x}{10,500}$

   $21x = 10,500$

   $x = 500$

5. 216 voted to strike

   3 strikers + 2 nonstrikers = 5 total

   $\dfrac{\text{strikers}}{\text{total}}$ $\dfrac{3}{5} = \dfrac{x}{360}$

   $5x = 1080$

   $x = 216$

6. 250 people passed

   $\dfrac{\text{passed}}{\text{total}}$ $\dfrac{5}{6} = \dfrac{x}{300}$

   $6x = 1500$

   $x = 250$

7. 30 inches long

   $\dfrac{\text{short}}{\text{long}}$ $\dfrac{4}{6} = \dfrac{20}{x}$

   $4x = 120$

   $x = 30$

8. 12 gallons of gray paint

   3 blue + 2 gray = 5 total

   $\dfrac{\text{gray}}{\text{total}}$ $\dfrac{2}{5} = \dfrac{x}{30}$

   $5x = 60$

   $x = 12$

9. (4) = $\dfrac{2 \times 12}{3}$

   $\dfrac{\text{sugar}}{\text{flour}}$ $\dfrac{2}{3} = \dfrac{x}{12}$

   $3x = 2 \times 12$

   $x = \dfrac{2 \times 12}{3}$

10. (2) = $\dfrac{90 \times 8}{12}$

   $\dfrac{\text{apples}}{\text{cost}}$ $\dfrac{12}{90} = \dfrac{8}{x}$

   $12x = 90 \times 8$

   $x = \dfrac{90 \times 8}{12}$

Ratio and Proportion Review, page 145

Part I

1. $48:60 = 4:5$

2. $1.6:6.4 = 1:4$

3. $75:35 = 15:7$

4. $x = 3$ $\dfrac{x}{9} = \dfrac{12}{36}$

$$36x = 108$$
$$x = 3$$

5. $s = 70$ $\dfrac{2}{7} = \dfrac{20}{s}$

$$2s = 140$$
$$s = 70$$

6. $n = 28\dfrac{4}{5}$ $\dfrac{8}{n} = \dfrac{5}{18}$

$$5n = 144$$
$$n = 28\dfrac{4}{5}$$

7. (3) 44   2 leave + 3 stay = 5 total

$$\dfrac{\text{leave}}{\text{total}} \quad \dfrac{2}{5} = \dfrac{x}{110}$$
$$5x = 220$$
$$x = 44$$

8. (2) 28   1 empty + 4 occupied = 5 total

$$\dfrac{\text{empty}}{\text{total}} \quad \dfrac{1}{5} = \dfrac{x}{140}$$
$$5x = 140$$
$$x = 28$$

9. 21 $\dfrac{\text{acres}}{\text{yield}} \quad \dfrac{35}{3150} = \dfrac{x}{1890}$

$$3150x = 66{,}150$$
$$x = 21$$

10. 24   2 delayed + 7 on time = 9 total

$$\dfrac{\text{delayed}}{\text{total}} \quad \dfrac{2}{9} = \dfrac{x}{108}$$
$$9x = 216$$
$$x = 24$$

Part II

11. $\dfrac{3}{2}$ $\dfrac{42}{28} = \dfrac{3}{2}$

12. $\dfrac{2}{5}$ 42 own + 28 rent = 70 total

$$\dfrac{\text{rent}}{\text{own}} \quad \dfrac{28}{70} = \dfrac{2}{5}$$

13. $\dfrac{3}{5}$ $\dfrac{\text{own}}{\text{total}}$ $\dfrac{42}{70} = \dfrac{3}{5}$

14. (3) 9:36   The other ratios simplify to 1:3.

15. (5) $5.10 $\dfrac{\text{feet}}{\text{cost}}$ $\dfrac{6}{3.40} = \dfrac{9}{x}$
$$6x = 30.60$$
$$x = 5.10$$

16. (2) $4\dfrac{1}{3}$ $\dfrac{\text{inches}}{\text{miles}}$ $\dfrac{2}{150} = \dfrac{x}{325}$
$$150x = 650$$
$$x = 4\dfrac{1}{3}$$

17. (3) $5\dfrac{1}{3}$ $\dfrac{\text{miles}}{\text{hour}}$ $\dfrac{450}{2} = \dfrac{1200}{x}$
$$450x = 2400$$
$$x = 5\dfrac{1}{3}$$

18. (4) 35 $\dfrac{\text{green}}{\text{white}}$ $\dfrac{5}{2} = \dfrac{x}{14}$
$$2x = 70$$
$$x = 35$$

19. (3) $\dfrac{3 \times 12}{5}$ $\dfrac{\text{width}}{\text{length}}$ $\dfrac{3}{5} = \dfrac{x}{12}$
$$5x = 3 \times 12$$
$$x = \dfrac{3 \times 12}{5}$$

20. (1) $\dfrac{2 \times 100}{15}$ $\dfrac{\text{parts}}{\text{hours}}$ $\dfrac{15}{2} = \dfrac{100}{x}$
$$15x = 2 \times 100$$
$$x = \dfrac{2 \times 100}{15}$$

Chapter 6

Exercise 1, page 149

1. 60%   75%   99%
2. 110%   200%
3. 4%   15%   20%
4. 100
5. 100
6. 100
7. 50
8. 300

Exercise 2, page 151

1. 9% = 0.09   24% = 0.24
   100% = 1   0.3% = 0.003
2. $87\dfrac{1}{2}\% = 0.87\dfrac{1}{2}$ $8\dfrac{1}{3}\% = 0.08\dfrac{1}{3}$
   0.15% = 0.0015   275% = 2.75
3. 2.7% = 0.027   3.95% = 0.0395
   57% = 0.57   1000% = 10
4. 150% = 1.5   12% = 0.12
   99% = 0.99   4% = 0.04

Exercise 3, page 152

1. 0.81 = 81% $0.37\dfrac{1}{2} = 37\dfrac{1}{2}\%$
   0.5 = 50%   0.004 = 0.4%
2. 0.09 = 9%   0.217 = 21.7%
   0.03 = 3% $0.33\dfrac{1}{3} = 33\dfrac{1}{3}\%$
3. 2.1 = 210%   4.85 = 485%
   3.25 = 325%   0.015 = 1.5%
4. 0.16 = 16%   0.4 = 40%
   1.75 = 175%   4.5 = 450%

Exercise 4, page 153

1. $\dfrac{45}{100} = \dfrac{9}{20}$ $37\dfrac{1}{2} \div 100 = \dfrac{75}{2} \div \dfrac{100}{1} = \dfrac{75}{2} \times \dfrac{1}{\overset{3}{\underset{4}{100}}} = \dfrac{3}{8}$

   $\dfrac{8}{100} = \dfrac{2}{25}$ $\dfrac{2}{100} = \dfrac{1}{50}$

2. $83\dfrac{1}{3} \div 100 = \dfrac{250}{3} \div \dfrac{100}{1} = \dfrac{\overset{5}{250}}{3} \times \dfrac{1}{\underset{2}{100}} = \dfrac{5}{6}$

   $\dfrac{24}{100} = \dfrac{6}{25}$

   $33\dfrac{1}{3} \div 100 = \dfrac{100}{3} \div \dfrac{100}{1} = \dfrac{\overset{1}{100}}{3} \times \dfrac{1}{\underset{1}{100}} = \dfrac{1}{3}$

   $\dfrac{80}{100} = \dfrac{4}{5}$

3. $\frac{150}{100} = \frac{3}{2}$ or $1\frac{1}{2}$

$12\frac{1}{2} \div 100 = \frac{25}{2} \div \frac{100}{1} = \frac{25}{2} \times \frac{1}{100}_4 = \frac{1}{8}$

$\frac{96}{100} = \frac{24}{25}$ $\qquad$ $\frac{5}{100} = \frac{1}{20}$

4. $\frac{90}{100} = \frac{9}{10}$ $\qquad$ $\frac{325}{100} = \frac{13}{4}$ or $3\frac{1}{4}$

$1\frac{1}{2} \div 100 = \frac{3}{2} \div \frac{100}{1} = \frac{3}{2} \times \frac{1}{100} = \frac{3}{200}$

$\frac{85}{100} = \frac{17}{20}$

Exercise 5, page 154

1. $\frac{1}{5_1} \times \frac{\overset{20}{\cancel{100}}\%}{1} = 20\%$

$\frac{5}{6_3} \times \frac{\overset{50}{\cancel{100}}\%}{1} = \frac{250}{3} = 83\frac{1}{3}\%$

$\frac{3}{8_2} \times \frac{\overset{25}{\cancel{100}}\%}{1} = \frac{75}{2} = 37\frac{1}{2}\%$

$\frac{2}{3} \times \frac{100\%}{1} = \frac{200}{3} = 66\frac{2}{3}\%$

2. $\frac{7}{4_1} \times \frac{\overset{10}{\cancel{100}}\%}{1} = 175\%$

$\frac{9}{10_1} \times \frac{\overset{10}{\cancel{100}}\%}{1} = 90\%$

$\frac{5}{12_3} \times \frac{\overset{25}{\cancel{100}}\%}{1} = \frac{125}{3} = 41\frac{2}{3}\%$

$\frac{6}{7} \times \frac{100\%}{1} = \frac{600}{7} = 85\frac{5}{7}\%$

3. $\frac{1}{6_3} \times \frac{\overset{50}{\cancel{100}}\%}{1} = \frac{50}{3} = 16\frac{2}{3}\%$

$2\frac{1}{2} = \frac{5}{2_1} \times \frac{\overset{50}{\cancel{100}}\%}{1} = 250\%$

$\frac{1}{12_3} \times \frac{\overset{25}{\cancel{100}}\%}{1} = \frac{25}{3} = 8\frac{1}{3}\%$

$3\frac{1}{4} = \frac{13}{4_1} \times \frac{\overset{25}{\cancel{100}}\%}{1} = 325\%$

4. $1\frac{1}{2} = \frac{3}{2_1} \times \frac{\overset{50}{\cancel{100}}\%}{1} = 150\%$

$\frac{9}{8_2} \times \frac{\overset{25}{\cancel{100}}\%}{1} = \frac{225}{2} = 112\frac{1}{2}\%$

$\frac{4}{3} \times \frac{100\%}{1} = \frac{400}{3} = 133\frac{1}{3}\%$

$5\frac{1}{10} = \frac{51}{10_1} \times \frac{\overset{10}{\cancel{100}}\%}{1} = 510\%$

Exercise 6, page 155

Percent	Decimal	Fraction
25%	0.25	$\frac{1}{4}$
50%	0.5	$\frac{1}{2}$
75%	0.75	$\frac{3}{4}$
$12\frac{1}{2}\%$	0.125 or $0.12\frac{1}{2}$	$\frac{1}{8}$
$37\frac{1}{2}\%$	0.375 or $0.37\frac{1}{2}$	$\frac{3}{8}$
$62\frac{1}{2}\%$	0.625 or $0.62\frac{1}{2}$	$\frac{5}{8}$
$87\frac{1}{2}\%$	0.875 or $0.87\frac{1}{2}$	$\frac{7}{8}$
20%	0.2	$\frac{1}{5}$
40%	0.4	$\frac{2}{5}$
60%	0.6	$\frac{3}{5}$
80%	0.8	$\frac{4}{5}$
10%	0.1	$\frac{1}{10}$
90%	0.9	$\frac{9}{10}$
$33\frac{1}{3}\%$	$0.33\frac{1}{3}$	$\frac{1}{3}$
$66\frac{2}{3}\%$	$0.66\frac{2}{3}$	$\frac{2}{3}$

Exercise 7, page 157

1. $0.25 \times 80 = 20$ $\qquad$ $0.6 \times 75 = 45$
2. $0.5 \times 260 = 130$ $\qquad$ $0.1 \times 420 = 42$

3. $0.9 \times 600 = 540$ $2 \times 35 = 70$

4. $0.045 \times 400 = 18$ $0.125 \times 96 = 12$

5. $\dfrac{3}{\cancel{8}} \times \dfrac{\overset{30}{\cancel{240}}}{1} = 90$ $\dfrac{1}{\cancel{6}} \times \dfrac{\overset{20}{\cancel{120}}}{1} = 20$

6. $\dfrac{1}{\cancel{3}} \times \dfrac{\overset{50}{\cancel{150}}}{1} = 50$ $\dfrac{7}{\cancel{8}} \times \dfrac{\overset{8}{\cancel{64}}}{1} = 56$

7. $\dfrac{3}{\cancel{2}} \times \dfrac{\overset{40}{\cancel{80}}}{1} = 120$ $\dfrac{2}{\cancel{3}} \times \dfrac{\overset{29}{\cancel{87}}}{1} = 58$

8. (4) $\dfrac{2}{24}$ Each of the other answers is equal to 12.

9. $675   75\% = 0.75   0.75 \times \$900 = \$675$

10. 96 people $80\% = 0.8$ $0.8 \times 120 = 96$

Exercise 8, page 159

1. 25% of $48 = \dfrac{48}{4} = 12$

   50% of $280 = \dfrac{280}{2} = 140$

2. 20% of $65 = \dfrac{65}{5} = 13$

   $33\dfrac{1}{3}\%$ of $360 = \dfrac{360}{3} = 120$

3. 10% of $80 = \dfrac{80}{10} = 8$

   $16\dfrac{2}{3}\%$ of $180 = \dfrac{180}{6} = 30$

4. 50% of $150 = \dfrac{150}{2} = 75$

   10% of $390 = \dfrac{390}{10} = 39$

5. 20% of $50 = \dfrac{50}{5} = 10$

   $33\dfrac{1}{3}\%$ of $210 = \dfrac{210}{3} = 70$

6. $16\dfrac{2}{3}\%$ of $720 = \dfrac{720}{6} = 120$

   $12\dfrac{1}{2}\%$ of $24 = \dfrac{24}{8} = 3$

7. 10% of $460 = 46$ $4 \times 46 = 184$
   10% of $1200 = 120$ $3 \times 120 = 360$

8. 10% of $\$110 = \$11$ $8 \times \$11 = \$88$
   10% of $\$2000 = \$200$ $6 \times \$200 = \$1200$

Exercise 9, page 160

1. $\dfrac{9}{36} = \dfrac{1}{4} = 25\%$ $\dfrac{7}{35} = \dfrac{1}{5} = 20\%$

2. $\dfrac{50}{75} = \dfrac{2}{3} = 66\dfrac{2}{3}\%$ $\dfrac{16}{40} = \dfrac{2}{5} = 40\%$

3. $\dfrac{120}{160} = \dfrac{3}{4} = 75\%$ $\dfrac{17}{34} = \dfrac{1}{2} = 50\%$

4. $\dfrac{23}{230} = \dfrac{1}{10} = 10\%$ $\dfrac{240}{300} = \dfrac{4}{5} = 80\%$

5. $\dfrac{15}{45} = \dfrac{1}{3} = 33\dfrac{1}{3}\%$ $\dfrac{70}{420} = \dfrac{1}{6} = 16\dfrac{2}{3}\%$

6. $\dfrac{57}{57} = 1 = 100\%$ $\dfrac{110}{55} = 2 = 200\%$

7. $\dfrac{3}{12} = \dfrac{1}{4} = 25\%$

8. $\dfrac{2}{40} = \dfrac{1}{20} = 5\%$

Exercise 10, page 161

1. $50\% = \dfrac{1}{2}$ $18 \div \dfrac{1}{2} = 18 \times 2 = 36$

   $25\% = \dfrac{1}{4}$ $30 \div \dfrac{1}{4} = 30 \times 4 = 120$

2. $75\% = \dfrac{3}{4}$ $45 \div \dfrac{3}{4} = 45 \times \dfrac{4}{3} = 60$

   $33\dfrac{1}{3}\% = \dfrac{1}{3}$ $25 \div \dfrac{1}{3} = 25 \times 3 = 75$

3. $40\% = \dfrac{2}{5}$ $60 \div \dfrac{2}{5} = 60 \times \dfrac{5}{2} = 150$

   $10\% = \dfrac{1}{10}$ $50 \div \dfrac{1}{10} = 50 \times 10 = 500$

4. $16\dfrac{2}{3}\% = \dfrac{1}{6}$ $30 \div \dfrac{1}{6} = 30 \times 6 = 180$

   $37\dfrac{1}{2}\% = \dfrac{3}{8}$ $90 \div \dfrac{3}{8} = 90 \times \dfrac{8}{3} = 240$

5. $80\% = \dfrac{4}{5}$ $240 \div \dfrac{4}{5} = 240 \times \dfrac{5}{4} = 300$

   $150\% = \dfrac{3}{2}$ $60 \div \dfrac{3}{2} = 60 \times \dfrac{2}{3} = 40$

6. $5\% = 0.05$ $\$150 \div 0.05 = \$3000$

7. $80\% = 0.8$ $20 \div 0.8 = 25$ pounds

Exercise 11, page 162

1. % $\dfrac{16}{32} = \dfrac{1}{2} = 50\%$ P $80\% = 0.8$ $0.8 \times 90 = 72$

2. W $60\% = \dfrac{3}{5}$ $30 \div \dfrac{3}{5} = \dfrac{\overset{10}{\cancel{30}}}{1} \times \dfrac{5}{\cancel{3}} = \dfrac{50}{1} = 50$

   P $4\dfrac{1}{2}\% = 0.045$ $0.045 \times 800 = 36$

3. % $\dfrac{14}{50} = \dfrac{7}{25} = 28\%$

   % $\dfrac{15}{45} = \dfrac{1}{3} = 33\dfrac{1}{3}\%$

4. P $3.6\% = 0.036$ $0.036 \times 900 = 32.4$

   % $\dfrac{120}{80} = \dfrac{3}{2} = 150\%$

5. W $33\frac{1}{3}\% = \frac{1}{3}$ $45 \div \frac{1}{3} = 45 \times 3 = 135$

   P $8.6\% = 0.086$ $0.086 \times 200 = 17.2$

6. P $20\% = 0.2$ $0.2 \times 60 = 12$

   % $\frac{30}{40} = \frac{3}{4} = 75\%$

7. % $\frac{72}{480} = \frac{9}{60} = \frac{3}{20} = 15\%$

8. P $8\% = 0.08$ $0.08 \times \$129{,}000 = \$10{,}320$

9. W $60\% = 0.6$ $\$12{,}000 \div 0.6 = \$20{,}000$

Exercise 12, page 164

1. $P = \% \times W = 0.25 \times 96 = 24$

   $\% = \frac{P}{W} = \frac{35}{56} = \frac{5}{8} = 62\frac{1}{2}\%$

2. $W = \frac{P}{\%} = \frac{15}{0.2} = 75$

   $P = \% \times W = 0.032 \times 600 = 19.2$

3. $\% = \frac{P}{W} = \frac{72}{80} = \frac{9}{10} = 90\%$

   $\% = \frac{P}{W} = \frac{34}{68} = \frac{1}{2} = 50\%$

4. $P = \% \times W = 0.18 \times 300 = 54$

   $\% = \frac{P}{W} = \frac{70}{210} = 33\frac{1}{3}\%$

5. $W = \frac{P}{\%} = \frac{120}{0.75} = 160$

   $P = \% \times W = 0.09 \times 1600 = 144$

6. $P = \% \times W = \frac{1}{8} \times 640 = 80$

   $\% = \frac{P}{W} = \frac{60}{75} = \frac{4}{5} = 80\%$

Exercise 13, page 166

1. % 75%

   $\dfrac{\text{part}}{\text{whole}}$ $\dfrac{18}{24} = \dfrac{x}{100}$

   $24x = 1800$

   $x = 75\%$

2. P $6,500

   $\dfrac{\text{part}}{\text{whole}}$ $\dfrac{x}{65{,}000} = \dfrac{10}{100}$

   $100x = 650{,}000$

   $x = \$6{,}500$

3. W $480

   $\dfrac{\text{part}}{\text{whole}}$ $\dfrac{120}{x} = \dfrac{25}{100}$

   $25x = 12{,}000$

   $x = \$480$

4. P 63 employees

   $\dfrac{\text{part}}{\text{whole}}$ $\dfrac{x}{90} = \dfrac{70}{100}$

   $100x = 6300$

   $x = 63$

5. % 15%

   $\dfrac{\text{part}}{\text{whole}}$ $\dfrac{6}{40} = \dfrac{x}{100}$

   $40x = 600$

   $x = 15\%$

6. P 27 employees

   $\dfrac{\text{part}}{\text{whole}}$ $\dfrac{x}{90} = \dfrac{30}{100}$

   $100x = 2700$

   $x = 27$

Exercise 14, page 168

1. $0.15 \times \$40 = \$6$

2. $\dfrac{\$9{,}000}{\$12{,}000} = \dfrac{3}{4} = 75\%$

3. $0.21 \times \$440 = \$92.40$

4. $\begin{array}{r} 21.5 \text{ pounds} \\ 0.8\,\overline{)172.0\,} \end{array}$

5. $0.06 \times \$240 = \$14.40$

6. $\begin{array}{r} 24 \text{ people} \\ 0.75\,\overline{)18.00\,} \end{array}$

7. (3) 25%

   Round each number to the nearest hundred.
   $\$2419 \rightarrow \$2400$ and $\$595 \rightarrow \$600$

   $\dfrac{\$600}{\$2400} = \dfrac{1}{4} = 25\%$

8. (4) 30%

   $\dfrac{\$6}{\$20} = \dfrac{3}{10} = 30\%$

9. (2) $345.60

   $0.09 \times \$3840 = \$345.60$

Exercise 15, page 170

1. $32.50
   $0.3 \times \$25 = \$7.50$ $\$25 + \$7.50 = \$32.50$

2. 1200 people
   $0.6 \times 750 = 450$ $750 + 450 = 1200$

3. $650
   $25\% = \frac{1}{4}$ $\frac{1}{4} \times \$31,200 = \$7,800$
   $\$7,800 \div 12 = \$650$

4. 3200 voters
   $0.6\overline{)4800.0}$ $\begin{array}{r}800\ 0\end{array}$ $8000 - 4800 = 3200$

5. $2070
   $0.15 \times \$1800 = \$\ 270$
   $36 \times \$50\ \ \ = \$1800$
   total $\ \ \ \ \ \ \ \ \ = \$2070$

6. (5) 4950
   $1.25 \times 2200 = 2750$
   $2200 + 2750 = 4950$

7. (5) $700
   $0.65 \times \$2000 = \$1300$ $\$2000 - \$1300 = \$700$

8. (3) $29,025
   10% raise $= 0.1 \times \$2250 = \$225$
   $\$2250 + \$225 = \$2475$
   3 months $\times \$2250$/month $= \$\ 6,750$
   9 months $\times \$2475$/month $= \overline{\$22,275}$
   total $\ \ \ \ \ \ \ \ \ \ \ \ \ \ \ \ = \$29,025$

9. (1) $\$2250 - 0.15 \times \$2250$

10. (5) Not enough information is given.
    You do not know the percent withheld for
    state tax.

Exercise 16, page 173

1. $12\frac{1}{2}\%$ $\begin{array}{r}\$0.99 \\ -\ 0.88 \\ \hline \$0.11\end{array}$ $\frac{\$0.11}{\$0.88} = \frac{1}{8} = 12\frac{1}{2}\%$

2. 25% $\begin{array}{r}\$1200 \\ -\ 900 \\ \hline \$\ 300\end{array}$ $\frac{\$300}{\$1200} = \frac{1}{4} = 25\%$

3. 36% $\begin{array}{r}68 \\ -\ 50 \\ \hline 18\end{array}$ $\frac{18}{50} = \frac{9}{25}$ $\frac{9}{25} \times \frac{\overset{4}{\cancel{100}}}{1} = \frac{36}{1} = 36\%$

4. $8\frac{1}{3}\%$ $\begin{array}{r}\$600 \\ -\ 550 \\ \hline \$\ 50\end{array}$ $\frac{50}{600} = \frac{1}{12}$ $\frac{1}{\underset{3}{\cancel{12}}} \times \frac{\overset{25}{\cancel{100}}}{1} = \frac{25}{3} = 8\frac{1}{3}\%$

5. 140% $\begin{array}{r}\$120,000 \\ -\ 50,000 \\ \hline \$\ 70,000\end{array}$ $\frac{\$70,000}{\$50,000} = \frac{7}{5}$

   $\frac{7}{\cancel{5}} \times \frac{\overset{20}{\cancel{100}}}{1} = \frac{140}{1} = 140\%$

6. 8% $\begin{array}{r}\$3600 \\ -\ 3312 \\ \hline \$\ 288\end{array}$ $\frac{\$288}{\$3600} = \frac{48}{600} = \frac{8}{100} = 8\%$

7. (2) $\frac{1500 - 1200}{1200} \times 100\%$

8. (4) 20%   Round each amount to the nearest $10.
   $\$298.99 \rightarrow \$300$ and $\$239.99 \rightarrow \$240$
   $\begin{array}{r}\$300 \\ -\ 240 \\ \hline \$\ 60\end{array}$ $\frac{\$60}{\$300} = \frac{1}{5} = 20\%$

Exercise 17, page 175

1. 75 members $0.25 \times 1500 = 375$
   $0.2 \times 375 = 75$

2. $36.90 $0.18 \times \$50 = \$9$
   $\begin{array}{r}\$50 \\ -\ 9 \\ \hline \$41\end{array}$

   $0.1 \times \$41 = \$4.10$
   $\begin{array}{r}\$41.00 \\ -\ 4.10 \\ \hline \$36.90\end{array}$

3. $1,440 $0.6 \times \$120,000 = \$72,000$
   $0.02 \times \$72,000 = \$1,440$

4. $12.45 $12\% + 5\% = 17\%$
   $0.17 \times \$15 = \$2.55$ $\begin{array}{r}\$15.00 \\ -\ 2.55 \\ \hline \$12.45\end{array}$

5. 10 Hispanic students $30\% + 45\% = 75\%$
   $100\% - 75\% = 25\%$
   $\frac{1}{4} \times 40 = 10$

6. $2400 $10\% + 5\% + 5\% = 20\%$
   $0.2 \times \$3000 = \$600$
   $\begin{array}{r}\$3000 \\ -\ 600 \\ \hline \$2400\end{array}$

7. 36 people $\quad 0.2 \times 240 = 48$

$$75\% = \frac{3}{4} \quad \frac{3}{4} \times 48 = 36$$

8. 8,750 accidents $\quad 0.25 \times 100,000 = 25,000$

$$0.35 \times 25,000 = 8,750$$

Exercise 18, page 177

1. $375 $\quad$ interest $= \$3000 \times 0.125 \times 1$

interest $= \$375$

2. $842 $\quad$ interest $= \dfrac{\overset{8}{\cancel{\$800}}}{1} \times \dfrac{5\,1/4}{\cancel{100}}$

interest $= \$42$

$\$800 + \$42 = \$842$

3. $900 $\quad$ interest $= \dfrac{\overset{50}{\cancel{\$5000}}}{1} \times \dfrac{9}{\cancel{100}} \times \dfrac{2}{1}$

interest $= \$900$

4. $36 $\quad$ 9 months $= \dfrac{9}{12} = \dfrac{3}{4}$ year

interest $= \$800 \times 0.06 \times \dfrac{3}{4}$

interest $= \$36$

5. $51.75 $\quad$ 6 months $= \dfrac{6}{12} = \dfrac{1}{2}$ year

interest $= \$900 \times 0.115 \times \dfrac{1}{2}$

interest $= \$51.75$

6. $105 $\quad$ 1 year 6 months $= 1\dfrac{6}{12} = 1\dfrac{1}{2} =$

$\dfrac{3}{2}$ years

interest $= \dfrac{\overset{5}{\cancel{\$500}}}{1} \times \dfrac{\overset{7}{\cancel{14}}}{\cancel{100}} \times \dfrac{3}{\cancel{2}}$

interest $= \$105$

7. $2300 $\quad$ 2 years 6 months $= 2\dfrac{6}{12} = 2\dfrac{1}{2} =$

$\dfrac{5}{2}$ years

interest $= \dfrac{\overset{20}{\cancel{\$2000}}}{1} \times \dfrac{\overset{3}{\cancel{6}}}{\cancel{100}} \times \dfrac{5}{\cancel{2}}$

interest $= \$300$

$\$2000 + \$300 = \$2300$

8. $1125 $\quad$ 1 year 8 months $= 1\dfrac{8}{12} = 1\dfrac{2}{3} =$

$\dfrac{5}{3}$ years

interest $= \dfrac{\overset{9}{\cancel{\$900}}}{1} \times \dfrac{\overset{5}{\cancel{15}}}{\cancel{100}} \times \dfrac{5}{\cancel{3}}$

interest $= \$225$

$\$900 + 225 = \$1125$

9. $933 $\quad$ 2 years 4 months $= 2\dfrac{4}{12} = 2\dfrac{1}{3} =$

$\dfrac{7}{3}$ years

interest $= \dfrac{\overset{40}{\cancel{\$4000}}}{1} \times \dfrac{10}{\cancel{100}} \times \dfrac{7}{3} = \dfrac{2800}{3}$

interest $= \$933.33 \rightarrow \$933$

10. $1317 $\quad$ 9 months $= \dfrac{9}{12} = \dfrac{3}{4}$ year

interest $= \dfrac{\cancel{\$1200}}{1} \times \dfrac{13}{\cancel{100}} \times \dfrac{3}{\cancel{4}}$

interest $= \$117$

$\$1200 + \$117 = \$1317$

Percent Review, page 179

Part I

1. 1.86 $\qquad 0.062 \times 30 = 1.86$

2. 37.5 $\qquad \dfrac{7.5}{0.2} = 37.5$

3. 60% $\qquad \dfrac{21}{35} = \dfrac{3}{5} = 60\%$

4. 70% $\dfrac{\$1400}{\$2000} = \dfrac{7}{10} = 70\%$

5. 10%
$$\begin{array}{r} \$1.80 \\ -\,1.62 \\ \hline \$0.18 \end{array}$$
$\dfrac{\$0.18}{\$1.80} = \dfrac{1}{10} = 10\%$

6. $27   9 months $= \dfrac{9}{12} = \dfrac{3}{4}$ year

$\dfrac{\overset{9}{\cancel{\$450}}}{1} \times \dfrac{\overset{2}{\cancel{8}}}{\underset{2}{\cancel{100}}} \times \dfrac{3}{\underset{1}{\cancel{4}}} = \dfrac{54}{2} = \$27$

7. (3) 768 $75\% = \dfrac{3}{4}$

$\dfrac{3}{\cancel{4}} \times \dfrac{\overset{320}{\cancel{1280}}}{1} = 960 \qquad 80\% = \dfrac{4}{5}$

$\dfrac{4}{\cancel{5}} \times \dfrac{\overset{192}{\cancel{960}}}{1} = 768$

8. (2) $786.70
$$\begin{array}{r} \$695 \\ \times\,0.06 \\ \hline \$41.70 \end{array} \qquad \begin{array}{lr} & \$695.00 \\ \text{tax} & 41.70 \\ \text{shipping} & +\,50.00 \\ \hline \text{total} & \$786.70 \end{array}$$

9. (2) $75 $\$749 \times 0.1 = \$74.90 \rightarrow \$75$

10. (4) $773 $\$749 + \$12 + \$12 = \$773$

Part II

11. $\dfrac{7}{20}$ $35\% = \dfrac{35}{100} = \dfrac{7}{20}$

12. 0.048 $4.8\% = 0.048$

13. (5) 60%

14. (5) Divide the number by 5.

15. (4) $\dfrac{56}{0.125}$ Each of the other choices equals 7.

16. (3) $\$350 + 0.06 \times \$350$

17. (3) 10%   Round each number to the nearest dollar.
$\$39.95 \rightarrow \$40$ and $\$35.89 \rightarrow \$36$
$$\begin{array}{r} \$\,40 \\ -36 \\ \hline \$\;\,4 \end{array} \qquad \dfrac{\text{change}}{\text{original}} = \dfrac{\$4}{\$40} = \dfrac{1}{10} = 10\%$$

18. (5) $\$2000 \times 0.08 \times \dfrac{1}{2}$

19. (3) $1.03 \times \$269$ billion
Expenditures will be 100% + 3% more, or $1.03 \times \$269$ billion.

20. (4) $\$1.7 \times 10^{12}$
The decimal is moved 12 places to the left.

Chapter 7

1. $\dfrac{18}{36} = \dfrac{1}{2}$ yard   8 hours $= \dfrac{8}{24} = \dfrac{1}{3}$ day

2. $\dfrac{40}{60} = \dfrac{2}{3}$ hour $\dfrac{12}{16} = \dfrac{3}{4}$ pound

3. $\dfrac{9}{12} = \dfrac{3}{4}$ foot $\dfrac{2}{4} = \dfrac{1}{2}$ gallon

4. $\dfrac{500}{2000} = \dfrac{1}{4}$ ton $\dfrac{528}{5280} = \dfrac{1}{10}$ mile

5. $\frac{1}{2}$ pint $\qquad$ $\frac{5}{60} = \frac{1}{12}$ hour

6. $\frac{5}{7}$ week $\qquad$ $\frac{8}{12} = \frac{2}{3}$ foot

7. $3 \times 16 = 48$ ounces $\qquad$ $4 \times 12 = 48$ inches

8. $5 \times 60 = 300$ seconds $\qquad$ $2 \times 3 = 6$ feet

9. $3 \times 2000 = 6000$ pounds $\qquad$ $4 \times 24 = 96$ hours

10. $1\frac{1}{2} \times 5280 = 7920$ feet $\qquad$ $5 \times 4 = 20$ quarts

11. 33 jars $\qquad$ $\frac{1 \text{ gal}}{4 \text{ qt}} = \frac{x}{130 \text{ qt}}$

$4x = 130$

$x = 32\frac{1}{2}$ jars, or 33 complete jars.

12. 72 hr $\qquad$ $\frac{1 \text{ day}}{24 \text{ hr}} = \frac{3 \text{ days}}{x}$

$1x = 72\text{hr}$

13. $\frac{3}{4}$ hr $\qquad$ $\frac{1 \text{ hr}}{60 \text{ min}} = \frac{x}{45 \text{ min}}$

$60x = 45$

$x = \frac{45}{60} = \frac{3}{4}$ hr

14. 2 mi $\qquad$ $\frac{1 \text{ mi}}{5280 \text{ ft}} = \frac{x}{10,560 \text{ ft}}$

$5280x = 10,560$

$x = 2$ mi

15. 12 trips $\qquad$ $\frac{1 \text{ ton}}{2000} = \frac{3}{x}$

$1x = 6000$

$6000 \div 500 = 12$ trips

Exercise 2, page 187

1. 1000

2. $\frac{1}{100}$

3. $\frac{1}{1000}$

4. $1.65 \times 1000 = 1650$ grams
   $9 \times 100 = 900$ centimeters

5. $3.2 \times 1000 = 3200$ milliliters
   $4 \times 1000 = 4000$ meters

6. $0.6 \times 1000 = 600$ grams
   $0.25 \times 1000 = 250$ milliliters

7. $80 \div 100 = 0.8$ meter
   $795 \div 1000 = 0.795$ kilogram

8. $500 \div 1000 = 0.5$ kilometer
   $380 \div 1000 = 0.38$ liter

Exercise 3, page 189

1. $\frac{1 \text{ lb}}{16 \text{ oz}} = \frac{x}{20}$

   $16x = 20$

   $x = 1\frac{4}{16} = 1\frac{1}{4}$ lb

2. $\frac{1 \text{ m}}{100 \text{ cm}} = \frac{x}{35}$

   $100x = 35$

   $x = \frac{35}{100} = 0.35$ m

3. $\frac{1 \text{ hr}}{60 \text{ min}} = \frac{x}{150}$

   $60x = 150$

   $x = 2\frac{30}{60} = 2\frac{1}{2}$ hr

4. $\frac{1 \text{ ft}}{12 \text{ in.}} = \frac{x}{75}$

   $12x = 75$

   $x = 6\frac{3}{12} = 6\frac{1}{4}$ ft

5. $\frac{1 \text{ L}}{1000 \text{ mL}} = \frac{x}{850}$

   $1000x = 850$

   $x = \frac{850}{1000} = 0.850$ or 0.85 L

6. $\frac{1\text{qt}}{2\text{pt}} = \frac{9}{x}$

   $1x = 18$

   $x = 18$ pt

7. $\frac{1 \text{ lb}}{16 \text{ oz}} = \frac{1 \, 3/4}{x}$

   $1x = 1\frac{3}{4} \times 16$

   $x = 28$ oz

8. $\frac{1 \text{ ton}}{2000 \text{ lb}} = \frac{x}{400}$

   $2000x = 400$

   $x = \frac{400}{2000} = \frac{1}{5}$ T

Exercise 4, page 190

1. 82 kilograms $\qquad$ $180 \times 0.453 = 81.54 \rightarrow 82$ kg

2. 121 pounds $\qquad$ $55 \times 2.2 = 121$ pounds

3. 168 centimeters   5 feet = 5 × 12 = 60 inches
   60 in. + 6 in. = 66 in.
   66 × 2.54 = 167.64 → 168 cm

4. 1011 kilometers   632 × 1.6 = 1011.2 → 1011 km

5. 335 miles   540 × 0.62 = 334.8 → 335 miles

6. 22 centimeters $8\frac{1}{2}$ × 2.54 = 21.59 → 22 cm

   28 centimeters   11 × 2.54 = 27.94 → 28 cm

Exercise 5, page 192

1. J = $\frac{7}{8}$ in.

2. K = $1\frac{1}{4}$ in.

3. L = $3\frac{1}{2}$ in.

4. M = $4\frac{1}{8}$ in.

5. N = $5\frac{5}{8}$ in.

6. $4\frac{3}{8}$ in. $5\frac{5}{8} - 1\frac{1}{4} = 5\frac{5}{8} - 1\frac{2}{8} = 4\frac{3}{8}$ in.

7. P = 2.5 cm

8. Q = 4 cm

9. R = 6.3 cm

10. S = 9.2 cm

11. T = 13.9 cm

12. 6.7 cm   9.2 − 2.5 = 6.7 cm

13. 36 amperes

14. 14 volts

15. $\frac{1}{10} \times 90 = 9$ seconds

Measurement Review, page 194

Part I

1. $\frac{22}{36} = \frac{11}{18}$

2. 115 cm = 1.15 m

3. (2) $10.80   2 lb 4 oz = $2\frac{4}{16} = 2\frac{1}{4}$ lb

   $2\frac{1}{4} \times \$4.80 = \frac{9}{4} \times \$4.80 = \$10.80$

4. (3) 185   4.00 − 2.15 = 1.85 m

   1.85 × 100 = 185 cm

5. (2) 4   3 yd 18 in. = $3\frac{18}{36} = 3\frac{1}{2}$ yd

   $15 \div 3\frac{1}{2} = 15 \div \frac{7}{2} = 15 \times \frac{2}{7} = \frac{30}{7} = 4\frac{2}{7}$

   He can make 4 complete suits.

6. (1) 42.9   36.5 + 42.2 + 50.1 = 128.8

   $\frac{128.8}{3} = 42.93 \to 42.9$

Part II

7. (4) $2\frac{5}{8}$

8. (5) $1\frac{3}{8}$ $S = \frac{7}{8}$ in. and $T = 2\frac{1}{4}$ in.

$$2\frac{1}{4} - \frac{7}{8} = 2\frac{2}{8} - \frac{7}{8} = 1\frac{10}{8} - \frac{7}{8} = 1\frac{3}{8}$$

9. (4) $\frac{2.5 + 0.96 + 1.2}{3}$

10. 7.1

11. 3.8 $X = 2.6$ cm and $Y = 6.4$ cm
$6.4 - 2.6 = 3.8$

12. (5) $\frac{5 \times 14}{16}$

13. (4) 37

14. (3) 84

Chapter 8

Exercise 1, page 198

1. five
2. 15%
3. 19 and under
4. $25\% = \frac{1}{4}$
5. $0.15 \times 500,000 = 75,000$
6. $0.48
7. $0.10 out of a dollar $= \frac{10}{100} = 10\%$
8. $0.34 is close to $0.33 $\frac{1}{3} = \frac{1}{3}$ of the total
9. 10% of $1,800,000,000,000 = $180,000,000,000
10. 1.8×10^{11}
11. (1) Individual income tax and social security make up more than 80% of the budget.
    48% + 34% = 82%
12. (1) $\frac{1}{4}$ 24% is close to $25\% = \frac{1}{4}$
13. (3) coal and nuclear
    Coal went from 46% to 57% and nuclear from 2% to 20%.
14. (5) $\frac{3}{10}$ $20\% + 9\% = 29\% \rightarrow 30\% = \frac{3}{10}$
15. (4) 10 times $\frac{20\%}{2\%} = 10$

Exercise 2, page 202

1. (2) 400
2. (1) 900
3. (5) 1998
4. (5) 1800   400 + 1400 = 1800
5. (3) 600   1400 − 800 = 600
6. (3) The number of morning dailies has increased while the number of evening dailies has decreased.
7. West
8. Northeast
9. Midwest and South
10. (4) 675 $\frac{300,000}{100,000} = 3$ $225 \times 3 = 675$
11. (2) 95 $\frac{50,000}{100,000} = \frac{1}{2}$ $\frac{1}{2} \times 190 = 95$
12. (5) 2,800 $\frac{1,000,000}{100,000} = 10$ $10 \times 280 = 2800$

Exercise 3, page 206

1. (1) more than 70%
2. (5) 1860
3. (3) 1880–1900
4. (4) 1940–1960
5. (5) less than 5%
6. (1) 1990
7. (2) 500 million
8. (5) 1996–1997
9. (4) 1996–1997
10. (1) Shipments of CDs have increased while shipments of cassettes have decreased.

Exercise 4, page 210

1. England
2. 69.1%
3. $2.04 $3.75 − $1.71 = $2.04
4. $3.33 $4.37 × 0.762 = $3.32994 → $3.33
5. (4) 15 × $3.52 × 0.679
6. 1980
7. $\frac{1}{5}$ $20\% = \frac{20}{100} = \frac{1}{5}$
8. 1:2   17:34 = 1:2
9. 684   0.57 × 1200 = 684
10. (4) The percent of men who are liberal has decreased since 1970.
    The table does not separate the categories of political views by sex.

Exercise 5, page 214

1. $\frac{1}{5}$
2. $\frac{1}{5}$
3. $\frac{2}{5}$
4. $\frac{3}{5}$ The three odd numbers are 1, 3, and 5.
5. $\frac{1}{6}$
6. $\frac{3}{6} = \frac{1}{2}$
7. $\frac{2}{6} = \frac{1}{3}$
8. $\frac{16}{20} = \frac{4}{5}$
9. $\frac{6}{300} = \frac{1}{50}$
10. $\frac{6}{16} = \frac{3}{8}$

Exercise 6, page 215

1. $\frac{2}{6} = \frac{1}{3}$
2. $\frac{2}{5}$
3. $\frac{2}{4} = \frac{1}{2}$
4. $\frac{3}{12} = \frac{1}{4}$ There are 6 + 3 + 1 + 2 = 12 pairs of socks.
5. $\frac{1}{11}$ There are now 6 + 3 + 1 + 1 = 11 pairs of socks.
6. $\frac{1}{10}$ There are now 5 + 3 + 1 + 1 = 10 pairs of socks.
7. $\frac{1}{8}$
8. $\frac{1}{7}$ There are now 1 + 2 + 4 = 7 cans of paint.
9. $\frac{4}{6} = \frac{2}{3}$ There are now 1 + 1 + 4 = 6 cans of paint.
10. $\frac{2}{1000} = \frac{1}{500}$
11. $\frac{6}{1000} = \frac{3}{500}$
12. $\frac{10}{30} = \frac{1}{3}$ There are 30 possible days in April on which to be born. There are 10 days after the 20th.

Exercise 7, page 218

1. Miller
2. Brown and Lane
3. 10
4. 27   4 + 5 + 3 + 1 + 2 + 3 + 2 + 1 + 4 + 2 = 27
5. 2.7 $\frac{27}{10} = 2.7$
6. 2.5   1 1 2 2 <u>2</u> <u>3</u> 3 4 4 5
            $\frac{2+3}{2} = \frac{5}{2} = 2.5$
7. 2   2 occurs three times.
8. 6
9. 35   6 + 12 + 10 + 4 + 3 = 35
10. 80−89
11. 17   10 + 4 + 3 = 17
12. 18   12 + 6 = 18

Data Analysis, Statistics, and Probability Review, page 220

Part I

1. $3600

2. 1999

3. $\frac{1}{4}$ 15% + 10% = 25% = $\frac{1}{4}$

4. (3) $136   0.04 × $3400 = $136

5. (4) $1020   0.3 × $3400 = $1020

6. (4) about $3200
   Monthly income in 2001 was $3600. It fell to $3400 in 2002. If the trend continues, monthly income in 2003 will be $3200.

7. about 250 million

8. 2000

9. 25 million

10. (5) 83 million
    0.3 × 275 million = 82.5 or about 83 million

11. (4) 76 million 0.2 × 380 million = 76 million

12. (5) 65+

Part II

13. $\frac{3}{9} = \frac{1}{3}$ 6 + 3 = 9 total $\frac{3 \text{ red}}{9 \text{ total}}$

14. $\frac{5}{8}$ 9 − 1 = 8 total $\frac{5 \text{ blue}}{8 \text{ total}}$

15. (4) 20   1 + 5 + 9 + 3 + 2 = 20

16. 5 ft 6 in. to 5 ft 9 in.

17. $\frac{3}{10}$
    5 + 1 = 6 students over 5 ft 6 in. $\frac{6}{20} = \frac{3}{10}$

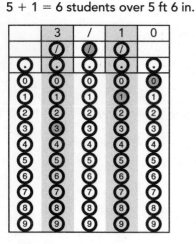

18. $\frac{1}{4}$
    3 + 2 = 5 students under 5 ft 6 in. $\frac{5}{20} = \frac{1}{4}$

Chapter 9

Exercise 1, page 226

1. c

2. a

3. e

4. b

5. d

6. acute   right   obtuse

7. reflex   right   straight

8. acute   obtuse   reflex

9. straight   right   acute

10. acute   right   obtuse

11. acute   straight   obtuse

12. reflex   reflex   acute

13. a protractor

14. 360° ÷ 12 = 30°   2 × 30° = 60°
    3 × 30° = 90°   4 × 30° = 120°

15. The angle halfway between 2:00 and 3:00 is $\frac{1}{2}$ of 30° = 15°.

    The angle from 3:00 to 6:00 is 3 × 30° = 90°.
    The total is 15° + 90° = 105°.

Exercise 2, page 230

1. 90° − 48° = 42°

2. 180° − 48° = 132°

3. 90° − 25° = 65°

4. 180° − 63° = 117°

5. $\angle w$

6. 360°

7. 180° − 75° = 105°

8. 180° − 119° = 61°

9. obtuse

   The supplement of an angle that measures *less than 90°* must be *greater than 90°* since the sum of the two angles is 180°.

10. 180° − 45° = 135°

11. 37°   Vertical angles are equal.

12. 180° − 110.5° = 69.5°

13. 138° − 47° = 91°

14. 30°   All the acute angles are equal when a transversal crosses parallel lines.

15. $\angle v$, $\angle w$, and $\angle z$ are the other obtuse angles.

Exercise 3, page 233

1. triangle
2. square
3. diameter
4. circumference
5. diameter
6. square   trapezoid   rectangle
7. triangle   rhombus   parallelogram
8. *FG* (or *GF*)
9. *GH* (or *HG*)
10. *FG* and *EH*
11. 90°

12. $\frac{36}{2} = 18$ inches

13. 7.5 × 2 = 15 feet

Exercise 4, page 236

1. rectangle   triangle   square

   $P = 2l + 2w$ $P = s_1 + s_2 + s_3$ $P = 4s$

   $P = 2(52) + 2(37)$ $P = 19 + 19 + 19$ $P = 4(8)$

   $P = 104 + 74$ $P = 57$ cm $P = 32$ yd

   $P = 178$ ft

2. rectangle   square

   $P = 2l + 2w$ $P = 4s$

   $P = 2(2\frac{3}{4}) + 2(1\frac{1}{2})$ $P = 4(\frac{1}{2})$

   $P = 5\frac{1}{2} + 3$ $P = 2$ in.

   $P = 8\frac{1}{2}$ in.

triangle

$P = s_1 + s_2 + s_3$

$P = 10\frac{1}{2} + 9\frac{1}{4} + 7\frac{3}{4}$

$P = 26\frac{6}{4}$

$P = 27\frac{1}{2}$ in.

3. rectangle   square   triangle

   $P = 2l + 2w$ $P = 4s$ $P = s_1 + s_2 + s_3$

   $P = 2(6.3) + 2(5.2)$ $P = 4(1.75)$ $P = 13 + 13 + 9$

   $P = 12.6 + 10.4$ $P = 7$ m $P = 35$ ft

   $P = 23$ cm

4. circle   circle   circle

   $C = \pi d$ $d = 2r = 2(20) = 40$ in. $C = \pi d$

   $C = 3.14(10)$ $C = \pi d$ $C = 3.14(3)$

   $C = 31.4$ yd $C = 3.14(40)$ $C = 9.42$ ft

                              $C = 125.6$ in.

5. $d = 2r = 2(7) = 14$ in.

   $C = \pi d$

   $C = \frac{22}{\overset{1}{7}} \times \frac{\overset{2}{14}}{1} = \frac{44}{1} = 44$ in.

6. (4) 4 × 20 ft   The other answers all equal 70 ft.

7. (3) $P = 6s$ Since all six sides are the same, multiply 6 by the measurement of one side.

8. (1) 2(1.6) + 2.4

Exercise 5, page 238

1. (4) 31.4 ft   3 × 10 = 30 ft

2. (3) 12.6 yd   3 × 4 = 12 yd

3. (2) 6.9 m   3 × 2.2 = 6.6 m

4. (3) 37.7 in.   3 × 12 = 36 in.

5. (2) 157 in.   3 × 50 = 150 in.

6. (1) 3.1 ft   3 × 1 = 3 ft

7. (1) 300 in.   3 × 96 = 288 in.

Exercise 6, page 239

1. $P = 2l + 2w$
   $P = 2(10) + 2(8)$
   $P = 20 + 16$
   $P = 36$ in.

2. width $= \frac{1}{2}(26) = 13$ m

   $P = 2l + 2w$
   $P = 2(26) + 2(13)$
   $P = 52 + 26$
   $P = 78$ m

3. To find one side, divide the perimeter by 4.

   $\frac{100}{4} = 25$ in.

   25 in. $= \frac{25}{12} = 2$ ft 1 in.

4. $P = 2l + 2w$
   $P = 2(36) + 2(42)$
   $P = 72 + 84$
   $P = 156$ in.

5. $\frac{156}{12} = 13$ ft for one window

   $13 \times 6 = 78$ ft for six windows

6. $78 \times \$0.60 = \$46.80$

7. $C = \pi d$
   $C = 3.14(50)$
   $C = 157$ ft
   $157 \times 12 = 1884$ inches

   $\frac{1884}{9 \text{ inches per brick}} = 209.33$ or 210 bricks

   (Round *up* to find the number of bricks.)

8. $P = 2l + 2w$
   $P = 2(72) + 2(30)$
   $P = 144 + 60$
   $P = 204$ in.

   $\frac{204}{12} = 17$ ft

9. Top: $\frac{1}{2}\pi d = \frac{1}{2}(3.14)(20) = 31.4$ in.

   Bottom: $2l + w = 2(30) + 20 = 80$ in.
   Total: $31.4 + 80 = 111.4 \rightarrow 112$ in.

10. (2) $2(25) + 2(15)$

Exercise 7, page 244

These answers use formulas written with letter abbreviations rather than words.

1. rectangle

   $A = lw$
   $A = 15(12)$
   $A = 180$ sq ft

   square

   $A = s^2$
   $A = 14^2$
   $A = 196$ sq ft

   triangle

   $A = \frac{1}{2}bh$

   $A = \frac{1}{2}(11)(6)$

   $A = 33$ sq in.

2. circle

   $A = \pi r^2$
   $A = 3.14(10)^2$
   $A = 3.14(100)$
   $A = 314$ sq yd

   parallelogram

   $A = bh$
   $A = 20 \times 12$
   $A = 240$ sq in.

   trapezoid

   $A = \frac{1}{2}(b_1 + b_2)h$

   $A = \frac{1}{2}(20 + 14)12$

   $A = \frac{1}{2}(34)12$

   $A = 204$ sq in.

3. rectangle

   $A = lw$
   $A = 8 \times 3\frac{1}{2}$
   $A = 28$ sq in.

   circle

   $r = \frac{4}{2} = 2$ yd
   $A = \pi r^2$

   $A = 3.14(2)^2$
   $A = 12.56$ sq yd

   square

   $A = s^2$
   $A = (6.5)^2$
   $A = 42.25$ m²

4. triangle   trapezoid

$A = \frac{1}{2}bh$ $A = \frac{1}{2}(b_1 + b_2)h$

$A = \frac{1}{2}(7)(9)$ $A = \frac{1}{2}(12 + 14)10$

$A = 31\frac{1}{2}$ cm² $A = \frac{1}{2}(26)10$

    $A = 130$ sq ft

circle

$A = \pi r^2$
$A = 3.14(0.5)^2$
$A = 3.14(0.25)$
$A = 0.785$ m²

5. parallelogram   rectangle

$A = bh$ $A = lw$
$A = 11 \times 6$ $A = 12.5 \times 8$
$A = 66$ sq in. $A = 100$ sq yd

trapezoid

$A = \frac{1}{2}(b_1 + b_2)h$
$A = \frac{1}{2}(20 + 30)15$
$A = 375$ sq ft

6. square   rectangle

$A = s^2$ $A = lw$
$A = (1.5)^2$ $A = 28 \times 10$
$A = 2.25$ m² $A = 280$ sq in.

circle

$r = \frac{100}{2} = 50$ in.

$A = \pi r^2$
$A = 3.14(50)^2$
$A = 3.14(2500)$
$A = 7850$ sq in.

7. (3) $\left(\frac{5}{8}\right)^2$

8. (4) Find the average of 7 and 9. Then multiply by 6.

9. (5) $\frac{1}{2}(12 \times 9)$

10. (3) 9   1 yard = 3 feet $A = s^2 = 3^2 = 9$ sq ft

Exercise 8, page 247

1. $A = lw$
$A = 10 \times 8$
$A = 80$ sq in.
2. 1 yd = 3 ft
$A = lw$
$A = 18 \times 3$
$A = 54$ sq ft
3. 18 ft $= \frac{18}{3} = 6$ yd
12 ft $= \frac{12}{3} = 4$ yd
$A = lw$
$A = 6 \times 4$
$A = 24$ sq yd
4. $A = \frac{1}{2}(b_1 + b_2)h$
$A = \frac{1}{2}(16 + 12)10$
$A = \frac{1}{2}(28)10$
$A = 140$ sq ft
5. $A = lw$
$A = 40 \times 25$
$A = 1000$ sq ft
$\frac{1000}{200} = 5$ gallons
6. 12 ft $= \frac{12}{3} = 4$ yd
9 ft $= \frac{9}{3} = 3$ yd
$A = \frac{1}{2}bh$
$A = \frac{1}{2}(4)3$
$A = 6$ sq yd
7. $A = lw$
$A = 8 \times 6$
$A = 48$ sq ft
3 windows $= 3 \times 48 = 144$ sq ft
1 sq yd $= 3 \times 3 = 9$ sq ft
$\frac{144}{9} = 16$ sq yd
8. $A = \pi r^2$
$A = 3.14(20)^2$
$A = 3.14(400)$
$A = 1256$ sq ft
9. total area $= lw = 50 \times 30 = 1500$ sq ft
pool area $= lw = 34 \times 18 = \underline{612 \text{ sq ft}}$
walkway $= \underline{888 \text{ sq ft}}$
10. (5) $60 \times 25 - 15 \times 12$
11. (4) $12^2 - \pi(4^2)$
12. (1) $20 \times 12 - 7 \times 3 - 8 \times 5$

13. (3) $\frac{A5}{3} \times \frac{B5}{3}$

The length and width are both in feet. Divide each by 3 to get yards. Then multiply length by width.

14. (5) C5 × D5

Multiply the area of the room in square yards by the cost per square yard.

Exercise 9, page 251

1. cylinder   rectangular solid   sphere
2. square pyramid   cone   cube
3. $A = lw$
   $A = 24 \times 16$
   $A = 384$ sq in.
4. $A = \pi r^2$
   $A = 3.14(30)^2$
   $A = 3.14(900)$
   $A = 2826$ cm^2
5. $A = s^2$
   $A = (1.6)^2$
   $A = 2.56$ m^2
6. $A = s^2$
   $A = 9^2$
   $A = 81$ sq in.
7. A cube has 6 faces.
   $6 \times 81 = 486$ sq in.
8. (2) $2(5 \times 8) + 2(5 \times 10) + 2(8 \times 10)$

Exercise 10, page 254

1. rectangular solid   cube
   $V = lwh$ $V = e^3$
   $V = 15 \times 12 \times 9$ $V = 8^3$
   $V = 1620$ cu in. $V = 512$ cu in.

   cylinder
   $V = \pi r^2 h$
   $V = 3.14 \times 10^2 \times 20$
   $V = 3.14 \times 100 \times 20$
   $V = 6280$ cu ft

2. square pyramid   rectangular solid
   $V = \frac{1}{3} e^2 h$ $V = lwh$
   $V = \frac{1}{3} \times 6^2 \times 8$ $V = 8 \times 3 \times 12$
   $V = \frac{1}{3} \times 36 \times 8$ $V = 288$ cu ft
   $V = 96$ cu ft

   cone
   $V = \frac{1}{3} \pi r^2 h$
   $V = \frac{1}{3} \times 3.14 \times 4^2 \times 9$
   $V = \frac{1}{3} \times 3.14 \times 16 \times 9$
   $V = 150.72$ cu in.

3. cylinder   cube
   $V = \pi r^2 h$ $V = e^3$
   $V = 3.14 \times 1^2 \times 3$ $V = (\frac{1}{2})^3$
   $V = 3.14 \times 1 \times 3$ $V = \frac{1}{8}$ cu in.
   $V = 9.42$ cu ft

   square pyramid
   $V = \frac{1}{3} e^2 h$
   $V = \frac{1}{3} \times 15^2 \times 20$
   $V = \frac{1}{3} \times 225 \times 20$
   $V = 1500$ cu in.

4. cube   cone
   $V = e^3$ $V = \frac{1}{3}\pi r^2 h$
   $V = (1.2)^3$ $V = \frac{1}{3} \times 3.14 \times 10^2 \times 30$
   $V = 1.728$ m^3 $V = \frac{1}{3} \times 3.14 \times 100 \times 30$
                  $V = 3140$ cm^3

   rectangular solid
   $V = lwh$
   $V = 3 \times 3 \times \frac{1}{2}$
   $V = 4\frac{1}{2}$ cu ft

5. $V = \pi r^2 h$
   $V = 3.14 \times (0.4)^2 \times 1.5$
   $V = 3.14 \times 0.16 \times 1.5$
   $V = 0.7536$ m^3

6. $V = \frac{4}{3}\pi r^3$
   $V = \frac{4}{3} \times 3.14 \times 3^3$
   $V = \frac{4}{3} \times 3.14 \times 27$
   $V = 113.04 \rightarrow 113$ cu in.

7. (4) $1\frac{1}{4} \times 1\frac{1}{4} \times 1\frac{1}{4}$

Exercise 11, page 257

1. $P = 10 + 11 + 3 + 5 + 7 + 6 = 42$ in.

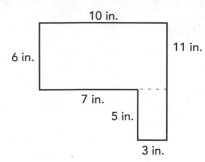

2. $A(I) = lw = 10 \times 6 = 60$ sq in.
   $A(II) = lw = 5 \times 3 = \underline{15 \text{ sq in.}}$
   Total $= 75$ sq in.

3. Area (top) $= lw = 9 \times 8 = 72$ sq ft
   Area (bottom) $= lw = 18 \times 12 = \underline{216 \text{ sq ft}}$
   Area (total) $= 288$ sq ft

4. 5 ft $= 5 \times 12 = 60$ in.

   $\dfrac{\text{area of table}}{\text{area of 1 tile}}$ $\dfrac{\overset{15}{\cancel{60}} \times \overset{15}{\cancel{60}}}{\underset{1}{\cancel{4}} \times \underset{1}{\cancel{4}}} = 225$ tiles

5. $\dfrac{\text{area of lawn}}{\text{area for 1 box}}$ $\dfrac{\overset{1}{\cancel{100}} \times \overset{20}{\cancel{80}}}{\underset{1}{\cancel{400}}} = 20$ boxes

6. $\dfrac{\text{area of floor}}{\text{area of 1 tile}}$ $\dfrac{\overset{10}{\cancel{20}} \times \overset{7}{\cancel{14}}}{\underset{1}{\cancel{2}} \times \underset{1}{\cancel{2}}} = 70$ carpet tiles

7. $V = lwh$
   $V = 4 \times 2.25 \times 1.5$
   $V = 13.5$ m³

8. 2 ft $= 2 \times 12 = 24$ inches $\quad V = lwh$
   $V = 24 \times 6 \times 6$
   $V = 864$ cu in.

9. 1 ft $= 12$ inches

   $\dfrac{\text{volume of carton}}{\text{volume of small box}}$ $\dfrac{\overset{2}{\cancel{24}} \times \cancel{6} \times \overset{1}{6}}{\underset{1}{\cancel{12}} \times \cancel{6} \times 1} = 12$ boxes

10. (2) the amount of dirt in each truckload

11. (1) $15 \times 10 \times 10 - \pi \times 3^2 \times 15$

12. (4) 225π $\qquad r = \dfrac{30}{2} = 15$ in.

    $A = \pi r^2 = \pi(15)^2 = 225\pi$

    Notice that no number value is substituted for π.

Exercise 12, page 261

1. scalene   right   isosceles
2. equilateral   isosceles   scalene
3. scalene   equilateral   right and isosceles
4. $65° + 25° = 90°$ $\qquad 180° - 90° = 90°$
5. right
6. hypotenuse
7. $65° + 50° = 115°$ $\qquad 180° - 115° = 65°$
8. isosceles   There are two 65° angles.
9. $30° + 60° = 90°$ $\qquad 180° - 90° = 90°$
10. right
11. $180° - 82° = 98°$ $\qquad \dfrac{98°}{2} = 49°$
12. $63° \times 2 = 126°$ $\qquad 180° - 126° = 54°$
13. isosceles $5 + 8 = 13$ inches
    $21 - 13 = 8$ inches
    Two sides are equal.
14. scalene $25° + 35° = 60°$
    $180° - 60° = 120°$
    The three angles are different.
15. scalene $4 + 5 = 9$ inches
    $16 - 9 = 7$ inches
    The three sides are different.
16. $90°$
    The right angle measures 90°. The other two angles must add up to 90° to make a total of 180° for all three angles.
17. $110°$
    $45° + 65° = 110°$
    $180° - 110° = 70° =$ the third angle of the triangle
    $\angle x$ is the supplement of 70°.
    $180° - 70° = 110°$

Exercise 13, page 265

1. no
   For the larger rectangle,
   base:height $= 12:6 = 2:1$
   For the smaller rectangle,
   base:height $= 3:1$
   The sides are not proportional.

2. yes
   For the smaller rectangle,
   base:height $= 10:8 = 5:4$
   For the larger rectangle,
   base:height $= 15:12 = 5:4$
   The sides are proportional.

3. yes

$45° + 85° = 130°$ $180° − 130° = 50° = \angle O$

$50° + 45° = 95°$ $180° − 95° = 85° = \angle R$

Each triangle has angles of 45°, 50°, and 85°.

4. no

$60° + 50° = 110°$ $180° − 110° = 70° = \angle C$

$50° + 80° = 130°$ $180° − 130° = 50° = \angle F$

The angles in the two triangles are not the same.

5. yes

Find the ratio of one of the equal sides to the base for each triangle.

For the smaller triangle, 6:4 = 3:2

For the larger triangle, 15:10 = 3:2

The sides are proportional.

6. yes

$90° + 50° = 140°$ $180° − 140° = 40° = \angle L$

$90° + 40° = 130°$ $180° − 130° = 50° = \angle N$

Each triangle has angles of 40°, 50°, and 90°.

7. 21 inches $\dfrac{8}{12} = \dfrac{14}{x}$

$8x = 168$

$x = 21$

8. yes

$\angle SUT = \angle VUW$ because they are vertical.

$\angle S = \angle W$ because they are both right angles.

If you subtract the sum of one right angle and one of the vertical angles from 180°, you get the same third angle for each triangle.

9. 40 feet $\dfrac{8}{12} = \dfrac{x}{60}$

$12x = 480$

$x = 40$

10. yes

Each triangle has a right angle, and the triangles share $\angle C$.

If you subtract the sum of a right angle and $\angle C$ from 180°, you get the same third angle.

11. 10 inches

The length of $AC = 15 + 10 = 25$ inches.

$$\frac{6}{15} = \frac{x}{25}$$

$15x = 150$

$x = 10$

12. (2) 6:5 = x:65

Exercise 14, page 269

1. side PQ

2. $\angle R$

3. side MO

4. $\angle N$

5. (2) $MO \cong PR$

6. (3) $\angle N \cong \angle Q$

7. no

The angles in one triangle correspond to the others, but you know nothing about the lengths of the sides.

8. yes

The missing angle in the second triangle is $180° − (60° + 45°) = 180° − 105° = 75°$.

This satisfies the ASA requirement.

9. no The corresponding sides are not congruent.

10. (1) $AC \cong DF$ This satisfies the ASA requirement.

11. (2) $\angle X \cong \angle S$ This satisfies the SAS requirement.

12. (1) $GI \cong JL$ This satisfies the SSS requirement.

Exercise 15, page 273

1. $a^2 + b^2 = c^2$

$30^2 + 40^2 = c^2$

$900 + 1600 = c^2$

$2500 = c^2$

$\sqrt{2500} = c$

$50 \text{ ft} = c$

2. $a^2 + b^2 = c^2$

$10^2 + 24^2 = c^2$

$100 + 576 = c^2$

$676 = c^2$

$\sqrt{676} = c$

$26 \text{ in.} = c$

3. $a^2 + b^2 = c^2$

$12^2 + 5^2 = c^2$

$144 + 25 = c^2$

$169 = c^2$

$\sqrt{169} = c$

$13 \text{ in.} = c$

4. $a^2 + b^2 = c^2$

$12^2 + 16^2 = c^2$

$144 + 256 = c^2$

$400 = c^2$

$\sqrt{400} = c$

$20 \text{ yd} = c$

5. $a^2 + b^2 = c^2$

$60^2 + 45^2 = c^2$

$3600 + 2025 = c^2$

$5625 = c^2$

$\sqrt{5625} = c$

$75 \text{ mi} = c$

6. (5) $\sqrt{30^2 − 18^2}$

7. (3) 30

$a^2 + b^2 = c^2$
$a^2 + 16^2 = 34^2$
$a^2 + 256 = 1156$
$a^2 = 900$
$a = \sqrt{900}$
$a = 30$

8. (2) 15

$a^2 + b^2 = c^2$
$a^2 + 8^2 = 17^2$
$a^2 + 64 = 289$
$a^2 = 225$
$a = \sqrt{225}$
$a = 15$

9. (4) 60

$a^2 + b^2 = c^2$
$48^2 + 36^2 = c^2$
$2304 + 1296 = c^2$
$3600 = c^2$
$\sqrt{3600} = c$
$60 = c$

10. (3) $\sqrt{15^2 + 36^2}$

Basic Geometry Review, page 276

Part I

1. $32\frac{1}{2}$ in.
$P = 2l + 2w = 2(12) + 2(4\frac{1}{4}) = 24 + 8\frac{1}{2} = 32\frac{1}{2}$ in.

2. 116° $180° - 64° = 116°$

3. 13 m $P = 5.8 + 4 + 3.2 = 13$ m

4. 94 ft $C = \pi d = 3.14(30) = 94.2 \rightarrow 94$ ft

5. 525 cu in.
$V = lwh = (15)(3\frac{1}{2})(10) = 525$ cu in.

6. 154 sq in.
$A = \pi r^2 = 3.14 \times 7^2 = 3.14 \times 49 =$
$153.86 \rightarrow 154$ sq in.

7. 12.8 m $P = 4s = 4 \times 3.2 = 12.8$ m

8. 92.5 cm² $A = lw = 12.5 \times 7.4 = 92.5$ cm²

9. $\frac{9}{16}$ sq in. $A = s^2 = \frac{3}{4} \times \frac{3}{4} = \frac{9}{16}$ sq in.

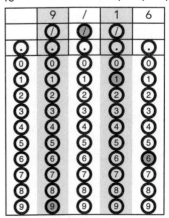

10. 5.4 cm²
$A = \frac{1}{2}bh = \frac{1}{2} \times 4 \times 2.7 = 5.4$ cm²

11. (3)   216
Find the missing measurements.
Add each side.
$P = 30 + 15 + 18 + 9 + 12 + 24 = 108$ ft

Each tile strip is 6 inches, or $\frac{1}{2}$ foot.

You need $108 \div \frac{1}{2} = 108 \times 2 = 216$ strips.

12. (2)   62

$\dfrac{\text{area of large rectangle}}{\text{area of 1 square yard}}$ $\dfrac{\overset{10}{30} \times \overset{5}{15}}{\underset{1}{3} \times \underset{1}{3}} = 50$ sq yd

$\dfrac{\text{area of small rectangle}}{\text{area of 1 square yard}}$ $\dfrac{\overset{4}{12} \times \overset{3}{9}}{\underset{1}{3} \times \underset{1}{3}} = 12$ sq yd

total = 62 sq yd

13. (1)   3348
volume of large section =
$lwh = 30 \times 15 \times 6 = 2700$ cu ft
volume of small section =
$lwh = 12 \times 9 \times 6 = 648$ cu ft
total = 3348 cu ft

14. (2) 3.6 $\dfrac{\text{height}}{\text{base}}$ $\dfrac{12}{10} = \dfrac{x}{3}$

$10x = 36$
$x = 3.6$ ft

15. (1) 15

$a^2 + b^2 = c^2$
$a^2 + 36^2 = 39^2$
$a^2 + 1296 = 1521$
$a^2 = 225$
$a = \sqrt{225}$
$a = 15$

Part II

16. circumference
17. 15 inches $r = \frac{30}{2} = 15$ inches
18. $\angle h$
19. 118° $180° - 62° = 118°$
20. $\angle b, \angle c, \angle f,$ and $\angle g$
21. (2) horizontal and parallel
22. (1) acute $180° - 128° = 52°$
23. (4) $2(3.5) + 2(1.8)$
    $P = 2l + 2w = 2(3.5) + 2(1.8)$
24. (3) $(2 \times 20) + (2 \times 8) - 4$
    Find the perimeter, $P = 2l + 2w$.
    Then subtract 4, the width of the walkway.
25. (4) $\frac{1}{2}(20 + 30) \times 15$ $A = \frac{1}{2}(b_1 + b_2)h$

    $A = \frac{1}{2}(20 + 30) \times 15$

26. (2) 1200π $r = \frac{20}{2} = 10$ cm

    $V = \pi r^2 h$
    $V = \pi(10)^2 \times 12$
    $V = \pi \times 100 \times 12$
    $V = 1200\pi$

    Notice that no value is substituted for π.

27. (4) right $33° + 57° = 90°$ $180° - 90° = 90°$
    A triangle with one right angle is a right triangle.
28. (3) $GI \cong JL$
    This satisfies the Angle Side Angle requirement
    for congruence.

29. 114.5° $180° - 65.5° = 114.5°$

30. 300 $\dfrac{\text{area of tabletop}}{\text{area of 1 tile}} = \dfrac{\overset{20}{\cancel{40}} \times \overset{15}{\cancel{30}}}{\underset{1}{\cancel{2}} \times \underset{1}{\cancel{2}}} = 300$ tiles

Chapter 10

Exercise 1, page 282

1. J   D   B   A   F
2. G   I   H   C   E

3. $-9 < -2$ $+3 > -5$ $-1 < +1$
4. $5 = +5$ $12 > -3$ $-1 > -2$
5. $+8 > -8$ $-7 > -10$ $2 > -3$

6. $|-8|$
7. $+3$

Exercise 2, page 284

1. $-9 - 3 = -12$
   $+7 - 15 = -8$
   $-32 + 15 = -17$

2. $+8 - 6 = +2$
   $+12 + 1 = +13$
   $-7 - 13 = -20$

3. $+11 - 24 = -13$
   $+16 - 5 = +11$
   $-13 - 14 = -27$

4. $+6 + (-11) = -5$
   $+14 + (-14) = 0$
   $-8 + (-7) = -15$

5. $(-12) + (-13) = -25$
   $(+8) + (-7) = +1$
   $(-9) + (+8) = -1$

6. $+5 - 8 + 9 = +14 - 8 = +6$
   $+8 - 6 - 5 = +8 - 11 = -3$

7. $-18 - 2 + 6 = -20 + 6 = -14$
   $-3 - 9 - 4 = -16$

8. $(-9) + (-4) + (+8) = -13 + 8 = -5$
   $(-1) + (-8) + (+6) = -9 + 6 = -3$

9. $(-10) + (-3) + (-8) = -21$
   $(+7) + (+11) + (-2) = +18 - 2 = +16$

10. $(3) -10 - 4 = -14$

Exercise 3, page 286

1. $(+6) - (+4)= +6 - 4 = +2$
   $(-8) - (+7)= -8 - 7 = -15$
   $(-9) - (-8) =-9 + 8 = -1$

2. $(+10) - (-9) = +10 + 9 = +19$
   $(+8) - (7) = +8 - 7 = +1$
   $(-9) - (-9) = -9 + 9 = 0$

3. $(-10) - (+12) = -10 - 12 = -22$
   $(+6) - (-7) = +6 + 7 = +13$
   $(-11) - (-8) = -11 + 8 = -3$

4. $(+20) - (-3) = +20 + 3 = +23$
   $(-18) - (+4) = -18 - 4 = -22$
   $(+5) - (-1) = +5 + 1 = +6$

5. $(-11) + (-3) - (-6) =$
   $-11 - 3 + 6 = -14 + 6 = -8$
   $(+6) - (-3) + (-2) =$
   $+6 + 3 - 2 = +9 - 2 = +7$

6. $(-9) - (+4) - (+10) =$
   $-9 - 4 - 10 = -23$
   $(-15) - (20) + (+6) =$
   $-15 - 20 + 6 = -35 + 6 = -29$

7. $(-8) + (-13) - (+6) =$
   $-8 - 13 - 6 = -27$
   $(-3) + (-4) - (-5) - (-6) =$
   $-3 - 4 + 5 + 6 = -7 + 11 = +4$

8. (2) $(-17) - (+7) = -17 - 7 = -24$

9. (2) $(-\$120) + (-\$50) = -\$120 - \$50 = -\$170$

10. (1) $(-\$200) + (+\$75) = -\$200 + \$75 = -\$125$

Exercise 4, page 288

1. $(-2)(+9) = -18$
   $(-6)(-6) = +36$
   $(+5)(-9) = -45$

2. $(+8)(3) = +24$
   $(-10)(7) = -70$
   $(+18)(-2) = -36$

3. $-7 \cdot -4 = +28$
   $24 \cdot -\frac{1}{2} = -12$
   $-0.1 \cdot -6 = +0.6$

4. $-\frac{3}{4} \cdot 12 = -9$
   $18 \cdot \frac{2}{3} = +12$
   $-11 \cdot -5 = +55$

5. $(-7)(6)(-2) = +84$
   $(+5)(+4)(-2) = -40$

6. $(4)(-2)(-1)(-6) = -48$
   $(10)(-\frac{1}{2})(3)(-1) = +15$

7. $(2)(-3)(5)(-\frac{1}{3}) = +10$
   $8(-3)(5)(\frac{1}{4}) = -30$

8. $(-6)^2 = (-6)(-6) = +36$
   $(-5)^3 = (-5)(-5)(-5) = -125$

9. (3) $(+3)(-6) = -18$
10. (2) $(6)(-\$20) = -\$120$

Exercise 5, page 290

1. $\frac{-40}{-20} = +2$ $\frac{-12}{+6} = -2$ $\frac{72}{-9} = -8$

2. $\frac{+16}{-24} = -\frac{2}{3}$ $\frac{-15}{+5} = -3$ $\frac{30}{-36} = -\frac{5}{6}$

3. $\frac{-108}{-9} = +12$ $\frac{-48}{-60} = \frac{4}{5}$ $\frac{+65}{-5} = -13$

4. $\frac{-63}{+35} = \frac{-9}{5}$ or $-1\frac{4}{5}$ $\frac{75}{-100} = -\frac{3}{4}$ $\frac{-15}{-150} = +\frac{1}{10}$

5. (1) $\frac{-20}{5} = -4$

6. (2) $\frac{-15}{5} = -3$

7. (3) $\frac{-\$450}{-\$1.50} = 300$

Exercise 6, page 291

1. $-4(13-8) = -4(5) = -20$
   $-5 + (-8)(-6) = -5 + 48 = +43$

2. $(12)(-2) + (-1)(-15) = -24 + (+15) = -9$
   $(-8)^2 - (-5)^2 = +64 - (+25) = 64 - 25 = +39$

3. $\frac{-8}{4} + \frac{15}{-3} = -2 - 5 = -7$
   $(-3)(5) + \frac{6}{-2} = -15 + (-3) = -18$

4. $-6 + \frac{30}{5} = -6 + 6 = 0$
   $\frac{-36}{9} - (-10) = -4 + 10 = +6$

5. $(-2)(-8) + (-9)(7) = +16 + (-63) = -47$
   $(15)(-1) - 9 = -15 - 9 = -24$

6. $(-7)(+20) + (10)^2 = -140 + 100 = -40$
   $2(-4 + 3 - 7) = 2(-11 + 3) = 2(-8) = -16$

7. $9(8 - 12) = 9(-4) = -36$
   $\frac{24 - 6}{-2} = \frac{18}{-2} = -9$

8. $\sqrt{29 - 4} - (-3) = \sqrt{25} + 3 = 5 + 3 = +8$
   $\frac{15 - 3}{-4 - 2} = \frac{12}{-6} = -2$

9. $\frac{(-20) - (-21)}{5 - 7} = \frac{-20 + 21}{-2} = -\frac{1}{2}$
   $\frac{-96}{-8} + (-3)^2 = +12 + 9 = +21$

10. $\frac{+9 - 7 - 5}{-3} = \frac{+9 - 12}{-3} = \frac{-3}{-3} = +1$
    $(8 - 14)^2 - (-6)^2 = (-6)^2 - 36 = 36 - 36 = 0$

Exercise 7, page 293

1. $6m + m = 7m$
   $5y - y = 4y$
   $7p - 6p = p$

2. $4a - 3 + 7a - 1 = 11a - 4$
   $x + 5x - 3x = 3x$
   $8z - 5 + 2z - 9 = 10z - 14$

3. $8 + 3y - 2 + 7y = 6 + 10y$, or $10y + 6$
   $7c - 4 + 5 - c = 6c + 1$
   $6k + 7 - 5k = k + 7$

4. $10s + 4s - 6s = 8s$
   $4n + 3 + n - 1 = 5n + 2$
   $6 + 8x + 5 - 9x = 11 - x$, or $-x + 11$

5. $2x + 3x + 1 + 2x + 2 = 7x + 3$
6. $7(4) + 3 = 28 + 3 = 31$
7. $2y + 3y + 1 + 2y + 3y + 1 = 10y + 2$
8. $10(6) + 2 = 60 + 2 = 62$

Exercise 8, page 294

1. $5(m + 2) = 5m + 10$
   $3(a - 1) + 4 = 3a - 3 + 4 = 3a + 1$

2. $2y + 3(y - 5) = 2y + 3y - 15 = 5y - 15$
   $2x + 1 + 5(x - 1) = 2x + 1 + 5x - 5 = 7x - 4$

3. $9 + 7(2a + 3) = 9 + 14a + 21 = 30 + 14a$
   or $14a + 30$
   $6(5a - 1) + 11 = 30a - 6 + 11 = 30a + 5$

4. $3c + 5(2c + 1) = 3c + 10c + 5 = 13c + 5$
   $8n - 2(3n + 1) = 8n - 6n - 2 = 2n - 2$

5. $10(p + 3) - 8p = 10p + 30 - 8p = 2p + 30$
   $s + 6(2s - 3) = s + 12s - 18 = 13s - 18$

6. $(5)\ 3x + 6$

7. $3(9) + 6 = 27 + 6 = 33$

Exercise 9, page 296

1.
$$f + 20 = 57$$
$$\underline{-20\quad -20}$$
$$f\qquad = 37$$

$$\frac{8y}{8} = \frac{96}{8}$$
$$y = 12$$

$$b - 19 = 28$$
$$\underline{+19\ +19}$$
$$b\qquad = 47$$

2.
$$\frac{x}{3} = 9$$
$$3 \cdot \frac{x}{3} = 9 \cdot 3$$
$$x = 27$$

$$33 = k - 8$$
$$\underline{+8\qquad +8}$$
$$41 = k$$

$$\frac{11}{2} = \frac{2d}{2}$$
$$5\frac{1}{2} = d,\ \text{or}$$
$$d = 5.5$$

3.
$$\frac{15p}{15} = \frac{75}{15}$$
$$p = 5$$

$$42 = t + 7$$
$$\underline{-7\qquad -7}$$
$$35 = t$$

$$18 = d - 6$$
$$\underline{+6\qquad +6}$$
$$24 = d$$

4.
$$9 = \frac{m}{4}$$
$$4 \cdot 9 = \frac{m}{4} \cdot 4$$
$$36 = m$$

$$\frac{25z}{25} = \frac{100}{25}$$
$$z = 4$$

$$n + 36 = 60$$
$$\underline{-36\ -36}$$
$$n\qquad = 24$$

5.
$$\frac{56}{8} = \frac{8x}{8}$$
$$7 = x$$

$$43 = r - 7$$
$$\underline{+7\qquad +7}$$
$$50 = r$$

$$\frac{a}{5} = 8$$
$$5 \cdot \frac{a}{5} = 8 \cdot 5$$
$$a = 40$$

6.
$$c - 4 = 27$$
$$\underline{+4\quad +4}$$
$$c\qquad = 31$$

$$m + 16 = 200$$
$$\underline{-16\quad -16}$$
$$m\qquad = 184$$

$$\frac{c}{9} = -2$$
$$9 \cdot \frac{c}{9} = -2 \cdot 9$$
$$c = -18$$

7.
$$\frac{12y}{12} = \frac{6}{12}$$
$$y = \frac{1}{2}\ \text{or}\ 0.5$$

$$-3 = a + 19$$
$$\underline{-19\qquad -19}$$
$$-22 = a$$

$$\frac{15r}{15} = \frac{9}{15}$$
$$r = \frac{3}{5}\ \text{or}\ 0.6$$

8. (4) Divide both sides of the equation by 1.5.

9. (4) Subtract 2.3 from both sides of the equation.

Exercise 10, page 298

1.

$$7m - 2 = 54$$
$$\underline{+2 \quad +2}$$
$$7m = 56$$
$$\frac{7m}{7} = \frac{56}{7}$$
$$m = 8$$

$$\frac{1}{3}p + 8 = 11$$
$$\underline{\phantom{\frac{1}{3}p}-8 \quad -8}$$
$$\frac{1}{3}p = 3$$
$$\frac{3}{1} \times \frac{1}{3}p = \frac{3}{1} \times \frac{3}{1}$$
$$p = 9$$

2.

$$\frac{a}{3} + 5 = 9$$
$$\underline{\phantom{\frac{a}{3}}-5 \quad -5}$$
$$\frac{a}{3} = 4$$
$$3 \cdot \frac{a}{3} = 4 \cdot 3$$
$$a = 12$$

$$40 = 13z + 14$$
$$\underline{-14 -14}$$
$$26 = 13z$$
$$\frac{26}{13} = \frac{13z}{13}$$
$$2 = z$$

3.

$$7 = \frac{c}{2} + 3$$
$$\underline{-3 \phantom{= \frac{c}{2}} -3}$$
$$4 = \frac{c}{2}$$
$$2 \cdot 4 = \frac{c}{2} \cdot 2$$
$$8 = c$$

$$2n + 3 = 11$$
$$\underline{-3 \quad -3}$$
$$2n = 8$$
$$\frac{2n}{2} = \frac{8}{2}$$
$$n = 4$$

4.

$$82 = 9d + 10$$
$$\underline{-10 -10}$$
$$72 = 9d$$
$$\frac{72}{9} = \frac{9d}{9}$$
$$8 = d$$

$$\frac{3}{4}y - 3 = 12$$
$$\underline{\phantom{\frac{3}{4}y}+3 \quad +3}$$
$$\frac{3}{4}y = 15$$
$$\frac{4}{3} \cdot \frac{3}{4}y = 15 \cdot \frac{4}{3}$$
$$y = 20$$

5.

$$25c - 17 = 183$$
$$\underline{+17 \quad +17}$$
$$25c = 200$$
$$\frac{25c}{25} = \frac{200}{25}$$
$$c = 8$$

$$39 = 16k - 9$$
$$\underline{+9 +9}$$
$$48 = 16k$$
$$\frac{48}{16} = \frac{16k}{16}$$
$$3 = k$$

6.

$$\frac{w}{2} - 7 = 3$$
$$\underline{\phantom{\frac{w}{2}}+7 \quad +7}$$
$$\frac{w}{2} = 10$$
$$2 \cdot \frac{w}{2} = 10 \cdot 2$$
$$w = 20$$

$$10 = 6a + 7$$
$$\underline{-7 -7}$$
$$3 = 6a$$
$$\frac{3}{6} = \frac{6a}{6}$$
$$\frac{1}{2} = a$$

7.

$$2 = 6x - 10$$
$$\underline{+10 +10}$$
$$12 = 6x$$
$$\frac{12}{6} = \frac{6x}{6}$$
$$2 = x$$

$$9r + 15 = 18$$
$$\underline{-15 \quad -15}$$
$$9r = 3$$
$$\frac{9r}{9} = \frac{3}{9}$$
$$r = \frac{1}{3}$$

8.

$$3y + 4 = 25$$
$$\underline{-4 \quad -4}$$
$$3y = 21$$
$$\frac{3y}{3} = \frac{21}{3}$$
$$y = 7$$

$$7 = 4n + 5$$
$$\underline{-5 -5}$$
$$2 = 4n$$
$$\frac{2}{4} = \frac{4n}{4}$$
$$\frac{1}{2} = n$$

Exercise 11, page 301

[Note: The solutions to the rest of the equations in this book use the shorter method of writing each step. Each line shows the *result* of performing an operation on the previous line.]

1.

$$5y - y = 19 + 9$$
$$4y = 28$$
$$y = 7$$

$$6f = 14 - f$$
$$7f = 14$$
$$f = 2$$

2.

$$6t + 8 + 4t = 58$$
$$10t + 8 = 58$$
$$10t = 50$$
$$t = 5$$

$$3 = y + 8y$$
$$3 = 9y$$
$$\frac{1}{3} = y$$

3.

$$9c = 44 - 2c$$
$$11c = 44$$
$$c = 4$$

$$8r + 17 = 5r + 32$$
$$3r + 17 = 32$$
$$3r = 15$$
$$r = 5$$

4.

$$8m = 2m + 30$$
$$6m = 30$$
$$m = 5$$

$$7n - 9 = 3n + 7$$
$$4n - 9 = 7$$
$$4n = 16$$
$$n = 4$$

5.

$$4a + 55 = 9a$$
$$55 = 5a$$
$$11 = a$$

$$6z + 11 = 5z + 20$$
$$z + 11 = 20$$
$$z = 9$$

6.

$$4p = p + 18$$
$$3p = 18$$
$$p = 6$$

$$5y - 4 = 2y + 77$$
$$3y - 4 = 77$$
$$3y = 81$$
$$y = 27$$

Exercise 12, page 302

1. $4(x - 2) + x = 27$ $3(y - 2) + 4 = 16$
    $4x - 8 + x = 27$ $3y - 6 + 4 = 16$
      $5x - 8 = 27$ $3y - 2 = 16$
         $5x = 35$ $3y = 18$
          $x = 7$ $y = 6$

2. $2a + 5(a + 3) = 99$ $8(s + 7) = 100 - 3s$
    $2a + 5a + 15 = 99$ $8s + 56 = 100 - 3s$
      $7a + 15 = 99$ $11s + 56 = 100$
         $7a = 84$ $11s = 44$
          $a = 12$ $s = 4$

3. $4(c + 4) = 61 + c$ $3(t + 10) = t + 90$
     $4c + 16 = 61 + c$ $3t + 30 = t + 90$
       $3c + 16 = 61$ $2t + 30 = 90$
          $3c = 45$ $2t = 60$
           $c = 15$ $t = 30$

4. $7(m - 8) = 2m + 4$ $5(m + 3) - 8 = 37$
     $7m - 56 = 2m + 4$ $5m + 15 - 8 = 37$
     $5m - 56 = 4$ $5m + 7 = 37$
       $5m = 60$ $5m = 30$
         $m = 12$ $m = 6$

5. $2(x + 6) - 3 = 11$ $9(y - 1) - 4y = 1$
    $2x + 12 - 3 = 11$ $9y - 9 - 4y = 1$
      $2x + 9 = 11$ $5y - 9 = 1$
         $2x = 2$ $5y = 10$
          $x = 1$ $y = 2$

Exercise 13, page 303

1. (3) 8 $6(8) - 3 = 48 - 3 = 45$
2. (2) 13 $2(13) + 1 = 26 + 1 = 27$
3. (4) 20 $\frac{20}{5} + 6 = 4 + 6 = 10$
4. (2) 9 $25 = 3(9) - 2 = 27 - 2$
5. (1) 7 $18 = 7 + 11$
6. (1) 12 $50 = 4(12) + 2 = 48 + 2$
7. (3) 8 $2(8 - 3) + 5 = 2(5) + 5 = 10 + 5 = 15$
8. (4) 9 $6(9 + 1) - 7 = 6(10) - 7 = 60 - 7 = 53$
9. (4) 5 $70 = 8(5 + 4) - 2 = 8(9) - 2 = 72 - 2$
10. (2) 12 $34 = 3(12 - 2) + 4 = 3(10) + 4 = 30 + 4$

Exercise 14, page 305

1. no $m - 6 > 1$
         $m > 7$
Since $m > 7$, m cannot equal 7.

2. yes $8r \leq 16$
          $r \leq 2$
Since r is less than or equal to 2, r can be 2.

3. yes $d + 7 \geq 2$
         $d \geq -5$
Since d is greater than or equal to -5, d can be -5.

4. yes $2f < 12$
          $f < 6$
Since f is less than 6, f can be 4.

5. (1) 4 $9c \leq 27$
          $c \leq 3$
Since c is less than or equal to 3, c cannot be 4.

6. $5m - 4 \leq 26$ $3n + 2 > 14$ $4p - 3 < 15$
    $5m \leq 30$ $3n > 12$ $4p < 18$
     $m \leq 6$ $n > 4$ $p < 4\frac{1}{2}$

7. $7c - 3 \leq 5c + 15$
   $2c - 3 \leq 15$
     $2c \leq 18$
      $c \leq 9$

   $8y + 1 < y + 22$
   $7y + 1 < 22$
    $7y < 21$
     $y < 3$

   $3(s - 2) \geq 2s + 10$
   $3s - 6 \geq 2s + 10$
    $s - 6 \geq 10$
     $s \geq 16$

8. $\frac{x}{3} + 5 \geq 7$ $5(a + 3) < 2(a - 6)$
    $\frac{x}{3} \geq 2$ $5a + 15 < 2a - 12$
    $x \geq 6$ $3a + 15 < -12$
                        $3a < -27$
                         $a < -9$

   $4w - 5 \leq 3w + 6$
    $w - 5 \leq 6$
      $w \leq 11$

9. (4) $x > -3$ $-2x < 6$
                     $x > -3$
Remember when you divide an inequality by a negative number, the direction of the inequality changes.

10. (1) $a \leq -7$ $-4a + 3 \geq 31$
                   $-4a \geq 28$
                     $a \leq -7$
Remember when you divide an inequality by a negative number, the direction of the inequality changes.

Exercise 15, page 307

1. $x + 9$ or $9 + x$
2. $7x$
3. $5x$
4. $x + 8$ or $8 + x$
5. $x - 10$
6. $x - 1$
7. $3/x$ or $\frac{3}{x}$
8. $x - 20$
9. $x/15$ or $\frac{x}{15}$
10. $x + \frac{1}{2}$
11. $x/2$ or $\frac{x}{2}$
12. $x + 4$ or $4 + x$
13. $\sqrt{x}$
14. x^3
15. $\frac{3}{5}x$

Exercise 16, page 308

1. $d + 2$ or $2 + d$
2. $s - 5$
3. $2\frac{1}{4}c$ or $\frac{9}{4}c$
4. $\frac{1}{5}i$ or $\frac{i}{5}$
5. $\frac{x}{6}$
6. $0.8t$ or $\frac{4}{5}t$ $80\% = 0.8$ or $\frac{4}{5}$
7. (4) $l - 2$
8. (5) $0.06m$
9. (2) $y - 10$
10. (2) $p - 15$

Exercise 17, page 310

1. (2) $a + 9 = 15$
2. (3) $\frac{2}{3}c = 12$
3. (1) $\frac{x}{3} = 20$
4. (2) $y - 16 = 10$
5. (3) $20 = 3m$
6. (2) $\frac{r}{7} = 4$
7. $x - 9 = 15$ $x = 24$
8. $6x = 27$ $x = 4\frac{1}{2}$
9. $\frac{x}{5} = 50$ $x = 250$

10. $3 = x - 5$ $8 = x$
11. $60 = \frac{3}{4}x$ $80 = x$
12. $7x = 84$ $x = 12$
13. $x - 40 = 290$ $x = \$330$
14. $\frac{x}{15} = 600$ $x = \$9000$
15. $\frac{x}{4} = 640$ $x = \$2560$
16. $0.75x = 90$ $x = 120$ people

Exercise 18, page 312

1. (2) $7m - 2$
2. (1) $\frac{x + 5}{4}$
3. (3) $a + 8a$
4. (1) $2(y + 6)$
5. (2) $\frac{n}{2} + 3$
6. (3) $7s - 2s$
7. (2) $2w + 6$
8. (1) $3p - 9$
9. $2x + 6$
10. $8x - 5$
11. $2x + 4x$
12. $\frac{x}{2} + 8$ or $\frac{1}{2}x + 8$
13. $\frac{x}{3} - 1$ or $\frac{1}{3}x - 1$
14. $15 - 3x$
15. $\frac{x + 7}{4}$ or $(x + 7)/4$
16. $10(x + 12)$

Exercise 19, page 314

1. $\frac{x}{2} - 5 = 6$
   $\frac{x}{2} = 11$
   $x = 22$
2. $3x + 4 = 19$
   $3x = 15$
   $x = 5$
3. $4x + 1 = 21$
   $4x = 20$
   $x = 5$
4. $2x - 9 = 7$
   $2x = 16$
   $x = 8$

5.　$6x + 3 = 12$
　　$6x = 9$
　　$x = 1\frac{1}{2}$

6.　$5x - 2 = 9$
　　$5x = 11$
　　$x = 2\frac{1}{5}$

7.　$3x - 1 = 5$
　　$3x = 6$
　　$x = 2$

8.　$4x - 2 = 18$
　　$4x = 20$
　　$x = 5$

9.　$2x + 1 = 13$
　　$2x = 12$
　　$x = 6$

10.　$6x + 10 = 34$
　　$6x = 24$
　　$x = 4$

11.　$\frac{x}{2} - 8 = 12$
　　$\frac{x}{2} = 20$
　　$x = 40$

12.　$\frac{x}{8} - 3 = 6$
　　$\frac{x}{8} = 9$
　　$x = 72$

13.　$2x - 7 = x + 3$
　　$x = 10$

Exercise 20, page 316

1.　13 and 14
　　first number = x　　　$x + x + 1 = 27$
　　second number = $x + 1$　$2x + 1 = 27$
　　　　　　　　　　　　　　$2x = 26$
　　　　　　　　　　　　　　$x = 13$
　　　　　　　　　　　　　　$x + 1 = 14$

2.　18, 20, and 22
　　first number = x　　　$x + x + 2 + x + 4 = 60$
　　second number = $x + 2$　$3x + 6 = 60$
　　third number = $x + 2 + 2$　$3x = 54$
　　　　　　　= $x + 4$　　　$x = 18$
　　　　　　　　　　　　　　$x + 2 = 20$
　　　　　　　　　　　　　　$x + 4 = 22$

3.　24 union workers
　　nonunion = x　　　　$6x - 8 = 4x$
　　union = $6x$　　　　　$6x = 4x + 8$
　　　　　　　　　　　　$2x = 8$
　　　　　　　　　　　　$x = 4$
　　　　　　　　　　　　$6x = 24$

4.　6 men and 18 women
　　men = x　　　　　　$3x - 2 = x + 10$
　　women = $3x$　　　　$2x = 12$
　　　　　　　　　　　　$x = 6$
　　　　　　　　　　　　$3x = 18$

5.　$2700
　　Juan's wage = x　　$x + 3x = 3600$
　　Felipe's wage = $3x$　$4x = 3600$
　　　　　　　　　　　　$x = 900$
　　　　　　　　　　　　$3x = 2700$

6.　24 hours
　　Jerry's hours = x　　$x + 2x + 2x + 6 = 51$
　　Jeff's hours = $2x$　　$5x + 6 = 51$
　　Paul's hours = $2x + 6$　$5x = 45$
　　　　　　　　　　　　$x = 9$
　　　　$2x + 6 = 2(9) + 6 = 18 + 6 = 24$

7.　$340
　　Rigbys' expenses = x
　　Millers' expenses = $x + 100$
　　Smiths' expenses = $2(x + 100)$
　　　　$x + x + 100 + 2(x + 100) = 580$
　　　　　$2x + 100 + 2x + 200 = 580$
　　　　　　　　$4x + 300 = 580$
　　　　　　　　　　$4x = 280$
　　　　　　　　　　　$x = 70$
　　$2(x + 100) = 2(70 + 100) = 2(170) = 340$

8.　40 years old
　　Jed's age = x　　　$x + 24 = 3x - 8$
　　Steve's age = $x + 24$　$32 = 2x$
　　　　　　　　　　　　$16 = x$
　　　　　　　　　　$16 + 24 = 40$

9.　55 hours
　　Tim's hours = x
　　Laura's hours = $x + 10$
　　Eric's hours = $2(x + 10)$
　　　　$x + x + 10 + 2(x + 10) = 210$
　　　　　$2x + 10 + 2x + 20 = 210$
　　　　　　　$4x + 30 = 210$
　　　　　　　　$4x = 180$
　　　　　　　　　$x = 45$
　　　　　　　$x + 10 = 55$

10. $552

deductions = x	x + 6x = 644
take−home = 6x	7x = 644
	x = 92
	6x = 552

Exercise 21, page 318

1. 45°

$$3x + 4x + 5x = 180$$
$$12x = 180$$
$$x = 15$$
$$3x = 45$$

2. 8 feet   width = x $2x + 2(2x) = 48$
length = 2x $2x + 4x = 48$
$$6x = 48$$
$$x = 8$$

3. 65°

$$x + 3x - 10 = 90$$
$$4x = 100$$
$$x = 25$$
$$3x - 10 = 75 - 10 = 65$$

4. 18 inches   width = 2x $2(2x) + 2(3x) = 60$
length = 3x $4x + 6x = 60$
$$10x = 60$$
$$x = 6$$
$$3x = 18$$

5. 108°

$$3x + 2x = 180$$
$$5x = 180$$
$$x = 36$$
$$3x = 3(36) = 108$$

6. 30 feet   width = 5x $2(5x) + 2(6x) = 110$
length = 6x $10x + 12x = 110$
$$22x = 110$$
$$x = 5$$
$$6x = 30$$

7. 110°

$$4x - 10 = 3x + 20$$
$$x = 30$$
$$4x - 10 = 4(30) - 10 = 120 - 10 = 110$$

8. 7 feet   width = x $2x + 2(x + 3) = 34$
length = x + 3 $2x + 2x + 6 = 34$
$$4x = 28$$
$$x = 7$$

9. 20°

$$6x + 3x = 180$$
$$9x = 180$$
$$x = 20$$
$$\angle X = 2(20) = 40$$
$$\angle XYW = 6(20) = 120$$
$$\angle W = 180 - 120 - 40 = 20$$

10. 8

$$4x = 2(3) + 2(x + 5)$$
$$4x = 6 + 2x + 10$$
$$2x = 16$$
$$x = 8$$

Basics of Algebra Review, page 320

Part I

1. −1 $+18 - 12 - 7 = +18 - 19 = -1$

2. −12 $(-8)(-3)(-\frac{1}{2}) = -12$

3. −216 $(-6)^3 = (-6)(-6)(-6) = -216$

4. −2 $+9 - (-3) + (-6) - (+8) =$
$+9 + 3 - 6 - 8 = +12 - 14 = -2$

5. 3x + 4 $8x + 7 - 5x - 3 = 3x + 4$

6. −17 $3(-7) + 4 = -21 + 4 = -17$

7. 1 $\frac{14 - 9}{8 - 3} = \frac{5}{5} = 1$

8. 8a + 11 $7(a + 2) - 3 + a = 7a + 14 - 3 + a =$
$8a + 11$

9. −5 $8(-2) + 11 = -16 + 11 = -5$

10. m = 21 $\frac{m}{3} + 1 = 8$
$$\frac{m}{3} = 7$$
$$m = 21$$

11. $c = 14$

$3(c - 8) = c + 4$
$3c - 24 = c + 4$
$2c - 24 = 4$
$2c = 28$
$c = 14$

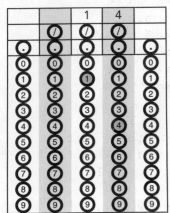

12. $n = 11$

$12.5 = n + 1.5$
$11 = n$

13. $a = 5$

$96 + 2a = a + 101$
$96 + a = 101$
$a = 5$

14. $z = 5$

$20 - 4z = 5z - 25$
$20 = 9z - 25$
$45 = 9z$
$5 = z$

15. $x \leq 8$

$9x - 5 \leq 7x + 11$
$2x - 5 \leq 11$
$2x \leq 16$
$x \leq 8$

Part II

16. (3) $-1\frac{3}{12}$ A negative number divided by a negative number is positive.

17. (5) 4

$4m - 3 > 17$
$4m > 20$
$m > 5$

The other answer choices are greater than 5.

18. (4) $10x + 2$ $P = 2x + 3x + 1 + 2x + 3x + 1 = 10x + 2$

19. (5) $9x - 5 = 6x + 7$

20. (1) 12

$10x - 7 = 101 + x$
$9x - 7 = 101$
$9x = 108$
$x = 12$

21. (2) $15

Joe's wage $= x$ and
Sam's wage $= x - 5$
$40x + 40(x - 5) = 1400$
$40x + 40x - 200 = 1400$
$80x = 1600$
$x = 20$
$x - 5 = 20 - 5 = 15$

22. (3) $1580

Tim's salary $= x$ and
Kate's salary $= x + 320$
$x + x + 320 = 2840$
$2x + 320 = 2840$
$2x = 2520$
$x = 1260$
$x + 320 = 1260 + 320 = 1580$

23. (4) $45°$

each base angle $= x$ and
the vertex angle $= 2x$
$x + x + 2x = 180$
$4x = 180$
$x = 45$

24. 70 women

men $= x$ and women $= x + 25$
$x + x + 25 = 115$
$2x + 25 = 115$
$2x = 90$
$x = 45$
$x + 25 = 45 + 25 = 70$ women

25. 50

$$2(2x) + 2(3x - 1) = 168$$
$$4x + 6x - 2 = 168$$
$$10x - 2 = 168$$
$$10x = 170$$
$$x = 17$$
$$3x - 1 = 3(17) - 1 = 51 - 1 = 50$$

Chapter 11

Exercise 1, page 325

1. A = (+9, +5)   G = (−7, −2)
    B = (+4, +10)   H = (−3, −8)
    C = (−2, +4)   I = (0, −7)
    D = (−6, +10)   J = (+6, −7)
    E = (−11, +3)   K = (+10, −3)
    F = (−10, 0)   L = (+12, 0)

2. F and L

3. C, D, and E

4. J and K

5.

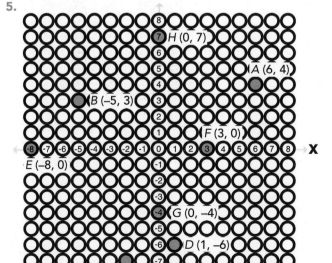

6. G and H

7. C

Exercise 2, page 327

1. A is 3 units above the x-axis.
    B is 5 units below the x-axis.
    The distance from A to B is 3 + 5 = 8.

2. B is 3 units to the right of the y-axis.
    C is 1 unit to the left of the y-axis.
    The distance from B to C is 3 + 1 = 4.

3. D = (−1, +3)

4. Area = lw = 8 × 4 = 32

5. E is 2 units to the left of the y-axis.
    F is 1 unit to the right of the y-axis.
    The distance from E to F is 2 + 1 = 3.

6. F is 1 unit above the x-axis.
    G is 3 units below the x-axis.
    The distance from F to G is 1 + 3 = 4.

7. $d = \sqrt{(x_2 - x_1)^2 + (y_2 - y_1)^2}$
    $= \sqrt{(-2 - 1)^2 + (1 - (-3))^2}$
    $= \sqrt{(-3)^2 + (4)^2}$
    $= \sqrt{9 + 16}$
    $= \sqrt{25}$
    $= 5$

8. Area $= \frac{1}{2}bh = \frac{1}{2}(3)(4) = 6$

9. $d = \sqrt{(x_2 - x_1)^2 + (y_2 - y_1)^2}$
    $= \sqrt{(2 - 6)^2 + (4 - 1)^2}$
    $= \sqrt{(-4)^2 + (3)^2}$
    $= \sqrt{16 + 9}$
    $= \sqrt{25}$
    $= 5$

10. $d = \sqrt{(x_2 - x_1)^2 + (y_2 - y_1)^2}$
    $= \sqrt{(-8 - 4)^2 + (2 - 7)^2}$
    $= \sqrt{(-12)^2 + (-5)^2}$
    $= \sqrt{144 + 25}$
    $= \sqrt{169}$
    $= 13$

11. $d = \sqrt{(x_2 - x_1)^2 + (y_2 - y_1)^2}$
    $= \sqrt{(-10 - 6)^2 + (-5 - 7)^2}$
    $= \sqrt{(-16)^2 + (-12)^2}$
    $= \sqrt{256 + 144}$
    $= \sqrt{400}$
    $= 20$

12. $(4) \sqrt{(9 - 3)^2 + (10 - 2)^2}$

Exercise 3, page 330

1. yes $y = 3x - 1 = 3(2) - 1 = 6 - 1 = 5$
(2, 5) is on the graph.

2. no $y = 4x - 5 = 4(3) - 5 = 12 - 5 = 7$
(3, 4) is not on the graph.

3. yes $y = \frac{x}{2} + 4 = \frac{6}{2} + 4 = 3 + 4 = 7$
(6, 7) is on the graph.

4. no $y = \frac{2}{3}x + 1 = \frac{2}{3}(3) + 1 = 2 + 1 = 3$
(3, 2) is not on the graph.

5. yes $y = -x + 3 = -8 + 3 = -5$
(8, −5) is on the graph.

6. yes $y = -\frac{x}{2} + 1 = -\frac{6}{2} + 1 = -3 + 1 = -2$
(6, −2) is on the graph.

7. $y = x + 3$
$y = 1 + 3 = 4$
$y = 4 + 3 = 7$
$y = -3 + 3 = 0$

x	y
1	4
4	7
−3	0

8. $y = 2x - 3$
$y = 2(5) - 3 = 10 - 3 = 7$
$y = 2(3) - 3 = 6 - 3 = 3$
$y = 2(0) - 3 = 0 - 3 = -3$

x	y
5	7
3	3
0	−3

9. $y = \frac{x}{3} + 1$
$y = \frac{6}{3} + 1 = 2 + 1 = 3$
$y = \frac{3}{3} + 1 = 1 + 1 = 2$
$y = \frac{-3}{3} + 1 = -1 + 1 = 0$

x	y
6	3
3	2
−3	0

10. $y = -x + 5$
$y = -8 + 5 = -3$
$y = -5 + 5 = 0$
$y = -1 + 5 = 4$

x	y
8	−3
5	0
1	4

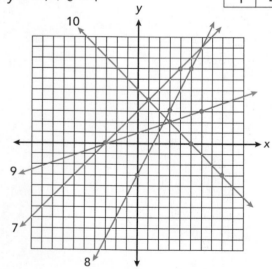

Exercise 4, page 334

1. slope $= \frac{8 - 2}{5 - 3} = \frac{6}{2} = 3$

2. slope $= \frac{9 - 5}{10 - 2} = \frac{4}{8} = \frac{1}{2}$

3. slope $= \frac{10 - 4}{-7 - 2} = \frac{6}{-9} = -\frac{2}{3}$

4. slope $= \frac{5 - (-3)}{-1 - 3} = \frac{5 + 3}{-4} = \frac{8}{-4} = -2$

5. (2) $x = +4$

6. (3) positive

7. 2 In the equation $y = mx + b$, m represents the slope.
In the equation $y = 2x - 4$, m is 2.

8. In the equation $y = mx + b$, b represents the y-intercept.

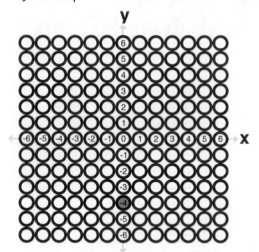

9. (4) $y = 2x + 5$ In the equation $y = mx + b$, b represents the y-intercept.
Only $y = 2x + 5$ has +5 in the place of b.

10. (−8, 0) Replace y with 0 in $y = \frac{x}{2} + 4$.
$$0 = \frac{x}{2} + 4$$
$$-4 = \frac{x}{2}$$
$$-8 = x$$

11. $\frac{3}{4}$ Substitute two corresponding values of x and y in the formula for slope.
$$y = \frac{6 - 3}{8 - 4} = \frac{3}{4}$$

12. (0, 0)

Exercise 5, page 337

1. $4x \cdot 3x = 12x^2$
   $2c(c - 5) = 2c^2 - 10c$
   $(-4a^2)(-6a^3) = 24a^5$

2. $m^3 \cdot m^4 = m^7$
   $n(7n + 4) = 7n^2 + 4n$
   $3s(s^2 - 2s) = 3s^3 - 6s^2$

3. $5t(6t - 1) = 30t^2 - 5t$

   $10x \cdot \frac{1}{2}x = 5x^2$

   $4d(d + 12) = 4d^2 + 48d$

4. (3) $x^2 + 4x$

5. $3(3 + 4) = 3(7) = 21$ or $3^2 + 4(3) = 9 + 12 = 21$

6. (5) $\frac{x^2}{2}$ $\frac{1}{2}x(x) = \frac{x^2}{2}$

7. $x = 8$ $\frac{x^2}{2} = 32$
   $x^2 = 64$
   $x = \sqrt{64}$
   $x = 8$

Exercise 6, page 338

1. $\frac{x^4}{x} = x^3$ $\frac{25y}{20y} = \frac{5}{4}$ $\frac{8c^2}{2c} = 4c$

2. $\frac{6a^4}{3a} = 2a^3$ $\frac{8x^5}{2x^3} = 4x^2$ $\frac{x^2y}{xy} = x$

3. $\frac{15mn}{5n} = 3m$

   $\frac{6a^3b^4}{9ab} = \frac{2a^2b^3}{3}$, or $\frac{2}{3}a^2b^3$

   $\frac{12s^4}{16s} = \frac{3s^3}{4}$, or $\frac{3}{4}s^3$

4. (4) $5x$ $\frac{20x^2}{4x} = 5x$

5. $x = 3$ centimeters $20x^2 = 180$
   $x^2 = 9$
   $x = \sqrt{9}$
   $x = 3$

Exercise 7, page 340

1. $9 = 3 \times 3$
   $10 = 2 \times 5$
   $15 = 3 \times 5$

2. $18 = 2 \times 3 \times 3$
   $20 = 2 \times 2 \times 5$
   $24 = 2 \times 2 \times 2 \times 3$

3. $25 = 5 \times 5$
   $30 = 2 \times 3 \times 5$
   $36 = 2 \times 2 \times 3 \times 3$

4. $40 = 2 \times 2 \times 2 \times 5$
   $50 = 2 \times 5 \times 5$
   $81 = 3 \times 3 \times 3 \times 3$

5. $4n + 4 = 4(n + 1)$ $3p - 6 = 3(p - 2)$
6. $15a - 10 = 5(3a - 2)$ $14c + 35 = 7(2c + 5)$
7. $6b + 8 = 2(3b + 4)$ $6f - 30 = 6(f - 5)$
8. $36y - 9 = 9(4y - 1)$ $16k + 56 = 8(2k + 7)$
9. $c^2 + 8c = c(c + 8)$ $d^2 + 4d = d(d + 4)$
10. $y^2 - 5y = y(y - 5)$ $n^2 - 8n = n(n - 8)$
11. $m^2 + 3m = m(m + 3)$ $p^2 - 2p = p(p - 2)$
12. $a^2 - 8a = a(a - 8)$ $s^2 + 9s = s(s + 9)$

Exercise 8, page 342

1. $\sqrt{27} = \sqrt{9 \cdot 3} = 3\sqrt{3}$
   $\sqrt{8} = \sqrt{4 \cdot 2} = 2\sqrt{2}$
   $\sqrt{20} = \sqrt{4 \cdot 5} = 2\sqrt{5}$

2. $\sqrt{150} = \sqrt{25 \cdot 6} = 5\sqrt{6}$
   $\sqrt{48} = \sqrt{16 \cdot 3} = 4\sqrt{3}$
   $\sqrt{50} = \sqrt{25 \cdot 2} = 5\sqrt{2}$

3. $\sqrt{12} \approx 3.5$
   $\sqrt{32} \approx 5.7$
   $\sqrt{200} \approx 14.1$

4. $a^2 + b^2 = c^2$ $a^2 + b^2 = c^2$ $a^2 + b^2 = c^2$
   $2^2 + 2^2 = c^2$ $2^2 + 1^2 = c^2$ $2^2 + 4^2 = c^2$
   $4 + 4 = c^2$ $4 + 1 = c^2$ $4 + 16 = c^2$
   $8 = c^2$ $5 = c^2$ $20 = c^2$
   $\sqrt{8} = c$ $\sqrt{5} = c$ $\sqrt{20} = c$
   $2.8 \approx c$ $2.2 \approx c$ $4.5 \approx c$

Exercise 9, page 344

1. YZ
2. XY

3. $\frac{YZ}{XZ} = \tan X$

4. $\frac{12}{13} = \cos M$

5. $\frac{5}{12} = \tan M$

6. $\frac{5}{13} = \sin M$

7. $\sin E = 1/\sqrt{5}$
8. $\cos E = 2/\sqrt{5}$
9. $\tan E = \frac{1}{2}$

	angle	sin	cos	tan
10.	30°	0.5	0.866	0.577
11.	45°	0.707	0.707	1.0
12.	60°	0.866	0.5	1.732
13.	75°	0.966	0.259	3.732

14. (3) $\tan 65° = \frac{x}{44}$

15. 94.4 feet

$\tan 65° = 2.145$

$2.145 = \frac{x}{44}$

$x = 94.38 \rightarrow 94.4$ feet

16. (4) $\cos 45° = \frac{7}{y}$

17. 9.9 $\cos 45° = 0.707$ $0.707 = \frac{7}{y}$

$y = \frac{7}{0.707} = 9.9009 \rightarrow 9.9$

Exercise 10, page 349

1. $y = 2x^2 - 5 = 2(2)^2 - 5 = 2(4) - 5 = 8 - 5 = 3$

2. $y = 2x^2 - 5 = 2(-3)^2 - 5 = 2(9) - 5 = 18 - 5 = 13$

3. $y = 2x^2 - 5 = 2(0)^2 - 5 = 2(0) - 5 = 0 - 5 = -5$

4. *yes*

When $x = 3$, $y = x^2 + x = 3^2 + 3 = 9 + 3 = 12$.

5. *yes*

When $x = 0$, $y = x^2 - 3x + 2 = 0^2 - 3(0) + 2 = 0 - 0 + 2 = 2$.

6. *no*

When $x = -4$, $y = x^2 - x - 6 = (-4)^2 - (-4) - 6 = 16 + 4 - 6 = 14$.

7. $y = x^2 + x + 1$

$y = 2^2 + 2 + 1 = 4 + 2 + 1 = 7$

$y = 1^2 + 1 + 1 = 1 + 1 + 1 = 3$

$y = 0^2 + 0 + 1 = 0 + 0 + 1 = 1$

$y = (-1)^2 + (-1) + 1 = 1 - 1 + 1 = 1$

$y = (-2)^2 + (-2) + 1 = 4 - 2 + 1 = 3$

$y = (-3)^2 + (-3) + 1 = 9 - 3 + 1 = 7$

x	y
2	7
1	3
0	1
−1	1
−2	3
−3	7

8. $y = x^2 - x + 3$

$y = 3^2 - 3 + 3 = 9 - 3 + 3 = 9$

$y = 2^2 - 2 + 3 = 4 - 2 + 3 = 5$

$y = 1^2 - 1 + 3 = 1 - 1 + 3 = 3$

$y = 0^2 - 0 + 3 = 0 - 0 + 3 = 3$

$y = (-1)^2 - (-1) + 3 = 1 + 1 + 3 = 5$

$y = (-2)^2 - (-2) + 3 = 4 + 2 + 3 = 9$

x	y
3	9
2	5
1	3
0	3
−1	5
−2	9

9. (3) $x = 6$ and $x = 8$

$x^2 - 14x + 48 = 0$

$6^2 - 14(6) + 48 = 0$

$36 - 84 + 48 = 0$ yes

$8^2 - 14(8) + 48 = 0$

$64 - 112 + 48 = 0$ yes

10. (1) $x = 5$ and $x = -2$

$x^2 - 3x - 10 = 0$

$5^2 - 3(5) - 10 = 0$

$25 - 15 - 10 = 0$ yes

$(-2)^2 - 3(-2) - 10 = 0$

$4 + 6 - 10 = 0$ yes

11. (4) $x = 4$ and $x = -3$

$x^2 - x - 12 = 0$

$4^2 - 4 - 12 = 0$

$16 - 4 - 12 = 0$ yes

$(-3)^2 - (-3) - 12 = 0$

$9 + 3 - 12 = 0$ yes

12. (1) $x = 8$ and $x = 1$

$x^2 - 9x + 8 = 0$

$8^2 - 9(8) + 8 = 0$

$64 - 72 + 8 = 0$ yes

$1^2 - 9(1) + 8 = 0$

$1 - 9 + 8 = 0$ yes

**Advanced Algebra and Geometry Review,
page 351**

Part I

1. 24 base = 5 + 3 = 8 and height = 3 + 3 = 6

    Area = $\frac{1}{2}bh = \frac{1}{2}(8)(6) = 24$

2. 14 $y = -3x + 2 = -3(-4) + 2 = +12 + 2 = 14$

3. yes $y = \frac{x}{2} + 4 = \frac{2}{2} + 4 = 1 + 4 = 5$

4. +1 slope = $\frac{6 - 2}{8 - 4} = \frac{4}{4} = +1$

5. yes

    $y = x^2 - 3x + 4 = 2^2 - 3(2) + 4 = 4 - 6 + 4 = 2$

6. 8   12 − 4 = 8

7. 10 $d = \sqrt{(x_2 - x_1)^2 + (y_2 - y_1)^2}$
        $= \sqrt{(12 - 4)^2 + (8 - 2)^2}$
        $= \sqrt{(8)^2 + (6)^2}$
        $= \sqrt{64 + 36}$
        $= \sqrt{100}$
        $= 10$

Part II

8.

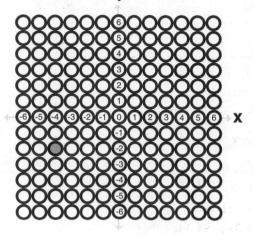

9. $2y^2$ $\frac{14\,xy^3}{7xy} = 2y^2$

10. $2 \times 2 \times 2 \times 5$

11. $4(3m - 4)$

12. $a(a + 9)$

13. $3\sqrt{5}$ $\sqrt{45} = \sqrt{9 \cdot 5} = 3\sqrt{5}$

14. (0, 6)

    When $x = 0$, $y = -4x + 6 = -4(0) + 6 = 0 + 6 = 6$

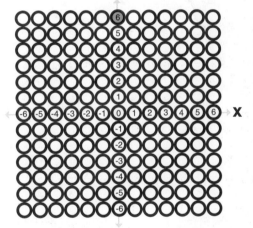

15. (2) (3, −7)

16. (5) $x^2 - 3x$ $A = lw = x(x - 3) = x^2 - 3x$

17. (2) $\frac{4}{5}$ $\cos A = \frac{\text{adjacent}}{\text{hypotenuse}} = \frac{8}{10} = \frac{4}{5}$

18. (4) $\frac{YZ}{XY}$ $\sin X = \frac{\text{opposite}}{\text{hypotenuse}}$

19. (1) $\tan 75° = \frac{x}{20}$ $\tan 75° = \frac{\text{opposite}}{\text{adjacent}}$

20. (2) $x = 4$ and $x = 11$ $x^2 - 15x + 44 = 0$
        $4^2 - 15(4) + 44 = 0$
        $16 - 60 + 44 = 0$ yes

        $11^2 - 15(11) + 44 = 0$
        $121 - 165 + 44 = 0$ yes

Formulas

AREA of a:

square	Area = side^2
rectangle	Area = length × width
parallelogram	Area = base × height
triangle	Area = $\frac{1}{2}$ × base × height
trapezoid	Area = $\frac{1}{2}$ × (base$_1$ + base$_2$) × height
circle	Area = π × radius^2; π is approximately equal to 3.14.

PERIMETER of a:

square	Perimeter = 4 × side
rectangle	Perimeter = 2 × length + 2 × width
triangle	Perimeter = side$_1$ + side$_2$ + side$_3$

CIRCUMFERENCE of a circle Circumference = π × diameter; π is approximately equal to 3.14.

VOLUME of a:

cube	Volume = edge^3
rectangular solid	Volume = length × width × height
square pyramid	Volume = $\frac{1}{3}$ × (base edge)^2 × height
cylinder	Volume = π × radius^2 × height; π is approximately equal to 3.14.
cone	Volume = $\frac{1}{3}$ × π x radius^2 × height; π is approximately equal to 3.14.

COORDINATE GEOMETRY distance between points = $\sqrt{(x_2 - x_1)^2 + (y_2 - y_1)^2}$;

(x_1, y_1) and (x_2, y_2) are two points in a plane.

slope of a line = $\frac{y_2 - y_1}{x_2 - x_1}$; (x_1, y_1) and (x_2, y_2) are two points on the line.

PYTHAGOREAN RELATIONSHIP

$a^2 + b^2 = c^2$; a and b are legs and c the hypotenuse of a right triangle.

MEASURES OF CENTRAL TENDENCY

mean = $\frac{x_1 + x_2 + \ldots + x_n}{n}$, where the x's are the values for which a mean is desired, and n is the total number of values for x.

median = the middle value of an odd number of _ordered_ scores, and halfway between the two middle values of an even number of _ordered_ scores.

SIMPLE INTEREST interest = principal × rate × time

DISTANCE distance = rate × time

TOTAL COST total cost = (number of units) × (price per unit)

Using a Calculator

The GED Mathematics Test permits the use of a calculator on half of the mathematics test. The Casio *fx*-260 scientific is the only calculator permitted with the test.

To turn the calculator on, press the [ON] key at the upper right or the red [AC] key. A small "DEG" will appear at the top center of the display, and "0." will appear at the right of the display.

To perform any arithmetic operation, enter the numbers and operating signs. Then press the [=] key when you finish.

Example 1 Find the answer to 8 + 5 on the calculator.

Press [8] [+] [5] [=]
The answer is [13.].

Example 2 Solve 32 − 6 on the calculator.

Press [3] [2] [−] [6] [=]
The answer is [26.].

Example 3 Find 4 × 79.

Press [4] [×] [7] [9] [=]
The answer is [316.].

Example 4 Divide 7)448.

Press [4] [4] [8] [÷] [7] [=]
The answer is [64.].

Example 5 Solve 2.3 − 4.8.

Press [2] [·] [3] [−] [4] [·] [8] [=]
The answer is [−2.5].

Example 6 Find $\sqrt{289}$.

Press [2] [8] [9] [SHIFT] [x^2]
The answer is [17.].

Example 7 Evaluate 4(9 − 2).

Press [4] [×] [[(---] [9] [−] [2] [---)]] [=]
The answer is [28.].

Glossary

absolute value the distance from a number to zero on the number line

acute angle an angle measuring less than 90°

adjacent angles angles that share one side

area a measure of the amount of surface on a closed plane figure

associative property for addition and multiplication, three numbers that can be grouped in any order. The sum or product will be the same. For any numbers a, b, and c, $(a + b) + c = a + (b + c)$ and $(ab)c = a(bc)$.

average the sum of a set of numbers divided by the number of numbers in the set. Another name for *mean*

B

base one of the factors in a power. For example, in 3^2 the base is 3 and the exponent is 2. In geometry, the side or face of a figure to which the height is drawn

C

circle a plane figure, each point of which is the same distance from the center

circumference the distance around a circle

common denominator for a set of fractions, a number into which each denominator can divide evenly

commutative property for addition and multiplication, numbers can be added or multiplied in any order. The sum or product will be the same. For any numbers a and b, $a + b = b + a$ and $ab = ba$.

complementary angles angles whose sum is 90°

cone a 3-dimensional figure whose base is a circle and whose height is the perpendicular distance from the base to the vertex

congruent figures geometric figures with exactly the same shape and the same size

consecutive one following the other. For example, 19 and 20 are consecutive numbers

coordinate plane a flat surface divided by a horizontal x-axis and a vertical y-axis

coordinates a pair of numbers in the form (x, y) that identify the distance of a point from the origin or center on the coordinate plane. The first number tells the distance to the left or right of the vertical axis, and the second number tells the distance above or below the horizontal axis.

cosine for an acute angle in a right triangle, the ratio of the adjacent side to the hypotenuse; abbreviated as *cos*

cube a 3-dimensional figure that contains six square faces. At each vertex, all sides meet at right angles.

cylinder a 3-dimensional figure that has both a circular base and a circular top, and whose height is the perpendicular distance from the top to the bottom

D

decimal a fraction in which the whole is divided into tenths, hundredths, thousandths, ten-thousandths, and so on

degree the unit of measurement for angles. One degree (1°) is $\frac{1}{360}$ of a circle.

denominator the bottom number in a fraction

diameter the distance across and through the center of a circle

difference the answer to a subtraction problem

digit one of the ten number symbols. The digits are 0, 1, 2, 3, 4, 5, 6, 7, 8, and 9.

distributive property when multiplying a number by a sum or a difference, you may first multiply each number in the sum or difference, or you can first find the sum or difference and then multiply. For any numbers a, b, and c, $a(b + c) = ab + bc$ and $a(b - c) = ab - ac$.

E

equation   a statement that two amounts are equal

equilateral triangle   a triangle with three equal sides and three equal angles, each measuring 60°

estimate   as a noun: an approximate value. As a verb: to find an approximate value

even number   a whole number that is evenly divisible by 2

exponent   a number that tells the power to which a base is raised. For example, in 3^2 the base is 3 and the exponent is 2.

F

factor   as a noun: a number that divides evenly into another number. As a verb: to write a number or an algebraic expression as a product of two or more terms

formula   a mathematical rule that tells the relationship between quantities

fraction   a part of a whole

G

gram   the standard unit of weight in the metric system

graph   a diagram that shows a relationship among numbers

grouping symbols   symbols such as parentheses or the fraction bar that tell which operations to do first

H

hypotenuse   in a right triangle, the side opposite (across from) the right angle

I

improper fraction   a fraction in which the numerator is greater than or equal to the denominator

inequality   a statement that two amounts are not equal. The symbols for inequalities are $<$ (less than), $>$ (greater than), $\leq$ (less than or equal to), and $\geq$ (greater than or equal to).

integer   positive and negative whole numbers and zero

intercept   the coordinates of the point where a line crosses the x- or y-axis of the coordinate plane

isosceles triangle   a triangle in which two sides have the same length. The two angles opposite the equal sides have the same measure.

L

legs   the two shorter sides in a right triangle

line   a straight path of points that continues in two opposite directions

line segment   a straight path of points with definite length, having two endpoints

linear equation   an equation whose graph is a straight line

liter   the standard unit of liquid measure in the metric system

M

mean   the sum of a set of numbers divided by the number of numbers in a set. Another name for *average*

median   a number in the middle of a set of numbers, or the mean of the two middle numbers in a set

meter   the standard unit of length in the metric system

mixed number   a number with both a whole number and a fraction

N

negative number   a number less than zero

number line   a line used to represent positive numbers, negative numbers, and zero

numerator   the top number in a fraction

O

obtuse angle   an angle that measures more than 90° and less than 180°

odd number   a whole number that is not evenly divisible by 2

P

parabola   the curve formed by the graph of a quadratic equation

parallel lines   lines that run in the same direction and do not cross

parallelogram   a four-sided figure with two pairs of parallel sides

perimeter   the distance around a closed plane figure

perpendicular lines   lines that intersect at a right angle

pi   the Greek letter π representing the ratio of the circumference of a circle to its diameter. The approximate value of π is 3.14, or $\frac{22}{7}$.

place value   the number that a digit stands for. For example, in 35.6, the digit 3 stands for 30 because 3 is in the tens place. The digit 6 stands for $\frac{6}{10}$ because 6 is in the tenths place.

plane   a flat surface

polygon   a closed plane figure formed by three or more line segments that meet only at their endpoints

positive number   a number greater than zero

power   a product of identical factors. For example, 3^2, or "3 to the second power", means 3×3. The base is 3 and the exponent is 2.

prime number   a number that is evenly divisible only by itself and 1

product   the answer to a multiplication problem

probability   the chance of an event happening, usually expressed as the ratio of the number of favorable outcomes to the total number of outcomes

proper fraction   a fraction in which the numerator is less than the denominator

proportion   a statement that two ratios (or fractions) are equal

protractor   a tool for measuring and drawing the degrees in an angle

Pythagorean relationship   for a right triangle, the square of the hypotenuse is equal to the sum of the squares of the other two sides. The formula is $a^2 + b^2 = c^2$, where a and b are the legs of a right triangle and c is the hypotenuse.

Q

quadratic equation   an equation in which at least one variable is raised to the second power

quadrilateral   a closed figure with four sides

quotient   the answer to a division problem

R

radius   the distance from the center of a circle to its circumference

ratio   a comparison of two numbers. A ratio may be written with a colon (:), as a fraction, or with the word *to*.

rectangle a four-sided figure with four right angles and with two pairs of parallel sides

rectangular solid a 3-dimensional figure in which each face is a rectangle

reducing expressing a fraction in lowest terms

reflex angle an angle that measures more than 180° and less than 360°

rhombus a four-sided figure with four equal sides

right angle an angle that measures exactly 90°

right triangle a triangle with one right angle

rounding making an estimate that is close to an original amount

S

scalene triangle a triangle with no equal sides and no equal angles

scientific notation a number written as the product of a number between 1 and 10 and a power of 10

similar figures geometric figures with the same shape but not necessarily the same size

sine for an acute angle in a right triangle, the ratio of the opposite side to the hypotenuse; abbreviated as *sin*

slope a measure of the "steepness" of a line on the coordinate plane. The slope is defined as the change in y values divided by the change in x values.

solid a 3-dimensional figure

sphere a 3-dimensional figure each point of which is an equal distance from the center

square a four-sided figure with four right angles, four equal sides, and two pairs of parallel sides

square pyramid a 3-dimensional figure whose base is a square and each of whose four triangular faces meet at a common point called the vertex

square root one of two equal factors of a number. The symbol for square root is $\sqrt{}$.

straight angle an angle that measures exactly 180°

sum the answer to an addition problem

supplementary angles angles whose sum is 180°

T

table an organized chart or list of numbers

tangent for an acute angle in a right triangle, the ratio of the opposite side to the adjacent side; abbreviated as *tan*

transversal a line that cuts across parallel lines, intersecting each of them

trapezoid a four-sided figure with one pair of parallel sides

triangle a closed plane figure with three sides and three angles

trigonometry the study of the relationship between pairs of sides in right triangles

U

unknown a symbol, usually a letter, that represents a solution to an equation. Also called a *variable*

V

variable a symbol, usually a letter, that represents a number. Also called an *unknown*

vertex the point where two sides of a closed figure or two sides of an angle meet

vertical angles angles formed when two lines intersect. Vertical angles lie across from each other and are equal.

volume the amount of space inside a 3-dimensional figure. Volume is usually measured in cubic units.

W

whole number a number that is evenly divisible by 1

Index